Third Edition

PROGRAM EVALUATION

Methods and Case Studies

EMIL J. POSAVAC

Loyola University of Chicago

RAYMOND G. CAREY

Parkside Associates, Inc.

Prentice Hall, Englewood Cliffs, New Jersey 07632

LIBRARY OF CONGRESS
Library of Congress Cataloging-in-Publication Data

Posavac, Emil J.
    Program evaluation : methods and case studies / Emil J. Posavac,
Raymond G. Carey. -- 3rd ed.
        p.   cm.
    Bibliography: p.
    Includes index.
    ISBN 0-13-730367-X
    1. Evaluation research (Social action programs)--United States.
I. Carey, Raymond G. II. Title.
H62.5.U5P62 1989
361.6'1'072--dc19   88-9794
                                                                     CIP

Editorial/production supervision: Word Crafters Editorial Services, Inc.
Cover design: Photo Plus Art
Manufacturing buyer: Ray Keating

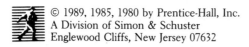 © 1989, 1985, 1980 by Prentice-Hall, Inc.
A Division of Simon & Schuster
Englewood Cliffs, New Jersey 07632

Printed in the United States of America
10 9 8 7 6 5 4 3 2 1

ISBN 0-13-730367-X

Prentice-Hall International (UK) Limited, *London*
Prentice-Hall of Australia Pty. Limited, *Sydney*
Prentice-Hall Canada Inc., *Toronto*
Prentice-Hall Hispanoamericana, S.A., *Mexico*
Prentice-Hall of India Private Limited, *New Delhi*
Prentice-Hall of Japan, Inc., *Tokyo*
Simon & Schuster Asia Pte. Ltd., *Singapore*
Editora Prentice-Hall do Brasil, Ltda., *Rio de Janeiro*

To
Wendy and Steve
Rita, Mike, and Mark

Contents

PART V: EFFECTIVE APPLICATION OF FINDINGS   245

13   The Evaluation Report: How to Get It Read   247

14   A Favorable Evaluation Climate:
How to Encourage Utilization   268

PART VI: CASE STUDIES   287

Acknowledgments

The following organizations and journals are thanked for permission to reprint or adapt material for this text: Institute for Program Evaluation, Inc., Roanoke, Virginia; *General Hospital Psychiatry*; *Journal of Alcohol & Drug Education*; *Evaluation Review*; *Evaluation*; *Evaluation & The Health Professions*; and American Psychological Association.

A number of secretaries and assistants have helped us in the preparation of the manuscript. At various times the following people have given much appreciated help: Carolyn Foraker, Karen Gianfortune, Bernadette Jaroch-Hagerman, and Susan Borkowski Lueger.

The authors are grateful to their respective institutions for encouragement during the writing of this text. The first author's contribution to the first edition was greatly facilitated by a sabbatical leave awarded by Loyola University of Chicago. The second author acknowledges with thanks the explicit support received from Lutheran General Hospital.

The authors also wish to express their appreciation for the helpful comments of the following reviewers: Amado M. Padilla, University of California at Los Angeles; Alan Siman, School of Social Work, San Diego State University; Ross F. Conner, University of California at Irvine; Brian T. Yates, American University; Myron Mast, School of Public Service, Grand Valley State Colleges; Clara Mayo, Boston University; Richard M. Wolf, Teachers College of Columbia University; Robert J. Calsyn, University of Missouri at St. Louis; Francis G. Caro, Institute for Social Welfare Research of the Community Service Society of New York; and Fred B. Bryant, Loyola University of Chicago. For the third edition: James R. Cook, The University of North Carolina at Charlotte; Mark W. Lipsey, Claremont Graduate School; and Melvin M. Mark, Pennsylvania State University.

The first author thanks his wife, Wendy Cook Posavac, for reading and commenting on the manuscript and for providing unfailing encouragement through all stages of this text's preparation. He also thanks his son, Steve, for accepting his father's obsession. The second author acknowledges with gratitude the contributions to his personal and professional development made by his parents, the late Elizabeth Carey and the late Raymond G. Carey.

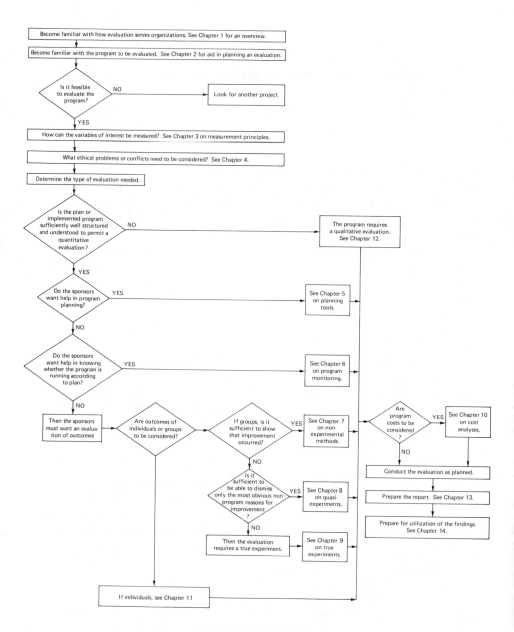

STEPS IN PROGRAM EVALUATION

part I

AN OVERVIEW
OF PROGRAM
EVALUATION

Education at Harvard University, job training at Leavenworth Prison, marriage counseling, blood pressure screening, school hot lunch services, the installation of safety equipment, and day care for preschoolers are formally organized ways that help people achieve their goals.

Of a myriad of services and products available in modern industrial societies, the greater proportion of workers and professionals are involved in meeting human needs for health care, education, training, counseling, emotional support, rehabilitation, and so on. The field of human services includes programs and facilities to help people lead more satisfying, healthier, safer, and more productive lives. Many of these needs have traditionally been met through the extended family or through voluntary charity; however, such needs increasingly are being met through organized, publicly funded efforts. These efforts are often called programs, and the methods used to plan, monitor, and improve such programs make up the field of program evaluation. The evaluation methods presented in this book are applicable to both the activities of nonprofit public and private agencies and to profit-making organizations.

Although scientific and engineering problems are important in industrial settings, success in business is often a question of success in managing human resources. Attempts to improve productivity, employee morale, or product quality all depend on good planning techniques, accurate feedback on the impact of the plan adopted, and utilization of that feedback. Furthermore, research on the need for and the effectiveness of a new product requires skills similar to those used by evaluators. Although this text and the examples it uses reflect the fact that most well-known program evaluations have been in publicly funded organizations, the principles of program evaluation have wide applicability.

The first four chapters of this book provide an orientation to the field and an overview of the methods and goals of program evaluation. In Chapter 1 we describe organizations and the types of programs and services offered. The people responsible for these organizations have many questions about how to plan the programs and judge their effectiveness. The contributions of program evaluation to the various stages of program development and implementation are illustrated.

An overview of the approach evaluators take in preparing to conduct program evaluations is provided in Chapter 2. Often program evaluations succeed or fail due to decisions made during the initial contacts with program managers or sponsors. The principles described apply to all the types of evaluations discussed and illustrated in later chapters.

Because program evaluation is essentially a science of information and its utilization, evaluators must be prepared to assess the quality of the information forming the basis of their work. In Chapter 3 the reader is shown the major ways of gathering information on service programs and how to judge the quality of information obtained. This presentation reflects the need for multiple sources of information in evaluation work; various sources have different strengths and weaknesses. The chapter should expand the reader's appreciation of measurement principles in applied settings.

When research is conducted in organizations serving people's educational, health, employment, emotional, and other needs, special care is exercised to protect the interests of the students, patients, employees, and clients of these organizations. Chapter 4 deals with such ethical issues as well as with the conflicts of interest that can arise when data are collected in organizational settings.

How This Book is Organized

The chapters of this book are arranged in a systematic fashion that reflects the steps followed in conducting a program evaluation. The flow chart that precedes this introduction provides a preview of what is to come. The reader can keep track of how each chapter fits into the organization of the text and can identify the major aspects of the program evaluator's responsibilities by referring to this figure now and as the course progresses.

We hope this text imparts some of the excitement of participating in the growing, developing field of program evaluation: the field is not fully defined, its techniques are varied, and conducting a program evaluation is challenging. We believe that it will continue to have a positive influence on our institutions and governmental agencies.

1

Program Evaluation
and Organizations

Program evaluation is a new and exciting applied social science. A productive society recognizes both the importance of human resources and the importance of providing human services in an efficient manner. Program evaluators provide information about human services in the same way accountants and auditors provide information about financial resources. The mission of program evaluation, or simply evaluation, is to assist in improving the quality of human services. More specifically, program evaluation is a collection of methods, skills, and sensitivities necessary to determine whether a human service is needed and likely to be used, whether it is sufficiently intense to meet the need identified, whether the service is offered as planned, and whether the human service actually does help people in need without undesirable side effects. Through these activities evaluators seek to help improve programs, utilizing concepts from psychology, sociology, administrative and policy sciences, economics, and education. Before discussing specific applications of program evaluation methods, we will describe the field as a whole and illustrate how evaluation and evaluators fit into organizations.

WHY PROGRAM EVALUATION DEVELOPED

Quality of Service Not Assumed

No longer is it assumed that well-meaning individuals or groups who institute a new health, education, training, rehabilitation, or other service actually help people. The rejection of the assumption that all human services help people receiving the service has made the efforts of many people who teach, counsel, provide medical care, or work with community groups more challenging—but possibly more productive. Today innovative programs as well as expansions of standard services can seldom be funded without some means of demonstrating that the costs of the service are justified by the improved state of the clientele. Although Congress initiated the requirement that services supported by federal grants be evaluated (see, for example, Neigher et al., 1982), the source of a program's funding has little effect on whether the program must be evaluated: It must.

The increasing use of social science methods to improve the effectiveness of human service programs and institutions made evaluation a "growth industry" during the 1970s (Guttentag, 1977). There were several reasons for this growth. Well-meaning, expensive, and ambitious attempts to overcome the effects of disadvantaged backgrounds during the middle and late 1960s were by and large ineffective; at least the impact of these efforts did not measure up to the optimistic expectations held by many program developers, government officials, as well as the general public (Cook and Shadish, 1986). During the 1970s considerable caution was expressed about beginning national programs whose effectiveness had not already been demonstrated. Boruch et al. (1983) show, however, that such warnings were often not heeded.

Besides the need to show that proposed programs will be effective, there are persistent needs to demonstrate that existing programs are worth having and are managed efficiently. Frequently, government programs are not explicitly terminated. Instead, new approaches to problems are implemented alongside of old programs. Some have suggested that programs be authorized for a specific length of time—five years, for example. After the specified period of time expires, the program goes out of existence unless its success has been documented and it has been reauthorized (Chelimsky, 1978). Although federal legislation has not been passed requiring this degree of evaluation of federal programs, this idea illustrates a rigorous use of program evaluation methods to guide legislation.

Difficulty in Defining and Measuring Results

Another reason why the demand for the evaluation of people-oriented services grew is that it is difficult to describe the intended outcomes of human service organizations as compared to those of product-oriented organizations. Whenever the intended outcome is hard to define, assessments of success are very complicated. Industrial firms make things that can be seen, weighed, and counted. Department stores, supermarkets, and bakeries sell merchandise. To evaluate the success of such organizations is easy—at least in theory. To judge success, it is necessary to determine whether the products were in fact made and sold, and whether the amount collected for the products exceeded the cost of making and selling them. In practice, these questions are complex, due to the nature of large businesses; however, the approach to judging the ultimate success of such an organization is easy to define and widely accepted. Of course, the ways of improving the profitability of a company require one to pay attention to the human resources of the organization.

The use of human resources is just as important as the use of financial resources; however, for many human services, the nature of the "products" is as difficult to describe as are the methods of assessing their quality. What are the goals of a remedial education program? How do we know that a child has obtained what a program was designed to offer? When is an injured person rehabilitated? What level of rehabilitation should be hoped for? If the state provides hot lunches to a school, but the children throw out the vegetables, is the program a failure? Should we change the menu or teach nutrition to the parents? If, after marriage counseling, a couple gets a divorce, was the counseling inadequate?

Regulation of Human Services

If human services were available only on a fee-for-service basis, evaluating them might be left to free-market forces. The services that were purchased would, by definition, be successful; unwanted services would fail because there would be few, if any, buyers. The free-market approach has not been permitted to govern the field of human services. There are two major reasons why this is so. First, it has been assumed that the public cannot easily differentiate between poor and good human service providers. How many patients, for example, can really tell when a physician is competent? For this reason, physicians and many other service providers are required to obtain a state license before providing services to people. Traditionally, qualifications for offering services were based on training; however, a trend is developing that would require a demonstration of skill before licensing.

A second reason why free-market forces do not control human services is that the recipient usually pays for the service indirectly. Private insurance companies, large charitable organizations, local governments, and, increasingly, federal and state governments cover the costs of many human services. Once a service program is developed, the intended recipients have little to say about how it is administered or what is provided. However, it is important that insurance and public funds be used wisely and productively. The need to demonstrate the effectiveness of human services is critical.

HOW PROGRAM EVALUATION IS USED IN ORGANIZATIONS

Types of Organizations Requiring Evaluations

The preceding paragraphs have been very general, and the reader may have had some difficulty knowing just what sort of activities are being discussed. The following is a brief discussion of the types of human services that can and ought to be evaluated.

Health care.   Hospitals, clinics, extended care facilities, nursing homes, mental health centers, and similar organizations sponsor many services for their patients and clients. Such facilities expend much money on services whose effectiveness has never been fully documented. Educational services for patients, some forms of psychotherapy, certain novel medical treatments, recreational programs, and innovative ways of treating medical/behavioral problems are among the types of health services that should be evaluated in some fashion. Common sense and good management practices call for the documentation of the effectiveness of such programs in order to justify the continued expenditure of funds.

Criminal justice.   Police departments, court systems, and prisons all sponsor programs to encourage respect for law enforcement, to develop citizen–law enforcement officer rapport, and to intervene in the lives of potential and convicted criminals. They also run many other programs to achieve varied goals. The effectiveness of these and other criminal justice programs is often questioned. Carefully done evaluations can aid both in the selection of new programs and in the improvement of existing programs.

Education.   Schools and colleges should evaluate the effectiveness of their teaching staffs as well as specific programs (such as enrichment and remedial programs). The effectiveness of new curricula should be assessed before dissemination to other schools.

Industry and business.   Training programs are widely used in all types of business. The effectiveness of such training programs should be monitored. Newly designed training programs are especially in need of evaluation. A new company-sponsored safety program, for example, would be an ideal program to evaluate using cost-benefit techniques, because both the cost of the program and the cost of accidents can be calculated.

Public administration.   Local communities support a variety of service programs. Preventive medicine (for example, blood pressure checks), park district programs, and fire safety inspections are among the varied service programs that are sponsored by local communities. Taypayers should be assured that the services reach the population for whom they were designed, that the recommendations of safety inspectors are followed, and that people in need of medical care are diagnosed and treated.

Various Kinds of Programs

Some human service programs are developed to help individuals with acute but temporary needs; others seek to correct or alleviate longstanding problems; and others help to prevent future problems or to develop the potential of students, workers, and managers.

Acute problems include the need for health care for injuries and for illnesses, the need for emotional and financial support after accidents or criminal attack, and the need for housing after a home or apartment fire. Such needs are pressing and must be met without delay if suffering is to be minimized, lives are to be saved, or worse emotional harm is to be averted. We are all aware of hospital care and emergency rooms, which alleviate physical needs. Acute needs of an emotional nature are sometimes met through community mental health crisis services. Some police departments try to help victims of crimes handle their emotional reactions. The help these programs offer is short term and must be quickly mobilized for maximum effectiveness.

Alcoholism counseling, drug abuse treatment programs, psychotherapy, physical rehabilitation, and training services in correctional facilities seek to help people with longstanding problems. There is a very high failure rate within such programs. Often both the cause and the actual nature of the problem are hard to define. Thus, the programs are difficult to design, hard to deliver, and confusing to evaluate. Evaluation of these services has traditionally been minimal. However, because the amount of money and human resources devoted to mental health and criminal justice programs is staggering, evaluation work in these fields is being encouraged, if not required, by funding bodies.

Some human services are designed to prevent problems. For example, law enforcement agencies suggest ways to make a home or a store less inviting to criminals; health education programs provide nutritional information to enable people to avoid certain health problems; and health screening programs detect illness or weakness that, if unchecked, could lead to serious disorders or even early death.

Educational programs constitute a major part of the human services industry. The products and goals of these programs are difficult to describe fully. Americans sponsor education at a variety of levels and for a variety of purposes from preschool through postgraduate work—and in a variety of settings from formal classrooms, to IBM management seminars, to the U.S. Army. People participate in educational programs to gain accreditation or become licensed to practice various occupations or professions, to learn specific skills, for enjoyment, for self-help, to enhance their social standing, and for intellectual and psychological growth. Accounting for the funds spent on education must take into consideration the specific purposes of the program being studied.

Programs developed to reduce the effects of economic disadvantages, including welfare, job-training, Medicare, Medicaid, and Social Security, were planned to help people maintain dignity and health despite limited financial resources. Some of these programs are politically controversial.

An issue that affects all the programs mentioned above is the growing technological revolution made possible by microelectronics. Wonders are promised by vendors of computers, new diagnostic equipment, communication systems, and so on. However, organizations considering the purchase of such equipment must first determine its value for their work. More than a few desk-top computers have remained unused. Furthermore, some technologically advanced systems have not performed well. Second, such equipment causes changes in work environments that may adversely influence employee morale. Third, organizations are becoming increasingly aware that choices must be made among available technologies, since few organizations can afford everything offered. Evaluators can help supply the information needed to make these choices.

Programs are delivered by a variety of agencies with very different characteristics. Human services can be administered as regional or national projects involving millions or even billions of dollars. At the other extreme, a program can be directed to a small group of people in a given institution over a very short time period.

We have purposely concentrated our discussions throughout this text on evaluations of the smaller programs likely to be encountered by evaluators working for school districts, hospitals, personnel departments, social service agencies, city or state governments, and so on. Although some national programs are described, the focus on smaller programs is useful in an introductory text because most readers are more familiar with local government or organization-level programs than they are with national programs. Johnston (1983) suggests that organization-level, in-house evaluators will carry the major responsibilities for program evaluation during the coming years, while the number of major, national evaluation projects will decrease. We do not intend to imply that the methods used to evaluate national projects are totally different from the methods used by the evaluator in a particular agency. However, it is likely that the complexity of the statistical analyses increases as the scale of the evaluation increases.

Although complex analytical tools are useful, the use of simpler techniques is sufficient for most evaluators and may produce greater utilization by administrators who find statistics to be an incomprehensible—if not intimidating—topic.

Some writers prefer to reserve the term *program* to refer to major government-funded human services (e.g., Cook, Leviton, and Shadish, 1985). As the preceding discussion indicates, this text uses the term in a more flexible manner, as do many other writers.

Reasons to Evaluate Programs

There are many reasons for conducting program evaluations. Among these reasons are:

- Fulfillment of accreditation requirements
- Accounting for funds
- Answering requests for information
- Choosing among possible programs
- Assisting staff in program development and improvement
- Learning about unintended effects of programs

The uses of evaluation will be described in more detail in the chapters on methods. At this point we discuss these major reasons only briefly.

First, many facilities are required to evaluate their programs for accreditation purposes. Colleges, hospitals, and mental health centers need accreditation to maintain viable facilities. Although a high level of effectiveness might not be required to maintain accreditation, the threat of the loss of accreditation helps maintain a certain quality of service.

Second, the vast majority of grant applications to government and philanthropic agencies require a discussion of the techniques to be used to evaluate the effectiveness of the activities supported by the grant. If a program to teach elderly people about nutrition is supported, the program administrators will be required to gather empirical evidence that the elderly are being reached and that the program has increased their nutritional knowledge and practices. If programs are to be accountable to government or charitable agencies (and, indirectly, to the public), it should be possible to show some results for the expenditure of funds.

A third reason to gather evaluative information is to facilitate the completion of the vast number of surveys government bureaus require for the continuation of funds. If an agency does not keep systematic records, each request for information will require a time-consuming manual search through files. If evaluation requirements are recognized and records are kept up in ways that are easily accessible, the evaluator will be a valuable member of the facility's staff.

Fourth, a variety of administrative decisions can be enhanced by evaluative data. An agency may be requested to expand its programs. However, budgets cannot be stretched to cover all the services that community residents or an enthusiastic staff suggest. Administrators are ultimately responsible for allocating resources. They must face questions such as: If job counseling is begun, what current service is to be eliminated or deemphasized? Is the proposed program suited to the needs of the local community? If evaluation activity has been a routine aspect of the facility, some material will already be at hand to help in the decision. In addition, if the principles of objective evaluation are accepted, it is more likely that an empirical approach to making decisions would be followed. An objective approach to decision making would be an improvement over the typical strategy of selecting programs on the basis of impressionistic and anecdotal evidence, or political pressures.

A fifth purpose of evaluation is to obtain information to improve practices and program structure. Providers of human services need information concerning how well they do their work. Also, evaluators can provide feedback on how well human service providers are viewed by those receiving the service. Good interpersonal relations are more important to human service providers than to people whose jobs require only superficial contact with people.

Sixth, some of a program's effects are intended, some are unintended. Just as effective medicines can have negative side effects, so too can useful and successful social programs. Scriven (1967) recommended *goal-free evaluations* as a way to learn about all program effects. For example, the introduction of Western, mechanized farming methods in some third-world nations has led to increased unemployment because farm tractors do the work of many laborers. An evaluation that focused only on the primary goal of the use of tractors, higher production per farmer, would overlook crucial negative, unintended effects.

What Program Evaluation Is Not

In seeking to define an area, it is helpful to describe what it does not include. Program evaluation is not to be confused with basic research or with individual assessment.

Basic research concerns questions of *theoretical* interest, without regard to immediate needs of people or organizations. In contrast, program evaluation tries to help people improve their effectiveness, assist administrators to make program-level decisions, and make it possible for programs to be accountable to the public. If evaluators do not provide information that is relevant to decisions, they are not fulfilling their major purpose. Furthermore, evaluation, but usually not basic research, is often done under time pressure and in settings (hospitals, courts, schools, training offices) designed for the delivery of a service, not for research.

If program evaluation is indeed a new social science with unique methods, it will require basic research on new evaluation methods and new procedures to encourage implementation of findings. Individuals creating such advances are essential to the practice of program evaluation; however, they do not fill the role of a program evaluator. Readers who have taken social science courses in which basic research is held up as an ideal may be surprised to find that the place of applications is so central in this text.

The second professional activity often confused with program evaluation is individual assessment. Educational psychologists, personnel workers, counseling psychologists, and others have traditionally provided diagnostic information for human service organizations. These people administer intelligence, aptitude, interest, achievement, personality, and other tests for the purpose of "evaluating" an individual's need for a service or one's qualifications for a job or for advancement. These activities are not part of the program evaluator's role. Some of the material in the following chapters refers to ways of measuring information about individuals. Information describing people will be derived from measures of performance in their jobs or from measures thought to be sensitive to changes caused by a human service program. For example, program evaluators might measure depression to find an effect of counseling or of another service, but not for the purpose of analyzing an individual's mental state.

Common Types of Evaluations

An evaluation of a program can be conducted from a number of points of view. This text divides evaluations in two ways: (1) according to the type of question asked about the program; and (2) according to the purpose of the evaluation.

The questions asked by evaluators can be classified into four general types: *need, process, outcome,* and *efficiency*. Each type of question leads to a particular focus and will be involved in our presentation.

The evaluation of need.   An assessment of need seeks to answer questions such as:

- What is the socioeconomic profile of the community?
- What are the particular needs of this community with respect to the type of program being considered (for example, health, mental health, employment, education, crime prevention)?
- What forms of service are likely to be attractive to this particular community?

The measurement of needs is a prerequisite to effective program planning. Today evaluators view planning as closely related to evaluation. Planning is, in fact, a form of evaluation—one that occurs before the program is implemented. The title of the journal, *Evaluation and Program Planning,* illustrates the close association of planning and evaluation.

In order to be a good advocate and a good planner, one must have correct information about need. Certain techniques are useful for measuring or estimating social needs. Although some of these techniques are less quantitative than are other aspects of evaluation, the accumulation and synthesis of information is a necessary aspect of need assessment. This text includes a brief discussion of the evaluation of need. Those readers who become involved in this area will find references to some key works on this subject at the end of Chapter 5.

The evaluation of process.   Once a program has been developed and begun, evaluators will turn to documenting the extent to which the program was implemented *as designed* and is serving the *target population*. One might think of process evaluation as an examination of the effort put into the program. The kinds of questions a process evaluation seeks to answer are:

- Is the program attracting a sufficient number of clients?
- Are clients representative of the target population?
- How much does the staff actually contact the clients?
- Does the workload of the staff match that planned?
- Are there differences among staff members in effort expended?

While the answers to these questions do not indicate whether the program is successful, they are still important; and anyone responsible for directing, funding, or expanding the program wants to hear them. It is conceivable that a good plan has been inadequately implemented or that a successful program is not serving the population it was commissioned and funded to serve. Early warnings about such problems provided by a process evaluation would give the directors an opportunity to redirect the program to give it a chance to be successful.

An extreme illustration of the need to verify the implementation of a program was provided by the finding that a Russian tractor factory was reported to be a model of efficiency when, in fact, construction problems had been so severe that it was not even built. To avoid criticism for failure, those who were responsible for having it built simply faked confirmation of construction and fabricated the production records ("The Potemkin Factory," 1980).

The information necessary for a process evaluation is often available in the agency; however, it is typically not in a usable form. Material describing the clients is on application or intake forms, but it might not be summarized. Details of services received are part of prose notes made by care givers and added to the files. Retrieving filed information requires a special effort and considerable expense. Process evaluations are best conducted when a system of reporting is designed to facilitate gathering and summarizing useful information. In Chapter 6 we illustrate the use of simple information systems for human service settings. References are provided for descriptions of more ambitious systems.

The evaluation of outcome. If a study of implementation does show that the program was successfully put into place, an assessment of the outcome achieved by the people in a program may become a major focus of evaluators. For example:

- Do the people who take a speed-reading course read fast?
- Do they read faster than those not taking the course?
- Can evidence be found that taking the course *causes* increased reading speeds?

Although it it reasonable to ask these questions, it will be clear just by the length of our treatment of outcome evaluation that it is difficult to identify the causes of behavioral changes observed in people. For example, many people begin psychotherapy during a life crisis. If several months later they feel better and seem better adjusted, the change may be due to therapy, to the natural resolution of the crisis, to a combination of both, or to something else entirely. If a change in on-the-job requirements is followed by better morale, can we say that the program change caused the better morale, or should we conclude that it was simply the attention of management that led to improved morale? Perhaps a better national economic outlook was the actual cause.

The presentation of methods will range from the very simple through the very complex. There are situations in which a research plan with many technical weaknesses will be quite appropriate for answering the questions facing administrators and public representatives at certain times. Other more demanding questions will require more complicated research plans. In fact, evaluators might work with more complicated research designs than do laboratory research scientists. This is true because laboratory social scientists can control some of the experiences of the people involved in the research. In contrast, evaluators gather data from people participating in actual, ongoing programs. Although these people are very interested in the benefits they can obtain from the program, their interest in the needs of the evaluators is marginal at best. The evaluators will be seen by some as requiring their energy and time without providing any service in return.

When designing and conducting outcome evaluations, evaluators need to define the ways to measure success. The evaluators of the national Head Start preschool program chose improved cognitive skills as the outcome of most interest. They were criticized as having defined the goals too narrowly, because health examinations and improved nutrition were also included in the program (Datta, 1976b). The definitions of successful outcome may well vary if we compare the opinions of various interested groups, such as the agency funding the program, the program staff, and the participants. A job-training program may be funded to provide job skills so that the long-term unemployed may obtain jobs with private companies. The staff, in contrast, may view the training as a reward for participation in local elections. Last, the trainees may view the program as a good, albeit temporary, job. Whose definition of outcome is to be used?

At times the outcome sought by one or more of the groups will be purposely hidden from evaluators. In politically sensitive settings careful evaluators will be in an uncomfortable position if publicly stated goals conflict with privately held goals. Developing methods to measure success is difficult when goals are clear; when they are hidden, evaluators' jobs are all the more difficult. We will discuss ethical concerns that are relevant when evaluators believe a program is using resources for purposes other than those intended. For example, in Dade County, Florida, an investigator charged that some funds for unemployed workers were used to hire relatives of politicians (*Time*, July 24, 1978). If the outcomes of programs are regularly evaluated, such misuse of money should be more readily discovered than it usually is.

Another problem centers on the issue of how long after participation the outcome is supposed to be maintained. People leaving a program typically return to the same environment that was at least partially responsible for their problems to begin with. The good intentions of alcoholics may not withstand the social pressures of their peers. Cigarettes are smoked by habit in a number of situations, such as after meals, or when one is worried or bored. Breaking down longstanding habits is very difficult. Although changes may be caused by an intensive program, the changes may only be superficial and dissolve in a matter of months, weeks, or days. If so, was the program a failure? Such questions about outcomes are treated in Chapters 7 through 10.

The evaluation of efficiency. While a program may help the participants, administrators and legislators must also address the issue of cost. Evaluations of efficiency raise the following questions:

- Does the program achieve its success at a reasonable cost?
- Can dollar values be assigned to the outcomes achieved?
- Does the program achieve a better level of success than other programs costing the same or less to administer?

There are often competing suggestions for the best ways to help people in need. Are people who are convicted of a crime in need of psychological counseling for emotional conflicts, moral instruction on values, vocational training for holding a job, or academic instruction to help them complete school? Institutions cannot do everything. Choices must be made among possible services. To make choices, the criteria on which to base the choice must be defined.

Two important criteria used to compare programs are effectiveness and cost. If two programs appear equally effective, then the less expensive program is getting more results per dollar. If the more expensive program is more effective, the problem becomes more difficult. Is the additional improvement worth the additional cost? Another complication is added because most programs seek to cause changes involving more than one characteristic. One program may spur improvement in several areas, and another may affect different characteristics. Weighing the relative effectiveness of two such programs is very difficult if the decision maker wishes to be objective. An introduction to cost-benefit and cost-effectiveness analyses is given in Chapter 12.

Note that there is a logical sequence in these evaluation questions and in the order of this text's chapters: without measuring need, programs cannot be planned rationally; without effective implementation, there can be no meaningful outcomes from the program; and without valued outcomes, there is no reason to worry about cost-effectiveness. A premature focus on an inappropriate evaluation question is likely to produce an evaluation with little value (Wholey, 1983).

PURPOSE OF PROGRAM EVALUATION

There really is only one major purpose for program evaluation activities, although this purpose is often broken down into several subpurposes. Human behavior is adaptive only when people obtain feedback from the environment. Our physical existence literally depends on the feedback within our bodies to regulate breathing and heart rate, levels of hormones and chemicals, eating and drinking, and so forth. Social behavior also requires feedback, but such feedback is not as dependable as that of our bodily systems. Delayed feedback, not clearly associated with the behavior causing it, is not very informative. Some writers have said that environmental problems are hard to solve because of the long delay between environmentally destructive policies and the feedback indicating a weakening of natural systems (Meadows and

Perelman, 1973). Program evaluation seeks to provide feedback in social systems.

What effect do social interventions such as jail sentences, nutrition counseling, community hotlines, crime prevention measures, or job-training programs have on the people expected to need these interventions? Figure 1.1 illustrates the place of program evaluation as the feedback loop in human service activities. Program evaluation can be a powerful tool for improving the effectiveness of organizations (Davis, 1982; Zammuto, 1982). The rational processes of assessing needs, measuring the implementation of programs to meet those needs, evaluating the achievement of carefully formed goals and objectives, and comparing the degree of achievement and the costs involved with those of similar programs serves to improve the use of human and material resources in organizations. Most evaluators subscribe to the idea that providing feedback to organizations will help those organizations meet the needs of their clients and remain effective and vital.

This general feedback principle often furthers two purposes. Evaluations can be done to strengthen the plans for services or their delivery, to raise the outcomes of programs, or to increase the efficiency of services; such evaluations are called *formative evaluations* (Scriven, 1967), because they are designed to help form the programs themselves. Evaluations may also help us decide whether a program should be started, continued, or chosen from among two or more alternatives; such evaluations are called *summative evaluations* (Scriven, 1967). There is a finality to summative evaluations; once the value of the program is assessed, it is possible that the program might be ended. In actuality, few evaluations really determine whether or not a program will be terminated (Cook, et al., 1985). There are many sources of information about programs available to administrators, legislators, and community leaders. Because program evaluations are only one of these sources, evaluators are not surprised when clear evaluation reports are not followed by specific decisions. Thus, nearly all evaluations are formative, ideally serving to improve the program evaluated.

Evaluations are also done for less than noble purposes (Kytle and Millman, 1986), some of which are discussed in the next chapter.

FIGURE 1.1 Schematic diagram of the place of evaluation as a feedback loop for a human service program.

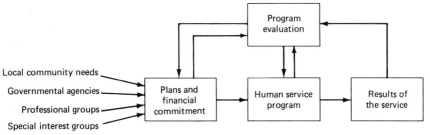

TRENDS MAKING EVALUATION NECESSARY

The growing interest in program evaluation is the result of several trends in American society. *Accountability* has become a word often heard in government and human service settings. Accountability refers to the justification of how resources have been used, and to the responsibility for achieving realistic results as an outcome of one's efforts (Scriven, 1981). The call for accountability seems to have resulted from the consumer movement, professionals' own desires to improve services, an awareness of good management practices, a recognition of the limits of society's ability to support human services, and legislation.

The Consumer Movement

In recent years a number of groups have been organized to make the needs of the consumer known to large corporations. This movement has had repercussions in human service fields. The philosophy behind this approach is summarized in the following comment: "The assumption that *operating* a service is equivalent to *rendering* service, and that both are equivalent to rendering *quality* service are no longer being honored as inherently valid" (Speer and Trapp, 1976, p. 217). The right of professionals to make unchallenged judgments has been curtailed. A form of medical care evaluation—malpractice suits and the threat of malpractice suits—has already altered the practice of medicine. No professional is above being held accountable. Government administrators, teachers, nurses, military officers, and even priests are among those whose performance is now being more closely analyzed. Increasingly, respect and acceptance have to be earned by performance, not by certification or status.

Professional Concern

The service providers themselves have often cooperated and provided leadership in the movement toward the evaluation of human services. In the early part of the twentieth century, American medical care received initial evaluation from the medical societies themselves. Such cooperation has its limits, however. An outcome evaluation conducted by the American College of Surgeons in the early decades of this century revealed such a poor level of outcome that the reports of this particular evaluation were destroyed (*National Standards for Community Mental Health Centers*, 1977). Medical outcome evaluation on a national scale was not attempted again until the 1970s. The evaluation activity of hospital and medical groups was further encouraged in 1965, when Congress mandated that a form of national health care review be implemented by hospitals participating in Medicare (Egdahl and Gertman, 1976).

Managerial Effectiveness

Good management procedures have become more widely used in human service fields. McConkey (1975), while serving as a statewide United Fund chairperson, was distressed to learn that some organizations requested funds but provided neither a description of their services nor evidence that the services produced positive outcomes. Human service administrators are much more aware of the necessity of effective management than they were in the past. The Crusade of Mercy (United Fund) of Chicago, Illinois, ran full-page ads picturing their "priorities committee." The caption under their picture stated that the "hardest noses of Chicago run the Crusade of Mercy." The caption went on to describe the auditing procedure used and how some agencies are dropped from support.

The reasons for tardy development of careful management procedures in human services may lie in two major areas: (1) the difficulty of specifying what the outcome of an effective human service should be; and (2) the origins of many human services in small charitable settings. Commercial firms can be clearer than can human service agencies about the goals they seek to attain. In addition, commercial managers have not had the "God-will-provide" attitude of the sincere but unsophisticated people who traditionally ran charity services. This is not to say that human service settings do or should act on the same values as business firms. Nevertheless, there is much to be learned from modern management methods.

Program evaluation in human services received impetus from the development of several data-oriented tools for managers. Tools for studying and improving the ways in which organizations function in accomplishing their purposes, such as operations research (Johnson, 1967) and systems analysis (FitzGerald, 1973), have helped evaluators with their work in human service organizations. Program evaluation can help managers learn which programs are successful and which programs are serving target populations. Such information can permit administrators to make more informed decisions.

Limitations on Resources

The recognition that society cannot fulfill every possible need that people may have requires that priorities be set. Which is more valuable—treatment of alcoholics in the workforce, or park programs for potentially delinquent children? Seldom are questions phrased so simply; however, the point to be made is important—devoting resources to one program means that these resources cannot be devoted to another program. Each program has its own supporters and beneficiaries. The conflicting wishes of these groups can make decision makers feel pulled in two, three, or more directions. Programs, of course, can be ranked on the basis of the power of the backers of the various programs. Still, it would be better to rank programs on the basis of their potential effectiveness. In this way the resources of society may be expended in a fairer and more useful manner than has traditionally been the case.

Legislative Mandates

The federal government has increasingly insisted on the evaluation of programs. The social programs of the federal government grew considerably during the 1960s and 1970s. Health, Education, and Welfare (HEW) programs required approximately $2 billion in 1953, which was 3 percent of the federal budget. By 1975 HEW programs made up 14 percent of the federal budget, not counting social security costs (*U.S. News & World Report*, 1975). Social programs have a reputation for costing more than they were expected to cost when initially planned. Medicare and Medicaid, for example, cost $39 billion in 1977 but only $6 billion in 1967 (*Newsweek*, 1977). Important for our purposes was the result of the congressional reaction to rapid cost escalation. Congress sought to contain Medicare costs by monitoring the time required for treatment and by examining the quality of treatment given (Gosfield, 1975). More recently, Medicare has paid hospitals a fixed amount on the basis of the illness being treated rather than the actual costs incurred. The "diagnostic-related groups" approach was developed to encourage hospitals to provide care in an efficient manner.

In addition to monitoring health care, the federal government has sought to limit the expansion of health care facilities. The belief that health care facilities are used whenever they are provided has often been voiced. It seems that more disease conditions "require" hospitalization when more inpatient facilities become available (Ball, 1978). If that is so, then careful planning—taking into consideration existing facilities and community need— must precede hospital expansion.

The government's role in evaluation is also evident in the requirement that recipients of educational or service grants be directed to evaluate their work. For example, the evaluation requirements in the Elementary and Secondary Education Act of 1965 (McLaughlin, 1974) encouraged the development of educational evaluation. Such requirements are often met with less than adequate research methods. However, we believe that thinking in evaluative terms is a step forward.

Although the federal government alone has the power to require steps to be taken to evaluate programs, other groups are becoming increasingly active. For example, Blue Cross and Blue Shield, administered by people in health care professions, have traditionally paid whatever bills were submitted by hospitals and doctors. These groups have become more strict about what charges will be honored. In 1977 some 20 medical/surgical procedures were listed by Blue Cross as ineffective and not be paid for, because research has shown that these procedures either provide no relief for patients or have been superseded by better diagnostic procedures (*Blue Shield News*, 1977).

THE ROLES OF EVALUATORS

Work Settings

Before actually describing the specifics of program evaluation, it would be worthwhile to describe where evaluators work. There are three major work settings for professional evaluators. Some evaluators work for the organization that desires certain programs to be evaluated. Such people are called "in-house evaluators." Because of the trends discussed in the previous section, program evaluation is necessary if administrators want their services to survive the competition for funds within their agency or within the city, state, or federal budget. It is undesirable for the evaluator to work under the manager of the service being evaluated; the explicit or implicit demand for favorable reports would be too severe (Cook, Leviton, and Shadish, 1985). Working for the central administration of a large organization that sponsors the services being evaluated helps to insulate the in-house evaluator from some of the pressure.

A second role is employment with governmental or regulatory agencies. The U.S. General Accounting Office, for example, is responsible to Congress for reports on how legislative programs are working out. The GAO's reports can influence legislation on welfare, health, education, and so forth. Some states have created evaluation units, often in the offices of the state auditor. The act creating the Legislative Auditor in Minnesota states that this official is to

> . . . determine the degree to which the activities and programs entered into or funded by the state are accomplishing their goals and objectives, including the evaluation of goals and objectives, measurement of program results and effectiveness, alternative means of achieving the same results, and efficiency in the allocation of resources ("Spotlight," 1982, p. 2).

Since states have responsibilities in the areas of education, health care, welfare, safety, highways, and so forth, evaluators in state offices work on a variety of topics. Since government-sponsored programs have supporters who carefully guard their turf, evaluations of government-based programs can be "explosive" (Nienstadt and Halemba, 1986).

The third major work setting for evaluators is private research firms. Such firms submit proposals in response to "Requests for proposals" announcing competitions for evaluations of governmental programs. The proposals are judged on the basis of cost and quality of methods proposed for the project. They are evaluated in much the same way as are competitive bids for construction projects; a contract for the project is given to the firm or evaluator group that has submitted the highest quality proposal within the allotted budget. (Some university faculty members conduct evaluations independently; they work in much the same way as evaluators who work with research firms.)

In addition to professional evaluators, many individuals in educational, personnel, training, rehabilitation, management, and corrections roles (among others) perform evaluations as part of their responsibilities. Readers who currently fill or intend to seek positions in such settings will find that the concepts and skills presented in this text are valuable in their work even if they never have a position labeled "evaluator."

Consultants Compared to In-House Evaluators

There are only two general ways an evaluator can relate to the organization needing the evaluation: (1) Evaluators can work for the organization and do a variety of evaluations; or (2) they can come to the organization from a research firm or a university to work on a specific program only. For the purposes of discussion, the terms *in-house evaluator* and *consultant* are used to summarize these two different roles. The particular role filled has implications for the size of the evaluation project attempted and for some of the characteristics of the research itself.

Factors related to competence. In terms of *knowledge about a program*, in-house evaluators have the advantage, since they have better access to program directors and to the organization's administration. A person who is physically present 40 hours a week is likely to see the program in action, to know the staff, and to learn about its reputation from other people in the organization. The information gained informally by a secretary in the cafeteria would be unavailable to a consultant not based in the organization. The more that is known about the actual workings of the program, the easier it is to ask the relevant questions in an evaluation.

The *technical expertise* of the evaluator is important. An in-house evaluator often works with a small group of two or three. Some evaluators work alone. However, working alone provides limited opportunities for helpful feedback. In contrast, the consultant may have the resources of a larger organization to draw upon.

A different facet of the question of technical expertise is suggested by the necessity of performing evaluation work in many different areas of an organization. During one period of two years, the authors of this text performed work on psychosomatic illness, stroke disability, a dietary supplement, patient satisfaction, medical education programs, and employee satisfaction, among other topics. It is challenging and stimulating to work in new areas; however, there is also a risk that inexperience in a given area may lead to oversimplifications. By selecting a consultant with experience in a specific program area, an organization may avoid the errors that may occur when an in-house evaluator faces a problem in a new area of the organization.

Personal qualities. There are personal qualities unrelated to technical competence that are important to evaluators. Evaluators can do more effective work if they are objective, trusted by administrators, and interested in improving the program being evaluated.

Being well known and, let us hope, having been found worthy of trust, in-house evaluators usually find program directors and staff more willing to devote time to the evaluation, to admit problems, and to share confidences than they would be with a consultant not previously known. Being trusted may make it possible for the evaluator to fulfull the organizational educator role suggested by Cronbach (1980).

An in-house evaluator can also be expected to have a *desire to improve the organization* sponsoring the program and paying the evaluator's salary. Although intentions are sometimes misunderstood, it is always in the best interests of evaluators to find ways to improve the organizations in which they work. Consultants might not have the same motivations, being less dependent for continuing support on the organization sponsoring the program.

On the other hand, whether or not one is dependent on the organization for a job may affect one's *objectivity*, which is important if reports are to be credible. The objectivity of in-house evaluators may be questioned because they may know the program designer and the staff delivering the service. It is not easy to criticize the work of a friend. The consultant, on the other hand, is unlikely to have developed personal relationships within the organization and thus may be more objective. An in-house evaluator may also hesitate to report critical findings because future work may be jeopardized. Research in an applied setting depends on the cooperation of many people. If they believe that negative results will come out of the project, the needed cooperation may be hard to obtain.

There is another side to the question, however. Evaluators will lose their credibility and, thus, their effectiveness if they ignore sensitive issues. The authors prepared a report that showed positive outcomes for the patients in a medical/psychological program (Carey and Posavac, 1977b). If the report had stopped there, it would have been welcomed. However, it went on to show that other patients obtained the same degree of positive benefit at less cost in a different program. This observation was not welcome. It is important to emphasize, though, that this short-term problem should be weighed against the likelihood that willingness to report negative or ambivalent findings will increase one's credibility in the long run.

The purpose of the evaluation required. Earlier in this chapter two purposes of evaluative studies were described—formative and summative. In-house and consultant evaluators can and do perform both types of evaluations. However, there are certain situations that are better served by one or the other type of evaluator. The in-house evaluator is likely to be more effective than a consultant in implementing procedures to follow for formative evaluations. Such evaluators will be available and committed enough to see the project through, and because formative evaluations cannot lead to a traumatic decision to end a program, negative results will not destroy the evaluator's role in the organization. If, in contrast, a summative evaluation is wanted because there is a strong suspicion that a program is failing, an outside evaluator will probably be more helpful than in-house personnel. A school board, knowing that it had to close one of three grade schools because enrollment had dropped, decided to select a consultant with no ties to the school district to recommend which school to close. The consultant performed an evaluation of efficiency for each school and recommended that the least efficient school be closed. Although there were some hard feelings, and a number of verbal attacks were leveled at the consultant and his report, the selection of the school to be closed was made and implemented with fewer difficulties than was the case in neighboring school districts making similar decisions, but relying entirely on local expertise.

Conflicts Between Evaluators and Organizations

Evaluators fill a position between (on one hand) the role of the research social scientist concerned about theory, the design of experiments, and the analysis of data—but for the most part uninvolved in the delivery of human services—and (on the other hand) the role of the practitioner dealing with people in need and seldom interested in or trained in the methods of data collection and analysis. Evaluators are able to read the language and to use the tools of the research social scientist. Research design, validation, reliability, statistical significance, and so forth are familiar to evaluators. In addition, the effective evaluator will be sensitive to the concerns and style of the service delivery staff. Finally, evaluators interact with administrators, who are ultimately responsible for the effectiveness and cost of the program. Because the field is still new and the tasks assigned to the evaluator are so varied, the role of the evaluator is not widely understood.

Participating in such a new field has advantages and disadvantages. The advantages include the intellectual stimulation provided by exposure to people serving various roles in human service programs and the satisfaction of seeing research methods used in ways that can be of potential benefit. The disadvantages include being viewed as intrusive and unnecessary by some service delivery personnel. As will be seen in the chapters that follow, the most effective evaluators show that they are allies of service providers, while at the same time asking searching questions and requiring documentation of answers. It must be recognized that evaluators might fail to see their own biases since they are affiliated with the organization offering the program (Cook, Leviton, and Shadish, 1985).

It is unfortunately true that shortsighted self-interest has opposed objective evaluation. Spinney (Isaacson, 1983) testified to Congress about how military planners ignored the findings of their own research and those of evaluation analysts when ambitious officers wanted pet projects funded. It should also be noted that some political orientations are opposed to government participation in many social services, regardless of the effectiveness of these governmental activities (Levin, 1982; Walsh, 1983). Campbell (1983), one of the early leaders in the evaluation field, has become concerned about the possibility of collecting valid information when people are threatened by an evaluation of their work or ideas. Others expect active, but changed, roles for evaluators in future years (Cronbach, 1980; Johnston, 1983; McClintock, 1983). These observers foresee a growth in the use of information prepared by people working in the organizations sponsoring the program or service. Furthermore, it seems likely that a responsible investment of resources by federal, state, and local governments, as well as by business and charitable organizations, will continue to require careful monitoring as well as evaluations of effectiveness (Rossi, 1983).

It is true that requirements to evaluate programs do not necessarily mean (1) that evaluations are uniformly good (they are not); (2) that evaluations are always utilized (they sometimes are ignored); or (3) that ineffective programs no longer exist (they do). However, many social scientists believe that the widespread requirement for evaluation, if coupled with increased sophistication in evaluation methods, will contribute to the achievement of the desirable goals of improving the effectiveness of social programs and making new programs more sensitive to the needs of the people to be served (Guttentag, 1977; Triandis, 1978; Wertheimer, 1978).

Getting a Job as an Evaluator

As mentioned above, many organizations conduct evaluations but do not call their evaluation activities "program evaluations." Some entry-level jobs go under the names "program analyst" or "planner." A number of graduate students have gotten such positions in city government during some phase of their studies. To get a job in program evaluation, one must sometimes be creative in suggesting how organizations can use an evaluator's skills. For example, one could draw an analogy between an auditor working with financial matters and an evaluator working with people-oriented issues. Just as one wouldn't run a business without adequate monitoring of cash flow, one really shouldn't run an organization without knowing how employees react to company policies and benefits, whether customers like the services, or if managers work better after being trained (Perloff, 1983).

In order to understand the problems of organizations that might hire an evaluator, it is helpful to learn something about the ways individuals in those organizations think. There are professional organizations for people in personnel, marketing, training, and so on; and the journals they publish can usually be found in libraries. Capper (1983) has suggested joining the organizations and meeting people in the businesses that might need evaluation skills. The crucial question is: How will evaluation improve the quality of the work done by the organization? To provide a credible answer, the evaluator must understand the needs of the organization.

People who are serious about getting started as evaluation consultants need brochures describing their services. Drawing up a brochure forces one to be clear about just what services can be offered to a business. Making appointments with directors of personnel, planning, training, and so on can be helpful, because this allows one to be seen. Having potential clients connect a face with a brochure helps develop credibility.

A number of people have suggested that conducting a project for free is a way of becoming known and demonstrating the value of program evaluation. Several students of the first author have been offered jobs after doing a class project for an organization.

Even after getting a job as an evaluator, it is still important to demonstrate that evaluation can help in running an effective program. Some managers will be threatened by the idea of someone collecting data on the effectiveness of their work groups. Still, becoming known in the organization as competent and trustworthy, and developing a broader knowledge of how feedback about effectiveness can help different aspects of the organization, will help keep a steady flow of work for the evaluation office.

Evaluation and Other Activities of an Organization

Professional interaction among people with similar interests is often beneficial to all concerned. An evaluator working alone will find it hard to grow and to develop professionally. If an organization is too small to employ more than one full-time evaluator, it may be wise to attach evaluation to another function of the organization. Four functions that are sometimes joined with evaluation are research, education, planning, and human resources.

Research. Some human service organizations routinely sponsor research directly with operating funds or indirectly with grant funds. Evaluation can become one function of the research team. For example, a police department was awarded a grant to study the effect of providing emotional support to the victims of crime. The social scientists responsible for that research would be excellent colleagues of an evaluator. University-affiliated hospitals carry on research. Individuals conducting research into psychiatric problems or emotional issues related to serious illness have interests similar enough to those of evaluators to serve as colleagues.

Education. Some organizations have joined the functions of education and evaluation. There is a longstanding precedent for this marriage in educational psychology. New study materials and curricula are evaluated before being widely used by schools. Universities are combining faculty development and evaluation into one office. Many organizations besides schools sponsor educational programs. For example, industries have safety education programs, apprenticeship programs, job-training programs for minorities, and so on. Sponsoring firms want to know if the programs are achieving their goals.

Planning. Planning is an activity in which evaluators can assist. It is common for service providers to serve as a planning group. This choice is wise; however, many direct-service providers are not data oriented, feel uncomfortable constructing need surveys, and may be unable to analyze the information obtained. Evaluators can help by showing them how effective the plans are likely to be and how consumers evaluate proposed projects or services. Sometimes evaluators can help planners simply by asking searching, hard-to-answer questions about the assumptions implicit in the plan for the program itself or for the implementation of the program.

Human resources.   Large businesses often have a vice-president of human resources. This office oversees all policies concerning hiring, compensation, and the professional development of employees. Compensation plans, training programs, management effectiveness seminars, and so forth all require evaluation if an organization is to be as effective as possible.

SUMMARY

National trends, such as the consumer movement, professional concern, increased managerial effectiveness, limitations on resources, and specific congressional mandates have converged to create a need for methods to make rational managerial and legislative decisions in human services. The social science methods of program evaluation include planning, program monitoring, outcome assessment, and benefit/cost considerations. Evaluators are quantitative social scientists working to improve the delivery of human services. Their efforts to effect such improvements are on a program level, not on the individual person/client/patient level frequently associated with human service organizations.

STUDY QUESTIONS

1. From newspaper and magazine articles, gather examples of the use of program evaluations in the formation of public policy. You might find articles dealing with medical care (malpractice, peer review, costs), education (children reading well or not reading well), program planning (need assessment), relative costs of programs with similar goals, or other issues.
2. What aspects of program evaluation might be used in organizational settings with which you are familiar? Illustrate.
3. List the advantages and disadvantages of making program evaluation a part of American human services delivery systems. Save your list, and when you have finished the text, consider how you might change the list.
4. Some people suggest that while society wants to believe that something is being done about social problems, most people really do not care if the programs actually have an impact on the problems. Consider the question of whether people really want to know if educational, welfare, health, and other services actually work.

FURTHER READING

DEMONE, H. W., AND HARSHBARGER, D. 1973.   The planning and administration of human services. In *Developments in human services,* vol. 1, ed. H. C. Schulberg, F. Baker, and S. R. Roen. New York: Behavioral Publications.
FAIRWEATHER, G. W., AND DAVIDSON, W. S. 1986.   *An introduction to community experimentation.* New York: McGraw-Hill.
WEISS, C. H. 1975.   Evaluation research in the political context. In *Handbook of evaluation research,* vol. 1, ed. E. L. Struening and M. Guttentag, chap. 2. Beverly Hills, Calif.: Sage.

2

Planning an Evaluation

Program evaluations begin in several different ways. Program personnel themselves may initiate the evaluation or seek to have an evaluation team conduct one. The funding agency or central management may require an evaluation of a sponsored or planned program. Or, an in-house evaluation department might suggest that the organization would benefit from an evaluation of a particular phase of its activities. In this case, a preliminary proposal would be submitted to the program sponsors or program director.

Whatever source of the initiative for the proposal, evaluators need to address a number of issues and make certain decisions before the collection of data begins. Before committing their resources, they need to learn about the goals and mechanics of the program, about the people who sponsor the program, about the program personnel, and about groups that may resist the evaluation of the program. After obtaining this information, evaluators must then decide whether an evaluation can be done. If the program is planned in a way that permits evaluation, then a decision needs to be made as to whether an evaluation should be done immediately, whether it should be done in the way in which it is proposed, or whether it should be done at all.

In the first part of this chapter, we provide an overview of the sequence and manner in which the above issues can be approached, identifying the steps to be taken between the time of the initial proposal and the beginning of data collection. The time and effort devoted to each step will vary, depending on the complexity of the program, the relationship of the evaluator to the program sponsors and personnel, and the urgency of time constraints. Some steps, such as selecting or developing measures, are very complex, and Chapter 3 treats them in more detail. In the second part of this chapter, we deal with potential sources of resistance to program evaluation.

SIX STEPS IN PLANNING AN EVALUATION

Step 1: Identify Relevant People

The first thing effective evaluators do is identify relevant people; that is, those who have a serious interest in the program and whose lives may potentially be affected by the evaluation. Relevant people are those who are heavily personally involved in the program, who derive some or all of their income from the program, whose future status or career might be affected by the quality of the program, or who are the clients or potential recipients of the program services. Such groups have been called stakeholders (Bryk, 1983), since they have a stake in the program and its evaluation.

Program personnel will usually be more personally involved in the program than either the sponsors or the clients. The program director will be a key person with whom evaluators will relate during the entire project. It will help to learn as much about the background, interest, attitudes, and reputation of the program director as possible. In addition, other people involved in the delivery of program services must not be overlooked. It is important to involve them in the planning stage so that they will assume ownership of the project and provide maximum support during the data collection stage (Bank, 1987). If possible, evaluators should learn about the relationship between the director and other program personnel, so that they can be dealt with more effectively during the planning meetings to be described below. For example, if the director manages in an authoritarian manner, it will be more difficult for evaluators to draw out the ideas of other personnel and determine when a consensus exists or when a power decision has been made by the director alone.

Program sponsors should be considered next. At times program personnel are the sponsors; in other cases sponsors will be funding agencies, governmental bodies, or administrators of the institution in which the program exists. Often there will be a single person with whom the evaluators are to relate. The funding agency may delegate one or two representatives to handle the commissioning and supervising of an evaluation project. In an institution such as a hospital, the program sponsor might be the vice-president or administrator to whom the program director reports and who is ultimately responsible for the management of the program. Contact with the program sponsor will be especially important during the initial stages of planning and at the end of the evaluation. At the beginning it is important that the sponsor fully supports the proposed evaluation and that all the program personnel are aware of that support. At the end of the evaluation, it is important that the report be presented to sponsors in such a way that it will be fully utilized in decision making. The presentation of the report and effective utilization of findings will be discussed more fully in Chapters 13 and 14.

Finally, the clients or recipients of the program services need to be identified. The amount and type of contact with the clients will depend on the nature of the program and of the evaluation. For example, if a cancer care unit is to be evaluated, are the program recipients only the cancer patients, or are the relatives of the patients also included? Are all cancer patients included, or only those with certain types of cancer?

Step 2: Arrange Preliminary Meetings

Before a final decision is made to undertake an evaluation, and before the writing of a detailed proposal, it is advisable to meet with relevant people to gather background information on five questions: (1) Who wants the evaluation? (2) What type of evaluation is desired? (3) Why do they want it? (4) When do they want it? and (5) What resources are available?

Who wants the evaluation? Ideally both the program sponsor and the program personnel desire to have the program evaluated. In this instance the evaluators will usually be interacting with competent people who are secure in their professional expertise, who are open to suggestions for improvement, and who welcome the opportunity to have documentation for what they feel is a successful program.

If the program sponsors initiate the evaluation proposal—either without the knowledge of or against the desires of the program personnel—the evaluators are faced with making the program personnel comfortable with the goals and methodology of the evaluation before data collection begins. If evaluators do not succeed in doing this, they face the possibility of open opposition or a lack of essential cooperation on the part of the program personnel. On the other hand, when the program personnel see the evaluators as "allies" rather than as "the enemy," they are more likely to give the evaluators both much-needed assistance in the difficult job of data collection and valuable insights into the interpretation of the data.

If the program personnel initiate the evaluation proposal—either without the knowledge of, or against the desires of, the program sponsors—the evaluators need to convince the sponsors of the usefulness of the evaluation, or it will be very difficult to have any worthwhile changes effected. Sponsors who do not assume ownership of the evaluation project during the planning stage are inclined to allow the finished reports to lie unused in their offices.

What type of evaluation is desired? Early in the evaluators' meetings with program sponsors and personnel, it will be clear that the term *program evaluation* does not have the same meaning for everyone. More often than not, program personnel will be thinking in terms of a formative evaluation that will help them modify and improve the program. On the other hand, program sponsors may desire a summative evaluation; they may be under pressure to divert resources to another program and must decide whether or not to continue the present program. Finally, some program personnel and sponsors will have little awareness of the whole concept of *program* evaluation and will therefore be expecting *individual* performance appraisal.

The task of evaluators at this point is to clarify the pertinent concepts for those who do not understand them and to help the relevant people decide what type of evaluation best meets their desires, needs, and resources. The choice is seldom between one type of evaluation and another. Often it is possible to incorporate some elements of various types of evaluations into the total scope of the project, depending on the complexity of the program goals and the resources available for the project. For example, in the evaluation of "Sesame Street" conducted by Cook et al. (1975), various types of assessment were included in the overall evaluation. They assessed (1) whether the program reached its target audience; (2) effectiveness by analysis of learning scores; (3) the magnitude of effects relative to the magnitude of the need that gave rise to the problem; (4) the ratio of benefits to cost; (5) the aspects of the complex home viewing situations that led to learning, and the conditions of TV viewing that most promote learning; and (6) the value of program objectives—that is, the importance of stimulating the growth of all social groups of preschool children versus that of narrowing the academic achievement gap between economically advantaged and disadvantaged children.

Why is the evaluation desired? Closely tied to the previous question is the issue of why evaluation is desired. The commissioning of an evaluation is rarely the product of an inquiring scientific spirit. More often it meets the needs of political forces. Program sponsors often need to satisfy constituents and want to keep politically advantageous programs alive. Effective evaluators will put a high priority on identifying the reasons why the evaluation is desired. Were there some groups in the organization who objected to the evaluation? What were their motives? Is there real commitment among the program personnel and program sponsors to using the results of the evaluation to improve decision making? Ideally, program personnel are seeking answers to pressing questions about the program's future: Should it be continued? Should it be expanded? Should it be modified? Evaluators expect that different stakeholder groups will have differing priorities: some want a smoothly functioning program, others want tips on making their work more effective, yet others want to see improvements in the service (Cook et al., 1985).

One aspect of the evaluators' role is to help both the sponsors and program personnel arrive at a consensus on the precise decision(s) to be made. For example, in the evaluation of a physical medicine and rehabilitation program (Carey and Posavac, 1978), the decision under consideration was not whether or not the program should be continued, because the program was generally recognized as useful and had abundant referrals both from physicians on the hospital staff and from physicians at other hospitals. However, the program personnel were concerned about patients who were discharged to their homes as apparent successes. They did not really know whether these patients maintained their levels of rehabilitation. After extended discussion it became clear that the primary focus of the evaluation was whether a follow-up program was needed for those patients who were discharged as successfully rehabilitated.

In other instances evaluations are conducted to determine how much of an impact a program has on other areas of the sponsoring institution. In such a case the program personnel are not decision oriented; rather, they seek to assure themselves that no serious side effects arise from the introduction of a new program. For example, the authors evaluated a hospital-based physician residency program in terms of its impact on other areas within the hospital. The study uncovered certain tensions and conflicts that might have developed into serious problems unless they were attended to immediately. The evaluators concluded the report with suggested corrective actions to be considered by the medical education committee.

Some evaluations done for public relations or political purposes are acceptable. For example, administrators may be reasonably certain that they have an effective program and may wish to generate greater support for that program. In other words, they desire greater visibility for the program with influential people who can provide increased political or financial support.

Evaluation may also be done solely to fulfill grant requirements. Many grants from governmental and private sources include an evaluation requirement. In this situation the decision to evaluate originates from pressure external to the program itself. For example, many projects funded by federal and state governments are required to be evaluated. The imposition of evaluation requirements is not without merit. When the need to ask evaluative questions is forced on people, they may become more self-critical than they would otherwise have been.

However, some reasons for program evaluation are undesirable. For example, an administrator may use program evaluation as a ploy to avoid making a decision. Administrators who are pressured about the viability of a given program can buy time by saying that the program is being evaluated; by giving as little support as possible to the evaluators, they ensure that the evaluation will take a long time to be completed. If there is a need to buy still more time when the evaluation is completed, administrators may appoint a committee to study the evaluation report. Evaluation is also inappropriate when administrators know what decisions they will make but wish to go through the charade of program evaluation to give their decision legitimacy.

When is the evaluation desired? The scope of an evaluation project can be limited by situational factors. If the evaluators are given a deadline, they may be forced to make choices that are not ideal. For example, measures specifically designed for a program may have to be foregone in favor of existing questionnaires or instruments, although these existing instruments may not be sufficiently reliable, valid, or applicable. The number of respondents or participants in the study may have to be limited, thereby decreasing the probability of detecting the true effect of the program. Adequate control groups may not be immediately available, although they might be available at a later date. Evaluators must decide whether they should proceed under less than ideal circumstances, delay the evaluation, or refuse to do the evaluation in order to avoid the possibility of generating misleading results. For example, Carey and Posavac (1979) were invited to plan an evaluation of a new cancer care center five months before it was introduced within an acute care hospital. A five-month lead time was not long enough to develop new measures for all the program objectives, nor to collect data from a large sample of cancer patients before the institution of the center. To save time, the evaluators measured patient moods with an existing instrument used in previous research with cancer patients.

Even when there is no absolute deadline, program personnel may be so eager for results that they request an early completion date. It is usually better not to commit oneself to a deadline that can be met only if everything occurs on schedule. Murphy's law ("If anything can go wrong, it will") is especially applicable in program evaluation: Data collectors become ill; respondents are unavailable; the mail is slow; computers break down when they are most needed. When an accurate estimated date for completion of the report must be made, careful estimates of the time required for each step in the project should be made. How much time is needed to find measures? To obtain program management agreement about methods? To schedule and interview the needed respondents? To analyze the information gathered? To write the report? Often considering each step in the process, one can arrive at a good estimate of the time required to complete the evaluation.

What resources are available?   Besides time, another situational factor that can limit an evaluation is the availability of resources. Grants only include a specified amount for the evaluation. Of course, in-house evaluators cannot be reckless with resources either. The assistance of program personnel or volunteers can hold down the expense of data collection.

Even if no formal contract is signed, it is advisable for evaluators to put into writing an exact list of what is covered and not covered in the cost estimate and to specify when payments should be made. The evaluator's understanding of his/her obligations should be sent to the program director and the manager of the institution sponsoring the program. Ideally, the manager will indicate in writing that the statement accurately summarizes the agreement. This approach does not indicate a lack of trust; it does recognize that the memories of busy people can fail. Honest misunderstandings as to what was agreed upon have led to hard feelings between evaluators and program directors.

Step 3: Assess the Evaluability of the Program

The next step is to decide whether an evaluation should be done. This process, referred to as an "evaluability assessment" (Schmidt, Scanlon, and Bell, 1979; Wholey, 1979), is intended to produce a reasoned basis for proceeding with an evaluation. Meetings with the stakeholders are held to learn about the conceptualization and the objectives of the program. Furthermore, the stakeholders will need to agree on the criteria of program success. If they do not agree about what makes a successful and an unsuccessful program, some types of evaluations are impossible to carry out. After such discussions, evaluators make a conscious decision to conduct or not conduct the evaluation.

A program is not ready to be evaluated until its theoretical basis has been developed, sufficient resources have been allotted, and sponsors are ready to implement it in a substantial fashion. Nor should an evaluation be undertaken when the expectations for the program are implausible, or if it is not feasible to collect the evidence required to demonstrate the effectiveness of the program. For example, before a Hospice Program for terminally ill people can be evaluated, the policy makers must agree on the answers to such questions as: What is the definition of a "terminally ill" patient? Are patients with only certain illnesses to be served? Is care for bereaved relatives to be included in the scope of Hospice services? Nor is a program evaluable if it is not ready to be implemented as planned. If, for example, a school had planned to introduce a computer course for its eighth-grade students involving a full-time instructor and ten computer terminals, it cannot be evaluated if there are only two terminals and a part-time instructor.

Horst et al. (1974) discuss some underlying causes of why those in charge of programs and those who evaluate them have not joined their efforts in a manner that more frequently results in program improvements. They suggest three underlying causes, which they say are not the responsibility of the evaluator: (1) a failure to define the problem addressed or the program intervention being made; (2) a lack of clear logic—that is, the connection between the program intervention and the immediate outcome is not understood clearly enough to permit testing; and (3) a lack of management—that is, those in charge of the program lack the authority or ability to follow through on evaluation results. Lipsey et al. (1985) reported that less than 30 percent of published evaluations described programs with theoretical formulations linking the program to the hoped for outcomes.

A helpful discipline to aid in deciding whether a program has a good theoretical basis is to try to construct an impact model showing how the elements of the program led to the changes in the program participants that the staff expects. Upon questioning, it may turn out that some programs are no more complicated than "we tell them what to do, and they will do it." On the basis of what you know about the health benefits of regular exercise and a balanced diet which is also low in sugar, fat, and salt, would you agree that knowledge is enough to motivate people? Many steps intervene between the provision of knowledge and actions. The steps can include the reinforcement of appropriate behaviors, social support, reminders, skill in applying knowledge, belief in the personal applicability of the information, and so forth. Discussions initiated by evaluators can reveal that planners have not developed a clear rationale on which to base a program or do not have the freedom to make changes in response to an evaluation. Recognizing such situations even before gathering any data is a contribution that evaluators can make (Cook and Shadish, 1986).

It is necessary to point out that at times evaluators do not have the freedom to decide not to conduct an evaluation. In-house evaluators may be assigned to conduct an evaluation. Consultants may accept a contract in order to maintain a staff, even if conditions are not perfect for carrying out the best evaluation. The main consideration is to make a conscious decision—not merely to drift into a project just because it is there. Chapter 4 suggests that when faced with an unevaluable program, an evaluator may be able to help program sponsors redefine an evaluation project.

Step 4: Examine the Literature

Evaluators often work on a wide variety of projects. An independent evaluator, for example, may evaluate a school system, then a community program for alcoholics, and then the organizational climate in a bank. Such an evaluator must become familiar with many types of organizations. Although this is difficult, some evaluators prefer such work; they enjoy the variety and do not like to restrict their efforts to a single area of interest.

Evaluators who specialize in limited areas have a less formidable task in drawing up a proposal. If they have been exclusively evaluating educational systems, mental health programs, or personnel problems in organizations, they develop an extensive knowledge of evaluation in their specialty. They can also build more easily on their own past research and contribute to the development of theory in that area.

However, when evaluators work in an area that is new for them, it is important to make a careful search of the literature before designing or developing new instruments. Evaluators should learn from the successes and failures of others and get a picture of the methodological, political, and practical difficulties that must be overcome.

Depending on the type of evaluation, computerized search services might be a good place to begin a search. MED-LINE, Psychological Abstracts Search and Retrieval (PASAR), and Educational Resource Information Center (ERIC) are three such useful systems. A search of professional journals recommended by program personnel is also helpful. After a few useful articles have been identified, the bibliographies of these articles will provide additional references.

While reading the articles, evaluators should keep these key questions in mind: Has any evaluation been done on this type of program? What designs were used? Were new measures developed? How reliable and valid were the measures? What type of statistical analysis was used? Was it appropriate? Is there a consensus among the findings of various studies? If there is conflict, is this due to sampling procedures, design, or interpretation of findings? What issues were not addressed or investigated?

Step 5: Determine the Methodology

After reviewing the literature, the evaluators are ready to make some methodological decisions regarding strategy and design, population and sampling procedures, control or comparison groups, measures, data collection, and statistical analysis. Separate chapters are devoted to some of these issues, but it is helpful to examine the main issues now so that the reader can better understand their interrelationships and how they fit into the planning stage of an evaluation.

Strategy and design. Strategy and design will largely be determined by the type of evaluation needed. Will the project be a need evaluation? A process evaluation? An outcome evaluation? An evaluation of cost effectiveness? Perhaps the project will include more than one kind of evaluation.

Strategy and design will also be influenced by whether the program is already in operation or whether it is still in the planning stage. If a new program is to be initiated, its effectiveness can be evaluated by gathering data on one or more occasions prior to the introduction of the program and comparing these data to information collected after its introduction. If the program can be introduced to some segments of a target population on a staggered basis, this is more desirable than introducing the program to the entire population at the same time. With this strategy evaluators can make multiple comparisons of the same group over time, and between groups. Whenever outcomes are measured, it is important to monitor the implementation of the various aspects of the program since failure to implement is a frequent reason for program failure.

Population and sampling. Once the target population (participants, respondents) has been identified, evaluators need to decide whether to use the entire population, a random sample, or a purposive sample.

One argument for including the entire population is political or psychological—namely, people may be offended if they were not included. For example, the organizational attitudes of hospital nurses toward their work and supervisors could be accurately measured by taking a stratified random sample from the various nursing services. However, experience has shown that the hospital climate survey itself has a positive impact on nurses' job satisfaction when all nurses are given the opportunity to express their views through the survey.

Sometimes it is best to select certain groups in order to examine particular evaluation questions. There may be concern about types of program participants or people with particular problems. Some writers suggest that evaluators take special care to be sure that participants from a variety of program settings are included. If the program is effective in different settings, one can have considerable confidence in the findings of an evaluation (Campbell, 1986). Thus, for example, an evaluation of a reading program in a large urban school system could be based on schools whose students represent different ethnic and economic backgrounds rather than making a random selection of students from all schools.

There are two main arguments for using a sample of participants rather than the entire population when the populations are large—namely, time and money. Program evaluation must be done within a budget and usually there are some time restraints. When Greeley (1972) studied the effects of the Vatican Council on Catholic priests in the United States, he quite properly used a 10 percent stratified random sample of the 55,000 Catholic priests. Greeley was able to get more than an 80 percent return from his sample and had sufficient numbers for studying subsets of the population. Because he chose to work with a sample rather than with the entire population, he kept within his budget and had the project completed in a reasonable time.

However sampling is to be done, evaluators expect that some people will drop out of the study. Thus, one usually seeks a larger sample than is essential for the evaluation. It is important to identify the characteristics of nonparticipants and those who drop out at various points of time. Both the attrition rate and the reasons for dropping out have a bearing on the conclusions to be made from the data collected.

If more than 50 percent of the target population or random sample is lost, the extrapolation of the findings to the entire population cannot be done with any confidence. Therefore, with a population of 1,000 respondents, evaluators will generally be able to make more valid interpretations if they take a 10 percent sample and expend the effort to obtain a 75 percent response rate ($N = 75$) than if they try to reach the entire population and obtain only a 30 percent response rate ($N = 300$).

The composition of the participant group will have an effect on subject dropout rates. For example, in a hospital setting it is more difficult to obtain a high percentage of returns from housekeeping personnel than from nursing personnel on a written employee questionnaire. This occurs because many housekeeping personnel have difficulty reading English. In contacting patients in the aforementioned cancer care center study, it was difficult to obtain an adequate response rate because of the serious physical conditions of the target population. Therefore, the questionnaires had to be as short and simple as possible in order to obtain a response rate of 50 percent or better.

Control and comparison groups. When participants are randomly assigned to a group where they do not receive the services of the program being evaluated, they constitute a true *control group.* When participants in a program are compared to a group not receiving the services of the program but not randomly assigned to a group, we speak of a *comparison group* (or a *nonequivalent control group*). If the goal of the evaluation is to determine whether the program caused a change in the participants, the ideal evaluation involves random assignment of participants to the treatment and control groups. (We will point out in later chapters that establishing causal evidence is often not the objective of program evaluations. See also Cronbach, 1982.)

Random assignment is frequently impossible; however, there may be ways to achieve the equivalent of this, even when the evaluators do not have total control of the situation. For example, in an evaluation of primary nursing in a hospital,[1] the evaluators did not have control over which patients were assigned to the units with primary nursing or to those with team nursing. However, investigation showed that all physicians allowed their patients to be assigned to medical units on the basis of bed availability. This meant that although the evaluators had no control over the assignment of patients, situational factors resulted in random assignment. Demographic records of the patients in each group demonstrated that this system of random assignment resulted in two groups that were reasonably comparable.

One way of strengthening the interpretation of findings when one cannot have true control groups is to have more than one comparison group. For example, this was of great value in the cancer care center evaluation previously mentioned. On some variables patients in the special cancer unit reported attitudes significantly more favorable than did one comparison group and significantly less favorable than did the other comparison group. On other criteria the patients in the special unit scored higher than both comparison groups. Therefore, with the use of two comparison groups, the evaluators were able to identify the advantages of the program with greater precision.

Evaluations need not always be comparative. In some settings there are absolute standards of performance or quality against which results can be compared. For example, one does not need a control group when monitoring the performance of orthopedic physicians in setting broken bones. Nor does one need a control group to tell whether immunization shots are correctly given to children since the shots and timing are standard and well-known. In other settings the performance criteria are not clearcut; in those settings it is often of value to measure the level of variables among people not in the program being evaluated.

Selection of measures. The key idea with respect to measurement is to plan for multiple measures from multiple sources. Obviously, one of the main sources of data in program evaluation is the client. However, clients can provide data in more than one way. Clients can provide self-report measures by responding to direct questions about their perceptions and satisfaction with the program. They can also take tests designed to measure attitudes or moods that might have been affected by the program. Some such tests are described in the next chapter.

The behavior of clients can also be a source of data. For example, satisfaction with a new job-training program might be measured by the percentage of applicants who drop out of the new program as compared to other programs.

Another important source of data is significant others, that is, those people who are in close contact with the clients—for example, spouses, rela-

[1]Primary nursing refers to a situation in which an individual nurse is assigned to give complete care to a few patients in a unit. It is distinguished from team nursing, in which a group of nurses works under a head nurse to provide care as needed to an entire unit of patients, perhaps alternating their responsibilities from day to day. Primary nurses work more closely with physicians in developing care plans and in discharge planning.

tives, or close friends. Under some circumstances their perceptions may have less danger of bias than those of the clients themselves. For example, Ellsworth (1979) developed a multiple-scale measure of the progress of mental health patients to be completed by the spouse or relative with whom the patient lived after discharge from the hospital.

Program personnel are a source of data. Because program people are often skilled professionals, their perceptions in some ways can have greater validity than the perceptions of either the clients or significant others. On the other hand, they may tend to be biased by their personal involvement in the program.

One must not overlook the evaluator's own observations which provide data that cannot be obtained in any other way. This point is expanded at length in Chapter 12 on qualitative methods. Finally, access to program records permits evaluators to gather information that is often useful.

The possibility that subgroups of program participants may respond differently to the program may suggest that a number of outcome variables should be measured. For example, evaluations of rehabilitation programs for stroke patients would be better if they included separate measures for daily activities (such as walking, eating, dressing, and so forth) and for speaking and understanding skills. Responses to rehabilitation are different depending on whether the stroke patient suffered neurological damage on the left or the right brain hemisphere. College students with different reasons for attending college (such as career preparation, intellectual broadening, or postponement of assuming adult responsibilities) will respond differently to various college programs.

Data collection. Who will handle the day-to-day mechanics of data collection? This will usually involve an on-site coordinator who will keep the program evaluators abreast of the whereabouts of the program clients, personnel, and other sources of data, so that they can be contacted at appropriate times by the evaluation team. This is ordinarily a thankless and tedious task, but a reliable person must handle it.

Data collectors need to be sensitive to the issue of confidentiality. First, confidential information must be kept confidential. If information was obtained with an understanding of confidentiality, it should not be released until explicit approval is obtained. Second, the obligation of others to keep information confidential must be respected. Evaluators do not have an ethical right to all information, even when it might have a bearing on the evaluation. Other values may at times conflict with the needs of evaluators. Care must be taken not to ask information from people in a manner they find to be an invasion of privacy.

Choice of statistics. In any type of evaluation, appropriate statistics that will demonstrate both the level of statistical significance and the magnitude of effects are needed. It is preferable to use statistical procedures that are simple, because the findings will be presented to program sponsors and personnel who often do not have a great deal of mathematical expertise. Nonevaluators should ideally be able to understand and to be convinced by the interpretation of the results; they should not merely be impressed by statistical sophistication. At times complicated analyses will be necessary. However, it is good to keep in mind that nonevaluators will usually be more comfortable with less-complicated statistics. One approach is to use statistical analyses that are as powerful as necessary, but to illustrate the conclusions drawn using percentages or—even better—graphs.

Final report. Finally, some thought should be given during the planning stage to the format of the final report. Graphs and bar charts are usually preferable to tables of statistics. Where tables of statistics are necessary, they should be kept to a minimum and put in an appendix. It is advisable to rough out a few tables or charts and use some estimated figures to see whether or not the type and amount of data are appropriate for the planned layout. Often a consideration of the style of the report will suggest changes in the plans for data collection and analysis. Chapter 13 is devoted to more complete discussion of evaluation reports.

Step 6: Present a Written Proposal

After reviewing the literature and thinking through the various methodological considerations outlined in Step 5, the evaluators are ready to prepare a written proposal for presentation to program personnel. The overall purpose is to be certain that the evaluators and program personnel agree on the nature and goals of the program, the type of evaluation desired, the measures of the program goals, and the readiness of the program for evaluation. It is psychologically important for the program personnel to fully understand the evaluation process, feel comfortable with it, and (if possible) be enthusiastic about it.

Some issues that were previously discussed during the initial meetings may have to be worked through once again. Program personnel may now see procedural problems that were not at first apparent. It may be necessary to delay the beginning of data collection either because they feel the program is not sufficiently operational to undergo evaluation or because the temporary presence of extraneous factors might interfere with the interpretation of data. For example, if the proposal calls for the collection of data from hospital patients on their reactions to resident physicians who make rounds with attending physicians, it would be advisable to collect this at a time when medical students are not also making rounds with resident and attending physicians. Otherwise, the patients might confuse the residents with medical students who have neither graduated from medical school nor are actually providing care to patients. The problem can be handled by delaying data collection until the months when the medical students are not present.

POTENTIAL SOURCES OF RESISTANCE
TO PROGRAM EVALUATION

Political and psychological factors can undermine an evaluation project. Some factors are based on genuine concerns, while others are based on misunderstandings of evaluation. Effective evaluators will identify these factors during the planning stage, bring them to the surface promptly, and resolve them gently and directly. Resistance will be very hard to resolve when the evaluation is planned as a summative assessment of the program's impact.

Expectations of a "Slam-Bang" Effect

Program personnel are generally enthusiastic and confident about the potential effects of their program. Because many program managers and staff members are enthusiastic and put forth much effort, they expect their new program to have dramatic results—a "slam-bang" effect. They will have a tendency to feel betrayed if evaluators are able to demonstrate only a moderate improvement over the old program. The difficulty can arise when the program that was replaced was already achieving its goals reasonably well and the new program is expected to improve on the replaced program.

One way to handle the high level of expectation is to help program personnel arrive at some rule of thumb for improvement that can reasonably be expected. For example, if elementary school students are reading at appropriate levels, a new reading program is unlikely to raise their reading levels very much. The sponsors of a new reading program should be satisfied if they raise the reading achievement just a little. Perhaps students will like reading better. Furthermore, a small improvement experienced by *many* people could have a major overall impact (Cook and Shadish, 1986).

There are other reasons why the expected "slam-bang" effect may not occur. Whenever a group of participants is chosen for comparison with a group of participants in a new program, the comparison group will almost always be receiving some kind of service. It is rare that participants in a new program are compared to a group that receives no service at all. When evaluators are comparing two modalities of services, both of which are considered good, it is unlikely that they will find great differences between the group receiving the new program and the comparison group receiving the standard service. For example, if a group of psychosomatic patients admitted to a special program in a hospital are compared to psychosomatic patients treated privately by physicians but without the benefit of the special program, both groups should improve—because both groups are receiving professional treatment. Often the value of such a program is better demonstrated by showing that the type of patient treated in the special program is more in need of the services offered and that improvement of equal magnitude is more difficult to attain with severely distressed patients. When this approach is explained to the staff, it may help to lower "slam-bang" expectations.

Self-Styled Experts in Evaluation

Frequently program personnel have had some experience working on a research project. Because of this experience, they may feel attached to a specific evaluation design. For example, they may insist on testing subjects prior to a treatment or new program, while the evaluators feel that a pretest may artificially sensitize the subjects to the treatment to be evaluated.

Self-styled experts may also want to use their own favorite measurement instrument, even when the professional evaluators feel that it will needlessly lengthen a questionnaire they judge to be adequate for measuring the goals of the program. Evaluators are advised to take the time to listen to such suggestions carefully and with an open mind; the ideas may have some merit. If the suggestions seem counterproductive or not feasible, evaluators should be gentle but firm in adhering to the design and measures they feel are appropriate. If evaluators give in to pressure against their better judgment, they will have no one to blame but themselves if the project is poorly executed.

Fear that Evaluations Will Inhibit Innovation

Personnel in human service organizations may worry that evaluation will interfere with innovation by inhibiting them from experimenting with new techniques. In both process and outcome evaluations, the staff may feel that evaluation permits absolutely no variation in the program during the period of data collection. This is partially true insofar as there cannot be major structural changes in the program that would alter the essential goals or nature of the program. However, the need for retaining program identity does not mean that clinicians or program personnel cannot be flexible in the day-to-day operation of the program within broad structural boundaries. Every program will have variability built into it. Evaluation will not limit this. However, it is wise not to attempt to evaluate a program that is just getting started; major changes can occur as staff become clearer about their objectives.

Fear that the Program Will Be Terminated

Although it is seldom true that a negative evaluation will lead to a program's termination (Cook and Shadish, 1986), it is possible that an evaluation could result in the curtailment or elimination of a program when results demonstrate that a given approach is not working out as expected. However, before sponsors can eliminate a program designed to meet a specific problem, they are ordinarily under some pressure to decide what to put in its place. Therefore, it is more likely that an evaluation, even an unfavorable one, will result in the refinement of a program rather than its elimination.

Early in the planning stage, effective evaluators will try to have program personnel view them as valuable and needed associates. Evaluators can often achieve this goal by describing their work in terms of "documenting success." Program sponsors are inclined to demand accountability from program personnel as a condition for funding. Evaluators are there to assist program personnel in fulfilling this obligation to the sponsors.

It is not always possible to dispel the threat of evaluation completely. The reputation of the evaluators for trustworthiness and competence is a valuable asset. One practice that will allay some anxiety is to promise the program personnel that they will see the final draft of a report and be asked for their suggestions and clarifications before it is sent to the sponsors. Nevertheless, evaluators will not be able to eliminate anxiety completely in people who are basically insecure or who have doubts about their own competence. In a good program these persons will be in the minority.

Fear that Information Will Be Abused

In addition to the fear that a program may be terminated, there may exist some concern that information gained about the performance of staff may be abused. Even competent clinicians, administrators, teachers, and other personnel are rightly concerned about merit reviews, future promotion, and career advancement. Past experience may have taught them to be wary of evaluators who have overstepped the boundaries of program evaluation or who have been careless about maintaining confidences. When procedures for access to data are clearly stated in the planning phase and then are carefully followed, evaluators build trust that may allay such worries. It is easy to lose trust and hard to regain it once it has been lost. Effective evaluators will not only explicitly try to convey the idea that program evaluation is distinct from individual performance appraisal, but they will carefully avoid speaking or acting in such a way that might even give the appearance that they are engaged in such an activity.

Fear that Qualitative Understanding May Be Supplanted

Clincians, teachers, probation officers, and other service personnel rightly feel that their day-to-day observations are a valuable source of input both for improving the functioning of a program and for evaluating its effect. They may feel that the evaluators' questionnaires, complicated research designs, and statistical techniques are less sensitive than are their own personal observations and evaluations. At times they are right.

However, the point to be made with program personnel is that their input is one very valuable source of evaluation data. Nevertheless, their subjective evaluations can be biased and can be strengthened by both quantitative and qualitative data gathered from other sources. Their subjective observations will be of greatest importance when the data are being interpreted. The ideal is not to eliminate either the quantitative or qualitative approaches but rather to integrate and blend the findings from both methodologies.

Evaluators will gain the confidence of managers and staff not only by being aware of this problem but also by articulating this awareness in such a manner that program staff members are reassured that the intricacies of human services have been appropriately addressed. Early in the planning stage, the program personnel can be assured that the evaluation will not begin until they have had the opportunity to carefully review the evaluation proposal and feed assured that their concerns in this area have been addressed properly.

Fear that Evaluation Drains Program Resources

The six sources of resistance described thus far are focused on various aspects of evaluation but not on the concept of evaluation itself. Some objections to evaluation strike at the very concept of program evaluation. The staff may charge that program evaluation drains money that could be spent on direct service. As the statement stands, it is true. However, the main question is whether evaluation can improve service. The alternative to spending money on evaluation is to risk spending money on services that are of doubtful value. Those who present this objection fail to face the reality that the day of accountability has arrived. Today it is hard to find a program funded either by government agencies or by private foundations that does not carry the stipulation that a certain amount of money in the grant be spent on evaluation.

Those who are not convinced by the accountability argument may be convinced by a more pragmatic one: evaluation research, if done well, may help spread a good idea and may result in attracting more money and resources to a program.

Fear of Losing Control of the Program

When evaluations are conducted by consultants or in-house evaluators, program managers and staff members may fear that they are losing control of their work. They may feel that the right to make decisions about the way the program is offered will be reduced. Such a fear is probably groundless; however, it is quite common. Staff members rightly realize that they not be able to control the information about the program that will be available to members of the administration of the organization housing the program. Unless the staff knows that the program is grossly inadequate, this fear may be reduced by working closely with the program so that evaluation shows strengths as well as possible weaknesses. Sometimes programs can use evaluations to gain control since the evaluation will give evidence to use in presenting the case for a larger allotment of resources for the program.

Fear that Evaluation Has Little Impact

Some critics of evaluation point out that frequently evaluation has very little impact on programs. There is a good deal of validity to this objection; evaluators have often been frustrated by seeing their reports set aside and disregarded.

However, evaluators should reflect on the hard reality that evaluation research is not a benign social science activity but rather a political decision-making tool. If relevant, evaluation results will be included among the other factors behind decisions. Because evaluation researchers work in a political context, the results of their work must be timely and relevant to decision making (Cronbach, 1982). Well-designed and carefully executed studies are valuable only when they speak to issues that are important to the organization. When evaluators fail to show how the evaluation is relevant, they have not completed their work.

In spite of the apparent validity of complaints about lack of impact, there is also some evidence that these complaints are overstated. First, evaluation studies have had a cumulative effect in certain areas. For example, the common finding that class size has marginal effects on learning may at first incline one to set aside the factor of class size as being of minimal importance. However, research done on schools in other countries has now shown that the marginal effect of class size holds only within the range of class sizes customarily found in American schools (Berk and Rossi, 1976). Therefore, it sometimes takes time before the significance of evaluation research can be put into perspective.

Second, evaluation research has some long-term value insofar as it challenges conventional wisdom. For example, the New Jersey negative income tax experiment boldly tested one of the oldest, most central economic assumptions. Most economists and politicians predicted that even a limited amount of guaranteed income would lead to massive malingering and a loss of motivation to work. The study yielded mixed results, some significantly at odds with expectations. For example, the findings indicated that a national program of guaranteed income at the benefit levels considered in this experiment would have only relatively small effects on the labor supply of male family heads (Haveman and Watts, 1976). The potential of evaluation research for challenging conventional wisdom is also illustrated by the Coleman Report (Coleman et al., 1966). This evaluation showed that schools make smaller contributions to the learning of children than does family background.

An unexpected benefit of the apparently limited impact of evaluation on programs has been the shift from summative evaluation to a greater emphasis on formative evaluation. This shift has helped to increase the involvement of evaluators in the planning stages of programs. This new emphasis and orientation of program evaluation is reflected in the subject matter and style of this text. Chapter 5 develops the role of the evaluator in program planning in greater detail.

SUMMARY

Following the six steps in planning an evaluation project serves to get the evaluation off to a good start. Note that the steps are suggested to help the evaluator to be responsive to the needs of the people most concerned about the evaluation. Responsive evaluators will have fewer problems with the resistances outlined in the second part of the chapter, compared to evaluators who seem less concerned about stakeholder needs.

STUDY QUESTIONS

1. As an outside consultant you are invited by a large manufacturing plant to evaluate a new training program for managers, called "Management Contact," which you are told applies the principles of transactional analysis to employer-employee relations. Explain the steps you would take and what you would need to know in approaching this job. What would be the major difficulties you would see?

2. Imagine that you are part of an evaluation team in the institutional research office of a major university. The chairperson of the department of psychology instructs you to evaluate a new graduate program called "Community Psychology." How would you approach this task? What would be the major pitfalls to avoid?

3. Suppose that you have been asked to evaluate the "Officer Friendly" program. You may recall from elementary school that a police officer comes to schools to talk to children about bike safety, dealing with strangers, how to call police, etc. The general goals for such a program include lowered accident rates among children and a better image of police officers. List the implicit theoretical assumptions that lie beneath those goals. In other words, what must happen for the goals of this program to be achieved?

FURTHER READING

BRINKERHOFF, R. O., ET AL. 1983. *Program evaluation: A practitioner's guide for trainers and educators—a design manual.* Boston: Kluwer-Nijhoff.

3

Measurement Principles and Tools

The selection of appropriate variables and strategies to measure those variables is of critical importance in designing an evaluation. The authors decided to present this subject here because these principles apply to all the forms of evaluation described in later chapters. The selection of measures is not easy, and a poor choice could reduce an otherwise well-planned evaluation to a futile endeavor. Each approach has advantages and disadvantages; therefore, a measurement approach useful in one evaluation may be inappropriate in another.

SOURCES OF DATA FOR EVALUATIONS

There are six major sources of data relevant to evaluations: (1) program records; (2) program participants; (3) staff delivering the program; (4) family members or other people with significant relationships to the participants; (5) observations of the evaluator; and (6) community-level indexes. The characteristics of the program to be evaluated, the questions addressed to the evaluator, and the resources available will determine which sources are used.

Program Records

A search of the program's records and files, its archives, can often provide reliable and inexpensive data for the evaluator. Archival data are most useful when the evaluation includes an examination of client characteristics, types of service provided, workload of the staff members, costs of providing services, or trends across long time intervals. When archival data are objective (for example, number of visits, type of service, or identity of the care-giver), the data will be very valid. On the other hand, diagnoses and other subjective entries may not be quite so valid. Furthermore, Krause and Jackson (1983) found that state summary records were quite inaccurate compared to an agency's own records. Two of the most important advantages of archival data are: (1) the measurement process does not affect the program participant; and (2) there can be no participant loss due to refusal or inability to participate. Some aspects of archival searches used as feedback material are discussed at greater length in Chapter 6.

Maintaining confidentiality is a problem that can become acute when using the program's records. Some evaluations using public documents need not be concerned with limiting access to the data. However, many evaluations utilize hospital, school, personnel, or counselor records that are clearly confidential. Some information in files may be damaging to a person's social and financial affairs. The inadvertent release of such data might even open evaluators to legal suits. In less sensitive situations a lack of sufficient care would make evaluators look unprofessional, and the resulting loss of credibility might result in their being denied access to records the next time it is requested. Evaluators cannot function without access to data.

There are a number of ways in which evaluators can protect the confidentiality of data used in the evaluation. For example, it is not always necessary to identify data by a person's name. At times researchers have used information to identify records that only the clients or patients themselves would recognize. For example, the first name and birthdate of a respondent's mother would provide a code for gathering all of the person's data together without using the person's name. If it might be necessary to contact the respondent in the future, the project director alone should keep a master list of the respondents' names and addresses and the associated code information. Some workers using very sensitive material have stored the names and code information in a different country. Most readers of this text will not be dealing with data that sensitive. For those who find themselves in sensitive positions, more sophisticated methods for guaranteeing confidentiality are discussed by Riecken and Boruch (1974) and by Campbell et al. (1977).

Program Participants

There are several reasons to look to program participants for evaluative information. First, the person who actually receives a service is often in an excellent position to evaluate many aspects of the program. The direct contact the clients have with the staff provides them with important knowledge about the program that no one else has. Second, only the clients have access to their own feelings about the program and staff. For example, after interviewing deinstitutionalized chronically ill psychiatric patients, Shadish et al. (1985)

concluded that the patients' sense of well-being was damaged by being released. Third, for many criteria the clients will be the most knowledgeable about their current state, especially at follow-up intervals. Further, they might well be the only available source of information about the use they make of additional follow-up services. A fourth advantage is that the information they provide is often relatively inexpensive to gather. Fifth, self-assessments have been found to be at least as accurate as other assessment approaches for a variety of behavioral and emotional dimensions (Shrauger and Osberg, 1981).

On the other side of the coin, certain participants may be too incapacitated to be valid sources of evaluation information. In planning an evaluation of a physical medicine and rehabilitation unit, one will quickly discover that few recent stroke victims can validly describe their own capabilities. Some are unable to talk, others have poor judgment, and others are so crushed emotionally by their impairments that it seems cruel to discuss their problems with them. Certain types of patients seeking psychotherapy cannot provide valid data; however, many others can.

Perhaps participants can provide good data for some aspects of the program but not others. General hospital patients usually know if rooms are clean, whether nurses and resident physicians treat them politely, and how long they have to wait outside the X-ray room. However, they cannot evaluate the choice of medication or the competence of their surgeons. Similarly, college students can report on whether a teacher returned tests promptly, held classes as scheduled, and lectured or led class discussions. It is very unlikely that many undergraduates can evaluate the accuracy of the information presented. In sum, participants can validly comment on objective aspects of the services given as well as their satisfaction with the services.

Evaluators are faced with the task of motivating the program participants to provide personal information about their attitudes and judgments. Participants may refuse to cooperate due to fear of public disclosure of personal information. Routinely, anonymity in reports is guaranteed. Many people do not understand the social scientist's disinterest in the personal facts about individuals, nor do they understand the necessity of using overall group averages and proportions in evaluation reports. They are familiar with the case study approach often used in popular newspaper and magazine discussions of medical, correctional, counseling, and educational programs. It is not surprising then that some respondents do not believe promises of anonymity. One respondent to a survey administered in a group setting without a way to identify the respondents wrote the following: "I have tried to be honest. I hope I don't lose my job." American society is going through a litigious and suspicious period. Evaluators cannot afford to give respondents cause to question their motives for requesting personal information.

Even when people are not afraid of public disclosure, they must still be motivated to spend time completing the forms and surveys. One approach is to appeal to the person's interest in improving the program being evaluated. Many people are sufficiently altruistic to be willing to share their feelings if they realize that their time can contribute to the improvement of services for others. However, they are not so altruistic that they will spend a long time or struggle with a poorly written survey.

Which program participants are most likely to cooperate? The experience of survey users is that those with the most favorable impressions of a program or facility are the most likely to respond. The 86 percent who responded to a lengthy survey on a chaplaincy internship were independently evaluated by their supervisors as having performed better during the internship year than the 14 percent who did not return the survey (Posavac, 1975). However, some very angry people may well write lengthy criticisms.

Participant information may be part of an evaluation in the form of vivid illustrations of very good staff performance, or, in contrast, very bad performance. Through case studies of teenagers Love (1986) showed that troubled adolescents were unlikely to fit into the mental health and welfare systems in a large city. Although a case study cannot show the extent of problems, it can show, for example, how specific program failures do occur.

Staff

Program staff people are important sources of data for evaluations. Staff members are trained to assess the degree of the participants' impairments and are in a good position to detect improvement. Also, they are the most likely to know how well a program is managed and how well the program runs on a day-to-day basis. On the negative side, staff members can be expected to be biased toward seeing improvement. After committing their efforts to helping people improve their skills or adjustment, it may be hard to accept failure.

Over and above these concerns, the evaluators need to recognize that evaluating a program is in some ways an evaluation of the staff's performance. Few people unhesitatingly welcome an evaluation of the effectiveness of the services they provide. Most people will be concerned about the use to which an evaluation will be put. If they are worried, they will resist the evaluation. Some college professors refuse to permit students conducting course evaluations to enter their classrooms. Some psychotherapists argue that checklists of symptoms and rating forms are blind to the crucial but subtle changes in a client that the therapist alone can sense. Because evaluation is not a developed science with unquestioned techniques (see Cronbach, 1977), it is easy to find weaknesses in the most carefully planned program evaluation. One way to reduce staff resistance is to provide some benefit for the staff as a byproduct of the evaluation of their program. Opportunities for improvement, workshops, and individual guidance, for example, should be tied in with an evaluation so that it is a learning experience. One must recognize that some evaluations have not been learning experiences. At times evaluators have been neglected to make a presentation to the staff of the program evaluated. Making a presentation to the staff is the least evaluators can do in return for the staff's cooperation.

Significant Others

If a program is designed to change the behavior (e.g., counseling and corrective programs) or the health of a person, family members will be affected. They must adjust their own behaviors as patients or clients change. Significant others see the recipients of human services (except for inpatients and prisoners) more frequently than the staff does, and they see the participants in natural settings, not merely in the short-term, artificial setting created by the program. Of course, family members may have biases just as staff members do; however, the direction of these biases may be hard to predict. In a comparison of nurses' ratings with spouses' ratings of the capabilities of stroke patients, we learned that nurses rated the patients as more proficient in performing daily activities (dressing, eating, grooming) than the spouses did. On the other hand, spouses rated the patients as being more proficient in cognitive tasks (speaking, reading, memory) than the nurses did.[1] In any program some family members will report more improvement than actually occurred, while others will report less. Because the focus is on program-level outcomes, not *individual* assessments, these idiosyncratic biases are less important than systematic biases such as those found with the stroke patients.

When requesting information about program participants from significant others, it is necessary to have the participants' permission beforehand. People vary in their willingness to have spouses or others provide personal information to the evaluation staff. In evaluations of hospitalized psychiatric inpatients, Ellsworth (1979) reports that 21 percent were too incapacitated to give or withhold permission, 19 percent refused the give permission, and 7 percent could not name a significant other to complete the evaluation forms. Therefore, a smaller proportion of the population can be assessed using the ratings of significant others as compared to the proportion who can provide self-ratings. Motivating respondents to cooperate will follow the lines previously mentioned—emphasizing the long-term improvement of the program for others. In seeking permission to contact a patient's or client's significant other, care should be taken that the request does not imply that good treatment in the program is contingent on the person's giving permission for such contact. Further, it is important that permission forms be written at a level that is comprehensible to the program participant. Often these forms are written at a level more suitable for a professional researcher (Gray, Cooke, and Tannenbaum, 1978).

Evaluator Observations

In some settings evaluations are conducted by sending a team of evaluators to make direct observations of the program. Colleges are accredited through

---

[1]For the interested reader, this finding was explained in the following fashion: Spouses, being familiar with the stroke patient, needed fewer cues for effective communication; however, like most people, stroke patients tend to perform grooming and self-care types of behaviors at a higher level for strangers than for family members.

a process that includes a several-day site visit by college deans and other administrators. The team's direct observations are combined with other information in preparing the evaluation report. The advantage of direct observations lies in the fact that people who are experts in the services provided by the program but are not involved in the program being evaluated, are the least biased sources of information (Endicott and Spitzer, 1975). As chapter 12 points out, observations of how the program really operates can be essential in understanding the program and making sense of the various forms of evaluative data.

Community Indexes

Some programs are planned to improve community-level variables. Examples of programs designed to influence the community include: a crime-reporting program designed to increase citizen participation in criminal surveillance and to change community-level indexes, such as arrest rates and crime rates; a reading program designed to raise the achievement levels of the children in a school district; and a citizen-developed project to monitor housing code violations thought to increase or maintain the quality of the housing in a neighborhood. Jason and Liotta (1982) used number of busy signals, time to answer a telephone call, and seconds on hold as measures of businesses' and community agencies' responsiveness to citizen needs.

The major difficulty with using community-level indexes is that there are many steps between the program and the hoped-for end results (Cook, Leviton, and Shadish, 1985). There are so many nonprogram variables influencing arrest rate, quality of housing, or reading level that an effective program may not be detectable. These influences are beyond the control of the staff. An evaluator who uses only community-level indexes in an outcome study may be left quite in the dark about the reasons for apparent failure or success.

Which Sources Should Be Used?

The choice of sources of data depends on the cost of obtaining data, the type of decision to be made on the basis of the evaluation, the size of the program, and the time available to conduct the evaluation. If a program needs feedback information, it is likely that records, participant attitudes, and family reports may be very helpful. If a decision is planned to expand (or to eliminate) an expensive, controversial program, the judgments and observations of outside experts may be the only source of data that will suffice. Such decisions must be made carefully on the basis of a widely accepted evaluation.

Regardless of the type of program or anticipated decision, evaluators should strive to use multiple measures from more than one source. In choosing multiple measures, it is especially important to select measures that are not likely to share the same biases. For example, a subjective assessment of the success of a program by a client may be mirrored by the subjective feelings of the client's spouse. If, on the other hand, a measure of subjective feelings is used with ratings of ability to function in specific settings or with objective achievement, evaluators are less likely to obtain sets of data with the same biases. When the same implication is drawn from a variety of sources, the evaluation will be treated as having greater credibility.

However, it also is possible that the multiple approaches will not agree. Shipley (1976) conducted an evaluation of a companion program for mentally ill patients. College students served as volunteer companions to discharged psychiatric patients. The volunteers, patients, and hospital staff all subjectively evaluated the program in quite glowing terms. However, more objective measures of the patients' behavior (by staff ratings and by frequency and duration of rehospitalizations) revealed quite *variable* reactions. Some patients apparently benefited, and others did not. His use of multiple measures led Shipley to a conclusion different from those of previous studies using only subjective attitude measures. In a similar vein Sullivan and Snowden (1981) found that staff, clients, standard tests, and agency files did not agree about the problems clients had. Evaluators need to be sensitive to the possibility that their selection of sources of data and of specific measures can lead to misleading conclusions.

The fact that evaluators frequently work with people trained in service delivery techniques, not in research methods, means that evaluators have considerable discretion in choosing the criteria of effectiveness and the analyses of those criteria. Berk (1977), Berk and Rossi (1976), and Zigler and Trickett (1978) go so far as to say that through their choice of variables and methods of analyses, evaluators can determine the results of an evaluation before it is conducted. Thus, to be fair to programs and to the consumers of program evaluations, evaluators must examine their own attitudes as they design an evaluation. Otherwise, their own biases may determine their findings. The following section describes the most important issues to consider when choosing assessment procedures.

PRINCIPLES IN CHOOSING ASSESSMENT PROCEDURES

Evaluators use several criteria in selecting methods of gathering the data required in an evaluation. Keeping these principles in mind while planning a study saves evaluators time and inconvenience later.

Multiple Variables

Evaluators usually recommend the use of multiple sources of information. It is also recommended that evaluators use multiple variables from their data sources; the elevation of a single variable to be *the* criterion of success can obscure an effect (Lipsey et al., 1985) and will probably corrupt it (Sechrest, 1984). A grisly example is the variable "body count" used in daily reports on the Vietnam War. The nature of the war made it hard to claim territorial gains. Thus, dead enemy soldiers were to be counted as a measure of the success of friendly forces. It became apparent that focusing on this variable led to its being inflated by counting every death as that of an enemy, even when those killed were civilians not taking part in the fighting. Barbour and Wolfson (1973) describe the difficulty of defining productivity of police officers. Concentrating on arrests may unintentionally encourage poor practices in gathering evidence necessary for convictions; or police officers may make arrests when the interests of justice would be better served without an arrest. Turner (1977) described the effect of a poorly defined criterion for mental health workers who refer clients to other public agencies. The criterion of successful referrals was defined as "90 percent of referred clients actually make contact with the new agency." The evaluator quickly learned that the mental health workers were escorting the individuals to the other agencies. Although the workers were scoring well on the criterion of successful referral—those referred to other agencies did make contact—other aspects of their work were left unfinished.

One way to avoid corrupting the criteria chosen and to avoid distorting the operation of a human service system is to use multiple variables. It is especially important that the variables serve as a check on one another. Thus, *both* arrest rate and conviction rate should be used as the measures of police productivity. Percentage of successful referrals *and* number of clients served should be used as criteria for assessing the work of a mental health worker screening people in need of various services.

An additional important reason to use multiple variables is that different variables are affected by different sources of error. If the multiple variables are measured in ways that are similar and if they come from the same source (for example, program participants), it may turn out that all the variables are affected by the same biases. When this happens, the extra effort is probably of little value. By using several variables, assessed by different methods from different sources of data, stakeholders can trust implications drawn from the convergence of these various sources of data (Mark and Shotland, 1987).

Important Variables

Because program evaluation is an applied social science, the variables to be measured must be relevant to the specific informational needs of facility management, community representatives, those responsible for budgets, and others. Thus, in planning an evaluation, evaluators must learn what questions are pressing and are as yet unanswered. The variables to be measured are then chosen on the basis of their importance to the questions facing administrators, staff, and other stakeholders.

The time at which a variable is measured may determine whether it provides appropriate information. The impact of educational services can often be assessed at the end of a program. Other human services are provided with the goal of altering the course of a person's life. Thus, the success of a program for juvenile delinquents can be better judged by the degree to which participants stay out of trouble with the law over a period of time. The participant's status at the end of a program is less informative than his or her status three or six months later. Still other programs should be evaluated on the basis of their success over a period of years.

The major way to approach selecting important and relevant variables is through discussions with staff and managers. If there is no decision to be affected by the variable, regardless of its value, or if no program standards mention the variable, then it probably is not important or relevant to the evaluation. If the location of the program participants' homes is not at all important to administrators, evaluators probably will not record it. However, at times evaluators may feel that a variable *should* be important and would be seen as important once summarized. Evaluators should not feel completely limited to recording just the information program managers and staff recognize as important. In other chapters we point out specific instances in which information that was not requested came as a surprise to the program staff. Furthermore, unintended negative side effects, which will certainly not be mentioned in program goals, should be considered.

Sensitivity to Change

There are two general types of measures of psychological and intellectual variables. One type seeks to assess an individual's general, typical level on some variable, and the other type seeks to assess current mood or achievement. Some writers have called the first type a measure of *trait* (Spielberger, 1972). The other type of measure has been developed to assess effects that trait instruments seek to minimize. Such an instrument is called a measure of *state*. A measure of state seeks to assess the individual's current level on a variable. The extent to which a measure of state is influenced by the individual's typical way of being is defined as a weakness of such a measure.

The distinction between intelligence tests and classroom tests may help to illustrate this point. Before a course few class members are expected to score well on a test covering the course material. However, after the course students are expected to do well if they have mastered the course material. The classroom test should be sensitive to the changes that have occurred in the skills of the students. Fairly stable characteristics of the students (such as intelligence) should not be primary factors leading to differences among the students' classroom test scores. In contrast, stable characteristics are expected to lie behind the differences obtained using standard intelligence tests. Although intelligence is certainly not fixed and does change in response to many environmental influences, the developers of intelligence tests sought to find test items that were minimally influenced by the individual's mood and immediate situation. It is not possible for a test to be completely unaffected by a person's habitual way of acting prior to entering the program; however, when measuring program outcome, the goal is to use instruments least affected by stable prior conditions and thus most likely to detect real changes in participants.

Evaluators usually choose measures of program output that are maximally sensitive to change, because change is what evaluators are trying to detect. This point is especially important in the evaluation of various forms of psychotherapy; therapists, who are so familiar with standardized personality tests, often approach program evaluation in the same manner as they approach individual client assessment. Individual assessment instruments are designed to measure personality and intelligence traits. Tests that show marked sensitivity to situational differences are not desirable for personality and intelligence measurement. In contrast, evaluators want a measurement instrument that is sensitive to respondents' current (hopefully improved) state. Using a trait measure to detect change puts the program at a considerable disadvantage by needlessly raising the probability of overlooking the change that did in fact occur.

Several methods can be used to check on the expected sensitivity of a measure. Previous effective use of the dependent variables with evaluations of similar programs would give one confidence that a variable is sufficiently sensitive. If the variable is to be assessed using a newly developed measure, evaluators might look for existing groups which differ on the variable to be measured. If a procedure to measure scientific reasoning does not distinguish students in a physics class from those in an English class, one would not expect it to be useful as an outcome measure for an evaluation of an innovative science curriculum (see Lipsey, 1983).

A final point about sensitivity to change was alluded to in the previous chapter—very good performance is hard to improve. Just as it is harder to go from an A to a perfect paper than it is to go from a C to a C+, it is hard to improve a program participant's condition or level of satisfaction if the program is already fairly effective and well received. In such a setting the criteria of success cannot change much. Evaluations dependent on detecting such small changes will usually conclude that the innovative program is no better than the old one, even when the innovative program is indeed better. There are statistical approaches to dealing with such situations; however, they are beyond the scope of this text.

Valid Measures

In an evaluation the instruments must validly measure the behaviors the program is designed to change. These behaviors may be the ultimate criteria behaviors (such as long life, better adjustment, employment) or more immediate behaviors that are believed to be useful in achieving the planned long-term outcomes (such as higher quality work and improved leadership practices).

In order to assure themselves of the validity of chosen measures, evaluators should share the measures with the program staff. If staff members have not approved the measures, they may later disown a negative evaluation as being based on invalid tools. Implementation of suggestions for program change may be strongly resisted if staff members did not share in the choice of instruments. However, evaluators must not depend totally on the staff members to suggest the measures, because program staff members are often inexperienced in social science methodology.

In general, any measurement tool will be more likely to have acceptable validity if the tool focuses on objective behavior rather than on undefined or vague terms. Objective behaviors (such as "late to work less than one day out of the week" or "speaks in groups") are more likely to be measured validly than less precise criteria (such as "is punctual" or "is assertive"), regardless of what specific measurement approach is chosen. Mager (1972) presents an informal but thorough discussion of the usefulness of behavioral criteria rather than personality trait words in specifying the achievement of a goal.

Some variables may appear to be valid when in fact they are very misleading. Campbell (1969) presented several measures of the frequencies of types of crime in Chicago plotted over time. In 1957 a liberal, highly regarded person was installed as chief of police. The year after his term began, official statistics on the number of thefts under $50 increased dramatically. Did the new chief cause a crime wave? Not likely. Instead, his reforms led to a more thorough reporting of crime and perhaps some reclassification of crimes. A check on the interpretation that the chief caused a crime wave was provided by the homicide rate. Homicides seldom go unreported and cannot be reclassified into a different crime category. When frequency of homicides was plotted over time, there was no noticeable change after the chief began. A very similar increase in crime statistics in Chicago occurred in the early months of 1983, when reporting standards were again improved ("Good news," 1983). Evaluators try to select and interpret variables carefully in order to avoid a misleading conclusion based on a poor choice of performance criteria.

Reliable Measures

Social behaviors cannot be measured perfectly because such measurements are affected by the respondent's mood, attitude, and understanding of directions—things that are extraneous to the behavior of interest. The degree to which people who are theoretically equivalent on a social variable such as depression actually score the same on a test is the test's reliability. In somewhat oversimplified terms, a reliable test will yield much the same values if administered twice within a short period of time. Reliability, like validity, is higher if the scores are minimally influenced by the passing mood of the person completing the instrument, whether that person is a program participant, staff member, or evaluator. The more reliable a measure is, the more likely it is to detect a difference between groups.

Variables referring to objective information and behavior are likely to be more reliable than subjective ratings or opinions. This does not mean to imply that ratings should never be used. We simply want to stress that it is harder to judge whether people are, for example, ambitious, than to record whether they have found jobs or have been promoted at work. Subjective ratings are usually less reliable since they are influenced not only by the behavior of the person being rated but also by the person doing the ratings.

Evaluators must appreciate the differences between the use of measures to estimate the general level of a *group* on some variable and their use to assess an *individual* on the variable. The greater the number of individuals whose responses are combined to estimate the level of the group, the more stable the estimate. Thus, surveys and other forms of measurement that would be rejected as insufficiently reliable to assess the views or behaviors of individuals may be very useful as measures of a group's views or behaviors. The following paragraphs illustrate the importance of the difference between estimating an individual's score and a group's score.

By using the standard deviation of a test and its reliability, it is possible to calculate a range of values that is likely to include the individual's true score. For example, assume that a person scored 105 on an IQ test with a standard deviation of 15 and a reliability of .95. The true scores of 68 percent of the people getting 105 will be between $105 \pm 15 \sqrt{1 - .95}$, or between 101.6 and 108.4. The standard deviation times the square root of 1 minus the reliability is called the *standard error of estimate* and is applied when an *individual's* score is the question of interest (see Brown, 1983).

On the other hand, when a *group's* mean score is to be estimated, the *standard error of the mean* is the statistic to be used, instead of the standard deviation as in the calculation given above. If a group of 81 people scored an average of 105 on the IQ test, the standard error of the mean is $15/\sqrt{81}$, or 1.67. We can conclude that 68 percent of such *groups* have true mean scores of between $105 \pm 1.67 \sqrt{1 - .95}$, or between 104.6 and 105.4. Compare this range with the range calculated in the previous paragraph. Even a measure with a reliability of only .40 would yield a sufficiently precise group estimate, although a test with such a low reliability would be inappropriate for use with individuals.[2]

There are a variety of reliability indexes that are reported in test manuals. Some are very relevant to evaluation work, and others are not useful for evaluators. The classic *test-retest* approach to reliability is not as important to evaluation as it is to the area of psychological assessment. The reason for this was alluded to in the section on sensitivity to change. Tests that are developed to be stable over time measure well-entrenched, habitual behaviors and are precisely the sort of tests evaluators do not want. Evaluators require measures of behaviors that are subject to change.

Split-half reliability, which is found by correlating the scores respondents earned on the odd-numbered test items with the scores earned on the even-numbered test items, is quite important to evaluators. Split-half reliability gauges the extent to which a psychological measure is homogeneous, that is, sensitive to one concept or characteristic rather than to a mixture of things. If a reading program is to be evaluated, the instrument to measure reading achievement should not include items requiring broad general knowledge or quantitative skills.

---

[2]Readers wishing more details on these points should examine an introductory statistics text, such as McCall (1986), and a testing text, such as Brown (1983).

Evaluators also look for *interrater reliability*, that is, agreement between independent raters. Often the criteria of success of a program include ratings made by professionals or relatives. An instrument that yields similar ratings when used by different observers is usually better than one that yields quite different values. Obviously, if the observers view the rated individuals in very different situations—at home versus in school—low interrater reliability may tell us more about the differences in situations than about the reliabilities of the ratings.

Nonreactive Measures

The mere act of requesting information from people or observing people can influence the behavior being studied. Measurement instruments will create questions that some people have never considered before. Raising an issue may make people more aware of things they previously ignored. The test itself will bore some respondents, offend some, and please others. The greater the behavioral change created by the measurement instrument, the greater its *reactivity*. Measuring the effect of human services is not at all similar to making physical measurements of inanimate objects.

Usually evaluators do not want to select measurement procedures that influence the people studied. If the instruments have an impact, the evaluation loses some of its usefulness, because the outcomes may be different once the instruments are no longer used. Completely nonreactive measurement is an ideal seldom actually achieved. An extended discussion of reactivity has been prepared by Webb et al. (1981).

At times a tool becomes part of the program not only because it provides data but also because it influences those concerned to follow correct procedures; or it raises questions that need to be answered if the program is to be a success. Figure 11.3 is an example of an evaluation tool designed to cause staff members to do certain things that were previously overlooked. If the people giving care to alcoholics complete the form responsibly, they will not only provide evaluation data for the state board but will also be fulfilling crucial steps in the ideal treatment of alcoholics.

Cost-Effective Measures

In planning a program evaluation, the cost of the test materials and the costs of gathering data must not be forgotten. It is necessary to select instruments that will measure the required variables within acceptable cost limits. Several principles are usually true. First, time and money invested in making test materials attractive and easy to use will be repaid in higher response rates. Second, money spent on published forms will be small relative to the costs of the evaluation staff in collecting and analyzing the data. Third, because interviews cost far more than do other measurement approaches, interviews should not be used without considering all alternatives. Some evaluative questions can be answered without requiring extensive interviews. Other questions are too complicated to address in only a written form. At times, respondents will be unable to use written material, will need prompting or encouragement to respond, will not respond to written surveys, or may be expected to be defensive or misleading in answering written surveys.

Last, the effect of the instruments on participant loss must be considered. No participant would be lost to the research in a study of the program's records. Many participants, on the other hand, will be lost if a lengthy survey is mailed to people after they have left the program. Thus, an instrument that is itself inexpensive may not be cost effective (1) if evaluators must spend a considerable amount of time following up on many tardy respondents; or (2) if so few respond that the results are not representative of any group.

TYPES OF MEASURES

Evaluators employ several general types of measures. The major distinction among the approaches is the degree to which they depend on self-reported impressions versus objective observations. The principles just introduced will be used to describe the strengths and weaknesses of the approaches presented.

Written Surveys Completed by Program Participants

Probably the most widely used technique for evaluating programs is the written survey. The survey technique provides the most information per dollar or hour investment by the evaluation staff. Surveys are not expensive to reproduce or to buy. If they are complex and especially constructed for a particular evaluation, their cost will be higher. (Guidelines for writing survey items will be discussed later in this chapter.)

Surveys vary greatly in their reliability and validity because the topics they cover are so different. A survey asking former clients to give a global, subjective evaluation of their experience in therapy will not be highly reliable; responses will vary with the moods of the people responding or with the particular aspect of the service they think about. Similarly, students' evaluations of teachers may be influenced by whether a difficult assignment is due soon or whether test results have just been returned. On the other hand, a survey may yield quite reliable judgments if it focuses on current behavior, such as jobs held, further treatment sought, source of referral, and so on. Many of these same remarks apply to the validity of surveys as well. The more objective the material evaluators request, the more likely responses will be valid estimates of the issue in question.

The loss of participants to the evaluation may be large if the samples are mobile, if the survey is long, or if the participants feel ambivalent toward the program. Evaluators must be prepared to follow up a mailed survey with reminder letters or phone calls to those who do not return the survey within two weeks (Anderson and Berdie, 1975). If only a minority of the sample returns a survey, the responses of the whole sample cannot be estimated. Certainly, receiving returns from fewer than 50 percent of the sample makes the survey useless for many purposes—but not for all purposes, as will be mentioned later.

Regardless of how the survey is to be used, those who do not respond will still be different from those who return the survey. In one study the 66 percent who returned a survey about their experience in outpatient counseling participated in an average of 20.2 counseling sessions, and those who did not respond participated in an average of only 9.5 sessions (Posavac and Hartung, 1977). Experienced survey users expect to find such differences and recognize the limitations these differences impose on the certainty with which conclusions may be drawn.

Ratings of the Program Participants by Others

Ratings by people important in the program participants' lives can be used as measures of program success. As with surveys, ratings made by significant others may be very reliable if they focus on relatively objective behavior, such as absenteeism, participation in discussions, or physical health. On the other hand, they may be unreliable if they focus on undefined and vague variables, such as adjustment or success in the program. Our experience with forms mailed to spouses indicates that the return rate for forms mailed to significant others is similar to that of mailed self-report surveys.

The cost of ratings may be high if professional staff members are expected to perform numerous or detailed ratings. If ratings are done by nonprofessionals and are kept brief, the cost may be acceptably low. Who is expected to do the ratings will be related to how complete the data will be. Members of the evaluation team will probably complete nearly all the ratings planned; however, significant others may resent the intrusion of the team, and professional staff members may feel that the ratings are an oversimplification of their professional judgment. The best that evaluators can do is to keep the rating form easy to use and to stress that the focus of the study is to obtain documentation of program effectiveness—not information on personal affairs. If people are willing to take a long-range view, they will see that they have an ultimate self-interest in improving program effectiveness.

Interviews

Gathering evaluative information by personal interview is useful when evaluators need to develop an understanding of the program, when they want to obtain information from people with unique information, or when they are not at all sure what is most important to interviewees (Guba and Lincoln, 1981). Since interviewing is an expensive way to gather data, it is not done unless it is necessary. Interviewing is not simply shooting the breeze with program clients or staff; it is a difficult job that requires considerable preparation. Good interviewers are thoroughly familiar with the issues to be addressed in the interview sessions. At times, specific questions will be addressed to the respondents; in other situations the questions will be quite general. A more detailed discussion of interviews is given in Chapter 12 on qualitative methods.

An alternative to interviewing a participant face to face is a telephone interview. The cost of a telephone interview is much lower, and research indicates that the material obtained is of nearly equal validity (*ISR Newsletter*, 1978). A letter received before the telephone call explaining the need for the study and requesting cooperation may improve a respondent's receptivity.

Behavioral Observations

Probably the method with the most potential for providing valid information is the behavioral observation approach. The ultimate outcome of any program is expected to be behavioral change. Examples include better ways of handling anger, better performance on the job, or ability to write a theme. The goals of a program are often difficult to translate into behavioral terms, and people are usually unavailable for observations. However, when the behaviors are public, observations may be feasible. Actual seat belt usage was measured by observers at stop signs and stop lights in an evaluation of a television advertising campaign to increase the proportion of passenger-car users who use their seat belts (Robertson et al., 1974).

A complex observational procedure is described by Paul (1986) for evaluating residential treatment settings. By carefully defining the behaviors of interest, Paul and his co-workers were able to develop lists of behaviors that can be used in a very objective fashion. For example, 11 categories of body posture are listed (such as walking or sitting on the floor) and 16 types of pathological behavior (such as pacing) are listed. The observer enters the treatment setting on a random schedule, locates one patient, and records the behaviors of the patient at that moment. The procedure is repeated for each patient in that setting, then the observer leaves. Each patient's behavior is sampled several times each day. By obtaining these randomly selected samples of patient behaviors, the patients' baseline behaviors and responses to treatment can be charted. Since the definitions of the categories are quite objective, very reliable observations are made. Actual observations of the behaviors expected to be changed yield an evaluation of high credibility.

Achievement Tests

In conducting evaluations of educational programs, measuring cognitive and intellectual achievement will frequently be the method of choice. Evaluators of educational programs have a valuable resource in achievement tests. Achievement tests with high reliability are well developed and are widely accepted in educational settings (Anastasi, 1982). There is some concern about whether standard achievement tests validly measure the goals of some educational programs; however, these criticisms are mild compared to debate about measures of emotional state (Waskow and Perloff, 1975). When educational programs are assigned goals that include the development of both academic and social skills (see, for example, Datta, 1976b), evaluations of the outcome of educational programs cannot depend solely on achievement test scores. Evaluators are careful to avoid choosing measures of aptitudes or intelligence when looking for a measure of achievement. The former are constructed to measure stable cognitive traits whereas achievement tests are sensitive to specific skills or knowledge that would not be possessed just by being smart.

Published versus Specially Constructed Instruments

Published measures can be easily obtained, have probably been prepared more carefully than an individual evaluator can afford to do, and have been administered widely enough to have obtained norms. If evaluators have access to norms, the material gathered from program participants will be much more easily interpreted. This is especially true when similar groups of people not receiving the program are unavailable. Norms must be used cautiously, however, since program participants may be different from the people on whom the norms were based.

Waskow and Perloff (1975) prepared a description of the best set of change measures for use in mental health settings. For the most part these are published, validated measures specifically developed to measure change brought about by psychotherapy. In order to illustrate several types of measures, a few are discussed below.

Illustrative published measures. Ellsworth (1975) developed a set of scales that can be used to evaluate the outcome of mental health care. The Personal Adjustment and Roles Skills (PARS) scales are to be used by a person who lives with the client being treated. A spouse would be the most knowledgeable rater, but an adult son or daughter or a parent would certainly be quite acceptable. Pretreatment and posttreatment forms for both males and females are available. Ellsworth has recently developed a children's form of the PARS. A sample of items from the PARS is given in Figure 3.1. The items are oriented toward behaviors, not diagnoses.

One unique feature of the PARS is the development of change norms. Ellsworth has obtained PARS ratings of inpatients and outpatients at the beginning and 90 days after the end of psychotherapy. For people with a specific pretherapy PARS rating, the change norms indicate how much change can be expected. Using change norms, an evaluator can determine the extent of improvement without testing comparison groups. In essence, the norms provide information about a comparison group for users without access to people not in the program. The change norms also permit the comparison of types of treatment, therapists, or facilities, using the degree of improvement achieved by the clients receiving different forms of treatment.

A general rating scale for assessing the degree of overall psychological health is useful for mental health program evaluation. An unnamed global level-of-functioning scale was recommended by Carter and Newman (1976) for routine use in counseling or mental health centers. Figure 3.2 gives the nine levels of function ranging from nearly total dependence on others

INSTRUCTIONS:

A. Please describe the person's community adjustment during the past month by answering each question below.

B. Please answer every question even though you might feel unsure of your answer.

C. Mark your answer to each question by making an X in the box under your answer choice, like this:

| X |

Answer choices

DURING LAST MONTH, HAS SHE . . .	1 Rarely	2 Some-times	3 Usually	4 Always
1 . . . Shown consideration for you. Mark one answer for each question	☐	☐	☐	☐
2 . . . Shown interest in what you say (mark one answer)	☐	☐	☐	☐
3 . . . Been able to talk it through when angry	☐	☐	☐	☐
4 . . . Shown affection toward you	☐	☐	☐	☐
5 . . . Gotten along with family members	☐	☐	☐	☐

Answer choices

DURING LAST MONTH, HAS SHE . . .	1 Almost Never	2 Some-times	3 Often	4 Almost Always
6 . . . Acted restless and tense	☐	☐	☐	☐
7 . . . Said things looked discouraging or hopeless	☐	☐	☐	☐
8 . . . Had difficulty falling or remaining asleep	☐	☐	☐	☐
9 . . . Been nervous	☐	☐	☐	☐
10 . . . Talked about being afraid	☐	☐	☐	☐

FIGURE 3.1 Selected items from the Personal Adjustment and Role Skills Scale, Female Pretreatment Form. (Reproduced by permission of Institute for Program Evaluation, Inc. Copyright 1974 by IPEV, Inc.)

Nine Levels of Global Functioning

With regard to the balance among four areas of function (personal self-care, social, vocational/educational, and emotional symptoms), select the person's ability to function autonomously in the community. (Note levels 5 through 8 describe persons who are usually functioning satisfactorily, but for whom problems in one or more of the areas force some degree of dependency on a form of therapeutic intervention.)

LEVEL 1: Dysfunctional in all four areas and is almost totally dependent upon others to provide a supportive protective environment.

LEVEL 2: Not working; ordinary social unit cannot or will not tolerate the person; can perform minimal self-care functions but cannot assume most responsibilities or tolerate social encounters beyond restrictive settings (e.g., in group, play, or occupational therapy).

LEVEL 3: Not working; probably living in ordinary social unit but not without considerable strain on the person and/or on others in the household. Symptoms are such that movement in the community should be restricted or supervised.

LEVEL 4: Probably not working, although may be capable of working in a very protective setting; able to live in ordinary social unit and contribute to the daily routine of the household; can assume responsibility for all personal self-care matters; stressful social encounters ought to be avoided or carefully supervised.

LEVEL 5: Emotional stability and stress tolerance are sufficiently low that successful functioning in the social and/or vocational/educational realms is marginal. The person is barely able to hold on to either job or social unit, or both, without direct therapeutic intervention and a diminution of conflicts in either or both realms.

LEVEL 6: The person's vocational and/or social areas of functioning are stabilized, but only because of direct therapeutic intervention. Symptom presence and severity are probably sufficient to be both noticeable and somewhat disconcerting to the client and/or to those around the client in daily contact.

LEVEL 7: The person is functioning and coping well socially and vocationally (educationally); however, symptom recurrences are sufficiently frequent to necessitate some sort of regular therapeutic intervention.

LEVEL 8: Functioning well in all areas with little evidence of distress present. However, a history of symptom recurrence suggests periodic correspondence with the Center; e.g., a client may receive a medication check from a family physician, who then contacts the Center monthly, or the client returns for bimonthly social activities.

LEVEL 9: The person is functioning well in all areas and no contact with mental health services is recommended.

FIGURE 3.2 Definitions of nine levels of functioning on which to base global ratings of psychological functioning. Such definitions of levels could be adapted for use in a variety of educational, rehabilitation, or training settings. (Adapted from Carter and Newman, 1976).

through a healthy adjustment requiring no further contact with the mental health center. The dimensions of life that would be examined by a rater can be defined according to the needs of the client population. The original scale suggested that the following areas of life could be considered in making the rating of function: (a) personal self-care, (b) social functioning in ordinary social units and in the general community, (c) vocational or educational productivity, and (d) evidence of emotional stability and stress tolerance.

Although the scale in Figure 3.2 was prepared for a mental health setting, the principles used in constructing this scale apply to many other settings as well. The crucial characteristic is the development of behaviorally defined levels of function. For example, in a vocational setting a useful rating might concern how much supervision a trainee requires. A level of 1 might indicate that the trainee needs constant supervision with continuous oral instructions to complete the job. The highest rating might be given when the trainee can complete the job independently and can even handle major problems without assistance.

Published measures are most useful when the program is designed to help all participants to achieve similar outcomes. Many education programs seek to teach skills to children of similar ages regardless of where they attend school. Thus, similar or identical measures of educational program effectiveness can be used in schools at a variety of locations. This is also true of many mental health programs because most counselors seek to help clients to reduce anxiety and depression and to cope with the problems of life. For these reasons evaluators working in educational or mental health settings often use standardized measurement instruments when they seek to learn how well a program is meeting its goals. Similarly, evaluators in medical care facilities can utilize standard laboratory tests indicating healthy physical function. Nevertheless, many programs are designed to effect behaviors that are unique to a particular social system, or, if not unique, at least the planned outcomes of the program are not measured as routinely as are academic achievement, anxiety, work satisfaction, etc. In such cases, the evaluator is required to develop a program-specific measure of impact.

Preparing Special Measures

The major disadvantage of published measures is easy to imagine: the program being studied may have goals and purposes not related to any currently published material. For example, there are relatively few special hospital units specifically for nonterminal cancer patients. When the authors were asked to design materials to measure patient reaction to such a new unit, we found little in the literature to help. Once the evaluators have decided that no existing measure is appropriate, a new instrument must be prepared. However, evaluators must be realistic about how much time they can afford to put into the construction of new instruments. The time pressure of work in service settings precludes the routine development of innovative research instruments.

The format of a survey. The format of a survey will be an important factor in gaining the cooperation of respondents, analyzing the data, and interpreting the results. If the survey is to be self-administered, the layout must be attractive, uncluttered, and easy to use. A structured answer format is preferable to an open-ended question approach. If a structured survey format is adopted, the survey might still be cluttered if the questions each have different response alternatives. For example, mixing "Yes" and "No" questions, "Agree-Neutral-Disagree" attitude statements, and "Frequently-Seldom-Never" reports of past behavior will make the survey harder to complete. The greater the proportion of questions that can be answered in the same answer format, the better. Figure 3.3 contains an example of a specially prepared survey that violates good practices. The respondents must repeatedly figure out what type of answer is required of them. People inexperienced in preparing surveys often construct surveys that are difficult to use. Figure 3.4, in contrast, would be easy to complete. The degree of difficulty experienced in completing a survey will affect the proportion of respondents who will complete it. Not only does a standard response format encourage a greater response rate, but it also increases the ease with which the results can be presented and interpreted; since the results can be summarized on one table, comparisons can easily be made among survey items. The use of an unnecessary variety of response formats can cause as much confusion for readers of a report as it does for respondents to a survey.

When an evaluator seeks the actual words of program participants, and when the range of possible reactions are not known, surveys using open-ended questions are often useful. Patton (1980) used both a structured answer format survey and open-ended questions in evaluating an educational setting.

FIGURE 3.3 Example of survey items violating many of the principles of easy-to-use, self-administered surveys.

High School Evaluation Form

1. How do you like attending your high school? (Circle one.)

Very much	Much	OK	Little	Not at all
1	2	3	4	5

2. How would you describe your teachers? (Check one.)

_____ 1. Mostly excellent   _____ 4. Mostly marginal
_____ 2. Mostly good   _____ 5. Mostly poor
_____ 3. Half good/half marginal

3. To what extent would you agree with the following statement: The physical facilities of my high school (classrooms, halls, gym, lunchroom, etc.) are good.

Strongly disagree	Disagree	Neutral	Agree	Strongly agree

4. Are your teachers good teachers and willing to talk with students after regular classes?   Yes _____   No _____

5. What is the place of interscholastic team competition in your school?

_____ Not at all important
_____ Very important
_____ Not sure

A coronary patient faces many potential problems during the period of convalescence. Which issues did you encounter and how difficult was your adjustment? Circle your answers.

How much difficulty did (or do) you experience over these potential problems?	Does not apply	None	Little	Some	Much
1. Going back to work	DNA	N	L	S	M
2. Sexual activity	DNA	N	L	S	M
3. Smoking	DNA	N	L	S	M
4. Diet	DNA	N	L	S	M
5. Anxiety	DNA	N	L	S	M
6. Depression	DNA	N	L	S	M
7. Activity restrictions	DNA	N	L	S	M
8. Understanding my doctor	DNA	N	L	S	M
9. My spouse's reaction to my health	DNA	N	L	S	M
10. My family's reaction to my health	DNA	N	L	S	M
11. Other _____ (Please specify)			L	S	M

FIGURE 3.4 A section of a self-administered needs-assessment survey that is easy to use because standard alternatives are provided for each item.

The actual words of the respondents were presented in a way that made it impossible to ignore the unavoidably dry statistical summary of the closed-ended survey questions. At other times evaluators use open-ended questions because they do not know what specific questions to ask. Requesting personal reactions or suggestions for change are two instances in which evaluators do not want to restrict respondents' answers in any way. It is time-consuming to categorize and summarize free-form answers. Potential users of open-ended questions should consult materials on qualitative methods (Guba and Lincoln, 1981; Patton, 1980) for detailed directions on analyzing these answers.

Preparing survey items.   There are a number of useful guidelines for preparing survey items. The most important principle is to remember who is going to respond to the items. A statement that is clear to an evaluator may not be clear to someone reading it from a very different vantage point. Questions that have the best chance of being understood will be written clearly, simply, and concisely. Such statements cannot be prepared in one sitting. On the contrary, they must be written, scrutinized, criticized, rewritten, pretested, and rewritten. Items written one week will not seem as acceptable the following week. If the first draft cannot be improved, evaluators have not learned to criticize their own work.

There are several characteristics of clear survey items. The items should avoid negatives. Negatively worded sentences take more effort to read and are misunderstood more frequently than positively worded sentences. Double negatives are especially difficult to read. Well-written items use short, common words rather than less common or longer words. Good survey items focus on one issue. An item such as "My physical therapist was polite and competent" combines two issues. In this case it is possible to interpret an affirmative answer but not possible to interpret a negative answer. What should the director of the unit do if many people answer negatively—have a workshop on charm or on the latest physical therapy practices? Finally, we urge that survey items be grammatically correct.

Several practices can help to detect survey items that need improving. First, the sentence should be read aloud. Often awkward phrasing is more obvious when read aloud than when simply silently reviewed. Second, someone on the program staff should read the draft items. Third, evaluators should think critically of how to interpret each possible answer to the item. As mentioned above, sometimes one answer can be interpreted but another cannot. Fourth, if ambiguities remain, they will probably be detected if the revised draft is administered as an interview with several people from the population to be sampled.

SUMMARY

The most important concept in this chapter concerns the use of multiple measures from multiple sources. The use of multiple sources of information is one of the basic characteristics of valid and useful evaluations. When choosing measures of variables, evaluators should use the criteria of a good measurement instrument to evaluate the specific instruments selected. Is something *important* being measured? Is the measure *sensitive to change,* even small changes? Does the measure seem *valid, reliable,* and *cost effective?* Is *reactivity* to the instrument a problem?

STUDY QUESTIONS

1. The following questions violate some of the characteristics of well-phrased survey items. Improve the wording or the structured options of these questions.
   a. Would you like to continue receiving counseling at the ABC Mental Health Center? _____ Yes _____ No
   b. Is the warmth of the staff an important reason for your continued participation in the XYZ Center? _____ Yes _____ No
   c. Please rate the quality of the care you received in the recovery room after your recent surgery. _____ Excellent _____ Good _____ Fair _____ Poor
   d. Police officers do not really care about the feelings of the victims of a crime. _____ Strongly agree _____ Agree _____ Disagree _____ Strongly disagree
   e. The times that services are available during the day should be extended because people are waiting too long for appointments. _____ Yes _____ No
2. Rewrite the items in Figure 3.3 so that they have a common response format.
3. In planning an evaluation of the ALPHA County Community Mental Health Center, the Freudian counselors insist that the Rorschach Inkblot Test be administered at one-month intervals to current clients. What would your reaction be to this proposal?
4. When an evaluation of clinical services was planned, the evaluator introduced

the level-of-functioning scale given in Figure 3.2. Some clinicians resisted this suggestion by saying that the scale merely refers to coping behaviors, *not* to intrapsychic growth. What would you respond?

5. Suppose an unethical evaluator wanted to stack the deck in favor of getting a favorable evaluation of a program. What types of measures would one use to achieve this? In the reverse condition, what types of variables would one choose to increase the likelihood of an unfavorable evaluation?

FURTHER READING

NUNNALLY, J. C., AND DURHAM, R. L. 1975. Validity, reliability, and special problems of measurement in evaluation research. In *Handbook of evaluation research*, vol. 1., ed. E. L. Struening and M. Guttentag, chap. 10. Beverly Hills, Calif.: Sage.

NUNNALLY, J. C., AND WILSON, W. H. 1975. Method and theory for developing measures in evaluation research. In *Handbook of evaluation research*, vol. 1, ed. E. L. Struening and M. Guttentag, chap 9. Beverly Hills, Calif.: Sage.

SUDMAN, S., AND BRADBURN, N. M. 1982. *Asking questions*. San Francisco: Jossey-Bass.

WEISS, C. H. 1975. Interviewing in evaluation research. In *Handbook of evaluation research*, vol. 1., ed. E. L. Struening and M. Guttentag, chap. 11. Beverly Hills, Calif.: Sage.

The single best source of measures useful in educational settings is:

MITCHELL, E. J., JR., ED. 1985. *The 9th mental measurement yearbook*. Lincoln, Neb.: Buros Institute of Mental Measurements of the University of Nebraska, Lincoln.

There are many sources of variables and scales for someone who is developing an evaluation plan for a mental health facility. A few of the best are:

CARTER, D. E., AND NEWMAN, F. L. 1976. *A client-oriented system of mental health service delivery and program management: A workbook and guide*. Rockville, Md.: National Institute of Mental Health. DHEW Pub. No. (ADM) 76–307. U.S. Government Printing Office Stock No. 017-024-00523-1.

HAGEDORN, H. J. ET AL. 1976. *A working manual of simple program evaluation techniques for community mental health centers*. Rockville, Md.: National Institute of Mental Health. DHEW Pub. No. (ADM) 76–404. U.S. Government Printing Office Stock No. 017-024-00539-8.

HARGREAVES, W. A., ATTKISSON, C. C., AND SORENSEN, J. D., EDS. 1977. *Resource materials for community mental health program evaluation*. 2nd ed. Rockville, Md.: National Institute of Mental Health. DHEW Pub. No. (ADM) 77–328. U.S. Government Printing Office Stock No. 017-024-00554-1.

WASKOW, I. E., AND PERLOFF, M. B., EDS. 1975. *Psychotherapy change measures*. Rockville, Md.: National Institute of Mental Health. DHEW Pub. No. (ADM) 74–120. U.S. Government Printing Office Stock No. 1724-00397.

Sources for measures of attitudes on a variety of topics include the following collection:

MUELLER, D. J. 1986. *Measuring social attitudes: A handbook for researchers and practitioners*. New York: Teachers College Press.

4

Ethical Standards of Conducting Program Evaluations

Evaluators often find themselves in ethical conflicts seldom experienced by social scientists engaged in basic research. Illustrative dilemmas are provided in two hypothetical situations. Although these scenarios are hypothetical, experienced evaluators will be able to identify with the problems described in the following paragraphs.

A project that cannot be done well.   Evelyn Marshall works for a social science research firm, Evaluation, Inc. Her firm is interested in getting a contract to evaluate an early parole program instituted by a state legislature. The question to be answered is whether early parole leads to more or less lawful behavior after release from prison, as compared to the behavior of prisoners paroled after serving the normal time. Marshall realizes that the legislature wants an evaluation that will examine whether the program is causally related to a lowered arrest rate after release, and that the evaluation is needed within one year. However, she also learns that the parole board will not randomly assign prisoners to receive early parole and that there are legal reasons why random assignment may be impossible. Under these constraints Marshall knows 12 months is not a sufficiently long time to test the effectiveness of the program. Should she and her firm conduct the evaluation even though they cannot do what the legislators say they want?

Advocacy versus evaluation.   Morris Franklin has completed an evaluation of Central Community Mental Health Center's outreach program for high school students whose poor school performance is thought to be related to drug abuse. As typically occurs, Franklin found (a) evidence supporting the program's effectiveness (students, parents, and school administrators like the program); (b) evidence that doesn't support the program (grades of the participants did not improve); and (c) some ambivalent evidence that could be interpreted as favorable or unfavorable depending on one's point of view (program students hold more part-time jobs than those not in the program). Franklin's report was received well by his supervisor. Meetings were scheduled to address the participants' grades and the other problems that were uncovered. Evaluator Franklin felt that he had done a good job. Later that month, however, Franklin's supervisor asked him to write a proposal to the school board supporting an extension of the program to other high schools. When the negative findings were mentioned, his supervisor told him to ignore the negative findings and "to be upbeat." Would it be unethical to write the proposal and not mention the known weaknesses of the program that the evaluation detected?

STANDARDS FOR THE PRACTICE OF EVALUATION

The need for ethical standards in research and in program evaluation has been felt by a number of organizations and individuals. Professional organizations have developed extensive statements of what it means to provide service and to conduct research in an ethical manner (e.g., Ethical principles, 1981). The American Psychological Association (1982) devoted a considerable amount of time and resources to a detailed study of ethical and unethical research practices. This project resulted in a ten-point statement of ethical principles accompanied by a lengthy commentary describing the meaning of the principles, illustrating violations of the principles, and showing how responsible investigators protect the rights of research subjects.

This text interprets ethical standards for evaluators in a fashion that is even broader than that adopted by the American Psychological Association. Since the findings of a program evaluation may be applied in an organization, there are many more chances for the evaluator to violate ethical principles than there are for the basic researcher to do so. In recent years two statements describing principles evaluators should follow have been published. One set of principles was prepared by the Evaluation Research Society (Rossi, 1982), and one was drawn up by a committee sponsored by professional organizations, foundations, and governmental agencies interested in the evaluation of educational programs and projects (Joint Committee on Standards for Educational Evaluation, 1981). Although the latter work was prepared to improve evaluations of educational practice, the principles it sets forth apply to program evaluations in all types of settings.

This chapter includes material based on statements of ethical conduct in research, as well as descriptions of good program evaluation practices. The reason for combining these two issues in this chapter lies in the authors' belief that ethics in evaluation means more than honesty with money and data and respect for research subjects. We believe that evaluators have the responsibility to provide clear, useful, and accurate evaluation reports to the organizations for which they work. Furthermore, the evaluator has a responsibility to society to work in a way that has the potential to improve services for people. Ethics are more complicated for evaluators working in settings designed to help people than for basic researchers working on issues with little immediate relevance to organizations. This is not meant to imply that basic research is irrelevant to the needs of society. We simply mean that errors in basic research are less likely to be used in a setting that could harm people. There is a long route from a basic research study to an application; along this route there are many opportunities to identify erroneous findings. In contrast, poorly done evaluations have affected the provision of services to needy people, disrupted the staffs of service organizations, and encouraged the use of harmful experimental medical treatments. For these reasons, we view ethics in evaluation as including all aspects of conducting an evaluation—from initial planning through presentation of the results to interested parties.

The beginning evaluator can use statements of ethical principles to guide the planning, conduct, and reporting of evaluations. There may well be crucial choices required at all stages of a program evaluation. As Morris Franklin learned, evaluators may perform a very careful evaluation and feel that everything has gone well, only to discover that the dissemination of their findings will violate the ethical standards used to guide their work. Ethical issues for evaluators may be divided into five categories: treating people ethically, recognizing role conficts, maintaining scientific credibility, serving the needs of possible users of the evaluation, and avoiding negative side effects of evaluations.

ETHICAL ISSUES INVOLVED IN THE TREATMENT OF PEOPLE

The first responsibility of the evaluator, as it is with the basic researcher, is to protect people from harm. Since harm can be done to people in a variety of ways, concerned evaluators will guard against harm to program participants as well as to the staffs of programs evaluated.

Assignment to Program Groups

Often the first question that will concern an evaluator is whether any harm can come to someone receiving the program that is being evaluated. Although medical, educational, and social service programs are offered with the purpose of helping those who participate, sometimes programs have either no impact, or a negative impact. A controversial evaluation was reported by Sobell and Sobell (1978), who designed a program for alcoholics based on behavioristic principles that theoretically should have permitted alcoholics to drink at a moderate level after treatment. The principles underlying this program contradict the traditional assumption that alcoholics cannot drink without once again becoming dependent on alcohol (Burtle, 1979). It is not unethical to conduct an evaluation on such a project; however, the evaluator working with a treatment team using a disputed procedure should be sure that if the treatment fails, the program participants will receive adequate additional service so that they will not have been harmed by the evaluation. Pendery, Maltzman, and West (1982) have argued that Sobell and Sobell did not conduct sufficient follow-up research on the participants in the evaluation in order to learn whether controlled drinking worked for the participants in the program: many were back in the hospital within weeks or months of discharge from the controlled drinking therapy. Nevertheless, in the published version of the evaluation, the Sobells implied that this approach to treatment for alcoholism was a viable alternative to the traditional treatment, which emphasizes abstinence.

Informed Consent

Another way to protect the participant from harm is to obtain the prior agreement of potential program participants who will take part in the evaluation. This is especially important when the evaluator plans an evaluation based on the random assignment of program participants to different forms of treatment or to the control group not receiving the treatment. When people are asked for their agreement, it is important for them to understand the request—that is, for their consent to be "informed." Informed consent means that potential participants themselves be allowed to make the decision about whether to participate, and that sufficient information about the program be provided to enable them to weigh all alternatives. If the person is misled or not given sufficient information about the risks involved, then informed consent has not been obtained, even if the person has signed an agreement to participate.

Seeking to give enough information to enable people to give informed consent may create an additional ethical dilemma for the evaluator. It may be that a control group, not receiving the new service under study, will feel in competition with the treatment group or, alternatively, will feel unfairly deprived (Cook and Campbell, 1979). If informed consent procedures have the potential to change the behavior of the nonprogram (or traditional program) group, then the validity of the evaluation will be threatened. There is no clear way to resolve such an ethical tangle. One approach, adopted by the American Psychological Association, is to consider the costs involved to the participants being studied. For example, Mexican-American women applying for family planning services were randomly assigned to a treatment group (oral contraceptives) or to a control group (dummy, look-alike pills) (Bok, 1974). The high costs of being in the control group, ten pregnancies, argues that these uninformed women should have been given complete information about this study. Such gross violations of ethical principles in research and evaluation are far less frequent in recent years than they were in the past.

Confidentiality

Information gathered during the course of an evaluation is to be treated with the utmost care. Whether the information is about program participants or employees, evaluators violate ethical principles if they conduct the research in a manner that violates people's privacy. This point was discussed in the previous chapter and will be stressed again in the chapter on the use of monitoring systems.

ROLE CONFLICTS FACING EVALUATORS

Evaluators gather data for the purpose of placing a value on plans for, the implementation of, or the outcome of programs. Since people serving on the staff of these programs earn their living as well as gain psychological rewards from their work, it should not be surprising that the evaluation process will create conflicts for those involved in evaluating the quality of the services or procedures provided. The most common conflicts arise (a) because most in-house evaluators are part of the management team of the organization, but the work of evaluators involves many groups other than managers; (b) because evaluators seek to be as objective as they can but yet are often called upon to be advocates for the organization; and (c) because consultant evaluators need to win contracts to do research in order to maintain the financial health of their company, even when it is hard to complete the evaluation with the desirable scientific rigor. Each of these role conflicts is discussed more fully below.

The term *stakeholder* refers to those people who are involved with the program under evaluation—as clients, administrators, staff, and so on (Gold, 1983). The term comes from the idea that those who support or benefit from an endeavor have a stake in its success. Thus, the clients served by a program have a stake in the outcome of an evaluation; if the program is suspended, they may lose a needed service. The staffs of programs want their work recognized and need the income their jobs generate. A publicly funded program will have stakeholders in the government, and even the taxpaying public has a stake, regardless of whether people are aware of either the specific program or the evaluation that is being conducted. Other stakeholders can be identified by the reader. Evaluators ideally will serve all the relevant stakeholders, even though evaluators are usually employed by only one of the stakeholders—the organization management, in the case of the typical in-house evaluator, or a governmental agency, in the case of many consultant evaluators. In an important sense, a large proportion of evaluators' ethical dilemmas arises from conflicts of interest among the stakeholders involved with a program. Before conducting an evaluation, it is wise to consider all the people who might be affected by the outcome. As is stated in Chapter 2, it is crucial to form a clear idea of who wants a program evaluated before beginning an evaluation. However, the evaluator will have a better understanding of ethical issues if the needs of all the stakeholders are considered, whether they want an evaluation or not.

To illustrate the process of identifying the stakeholders of a program, consider the case of an evaluator charged with conducting an evaluation of a new method of sentencing convicted criminals. A state governor proposed and the legislature passed a sentencing procedure for certain crimes called "Class X crimes." The legislation was passed because there is a widely held opinion that the sentencing practices of judges are too lenient and are quite different from judge to judge. The legislation, in effect, took the question of length of jail sentence out of the judges' hands for certain crimes: a defendant judged guilty of a Class X crime now faced a sentence determined by law. Who were the stakeholders in this situation?

First, the state legislature that commissioned the evaluation was a stakeholder, since it wrote the law that was being evaluated. The governor had a stake in the outcome of the study, since he proposed the law. The governor would want all evaluations of his work to be favorable in order to enhance his chances of reelection. Those state legislators who favored the law likewise desired a favorable finding. In contrast, some legislators who opposed the law may have preferred to see their position vindicated by a finding that the law had not had its intended effect. All the citizens who look to the courts to assist in the job of preventing dangerous individuals from committing additional crimes had an interest in this work. Judges, too, had a stake in the findings of the study, since it was their day-to-day behavior that was being studied. Prison officials needed to be aware of evaluation findings, especially with respect to the possible influence of the new sentencing procedures on their facilities. Police officers also were interested to learn how the new sentencing procedures had been implemented. Defense lawyers, defendants, and the state attorney's office also had stakes in the outcome of the evaluation, since their strategies depend on how sentences are determined. Clearly, many groups care about the findings of program evaluations.

Effective evaluators take the range of stakeholders into account as they plan, conduct, and report their work. The conflicting expectations of different stakeholders can lead to ethical difficulties for evaluators. Anticipating these and other conflicts can spell the difference between intolerable problems—resulting in the evaluation becoming a political "football"—and a carefully planned, even if controversial, evaluation.

Evaluators should try to minimize conflicts among the wants of various stakeholders before the evaluation begins, since they are subject to less pressure if they can negotiate questions such as: Who will have access to results? What information is to be used? How would different patterns of data be interpreted? and so on. If the study is begun without settling these issues, the probability that different groups will manipulate the evaluation to suit their own purposes is increased. At times jealousies and disputes about ownership of information have made it impossible to conduct a credible evaluation. Stakeholders who do not want an evaluation conducted benefit from such an outcome; however, all others lose.

THE SCIENTIFIC QUALITY OF THE EVALUATION

Once the possibility of harm to program participants is minimized and potential role conflicts are explored, the evaluator can turn to ethical issues associated with the scientific quality of the evaluation project. It is the author's view that conducting evaluations that are invalid for the purpose for which they were commissioned is just as unethical as, for example, not protecting the confidentiality of information obtained from participants. The next sections cover the ethical ramifications of four of the most frequently found threats to the scientific validity of evaluations.

Valid Measurement Instruments

Evaluators in educational and mental health settings frequently use standardized, published tests in measuring the expected outcomes of the program being evaluated. The most well developed tests are the standardized achievement tests designed to estimate a child's progress in school. Because these tests are so well developed, there is a temptation to apply them even when they may not be appropriate to measure the outcomes of a program. In other words, one cannot simply ask if a measurement tool is valid: The most effective evaluators ask if a measurement tool is valid to assess program participants in a specific setting. Choosing an inappropriate way to measure a hypothesized outcome can obscure the effects of a program (Lipsey, et al., 1985) or, even worse, lead to a misleading conclusion. For example, an evaluation of a school program on ecology used as an outcome measure a standardized achievement subtest on science, including topics on hygiene, biology, and earth science (Joint Committee, 1981). This subtest was not appropriate for measuring the achievement of the students in the innovative ecology course. The evaluation's negative findings did not reflect the actual results of the program.

Evaluators will make mistakes, just as all people do. However, failing even to consider the specific content of the course and the actual material covered by the selected subtest can be considered unethical conduct on the part of a professional evaluator. It is unlikely that any standardized test exists to measure the achievement of students in an ecology course, because few such courses have been taught until recently: The evaluator should have recognized that. The school district would have been better off had the evaluation not been conducted at all; the program was saddled with a negative evaluation, which—although invalid—had to be explained by program supporters.

Skilled Data Collectors

It is likely that a standardized test can be competently administered by people with little training; however, many evaluations use information collected through personal interviews. Interviewing is not an easy job. Good interviewers possess skills and common sense that will permit them to obtain the information needed without injecting biases, and to maintain the good will of the person interviewed. It requires a degree of maturity and a respect for truth to be able to record and report attitudes at variance with one's own. An early study (Rice, 1929) found that two interviewers of destitute men were reporting very different answers to an interview question concerning why these men found themselves in their current condition. One interviewer repeatedly found that the men attributed their problems to alcohol; the other interviewer reported that the men said they were the victims of an unjust society. The fact that the first interviewer favored prohibition while the second was a Marxist suggests that the interviewer's reports were strongly influenced by their own political views.

It is not always easy to obtain the cooperation of the individuals to be interviewed. Guba and Lincoln (1981) note that interviewers need to exercise polite persistence as they seek to interview program participants. Carey (1974) interviewed terminally ill patients as part of an evaluation of hospital care for dying patients. It takes great sensitivity to conduct such interviews without appearing to care more about data than about the personal tragedies of the patients. Children present a very different type of problem. Interviewing children in a compensatory education program designed to improve self-confidence, study habits, and social skills requires patience and the ability to gain the cooperation of the children. An interviewer without experience in working with children may learn very little about their feelings, because children do not respond to the same demands as adults do. Indeed, if young children do not feel respected, they may not say anything at all! An evaluation cannot provide meaningful information with data that are inaccurate or incomplete.

Appropriate Research Design

One of the themes of this book is that the research design must fit the needs of those who will utilize the information. As later chapters will illustrate, different needs require more or less scientific rigor. However, once a need is articulated, it is unethical to conduct an evaluation if it is known at the outset that the planned evaluation cannot answer the questions that the sponsors of the evaluation put to the evaluator. This seems to be the ethical dilemma faced by Evelyn Marshall, as outlined in the introduction to this chapter. Although her company needs the work, and although the program should be evaluated, it seems unlikely that she can conduct an evaluation to answer the questions the state legislature has presented to her company.

At this point Marshall has at least three alternatives: (1) go ahead and do the evaluation, (2) decline to conduct the evaluation and hope that an alternative job comes by to keep her productively employed, or (3) negotiate on the actual questions to be addressed by the evaluation. The first alternative is unethical, and the second is risky for Marshall; the third may well prove productive. Frequently sponsors of evaluation are unskilled in research methods and do not know when they have given an evaluator an impossible assignment. It may be that the legislature does not really require an evaluation that traces the causes of any possible changes in parole procedures. What is actually needed may be only a careful documentation of the actual implementation of the new law. If negotiations reveal that implementation is the main issue, Marshall can conduct the evaluation; in fact, she can now do a better job than would have been possible fruitlessly trying to trace causal relationships.

Adequate Descriptions of Programs and Procedures

One of the basic characteristics of science is its public nature. Science is to be conducted in such a way that other scientists can evaluate the procedures used and conduct (replicate) the same research. Only in this way can errors in research be detected. Frequently evaluations are not described in sufficient detail to permit others to fully understand either the program or the evaluation procedures. Patton (1980) illustrated the advantage of describing the program as an aspect of conducting a program evaluation. He found that an evaluation of a program to help economically disadvantaged young mothers learn parenting and financial management skills concluded that the program was ineffective—even though the program was not implemented. If the evaluators had taken the effort to observe and describe the program as put into effect (not just as planned), they would have learned that there was so much political resistance, the program never even occurred. In a review of many evaluations, Lipsey et al. (1985) discovered that a large proportion of evaluations did not address implementation issues.

Besides describing the program, the evaluation procedures should be presented in enough detail so that others can understand how the evaluator obtained and analyzed information. As will be mentioned later, all interested parties will not want to know every detail. However, such detailed reports should be available to others who want to implement the program or who want to compare evaluations conducted in different settings. If it is impossible to compare evaluations because they are inadequately reported, one might wonder if the report writers were clear in their own minds about what was done.

In general, it is crucial that the evaluation be interpretable. Data sources and research design must be relevant to the purposes of the evaluation; data collectors need to be sufficiently skilled to provide accurate data; others should have access to a detailed description of the program and the evaluation procedures.

RECOGNIZING THE NEEDS OF ALL STAKEHOLDERS

The concept of stakeholders was introduced in the context of potential role conflicts for evaluators. Considering the different stakeholders is also important for making an evaluation as useful as possible for all those who may use or be influenced by the evaluation.

Program Managers Are Concerned with Efficiency

Those who are responsible for managing an organization are concerned about the efficiency of its services and operations. Profit-making firms must produce goods and services in an efficient manner; otherwise, competing firms will be able to serve customers at a lesser cost. In time inefficient firms will go out of business or be bought out by more efficient ones. Nonprofit human service agencies do not operate on the same principles as profit-making firms; however, effective managers still strive to provide the maximum amount of service possible to clients, students, or patients in their agencies. The most important aspect of an evaluation in a manager's judgment may frequently be information on the efficiency of the program. A later chapter will discuss the cost-benefit questions so important to managers.

An Evaluation Can Help the Staff

The needs of the staff will be best served if the evaluation can provide practical guidance, improving the effectiveness with which they serve clients, students, patients, or customers. An evaluation of the flow of information through a large division of a firm may reveal inefficiencies. If the staff is provided with viable alternatives to the current procedures, they will have been well served by the evaluation. A study of physician residents in a large hospital detected gaps in the services the residents provided to patients (Posavac, Carey, and Marin, 1980). For example, residents did not make good use of the social support services (for example, social work and chaplaincy) provided by the hospital for patients, and they had difficulty in maximizing the comfort of dying patients whose diseases could not be cured. Residents desiring to improve their skills could make use of this information by accepting appropriate training.

Obviously, recommendations that are not accompanied by an estimate of the resources required to carry them out are not realistic. Evaluators also know that an evaluation is a good vehicle for giving staff members recognition for good work. Evaluations that are unnecessarily one-sided neglect some legitimate needs of the staff—an important stakeholder group in an in-house evaluation.

Clients Can Be Served by an Evaluation

An effective evaluation must also consider the program participants. Clients frequently have no voice in the planning or implementation of either programs or evaluations. Upon reflection, this fact seems almost bizarre: The group most affected by programs is the least consulted. However, clients are not unified, they seldom have spokespersons, and they do not hire evaluators. Among the ways evaluators can fulfill their responsibility to clients is to compare the needs of the program participants with the services offered, to help the staff and manager better understand the needs of participants, and to structure recommendations around the clients' needs. It is not unknown for recommendations to be made without an adequate understanding of the client population. The needs of the manager and the staff have sometimes taken precedence over those of the client.

Another aspect of the stake students, patients, trainees, and others have in an evaluation is their interest in continuing to receive service during the evaluation. It is usually impossible to conduct an evaluation without causing any disruption in the work of the staff and in service to participants. Ethical concerns for the needs of program participants require that service disruption be minimized.

Community Members as Stakeholders

Most service agencies receive some of their financial support from the community by way of taxation or contributions, or indirectly through reductions in property taxes. In some ways the community is in the same position as the client population: the community is dispersed and does not have easily identifiable spokespersons. Perhaps the most ambitious approach to involving the community in the evaluation process is the citizen evaluation model developed for the National Institute of Mental Health (NIMH) (Zinober and Dinkel, 1981). Following procedures and using materials prepared by NIMH, community citizens can evaluate community mental health centers themselves. This approach is one way to ensure that the stake of the community will be recognized. While this endeavor requires the commitment of citizens, it can—and has—been done (Albright, 1982).

Financial Backers

Human service agencies usually have the financial support of government bodies, charitable organizations, or foundations. In business organizations there are many management layers between an evaluator and the ultimate financial backers; however, costs and profits will be considered at all levels of the organization and will be a part of all evaluations. Groups that put up the money certainly have a stake in the success of the programs they support. Frequently governmental offices and foundations commission evaluations of programs receiving their support. In these instances their interests are probably well protected. Ethically planned in-house evaluations should also reflect the interests of the groups that supply the financial backing for the service agencies.

Figure 4.1 illustrates how stakeholders' views can lead to different conclusions, even when evaluating the same information.

AVOIDING POSSIBLE NEGATIVE SIDE EFFECTS OF EVALUATION PROCEDURES

Evaluators face a number of ethical issues related to the applied nature of their research. The ethical issues covered in this section are less central to

Differences in the views of various stakeholders are illustrated in the controversy over "workfare" programs, which require applicants for welfare to hold part-time, temporary jobs. The idea is that welfare recipients should do some work for the assistance they require. While they continue to look for steady work, they spend a week or two a month in public or nonprofit organizations doing jobs that would not have been filled by a regular employee.

Some critics say the program is shortsighted, that the people do not learn real work skills, and that the state does not adequately supervise these temporary "employees." Other critics say workfare merely requires welfare applicants to "sing for your supper," making welfare programs punitive. A public aid official counters by saying that some workfare participants need workfare to learn that holding a job requires coming to work, staying all day, not hitting anyone, and bathing before they go to work. Nonprofit service organizations report that the day-care, janitorial, and food service assistance they get through workfare has improved their services to other low-income people.

An evaluator would be hard pressed to gather data that would be acceptable to all stakeholders, because there are fundamental value conflicts that data will not resolve. (Source: Brotman, 1983.)

FIGURE 4.1   An illustration of how stakeholders' values can conflict.

the conduct of basic research; however, in the applied research arena these questions can take on immense importance both for evaluators and for the stakeholders affected by the evaluation study.

Can Someone Be Hurt by Inaccurate Findings?

Inaccurate findings can either show falsely positive findings—erroneously suggesting that the program is effective—or falsely negative findings—erroneously suggesting that the program is not effective. When such false conclusions are due to random statistical variation, the first false finding is called a Type I error, and the second is termed a Type II error. Such false conclusions can also be made when insufficient attention is paid to the design of an evaluation. Without careful thought, evaluations sometimes focus on the wrong variables or use too short a time span to show either positive or negative effects. At other times an evaluator's enthusiasm for a program may lead to falsely optimistic conclusions.

The possibly misleading work on alcoholism treatment by Sobell and Sobell (1978) has been discussed in the light of the follow-up study done by Pendery, Maltzman, and West (1982). It is possible that the treatment of alcoholics at other institutions may have been redesigned when therapists read of the apparently favorable results the Sobells claimed for the controlled drinking therapy. Basic researchers are cautioned to care for the safety and welfare of the people actually studied in an experiment. In addition, evaluators need to think about how program planners might use an evaluation of a program. Inadvertently encouraging the use of a harmful program due to insufficient care in conducting research is an ethical problem with which basic researchers need rarely be concerned; however, it is often an important issue for evaluators.

In contrast to falsely favorable evaluations, falsely negative evaluations can also harm people by encouraging the elimination of beneficial services. Lazar (1981) described one overlooked aspect of preschool programs such as Head Start. According to Lazar, Head Start, a summer preschool program for economically disadvantaged children, made its strongest contribution to the future school achievement of the children not by what it taught, but by the way it involved mothers in the education of their children. Showing mothers how to work with their children and introducing them to the school system encouraged them to develop a level of involvement with the education of their children often not found among lower income families. This involvement could have been achieved regardless of the actual content of the summer programs. Evaluations that focused only on the intellectual growth of the children during the eight-week program were too narrow. The falsely negative conclusions could have harmed other children if preschool programs had been eliminated. Comprehensive evaluations of programs such as Head Start have shown them to be effective (Darlington et al., 1980), in contrast to the initial study (Cicarelli et al., 1969).

Statistical Type II Errors

Type II errors (concluding that a program is ineffective when it is in fact effective) can occur because the sample of program participants involved in the evaluation was small or just happened to be atypical. Whenever measurements are made on a sample of people rather than on the whole population, and whenever measurement instruments are not perfectly reliable, random variation can produce Type II errors. Evaluators can seldom test whole populations, and the information sources available to evaluators are never perfectly reliable. Basic researchers worry about Type II errors because it is a waste of time to conduct research that yields inaccurate conclusions. However, Type II errors in a basic research study typically cause no harm to others. Evaluators, on the other hand, have an additional worry about random statistical errors: They do not want to falsely conclude that a valued program is ineffective. Thus, evaluators are much more concerned about Type II errors than are basic researchers (Lipsey et al., 1985; Schneider and Darcy, 1984).

Unfortunately, evaluators work in situations that make Type II errors very likely. In an attempt to reduce the demands made on program participants asked to provide data, short surveys may be used and the number of variables may be limited. To reduce the disruption of services, only a few participants may be tested. In other cases there may only be relatively few participants in an expensive program to be evaluated. Or the evaluator may not be given sufficient resources to measure the outcome variables on a large number of participants. In all such cases the possibility of making Type II errors is increased. After reviewing 122 published program evaluations, Lipsey et al. (1985) concluded that the research design of a large proportion of evaluations was too weak to detect even a moderately sized effect, not to mention a small effect.

Pay Attention to Unplanned Program Effects

Ethical evaluators are careful to examine the programs as implemented, not just as designed. One aspect of this issue is the low level of actual implementation of programs as already discussed. A second aspect of this issue involves possible negative side effects of a program. Just as physicians are concerned about side effects of medications, evaluators work most effectively when they are alert to unexpected negative features of a program. For example, welfare procedures may demean recipients, prison regulations may cause dependency leading to more difficulty in making decisions after release, and an arbitrary method of introducing improved working conditions may alienate employees. Such outcomes will, of course, never be found in the goals of the program as planned. In fact, program planners and managers might not even anticipate these results. One way to imagine possible negative side effects is to contact critics of the program. Although program supporters may view such contacts as unnecessary, evaluators can do more useful work if they detect important negative side effects of programs.

Chapman and Risley (1974) described a program whereby children were paid to pick up and turn in litter. The program developers did not expect the children to bring in bags of household garbage from their homes: the program staff refused to pay for these bags. The children then threw the household garbage into nearby yards, certainly an unwanted side effect. The program was revised so that payment was made not for bags full of litter but for cleaning up specified yards. Recognizing a negative side effect led to a better program. Table 4.1 includes some additional negative side effects of policies with desirable goals.

Unexamined Values Held by the Evaluator

Conflicts between the role of program advocate and the role of evaluator have already been mentioned. The evaluation may also be rendered less valid

TABLE 4.1. Seeking to Achieve Desirable Goals Has Led to Serious Side Effects Unexpected by the Program Developers.

DESIRABLE GOAL	PROGRAM	NEGATIVE SIDE EFFECT
Save gasoline	Reduce size of cars	Increase in injuries during accidents
Reduce auto pollution	Pollution control devices	Reduced gas mileage
Save energy	Burn waste forestry products for heat	Loss of nutrients currently returned to the soil
Improve food production in poor nations	Use fertilizers and farm machinery	Poor farmers who could not afford costs sold farms and became unemployed city dwellers

if values are assumed by the evaluator without examination. Sjoberg (1975) suggests that evaluators typically accept the existing power structure and adopt its values with little reflection. For example, embezzlement is not treated as a major crime because, according to Sjoberg, it is a middle- and upper-class crime. He also suggests that many teenagers are labeled delinquent because they violate the norms of those who hold the power in society. Sjoberg has highlighted an important issue for evaluators, whether or not one agrees with his examples. He has forcefully argued that one cannot serve the needs of all groups with a stake in the evaluation if the evaluator has implicitly adopted the values of the most powerful group involved with the evaluation. Clearly, it is difficult to recognize assumed values. One way to guard against the effcts of such implicit values is to avoid working with only the individuals planning or offering the service. Trying to learn what participants seek in the program may yield insights not gained in discussions with professionals.

Other unexamined values may be hidden in statistical analyses. Ball and Bogartz (1970) examined the overall mean achievement of children watching "Sesame Street" and concluded that the series was successful in achieving some of its goals. Cook et al. (1975), however, divided the children on the basis of socioeconomic background and concluded that the program was not effective. Among other things, the program was specifically designed to improve the cognitive skills of children from low socioeconomic areas. One reason the cast includes many members of minority groups is to increase the chances of children from minority groups watching the program. Nevertheless, Cook et al. learned that the cognitive skill gap between lower- and upper-class children who watched "Sesame Street" actually increased. Therefore, although watching the program had a positive impact, it did not provide the special help to disadvantaged children that was a fundamental goal of the program. Without a creative reanalysis of the evaluation, this important—but subtle—finding would have been overlooked. One ethical viewpoint asserts that when benefits are uneven, the least privileged group should benefit the most (Bunda, 1983).

SUMMARY

The major ethical issues involved in conducting research have been described under five topics: the protection of the people studied, the danger of role conflicts, threats to the scientific quality of evaluations, the varying needs of different groups who may be influenced by the evaluation, and negative side effects that may be related to the program or to the way of conducting the evaluation. Special emphasis was given to the applied and political nature of the settings in which program evaluations are conducted. The applied setting creates more ethical dilemmas than the basic research setting. Although these conflicts and limitations require evaluators to exercise considerable care in conducting evaluations, these issues make the role of the evaluator vital and exciting.

STUDY QUESTIONS

1. Analyze the different views of the various stakeholders who would be involved with a teacher evaluation procedure in a college or university.
2. Contrast the dangers of Type I and Type II errors in basic research versus those in program evaluation, with special regard to ethical considerations.
3. Some evaluators do not mention all negative or unfavorable findings in official evaluation reports, but do bring such issues to the attention of program managers during private meetings. What are the pros and cons of this practice?

FURTHER READING

JOINT COMMITTEE ON STANDARDS FOR EDUCATIONAL EVALUATION. 1981. *Standards for evaluations of educational programs, projects, and material.* New York: McGraw-Hill.

PERLOFF, R., AND PERLOFF, E., EDS. 1980. *Values, ethics, and standards in evaluation.* San Francisco: Jossey-Bass.

ROSSI, P. H., ED. 1982. *Standards for evaluation practice.* San Francisco: Jossey-Bass.

part II

EVALUATION IN PROGRAM PLANNING AND MONITORING

Chapter 1 described the need for program evaluation and the growing trend toward using evaluation methods to improve and to justify the offering of human service programs. An overview of the evaluator's role vis-á-vis service providers and organization administrators was given in Chapter 2. Measurement principles were discussed in Chapter 3 to emphasize that evaluators are research professionals who know how to approach the quantification of variables important to human services. In Chapter 4 ethical concerns and the evaluator's responsibilities were described.

In Part II the discussion of the specific tasks of evaluators is initiated. Evaluators can make contributions to the administration of programs without actually examining the effectiveness of human services in achieving goals. First, Chapter 5 shows how evaluators can participate in the planning of programs by using their social science skills to help planners find indicators of need and to quantify and summarize these indicators. Second, evaluators can assist in monitoring a program to learn the extent to which it has been implemented as planned. Administrators and representatives of the public want to know: Who gets what services from whom? Program evaluation methods, as illustrated in Chapter 6, can be applied to answer such a question. Less quantitative approaches to planning and monitoring the implementation of programs are discussed later in Chapter 12.

5

Evaluation in Program Planning

What sort of help can a person trained in social science methods provide to planners of human services? How can a program evaluator do anything *before* there is a program? There are four general types of contributions to be made: (1) specifying the needs a program should meet; (2) helping to describe the goals and objectives of the program; (3) tracing the program activities step-by-step through to their intended impact in a conceptual model; and (4) selecting from among various possible programs.

Planning is required before any human service program is begun. Long before the doors of a service agency swing open, some people must shape the service according to their perceptions of the need for it and the best ways to meet those needs. A surprisingly large number of programs have been planned on the basis of little more than an influential person's impression of what a group needs. Whether the program is for alcoholics, malnourished children, or unemployed blue-collar workers, unverified subjective impressions often guide the planning of the program. Before we illustrate the methods an evaluator might use to help the planners of human services, a brief discussion of the problems faced by planning committees may be helpful. These comments are based on observations of meetings of planning committees made up of such human service providers as teachers, social workers, or nurses. Since individuals working in such positions are seldom trained in social science research techniques, evaluators have made valuable contributions to such planning groups.

THE EVALUATOR AND THE PLANNING COMMITTEE

What Planning Committees Want to Accomplish

There are two important general goals: to produce the best possible practical plan and to find a plan with broad-based support. Many planning sessions, however, follow the less than ideal patterns of planning either by administrative fiat or by means of dilatory, boring planning sessions. Both patterns may be caused by the lack of definitive information and the difficulty for any individual to grasp the total set of needs and program possibilities.

Unambiguous information is hard to obtain and, in fact, may not exist. Even experts in an area cannot know what policy is most likely to succeed. Evidence for following a given path can usually be found; however, often there is other evidence supporting a different course. After hearing experts use the expression "on one hand . . . but on the other hand," a Senate committee chairman expressed a desire for "one-armed scientists" (David, 1975). His desire was obviously facetious; however, it illustrates a crucial point—even when information is available, it will seldom point to a single plan to solve a problem.

Planning committees may have difficulty selecting the best plan because people are limited in how much information they can use at one time. To consider simultaneously all the variables involved is impossible. Fortunately, methods are available to break a decision down into parts or steps. The jargon word for this process is to *disaggregate* a decision. The suggestion to disaggregate is good advice when making any decision; however, planning committees may persist in grappling with the whole problem without seeing that aspects of the problem can be approached one at a time. The last section of this chapter describes how to disaggregate a decision.

The frustration of not seeing a clearly best way to solve a problem sometimes inhibits planning. When a committee tackles a complex problem, often no one structures the task for the committee. This lack of structure leads various individuals to either engage in small talk or push their own views. Once it becomes clear that the planning committee is not getting anywhere, an administrator may decide what the plans should be. The committee may actually be greatly relieved by such a move.

To be fair, some planning groups do not function well because they have access only to funds earmarked for certain purposes. Such groups work within a rather narrow range of options. However, the planning group still has a critical task; a human service program can take many specific forms, even within a narrow range of options.

Evaluators Can Help Program Planners

It is unfortunate that evaluators are so often consulted only after a program is already in place. Doubly unfortunate is the situation in which the evaluator is consulted after a program is suspected of being ineffective. Well-managed human service organizations are directed by managers who recognize the need for evaluation. Such managers may encourage evaluators to sit in on planning sessions; indeed, planning is much like evaluation. The planner merely uses a future tense (for example, *Will* the program help?), and the evaluator typically uses the past tense (for example, *Did* the program help?). If evaluators are involved early, planners have convenient access to knowledge about what can be evaluated objectively and at what cost. Such collaboration is likely to be helpful, because in many human services the innovators are not trained in management, research, or program evaluation methods. In addition, many administrators and planners do not have experience in conceptualizing program objectives in ways that encourage making observations and summarizing information that will provide corrective feedback to the program staff and managers. For example, the goals of many service programs are written in such general terms that it is impossible to know when the goal has been attained and when it has not. For example, the goals of "giving quality medical care," "reducing crime," and "opening meetings to the community" cannot be evaluated as phrased. When do you know "crime" has been "reduced"? What crimes? How much of a reduction would count? One percent? Ten percent? For how long must a reduction last? All these questions (and others) must be answered before a plan can be made and before an evaluation can be initiated. This type of questioning to clarify assumptions often reveals that plans are not complete (Cook and Shadish, 1986).

The next section of this chapter concerns some general issues evaluators should raise in planning sessions. Next, methods of carrying out an assessment of need are described. Last, a method to help planners divide a complex decision into manageable parts is presented.

GENERAL ISSUES TO ADDRESS IN PLANNING

Identifying the Intended Participants

While clearly identifying the population(s) to be served by a program is the most advisable first step in program planning, it is easy to evade this hard task. Some people talk about serving the needs of the "community." As long as a vague term is used, the various people involved in the planning may comfortably continue to "plan" while each holds a different view of the community to be served. Even worse, those without a clear idea of the community assume the others know who the community is. The evaluators can help the planning group to address this question. Nevertheless, they can expect foot dragging, because the task is both hard and anxiety-arousing. This is so because once a choice is made among the possibilities, the plan will attract critical attention; it is not difficult to hide weak plans in vague descriptions.

Carefully identifying those to be served is crucial—the needs of one group are different from the needs of another group. Further, an approach that may work with one group may not be effective with a different one. For example: Junior high school students have different social and academic needs than senior high school students: repeat offenders are less likely to benefit from a program that may benefit teenagers who have been convicted of one crime, although both may be correctly identified as "juvenile delinquents"; people from more privileged economic backgrounds probably expect human services to be housed in more attractive settings than do people used to less plush housing; and an elderly population needs different services from a mental health center than do teenage runaways.

One way to force oneself to be specific and clear is to put ideas down on paper and permit someone else to react to them. A chart summarizing the characteristics of a target population may be useful. A hospital planning an ambulatory care center may define the following groups as the target populations: the elderly; indigent or near-indigent families; children of all families requiring immunizations and other routine care; and newcomers to the local community. It is possible to obtain estimates of the sizes of these groups from local governments and census reports, as illustrated later in this chapter.

Identifying the Needs to Be Met

Successful programs seek to alleviate real problems that are recognized by the population to be served. Certainly, planners of human service programs are likely to do a better job if they know what the target population needs. There is a critical difference between the needs felt by a population and the needs professionals attibute to the population (Cagle and Banks, 1986; Conner, et al., 1985). If the target population does not recognize a need, the program will have to include an educational aspect. The staffs of screening and treatment programs for high blood pressure deal daily with people who do not recognize a need for care. When the disease first develops, elevated blood pressure usually does not produce felt symptoms; in addition, the treatment does have undesirable side effects (*Medical World News*, 1977). Because people expect to feel better, not worse, after taking medicine, many reject the treatment. A rejected treatment means a program failure, even though the medication is effective in prolonging the lives of the hypertensive patients by reducing the likelihood of strokes and other cardiovascular diseases.

A university English professor provides a second example of the disappointing results of not realizing that a target population may not construe a problem in the same way as a professional offering a service. She reasoned as follows: (1) Many college students do not write very well, and professors in many fields agree that improvement would be desirable; (2) English professors have only limited contact with students, compared to professors in the students' major fields; therefore (3) one way to improve student writing is to improve the ability of non-English faculty to grade, evaluate, and improve the writing done for non-English courses. She developed a series of workshops for non-English department faculty members involving a number of her departmental colleagues and obtained funds from the college dean for a guest speaker. The flaw in her plans was very basic. It was wrong to assume that people who complain want to act upon their complaints. Although many college professors complain about student writing ability, relatively few may be ready to involve themselves actively in the grading and counseling required to encourage improvement. Consequently, the attendance at the workshops and the lecture was primarily from the English department; non-English department faculty could be counted on the fingers of one hand. As a matter of fact, there were more graduate student evaluators present to observe the first workshop than there were faculty members from departments other than English. Other workshops were then canceled. The point should be clear: programs can be effective only when they meet real needs and when the target population agrees that it has those needs.

In assessing the need for a human service, it is very important to be objective—the extent of need is easy to overestimate. Nurses were concerned about the large number of stroke patients in a medium-sized hospital. They felt they were unable to meet these patients' needs without a special stroke unit. Because of these concerns, the administrators cooperated in a study of the severity of stroke patients in their hospital. It quickly became clear that there were actually very few stroke patients in the hospital. Those few admitted with possible strokes were usually discharged with much less severe diagnoses. In spite of the subjective feelings of many of the people on the staff of that hospital, there was no way to justify the added expense of a special stroke unit. The administration needed to deal with the concern of the staff, but in ways other than the institution of a new unit.

The Program's Resources

An evaluation of a proposed program will include an evaluation of the type of staff required. What training and experience should the staff members have? Will their training fit the actual needs of the people to be served? Is their work planned to use their talents effectively? Effective people may ultimately be ineffective if placed in situations for which they were not trained or if the situation restricts the use of their skills.

The staff must be housed in adequate facilities. If they lack appropriate areas in which to meet program participants as individuals or as groups, the program may be impossible to deliver. Work-training programs must have up-to-date equipment, or the training will not be useful to the trainees. The location of the facilities is also important; public transportation may be a necessity for the people to be served.

Expectations for the Program

Evaluators can also help planning committees specify the goals and objectives of the program. Program sponsors and funders are increasingly asking for a careful description of the objectives of new programs (Wholey, 1981). Without this emphasis it is next to impossible to determine whether the service was offered as planned or whether the service achieved what it was set up to do. Goals and objectives need to be described in ways that permit one to recognize when they have been achieved and when they have not. Otherwise, people cannot be held accountable for their work.

There are several levels at which goals can be written. Marshall (1979) illustrates these different levels for a manager who wanted to install a computerized inventory system. At one level her goals could be phrased in terms of obtaining the necessary hardware, programs, and training for her employees by certain dates. At a second level her goals would concern the actual functioning of her new inventory system. These goals might refer to the shortened time required to locate inventory items, and fewer items being out of stock. Third, her list of goals should take note of the actual purpose of the new inventory system: Customers should be more satisfied with her firm, and business should improve. Marshall emphasizes that planners should keep this third level of outcome goals clearly in mind as they work. Since there may be many ways to achieve better customer satisfaction, planners should not limit themselves to only one method before examining alternatives. However, once a course of action is selected, statements of goals at all levels are appropriate for good planning and for developing an accountability system. Figure 5.1 includes several examples of ways to state objectives. Note how it is essential that Level 1 goals be met before one can expect Level 2 goals to be met. Level 2 and Level 3 are similarly related.

VARIOUS LEVELS AT WHICH GOALS CAN BE WRITTEN

Level 1. An example of goals that refer to the acquisition of basic hardware and personnel for computerizing an inventory control system. This is a "start-up" objective. Nothing can happen without this being achieved.

The system will be installed in all forty-two companies in a six-year period— four in the first year, six in the second, and eight each year after.

Level 2. The ways to recognize the inventory system as working well are included in this second level of goal statements. The achievement of Level 1 goals does not guarantee achievement of Level 2 goals.

The system can handle 15,000 inventory items.

Items can be located using the system in an average of ten seconds, with no more than 5 percent of searches taking more than thirty seconds.

Level 3. Although achieving goals at the first two levels is crucial for the ultimate success of the project, there are additional goals that should be considered. The real reason for computerizing an inventory system is to make a difference for customers. These goals reflect whether the customers are getting better service from the company.

Delivery times will be reduced.

There will be 50 percent fewer items out of stock as compared to the current system.

Formal customer complaints about out-of-stock items and slow responses to customer requests for information will be reduced by 50 percent.

FIGURE 5.1 Objectives for a program should refer to all levels of the program. Implementation, function, and outcome goals are reflected in this illustration. (Adapted from Marshall, 1979.)

Evaluators not only help in developing statements of goals and objectives for planners, but they are also called upon to help estimate the degree of success the program will have in achieving these goals (Wholey, 1981). On the basis of completed evaluations, personal experience, and theoretical understanding, evaluators can help to explore the possibilities that a planned program can be put in place, that it will attract cooperation from the community, and that it will lead to the improvements hoped for. This process is called *developing an impact model* or *theory*. To evaluate program plans, planners need to describe why they believe that the service will effect the improvements wanted. Once one seeks to describe the process of change, starting with resources, through actual service delivered, to outcome, unwarranted assumptions are highlighted. It is not at all unusual for such inquiries to reveal the unarticulated core theory to be embarrassingly simple and to ignore fundamental psychological processes: many program "plans" are little more than telling others what is good for them. Information is important, but information alone is seldom enough to change behavior (Cook, Leviton, and Shadish, 1985).

It is not unusual for programs to be implemented that are simply too weak to have the impact planners thought likely (Quay, 1979; Sechrest, et al. 1979). For example, can a summer in a preschool program such as Head Start realistically be expected to provide the basic skills needed for doing schoolwork, when a child has spent five years in a severely impoverished home? Can 12 hours of psychological counseling really affect a prisoner's ability to get and hold a job after release? This approach to examining a program during the planning stages has been called *evaluability assessment* (Wholey, 1981) and *preformative evaluation* (Scriven, 1981). The last section of this chapter describes how to systematize these expectations.

When it appears that a program will be insufficient to meet the needs it is designed to serve, two paths are open. On one hand, the program's goals could be scaled down. It may be better to strive to meet realistic goals than to fail to meet overly optimistic ones. On the other hand, the program could be strengthened. Both paths may require that the entire program be reconsidered. Program sponsors might not be satisfied with scaling down their expectations, but strengthening the program may require the expenditure of more funds than the sponsors wish to provide. The evaluator's contribution to a better program is important in the long run; however, in the short run the suggestion that a program might not be sufficient for its purposes will not be joyfully received. Nevertheless, program plans examined in this way are likely to be more successful.

INFORMATION SOURCES FOR THE ASSESSMENT OF NEED

People who have participated in planning committees have complained that so much is unknown that their job is close to impossible. No one can make the planning committee's job easy; however, there are a number of techniques for gathering information that can reduce some of the planners' confusion. Sources of information that have proved useful include census data relevant to the need for human services, existing community agencies serving similar problems, surveys of residents of the community to be served, and knowledgeable people in the community, often called *key informants*.

Census Data

Census data are available for many years. Some of the items in the census surveys are relevant to program planning. This source has much to recommend it for use in program planning: it is usually considered reliable and valid; it is public when in summary form; and it is relatively inexpensive as compared to other types of data. The indexes in Figure 5.2 were derived from census information. This information was part of a needs assessment study utilized in a plan to expand mental health facilities in a group of rural counties. By comparing these indexes with similar variables for the whole state and for the nation, the extent of needs could be estimated. Census data will not be useful when planning a program in a rapidly expanding locality or within an organization.

Existing Services and Providers

Before launching a new facility or initiating a new program to provide additional services, the planning group should make an inventory of existing agencies in the area that offer similar or related services. Such a survey will help to avoid the duplication of services and to locate key informants who can provide good estimates of certain community needs. For example, there are a variety of sources where people seek the emotional support that could

---

Age distribution of population
Percentage of teenagers not in school
Percentage of black teenagers not in school
Percentage of working mothers of children under 18
Percentage of working mothers of preschool children
Percentage of aged persons living alone
Percentage of aged persons in poverty[a]
Percentage of extremely crowded housing units[b] without plumbing facilities
Percentage of large households[c] with low income
Percentage of female-headed families with children
Percentage of disabled persons not in institutions
Percentage of disabled persons not in institutions and unable to work

---

[a]Based on local income levels

[b]More than one person per room

[c]Six or more persons

FIGURE 5.2 Census data used in the needs assessment study prepared for the Spoon River Community Mental Health Center. (Source: *Community Mental Health Plan, Spoon River, Illinois.* Spoon River Community Mental Health Center, Inc., 1977.)

be provided by a mental health center. Clergy and physicians probably deal with more such people than do psychologists and psychiatrists (see Posavac and Hartung, 1977). There is a wide range of estimates of the percentage of people seeing physicians who basically are not physically ill. Some estimates are as high as two-thirds of all patients. The clergy of certain religious denominations spend much time with parish members experiencing crises. Thus, members of the clergy and physicians would be good key informants in plans for developing new mental health services.

Once the facilities and personnel currently offering a service are identified, an empirical study of the number of people who are being treated or served is often conducted. There are at least two approaches to estimating the number of people receiving a service. The most direct approach is to survey the appropriate individuals in the area. Physicians and clergy could be asked how many people they have served during the last month(s) who may require attention for certain mental health problems. The problem list would be kept short, because classifying people into a few categories would be less subject to error than asking informants to use finely defined categories. One needs survey presented only three categories: mental illness (defined very broadly to include "problems in living"), drug abuse, and alcohol problems. Specific services to children and to elderly adults are being stressed more than in the past. A persons-under-treatment survey may include a gross age categorization, such as 17 and under, 18 to 64, and 65 and over.

The number of people actually in programs can be ascertained from the existing programs. These values will often be more accurate than estimated values. Medical and mental health programs must keep accurate records, although such records will not be flawless. Programs filling social and recreational needs, such as park programs or centers for senior citizens, probably will have far less accurate records.

Since additional services are being planned, the number of people who were referred to other agencies would be of interest. Also of interest would be estimates of the numbers of people the current care giver would have liked to have referred to another service or agency but could not, because the service did not exist in or near the community. Such information is important; some individuals are already in appropriate programs, but others may be receiving services that are not closely related to their needs.

The difficulty of referring someone for care can also be useful in a needs assessment. Love (1986) used case studies of troubled teenagers to show how the structure of the welfare and mental health services in metropolitan Toronto made it impossible for an adolescent to get help even though his alcoholic father had thrown him out of his home. Unfortunately the unstable and, at times, aggressive 17-year-old had several recent addresses in different communities and needed several different services. It was unclear where he should have sought help, and only a few agencies could assist him with his multiple problems. Although the existence of compelling cases does not show the extent of an unfilled need, cases can show that human service reorganization or expansion may be needed to meet certain types of needs.

When estimating need for any type of program, the distinction between incidence of a problem and prevalence of a problem is worth making. Incidence refers to the number of times a problem is experienced. Prevalence refers to the number of people who have the problem at a given time. For example, the incidence rate of the common cold is high: many people get one during a year, perhaps more than once a year. However, people usually recover in several days, so the prevalence at any one time is low. The distinction is important: a response to a problem will be different depending on whether the problem is viewed as widespread but temporary, or less widespread but long lasting. For example, attempts to help unemployed people will be different depending on whether one believes that most unemployed individuals are merely between jobs or that unemployed people are likely to be out of work for a long period of time.

Simply documenting a need is not sufficient to show that people will leave the care giver from whom they currently obtain services. People do not view care givers as readily interchangeable—trust develops slowly. Offering a service for which there is an objective need is not the same as offering a service that people would prefer over what they currently use. The continued use of native healers by some Spanish-American residents of cities in the United States is an example of a preference for what is known over services offered by public agencies (Adler and Stone, 1979).

It is important to repeat a word of caution: informants, even quite knowledgeable ones, often overestimate need. Therefore, estimated needs must not be considered as actual needs without collaborative evidence. Estimated needs are not worthless values; however, they should be treated as estimates.

Community Resident Survey

The residents of a community have certain attitudes toward the development of human services and toward the particular services needed. Their attitudes can be part of the planning. If the service is relevant to all citizens, the community should ideally be surveyed systematically to obtain a representative sample of the opinions of the residents. Obtaining a truly representative sample is extremely difficult and thus expensive. Avoiding clearly biased samples, however, is possible if the planner is careful in the selection of community respondents. Interviewing only professionals, only low-income residents, or only elderly people would render the results quite useless. A compromise might be possible by using intact groups that are likely to be fairly representative of the community. Such a course would not be expensive, because intact groups completing a survey do not require much time from a survey administrator. Public schools and church groups are two sources of respondents that may be available to a planning group. Depending on the nature of the program being planned, special groups of likely users could be sought. For example, medical planners would want to contact emergency rooms and outpatient clinics. Because parenting programs are more likely to be used by new parents, the names of families with babies might be obtained from hospitals or churches. (Some facilities may not be willing to provide names, in order to protect the privacy of their members or patients.)

The form of the community survey requires some care in construction. When constructing a survey, it is important to remember its purpose: to assess the need for a service, the acceptability of a particular service, and the willingness of people to use the program or facility. Some surveys, however, are set up in such a way that a very high response in favor of the proposed facility is guaranteed. In attitude measurement this bias is called *acquiescence*. Acquiescence refers to the tendency of people to say yes to questions if the questions at all encourage such an answer. Some needs surveys have essentially listed various services and asked if such services "should" be available to people in the community who need it. Imagine being asked:

> Do you think (your hometown) should have an emergency service that provides immediate counseling any time of the day or night for people who are having a crisis with personal or family problems?

> Do you think it would be helpful to you to learn more about mental illness and where to get mental health services, or to be able to handle a specific situation?

Wouldn't you answer yes to these questions? Most people would. There is nothing terribly wrong about the questions in themselves, but there are some additional items that should be added to this type of question.

Without measuring intended use of services and without providing information on the costs of such services, the meaning of verbal support for developing new services is impossible to interpret. People can agree that a service *should* exist but feel that the need for it is so slight that they are unwilling to devote more than a token amount of money to it. If this were the case, a marked degree of assent to a question of need would be quite misleading. If few want to pay for a service, the fact that many think it should be available is irrelevant.

Another useful approach to an assessment of need is to estimate what use people intend to make of a service. If the assessment of need concerned mental health programs, the survey constructor would be careful not to ask personal questions respondents would be unwilling to answer honestly. The survey should seek to estimate whether individuals have looked for a similar service for themselves or for someone they know.

For some services the community survey would be especially helpful. For example, many burglaries and acts of vandalism go unreported because the victims feel there is little hope of regaining the stolen goods or that it is too much trouble to report the problem. If the community survey revealed that such hopelessness was widespread, the need for a new program might be even more compelling than the crime statistics themselves.

Whether a planned program is large or small, the principles described above can be used in assessments of need. The need for programs within large organizations, such as faculty development, student counseling, worker safety programs, and special hospital programs are among the kinds of small-scale programs for which needs should be documented before beginning the program. For each of these programs, a survey of those currently offering similar services, estimates of the number of those receiving similar services, and a survey of potential users would be valuable approaches to gathering information about need.

Once needs are defined validly, they become the basis for program planning and, subsequently, a basis for the development of program outcome measures. Sometimes the very methods used to examine needs can be used to show improvement in the target populations or communities. Standard achievement tests, for example, can show a need for improved instruction in reading as well as the impact of a program designed to improve reading skills.

A DECISION THEORY APPROACH TO PLANNING:
THE MULTI-ATTRIBUTE UTILITY (MAUT) METHOD

Having identified the general issues to be addressed in planning, and having described some of the tools for the assessment of need, we can now consider a practical approach by which evaluators can assist planners in choosing among possible programs. The method described in the remainder of this chapter is the Multi-Attribute Utility (MAUT) Method (Edwards, et al. 1975; Pitz and McKillip, 1984). This method is a technique derived from decision theory, which has been used for program planning, especially for allocating resources to competing human service programs. The method can also be adapted to making decisions of any kind, for example, in the purchase of new equipment, the choice of a new career, or personnel selection. However, in this book attention is focused on the use of the MAUT method for program planning. After first examining the basic purpose and design of the MAUT method, we shall outline and illustrate the method itself.

Basic Purpose and Design of the MAUT Method

The basic purpose of the MAUT method is to disaggregate a decision—that is, to separate the elements of a complicated decision and evaluate each element separately and to help people consider the strengths of alternative ways of meeting the needs identified. Instead of approaching a decision from a global viewpoint and beginning with a debate about the merits of competing programs, decision makers begin by reaching agreement on what they are trying to accomplish through the available programs. Having agreed on their overall goals, they then develop a consensus on the criteria to be used in judging the desirability of the competing programs. After having established this common ground, they can debate the merits of the programs in the light of the criteria established. This approach will in many cases narrow the focus to the exact area of disagreement and highlight the basic agreement among the planners.

A simplified version of decision disaggregation might be described as follows:

1. Decide on the appropriate criteria on which to base a decision. These criteria are values that the decision makers wish to maximize through the program. These criteria will guide their choice among available programs.
2. Weight the criteria to reflect their subjective importance to the decision makers. This procedure determines the relative importance of the values of the decision makers.
3. Evaluate each possible program on the basis of each criterion. This step enables the decision makers to pinpoint the strengths and weaknesses of each alternative program.
4. Combine the evaluations made on the basis of individual criteria into an overall judgment. This step shows the overall desirability or utility of each program.

Consider the example of a high school graduate choosing between attending College A and College B. Rather than trying to make the decision by stepping back and choosing a college on the basis of overall feelings, the student might choose to disaggregate the decision in the manner outlined in Figure 5.3. The student first identifies the criteria that reflect his or her values with respect to a college. In this instance the student identified acceptable cost, good academic reputation, attractive location, and good social opportunities.

Second, the student weighted the criteria to reflect their relative importance. As seen in Figure 5.3, the item called "social opportunities" was evaluated as least important and given a weight of 10. Location and academic reputation of the college were considered to be of equal importance, and both were thought to be twice as important as social opportunities. Therefore, they were given a weight of 20. Finally, cost was judged to be the most important

CRITERIA IN CHOOSING A COLLEGE (VALUES)	WEIGHT OF CRITERIA (IMPORTANCE)	RATING OF OPTIONS	
		COLLEGE A	COLLEGE B
Attending a college with:			
An acceptable cost	30	8	6
A good academic reputation	20	7	8
An attractive location	20	4	5
Good social opportunities	10	9	5

Computing desirability

College A's desirability: 30(8) + 20(7) + 20(4) + 10(9) = 550
College B's desirability: 30(6) + 20(8) + 20(5) + 10(5) = 490

Decision: Choose College A

FIGURE 5.3 Disaggregation of the selection of a college.

item and was given a weight of 30, which indicates that it is three times as important as social opportunities and half again as important as both location and academic reputation.

Third, each college was rated on a scale from 1 to 10 on each of the four criteria. The table shows that College A was judged more desirable on cost and social opportunities, while College B was judged more desirable on academic reputation and location.

Finally, the overall desirability (utility) of each college was determined in a quantitative manner by multiplying the rating on each criterion by its weight and adding the products for each college. The sum of the products equaled 550 for College A and 490 for College B. The decision was to choose College A.

When more than one decision maker is involved in a decision, the decision disaggregation method provides a system for combining their input in a manner that minimizes conflict. The decision makers begin by establishing common ground, agreeing on the criteria and the relative value of each before debating the merits of the available options. This procedure disciplines the discussion by identifying the areas of potential disagreement; that is, whether there is a difference in priority of values, in estimates of how much each option will maximize the values, or in both areas.

For example, suppose that in the above illustration the student's mother and father were to share in the selection of a college with their son or daughter. Rather than beginning the discussion with the parents declaring their preference for College B and the student opting for College A, they would begin by discussing their values and trying to agree on priorities before discussing the merits of either school. It would then become clear whether there was a conflict of values or rather a conflict of how well each college was judged to fulfill a common set of values.

The decision disaggregation method of decision making is really not a new concept; rather, it is an old idea with new terminology and extended application. Benjamin Franklin may have been among the earliest people to use a simplified MAUT approach in decision making (Dawes and Corrigan, 1974). In a letter to his friend Joseph Priestly dated September 19, 1772, Franklin suggested the following procedure for arriving at decisions:

> My way is to divide half a sheet of paper by a line into two columns; writing over the one *Pro*, and over the other *Con*. Then, during three or four days consideration, I put down under the different heads short hints of the different motives that at different times occur to me *for* and *against* the measure. When I have thus got them all together in one view, I endeavor to estimate the respective weights . . . [to] find at length where the balance lies. . . . And, though the weight of reasons cannot be taken with the precision of algebraic quantities, yet, when each is thus considered, separately and comparatively, and the whole matter lies before me, I think I can judge better, and am less liable to make a rash step: and in fact, I have found great advantage for this kind of equation, in what may be called *moral* or *prudential algebra* (Dawes and Corrigan, 1974, p. 95).

What Franklin called "prudential algebra" is a simplified MAUT approach, although he places less stress on the quantitative analysis and more on the qualitiative analysis of various arguments for and against a given measure.

Ten Steps of the MAUT Method

There are ten steps to the MAUT approach to measuring the relative usefulness of action alternatives. Edwards (1977) described the steps in detail. The steps are briefly summarized and explained below.

Step 1: Identify the organization whose utilities are to be maximized. In other words, what is the organization or person for whom the evaluation is being conducted? In the above example, the person for whom the evaluation was being conducted was the student planning to attend college.

Step 2: Identify the issue or issues to which the utilities needed are relevant. That is, what is the purpose of the evaluation? What decision is the organization or individual addressing? In the above example the decision to be addressed is the choice of college to attend.

Step 3: Identify the entities to be evaluated. The "entities to be evaluated" are the options or choices the organization or individual has at hand. The options may be action alternatives or programs designed to meet an organizational need. For example, should the high school graduate attend College A or College B?

Step 4: Identify the relevant dimensions of value. The "relevant dimensions of value" are the criteria on which the organization or individual will focus in order to make a choice between competing options or courses of action. They reflect organizational values as they are applied to the decision at hand. The dimensions should be clear and specific enough so that all the planners will understand them in the same way. In our example the cost of college might be further defined as tuition plus transportation and room and board, so that the statistics gathered on Colleges A and B would be comparable.

Finally, the criteria should be concrete enough to allow for accurate measurement. In our example "an acceptable cost" is the criterion that can be most objectively measured, and "good social opportunities" is a poorer criterion, since it must be measured in a vague, more subjective manner.

Step 5: Rank the dimensions in order of importance. After the dimensions have been selected in Step 4, the organizational representatives rank the dimensions in order of importance. Disagreement between representatives is almost certain at this step, and this disagreement should be resolved through discussion and consensus. It should be made clear that the order can, and probably will, be altered later on during the discussions that take place under Step 6. In the example "an acceptable cost" was rated first, "good academic reputation" second, "an attractive location" third, and "good social opportunities" fourth.

Step 6: Rate dimensions in importance, preserving ratios. The process begins by assigning the least important dimension a rating of 10. (The figure 10 is arbitrary, but allows for fine grading of subsequent dimensions while still retaining integer numbers.) Then the next least-important dimension is considered. If this dimension is considered to be twice as important as the previous one, it is given a rating of 20. If it is only half again as important, it is assigned a rating of 15. In fact, the representatives may decide that the second dimension rated is really no more important than the first dimension rated and give it a rating of 10 also, or even reverse the order of importance in light of further discussion. These ratings are called "weights" in Steps 7 to 9. As the process continues, many changes are likely to be made both in ranking and rating of dimensions. Such changes are acceptable and often desirable. Because the college-choice example was deliberately simplified, the following steps were not used in that example.

Step 7: Sum the importance weights, divide each by the sum, and multiply by 100. This is purely a computational step so that the ratings of all the dimensions will add up to 100. Edwards refers to this process as "normalizing" the weights. This process provides a clearer picture of the relative values of the weights given to each dimension, and makes subsequent calculation easier to manage.

During Step 7 the representatives will be able to recognize the reason for not including too many dimensions under Step 4. If there are too many dimensions, some will end up with trivially small weights that will, in effect, eliminate their impact on the decision. About six dimensions are ordinarily adequate and manageable. Lower ranked dimensions can also end up with trivial weights if more highly ranked dimensions are carelessly judged to be five or more times as important as the lower ranked ones.

Step 8: Measure the location of the entity being evaluated on each dimension. These "measurements" are judgments and usually are very subjective estimates. At times objective data may be available. Edwards suggests asking each representative to estimate the probability on a 0-to-100 scale that a given option will maximize each dimension. In other words, if a program is judged to have a high probability of fostering the value represented on a certain dimension, it might be assigned a 0.70 probability. If the program has a low probability of fostering the same value, it might be given a 0.20 probability. It is likely that all available options will be thought to have merit on each dimension of value. Therefore, it will seldom be appropriate to use 0. These estimates indicate how useful a course of action is in achieving the desired objectives. Thus, these probabilities are called utilities in discussions of the analysis of decisions.

Once again, there will probably be divergence of estimates by different representatives. However, through the MAUT process common ground has previously been established through agreement on the dimensions and their relative weights. As a result, disagreement is now narrowed to the estimate of each option's probability of maximizing a given dimension of value.

Step 9: Calculate utilities for entities. The equation is

$$U_i = \sum_j w_j u_{ij}$$

Remember that the sum of w_j equals 100. U_i is the aggregate utility for entity i; w_j is the normalized importance weight of dimension j from Step 7; and u_{ij} is the rescaled position of entity i on dimension j from Step 8 (Guttentag and Snapper, 1974, p. 58).

Stated simply, the total utility of each program or action alternative is obtained by multiplying the importance weight for each dimension (from Step 7) by the probability rating of an option on that dimension (from Step 8) and summing the products.

Step 10: Decide. If a single action alternative is to be chosen, the rule is simple: Maximize U_i. If a subset of alternatives is to be chosen, then the subset for which the sum of all U_i's is a maximum is best (Guttentag and Snapper, 1974).

If the decision makers want only one program and are indifferent to cost, the best decision will be the program with the highest aggregate utility, U_i. Since costs are usually important, the MAUT user needs to choose a method to handle costs. Cost can be handled in more than one manner. In the college-choice example, cost was a value dimension. If cost is not introduced as a value dimension, then the utility of each option is considered in light of the budget available. It may be possible to fund the two best options or programs. If the cost of the program with the highest utility exceeds the budget, then the program next in priority might be chosen. The problem of relating program plans, outcomes, and costs is complex. Chapter 10 discusses the problem in greater detail.

An Application of the MAUT Method

To understand more fully the ten steps of the MAUT method as described above, consider the example of a large manufacturing firm that is concerned with high turnover among its employees. The firm would like to build loyalty and trust among its employees so that there would be greater stability in the work force. The president of the firm invites the firm's four vice-presidents to meet and to suggest what steps should be taken. We assume that these managers have access to empirical information that suggests employees leave the firm because they perceive management policies to be arbitrary and unjust. At this point, a selection among the possible responses to this problem must be made. Suppose that one of the vice-presidents, who has been reading about decision making, suggests that they disaggregate their task. The vice-presidents decide to use the MAUT method to approach the problem.

Step 1. The organization whose utilities are to be maximized is the manufacturing firm. The firm will be represented by the vice-presidents.

Step 2. The issue to which the utilities are relevant is how the firm can best build the loyalty and trust of its employees.

Step 3. When the vice-presidents meet for the first time, they identify the available options or action alternatives. Let us suppose that they identify four possible courses of action:

1. Presidential visits to employees in their work areas.
2. "Skip-one" contact sessions (where employees have the chance to discuss their work life with their own supervisor's supervisor).
3. Training the supervisors and all management personnel to develop better supervisory skills.
4. Career-planning sessions for all employees.

Step 4 and Step 5. Next, the vice-presidents identify the following six dimensions of values that would guide their choice and then rank them (*Step 5*) in the following order:

1. Personalization of relationships.
2. Increased input by employees into the decision-making process.
3. Removal of fear of retribution from the communication network.
4. Increased job self-determintion.
5. Assurance to employees that the company followed through on previous employee recommendations.
6. Clarification of company goals.

Step 6. Next, the vice-presidents proceed to assign weights to each dimension. They give dimension 6 a value of 10 and then decide that dimension 5 is of equal importance; therefore, dimension 5 is also given a value of 10. Dimension 4 is considered and judged to be twice as important as either dimension 5 or 6; dimension 4, therefore, is given a weight of 20. In like manner, dimensions 3, 2, and 1 are assigned weights of 30, 45, and 55, respectively.

Step 7. The weights are normalized by dividing each by the sum of the six weights and then multiplying by 100. This process results in the following normalized weights:

DIMENSION	RAW WEIGHT	NORMALIZED WEIGHT
1	55	32
2	45	26
3	30	18
4	20	12
5	10	6
6	10	6
	170	100

Step 8. The group discusses the probability of each value dimension being maximized by each option. For example, option 1 (presidential visits) is given a 0.25 probability of maximizing dimension 1 (personalization or relationships); option 2 (skip-one contact sessions) is given a 0.50 probability; option 3 (training of supervisors), a 0.65 probability; and option 4 (career-planning sessions), a 0.50 probability. The process is repeated for the remaining five dimensions. The probabilities are all given in Figure 5.4.

Step 9. Utilities are calculated for each option by multiplying the weight of each dimension by its probability estimate. For example, option 3 receives the highest utility score: $32 (0.65) + 26(0.85) + 18(0.80) + 12(0.50) + 6(0.40) + 6(0.80) = 70.50$. Option 2 ranks second, with a utility score of 59; option 1 ranks third, with a utility score of 38. Finally, option 4 is last, with a score of 35. These calculations are summarized in Figure 5.4.

Step 10. Decide. In the supposition that a training program for supervisors (option 3) would consume all the available money and resources, the vice-presidents would probably recommend to the president that only option 3 be implemented. However, if enough resources are available to implement option 2 (skip-one contact sessions) as well, then option 2 might be recommended along with option 3. The skip-one contact sessions received a utility score (58) that was not too far behind the score for a training program for supervisors (70).

In the supposition that there are not enough resources available for option 3 (training for supervisors), then option 2 would be recommended as the best choice within the firm's budget. The remaining two options (presidential visits and career planning) received utility scores of 37.70 and 33.70, respectively, and are clearly judged to be less effective than either options 3 or 2.

Rather than rely solely on the recommendation of the vice-presidents, the president might be well advised to seek input from other stakeholder groups within the plant who would be affected by the decision. For example, the president might have a group representing first-line management and another group representing nonmanagerial employees meet separately to use the MAUT method to address the question of building employee trust and loyalty. If both groups arrive at the same conclusion as the vice-presidents,

OPTIONS (SPECIFIC ACTION PROPOSALS)		DIMENSIONS (VALUES) TO BE MAXIMIZED						UTILITY	FINAL RANK
		1	2	3	4	5	6		
	WEIGHTS =	32	26	18	12	6	6		
1. Presidential visits to employees in their work area	Probabilities =	0.25	0.30	0.75	0.00	0.70	0.70		
	Wts. × Probabilities =	8.00	7.80	13.50	0.00	4.20	4.20	37.70	3
2. Skip-one contact sessions	Probabilities =	0.50	0.60	0.75	0.50	0.50	0.70		
	Wts. × Probabilities =	16.00	15.60	13.50	6.00	3.00	4.20	58.30	2
3. Training of supervisors and management personnel to develop better supervisory skills	Probabilities =	0.65	0.85	0.80	0.50	0.40	0.80		
	Wts. × Probabilities =	20.80	22.10	14.40	6.00	2.40	4.80	70.50	1
4. Career-planning sessions for all employees	Probabilities =	0.50	0.15	0.20	0.75	0.10	0.10		
	Wts. × Probabilities =	16.00	3.90	3.60	9.00	0.60	0.60	33.70	4

FIGURE 5.4 Multi-Attribute Utility (MAUT) worksheet.

the president would have greater certainty that a supervisory training program would be accepted.

Use of the MAUT Model to Guide Evaluation

Not only is the MAUT model a guide to decision making but it also provides a means of focusing evaluation on the area where decisions must be made. Suppose that in the example just given, the president decides to proceed with a program to train supervisors and management personnel. However, the president questions how correct the vice-presidents were in the high probability (80 percent) they assigned to the effectiveness of the training of supervisors in removing fear of retribution from the communication network. The evaluation team can then focus its efforts on clarifying the degree to which fear of retribution is removed through supervisor training.

Subsequent evaluation will be needed to estimate the probability that the program did achieve its goals on one or more value dimensions. This could either confirm the wisdom of the choice of a given option or make the decision makers review their commitment to that option.

SUMMARY

Evaluators can contribute to the planning process by asking questions that help planners clarify the program's conceptual base and by assisting in the development of statements describing the ways the program is intended to be implemented and how it is to help the target population. Information on needs is collected from many sources, including official censuses, existing programs, and community or organizational surveys. Once information on needs is developed, a selection among possible programs is required. The chapter includes an example of a decision theory approach to program selection. The use of an explicit approach to program selection forces planners to examine different options as they may relate to the various desired results of the program. Evaluators can assist in this process by recommending such a structured approach and by providing information about what is already known on the basis of previous evaluations.

STUDY QUESTIONS

1. Assume that the following questions appeared in a community survey. Discuss the strong and weak points of each.
   a. Is it important that (your town) have a program for gifted children in the public schools?
   b. Would you use a nutrition information service if it were available in (your town)?
   c. Have you ever sought counseling help for yourself or for someone else?
2. A key informant survey on the nutritional needs of the children of a particular community included the individuals listed below. Describe the degree to which

each is a good or a poor source for information on the nutritional level of children of the community.

a. The mayor.
b. The members of the city council.
c. A private-practice physician.
d. The school nurse.
e. A restaurant owner.
f. The truant officer.
g. Day-care center teachers.
h. Elementary school teachers.
i. Senior high school teachers.

3. Assume that your college has a $50,000 grant to reduce crime on campus. Consider what sources of information about needs could be used. Then list the objectives such a program might attempt to achieve. Next list some possible specific actions that might be followed (for example, publicity campaign, new locks, escort service, and so on). Finally, draw up a MAUT decision matrix to choose among the possible programs.

4. Prepare an illustrative MAUT decision matrix as in Figure 5.4 to disaggregate a choice you must make or have recently made.

5. Under what conditions would an evaluation of need be threatening to an organization?

FURTHER READING

ATTKISSON, C. C., et al. eds. 1978. *Evaluation of human service programs.* New York: Academic Press.

EGAN, G. 1985. *Change agent skills in helping and human service settings.* Monterey, Calif.: Brooks/Cole.

McKILLIP, J. 1987. *Need analysis: Tools for human services and education.* Beverly Hills, Calif.: Sage.

PITZ, G. F., AND McKILLIP, J. 1984. *Decision analysis for program evaluators.* Beverly Hills, Calif.: Sage.

6

Monitoring the Operation of Programs

Program monitoring " . . . is the least acknowledged but probably most practiced category of evaluation" (ERS Standards Committee, 1982, p. 10). The most basic form of program evaluation is an examination of the program itself—its activities, the population it serves, and how it functions. Program monitoring includes an assessment of how much effort in the form of human and physical resources is invested in the program and whether the effort is expended as planned. The evaluation of effort is important; a program without sufficient resources cannot be expected to influence the participants in the program, and a program planned to meet one problem will be less useful when applied to a different problem. Careful program monitoring will yield "impressive results" according to Lipsey et al. (1985).

It is important, nevertheless, to note that an evaluation of the activities of a program cannot reveal whether the clients actually benefit from the program. Evaluation of the degree of successful outcome ultimately achieved requires approaches that differ from the methods described in this chapter. The methods illustrated here are called "administrative monitoring" (Poister, 1982). Assessing program results can be called, in contrast, "performance monitoring." Relating program outcomes to goals is discussed in Chapters 7 through 9.

Since a well-planned, well-staffed, and well-housed program may not function effectively, even evaluators commissioned to assess the quality of a program will inquire into its day-to-day performance. Businesses evaluate their performance by counting cash receipts at the end of the day and by performing inventories of stock at regular intervals. Human service managers need measures of activity similar to those available to commercial firms. The problem, of course, is that the ultimate products of human service programs, well-functioning people, are not nearly as objectively measured or as concrete as store inventories.

The place to begin is to ask whether the human service program has been implemented as planned. If well-designed advertisements encouraging seat belt use are not actually published or broadcast, there is no reason to evaluate the impact of the material. If drug abusers do not attend a drug abuse program, there is little need to ask whether the program reduced drug abuse. Systematic methods have only recently been developed to monitor medical care, counseling and psychotherapy, training, and other forms of human services. Some of these methods assess the degree to which previously specified optimal procedures are followed. In this chapter we do not address the question of following optimal procedures; that question is pursued in Chapter 7. At this point evaluation is limited to a description of the services that are actually delivered.

Managers need such information to facilitate their planning and decision making, to anticipate problems, and to justify the existence of the program. For example, if it is discovered that a population receiving assistance is not the one targeted, then the program is not serving the need it was designed to meet and may have to be altered. Striking differences in the contributions of different staff members or an unusually heavy client dropout rate would be other problems important to detect. Managers can act to correct problems only if they have adequate information. Thus, program monitoring usually serves a formative function for program managers. Without accurate information, problems may become apparent only when it is too late to correct them.

THE PROGRAM AUDIT AS A MEANS OF PROGRAM EVALUATION

Some evaluators have come to use the term *audit*, taken from accounting terminology, to describe the process of quantifying the amount of services rendered and the identity of program participants (Sells, 1975). Others simply refer to this activity as monitoring a program (Mechanic, 1975). To keep the term separate from the functions of accountants, the term *audit of services* is used to refer to a systematic examination of program inputs, or the effort put into a program.

Evaluators who conduct an audit of services gather information so that they can describe the program. A description of the program includes a profile of the clients coming into the program, a summary of the services given, workloads of the staff members, and sometimes clients' evaluations of the program. Program directors and staff sometimes believe they do not need quantified information to summarize the type and amount of services they provide and to whom these services are given. However, it is common knowledge among evaluators that the staff members' subjective beliefs about the program and clients are often in error.

In several studies in which the authors have participated, program staffs have been very wrong in describing the population served by the program. In an evaluation of an innovative organization of nursing on a hospital unit (Carey, 1979), the staff said that 90 percent of the patients would have one of three major problems: respiratory illnesses, diabetes, or hypertension. As part of the evaluation, the diagnoses of the patients on the unit were recorded. It turned out that only 20 percent of the patients were diagnosed as having one of these three ailments. Is it possible that service could be improved if the nurses realized that they were actually serving a very heterogeneous patient population? An educational program designed for a relatively homogeneous patient population cannot be very effective when given to a group containing individuals with many unique needs.

The description of the population served and the services rendered by a program fills several needs. First, the immediate needs of management may be most obvious. In order to manage a human service program effectively, it is necessary to know who receives what service from whom, and when the service is given. Managers fill their roles better the more they are able to anticipate and avoid crises. Second, an audit of services is a necessary prelude to rigorous study of the outcome of the services since the planned outcomes will not occur if services are not or only marginally provided. Third, knowing what is currently done provides a way to plan rationally.

A modest audit of services conducted between two specific dates can serve to aid planning or as a preliminary step in an outcome evaluation. The limited approach provides a snapshot of the program; the ongoing method provides a motion picture of the program. An examination of the program's records for a limited time period is undertaken to answer some particular questions about the level and types of services given; such information can give the planner and manager some directions to follow in program planning. In contrast, management needs require an ongoing information system and may well require the development of a system to obtain information routinely. Repeated descriptions of a program over fairly short time periods, such as one month, permit closer monitoring and allow adjustments to be made in the way the program is run. A procedure to summarize services on a regular basis is called a *management information system,* or MIS.

As with most dichotomies, this contrast between special, limited audits versus extended, routinized audits may break down in practice. However, the distinction is useful; programs have different needs at different times. If a manager needs information that is gathered repeatedly over short time intervals, an approach requiring hand retrieval of data would be overly expensive and slow. On the other hand, a small program may not be sophisticated enough to require a complex information system; in such cases a simpler, less ambitious procedure would be used. Some writers in program evaluation view the development of management information systems as a major part of the role of in-house program evaluators (for example, see Attkisson et al., 1978).

WHAT TO SUMMARIZE IN AN AUDIT OF SERVICES

There is no standard way to select and gather the information required to describe a program. Programs differ in the types of people served, the services given, and the type of institution offering the services. Evaluators bear in mind several points as they prepare an audit of services. These points are not explicit guides as to which information to gather or which procedures to use. Rather, they help evaluators focus on the issues that need to be addressed.

Relevant Information

The information gathered must be central to the purpose of the audit. Important information can help to set staff levels, to satisfy accreditation criteria, and to plan for space needs. Effective evaluators attempt to gather only information that is relevant to describing the program and how it functions. Many characteristics of clients and programs are not central to program decisions. Evaluators may find many potentially interesting questions to explore while doing an evaluation, such as the relationship of birth order to the probability of becoming a juvenile delinquent or the degree that students' right/left hand preferences are related to academic success. Such questions might well be important for theories of social development or brain function. If evaluators have the time to study issues of basic research, they may seek to explore some of these hypotheses. However, every bit of additional information recorded in an audit increases the cost of data collection and analysis.

Actual State of Program

A second point is that an audit must describe the actual state of the current program. Evaluators are careful to distinguish between the program as described and the program as administered. Many programs that look very good on paper fail, not because they were designed poorly but because the staff or the participants did not actually follow the design or the procedure as planned. In a large university with many commuting students, attempts were made to help freshmen become part of university life. In one program groups of 8 to 12 freshmen were invited into faculty homes for social evenings. A number of enthusiastic faculty members volunteered to take part in the program. One of the major findings of the evaluation was that in spite of this early enthusiasm on the part of the faculty, 40 percent of the faculty did not actually invite the students whose names they were given. Second, among the students who did receive invitations, 60 percent declined to attend. One particular faculty member prepared a fairly generous buffet dinner—only to discover as the evening passed that not one student was going to come. This program to involve students in the life of the campus did not need to be evaluated with an experimental design as planned. Merely noting the number of faculty who did not actually invite any students and the proportion of students who did not accept invitations was enough to show that the program was not being carried out. The program itself was very unlikely to reduce the number of freshman dropouts or to improve student morale. Without a careful study of the implementation of the program, administrative officers concerned with freshmen-dropout problems would have been at a loss to understand just what went wrong with the program.

The information necessary to describe the services rendered include (1) the type of service offered by the program (such as job training, group therapy, immunizations); (2) the extensiveness of the program (such as hours of training or therapy, skills to be learned, location of the program, facilities); and (3) the number of people participating in the service, especially the proportion of people completing the program.

Providers of Services

The preparation of an audit of services should include a description of who gives the services. In large hospital settings many care givers—such as physicians, nurses, and physical therapists—are licensed by the state for the particular job. In other human service settings, especially where pay is low, people with limited training are involved in giving the service. Counseling programs for drug addicts or former addicts are sometimes staffed by people who are neither trained nor psychologically equipped for the positions they are filling. It is also possible that the staff may be overqualified. An evaluation of a project staffed by volunteer lawyers to help ex-convicts readjust to community life found mixed results—the released prisoners looked to the volunteers for legal aid, not for general readjustment help. Thus, the legal training of the volunteers stood in the way of a truly effective program, in spite of sincere efforts (Berman, 1978).

Program Participants

A fourth major part of an audit includes a description of those who receive the services. If a program was well planned, the population to be served would have been specified carefully and the program tailored to meet the needs of that group. An audit should document the identity and the needs of the people using the service and compare these findings to the program plans. In other words, the fit between the program and the needs of those using it can be examined. If the fit is not good, changes or redirections for the program can be considered. If the agency never actually defined the group to be served, a description of the people using the agency may be especially enlightening.

The people using the program are routinely described by gender and age. The choice of additional information to be presented depends on the specific nature of the program. Such information may include where the people live, the major problems for which they are seeking help, the source of referral, ethnic background, and so forth.

The ease or difficulty people have in obtaining the service is an aspect of the description of those receiving the service. Since this information is seldom in agency files, it would be necessary to prepare a short survey to administer to people using the service. Questions asked should cover how much time elapsed between initial contact and first appointment, the mode of transportation used, parking availability (if required), and time necessary to wait for care. In preparing such a survey, one must be aware of differences in ease of access that are related to variables such as time of day (morning versus afternoon versus evening), day of the week (workdays versus weekends), type of service, and welfare status of the individual. It is unlikely that a facility would need to gather all this information routinely. Obtaining it soon after beginning the program and at later time periods as the facility changes or expands would be sufficient.

When audits are reported, evaluators have come to expect to be told that the results of the audit (and this is true of any evaluation for that matter) were already known. It is a common human tendency to assimilate new information without realizing that it does conflict with what was previously expected. An accomplished evaluator will not reveal the findings of evaluations before obtaining some information on what the staff and director expect the audit to show. Only in this way will an evaluator actually know whether the audit produced "nothing new" or whether the results did indeed yield new material. Furthermore, stakeholders are more likely to use information if they recognize some of their beliefs were incorrect. Correcting inaccurate beliefs needs to be done gently and with respect; otherwise the chances of utilization will drop to zero regardless of the quality of one's data or recommendations.

AN APPROACH TO PROVIDING REPEATED AUDITS

When setting out to prepare a method of providing periodic reports describing the way an agency functions, the evaluator needs to have a hand in designing the agency's records. Instead of using existing files, the evaluator can help the agency design recording and filing procedures that will be useful for evaluation and for routine agency needs. When records are designed for use in evaluations, it is quite economical to prepare the type of reports described in this chapter.

Existing Records of a Program

It would be impossible to perform an empirical evaluation of effort without adequate records. However, it is no secret that the records of human service agencies are often in abysmal condition. Inadequate records are frequent even in hospitals, where sloppy handwriting has resulted in fatal drug overdoses and the amputation of a healthy leg instead of a diseased one (Dixon, 1977). Why are charts and records in such poor condition? Record-keeping is a dull and time-consuming task. Individuals attracted to human service occupations often view record-keeping as time taken away from clients, students, or patients. In the very short run, that view may be correct. Furthermore, records were less important in the recent past, when impressionistic evaluations of success and effort were sufficient evaluations in many settings. The existence of this and other books on evaluation methods shows that impressionistic evaluations are no longer accepted as sufficient by regulatory and accrediting agencies. We hope readers will agree that in the long run, well-kept records (and evaluation, in general) will result in more effective attention to human service program participants.

Evaluators helping an agency to develop an ongoing plan for documenting the provision of services will probably first ask what material is available in the records as currently maintained. However, even agencies with highly detailed and carefully maintained records may not have all the information useful for program evaluation purposes. Such records often contain long narrative accounts of progress or disability. The reason narrative records are not useful is that they lack a common frame of reference.

People adopt widely differing point of view in defining success in human services. For example, the care giver, the program participant, and the community tend to define success in mental health care in quite different terms. People in the local community are distressed by public acting-out behavior. Communities do not want individuals around who wear unusual clothing, argue frequently with neighbors or shopkeepers, or tell passersby about hallucinations. The larger society wants individuals to keep up their living quarters, hold jobs, and, in general, behave responsibly. If mental health counseling or the provision of tranquilizers can keep people looking and acting relatively normal, society will consider the service successful and effective.

Therapists, on the other hand, have traditionally been less interested in day-to-day responsible behavior than in personality structure and emotional health. They would not view therapy as effective if it only assisted people to cope better or to conform passively to social norms. Instead, they would desire to detect greater autonomy, greater self-actualization, less guilt, and more frequent assertiveness. These are behaviors that are largely not observable by the community and not relevant to its evaluation of a mental health center.

Individuals receiving therapy may have an altogether different set of standards. They may evaluate therapy on the basis of whether they feel better about themselves. It is quite possible for clients to find a mode of adjustment that is acceptable to themselves but that would neither satisfy the therapist nor many members of the community.

Strupp and Handley (1977) have discussed these three points of view in more detail, especially with regard to negative outcomes in therapy. When individuals differ in their relative emphasis on these three points of view, free narrative reports will not be very useful to the evaluator. If the therapists also differ in theoretical orientations (such as Freudian versus behaviorist versus medical), the narratives will be even more difficult to compare and to summarize.

Increasing the Usefulness of Records

It is necessary for the program director and other information users to develop a list of essential information useful in managing and evaluating the program. A point repeatedly stressed in this book is that information is gathered only when it is useful. If there are legal requirements to obtain certain information, or if decisions are to be made on the basis of the information, then it should be gathered. Otherwise, the material need not be recorded, unless it is suspected that negative side effects are occurring.

Information should not be gathered simply to fill folders in file cabinets. Methods of summarizing the information must be developed to increase the usefulness of files. In different contexts, staff or managers have confidently assured evaluators that certain information was "in the files"—unfortunately, many files are incomplete. However, the major point is that in-the-files information is not useful information. Retrieving material from client folders is a time-consuming task. Further, it is a sensitive task: the privacy of the clients must be maintained. It is more efficient to develop a management information system that permits the routine summary of participant descriptors (that is, age, sex, disability) and service provided without manually going through file folders that often contain personal material important to the client and the care giver but irrelevant to the evaluator.

How Records Can Be Used in Process Evaluations

One useful approach might be to prepare monthly summaries of all new clients. Figure 6.1 is a form that could be used when people initially request counseling at a center offering outpatient counseling. It contains much of the same information many counselors request. Regardless of the size of the facility, a sheet such as this would become the first entry in the individual's file. Notice that the center personnel add some information themselves, such as an identification number and a problem code. Otherwise, the form could be self-administered.

To use this information most easily and effectively, it is necessary to have the material entered into a computer system. In order to maintain the client's privacy, it is necessary to have some of the material in Figure 6.1 on a second copy in a form that is not easily identifiable. A second copy can be obtained using two printed forms with carbon paper bound between the pages. Confidentiality can be maintained by making it impossible for the client's name, street address, telephone number, and other traceable material to print through. The information would be identified by the number added by the intake worker or secretary before the copies are sent to a data analyst. Figure 6.1 includes spaces to code type of problem(s) leading to a request for counseling.

The specific information to be gathered will depend on the needs of the particular human service agency preparing the system. Figure 6.2 contains a list of items that agencies would want to consider in preparing forms for gathering information about new clients.

Simply having some of the information in Figures 6.1 and 6.2 summarized each month or quarter would yield a more complete description of new clients than many agencies traditionally have available. For each calendar or fiscal year, the individual reports could be combined into a yearly profile of new clients.

PLEASE COMPLETE THIS FORM AND RETURN IT TO THE SECRETARY IN THE ENVELOPE PROVIDED. THE INFORMATION YOU GIVE US IS CONFIDENTIAL AND WILL BE CAREFULLY SECURED.

Name _____

Address _____

_____ zip _____

Telephone _____

Please do not write in boxes below:

☐☐☐☐☐☐☐

☐☐—☐☐—☐☐

Marital Status: (Circle one)
  1. Never married 2. Married now 3. Widowed 4. Divorced/Annulled 5. Separated

Sex:
  1. Female   2. Male   3. Couple application

Age: _____   Age of spouse if married now: _____

Who referred you to the center? (Circle one)
  1. Myself, friend, family   4. Hospital   7. Another agency
  2. Another client   5. Physician   8. Other _____
  3. Clergyman   6. Psychiatrist   _____

What problem(s) has prompted you to consider counseling at this center? ☐☐
_____ ☐☐
_____ ☐☐
_____ ☐☐

What form of counseling are you most interested in at this time? (Circle one)
  1. Individual   2. Family   3. Marital   4. Group

Who lives in your immediate family?
  Adults (give their relationship to you) _____ ☐☐
  _____ ☐☐
  Children (give ages)   _____ ☐☐
  _____ ☐☐

Have you previously received counseling from some other agency or counselor?
  1. Yes
  2. No

If "Yes" and if you do enter therapy with a counselor from the center, may we contact this person or agency about you?
  1. No
  2. Yes (Give name of counselor) _____

  Please sign _____

Where are you employed? _____

Please give the name and address of any insurance company that will meet part of your expenses at the center.

Name _____ Address _____ Ident. No. _____

FIGURE 6.1 An application form for potential clients of an outpatient counseling center.

Initial Information
Name
Address
Sex
Age
Educational level
Marital status
Family description
Ethnic background
Referral source
Problem(s) leading to request for services
Previous participation in similar human services programs
Insurance coverage
Veteran's benefits
Welfare status
Dates: Of initial application
When formal participation begun

Some information will be unique to the type of agency involved. For example:

Mental health services:	Previous hospitalizations
	Type and extent of therapy
	Current medication
	Previous diagnoses
	Alcoholism/Drug user
	Functional life status
	Identity of previous therapist
Criminal justice programs:	Status with court system
	Type of previous programs
	Location of programs
	Voluntary or forced participation
Job-training programs:	Jobs held, length of previous employment
	Income
	Reason for unemployment
	Types of previous job-training programs
	Location of programs
Educational programs:	School attending
	Grade level
	IQ or other standardized tests
	Location of previous programs

Ongoing information
Amount of service rendered (hours of therapy, courses completed, skills mastered)
When service given
Identity of care giver(s)
Functional status or adjustment during and at termination of service
Reason for termination
Degree of self-support
Fees charged
Referral made

FIGURE 6.2 Types of information an agency might include in the basic descriptive information gathered about those seeking service, as well as the type of information added as the service is given.

Figure 6.3 is an illustrative new client report for a given month. The report includes information important to a particular center. For example, one counseling center with which we are familiar seeks to be of service to community clergy when they are faced with parish members who have emotional problems that cannot be handled by brief supportive counseling. A variable included in a hypothetical report of new clients for this center would be source of referral. This center can document that it is fulfilling one of its

```
NEW CLIENTS FOR MAY 1984


GENDER AND AGE OF NEW CLIENTS
                                       N    %  AGE
   INDIVIDUAL CLIENTS      FEMALE      98   65   34
                          MALE         30   20   27
   COUPLES (TWO PEOPLE)                11   15   32
                                      ---  ---   --
     TOTAL NEW CLIENTS                139  100   32



MARITAL STATUS AND GENDER                        FEMALE   MALE
                          NEVER MARRIED             28      12
                          MARRIED NOW               48      15
                          WIDOWED                    3       0
                          DIVORCED,ANNULED          15       3
                          SEPARATED                  4       0


SOURCES OF REFERRAL                                 N       %
                          SELF,FRIEND, FAMILY       27      19
                          ANOTHER CLIENT             5       4
                          CLERGY                    67      48
                          HOSPITAL                  15      17
                          PSYCHIATRIST               2       1
                          ANOTHER SOURCE             3       2


PROBLEM CODE                                        N       %
                   MARITAL PROBLEMS                 80      58
                   INDIVIDUAL ADJUSTMENT ISSUES    128      92
                   PROBLEMS AT WORK                 30      22
                   PROBLEMS AT SCHOOL               8        6
                   PROBLEMS WITH CHILDREN           62      45
                   ALCOHOLISM, DRUG USE             28      20
                   UNDIAGNOSED PHYSICAL SYMPTOMS    16      12


SERVICE SOUGHT                                      N       %
                       INDIVIDUAL THERAPY           82      59
                       FAMILY THERAPY               15      11
                       MARITAL THERAPY              32      23
                       GROUP THERAPY                10       7


NUMBER(%) HAVING PREVIOUS PSYCHOTHERAPY  45 ( 32%)

NUMBER(%) EMPLOYED  92 ( 66%)
```

FIGURE 6.3 An illustrative monthly report describing applicants for outpatient counseling.

goals by showing that a large proportion of its referrals do indeed come from clergy. Age, sex, apparent problem, type of therapy desired, and location of residence are useful types of information in judging whether an agency is serving the population it was designed to serve.

The value of having summaries such as that shown in Figure 6.3 would be apparent to anyone who has worked in a large organization—it is necessary to let people know what you are doing. Program managers can more easily justify the continued existence of their programs if they are able to provide documentation of the number of people served, as well as brief demographic descriptions and the reasons clients give for seeking the service. Having information available also facilitates responding to requests for information. Frequently government agencies request material that may be available only by searching through the files. Chapman (1976) reported that the need to quickly prepare an extensive survey precipitated a crisis in a mental health center because much necessary information was not easily available. The crisis ultimately led the center to prepare an information system capable of routinely summarizing client characteristics as well as much additional information.

Following the Course of Service

The course of a service can be followed by preparing standard forms with spaces in which therapists can record certain information after each client contact. This short contact report does not take the place of the therapists' process notes, which are normally for the personal use of the therapist. Figure 6.4 is an example of such a contact report. The identification number would be used to match this report with other information about a particular client, such as information gathered at the beginning of therapy and from previous contact reports. The therapist identification number and therapy type are useful for documenting workload. The functional status ratings could be based on the procedure described in Chapter 3 (see Figure 3.2). Including the charges on this form would facilitate an automated billing system. Information about referral can be noted on this form, and a therapist may also indicate when a formal end of therapy has occurred.

To make more efficient use of the contact report in Figure 6.4, there should be copies for the therapist, the client, and the data analyst. All three copies could be made simultaneously. The client's copy and the data center's copy would not include all the information included in the therapist's copy. The copy for data processing would not include any of the printed labels included in Figure 6.4; it would not even indicate that the report referred to a therapy session. Figure 6.5 includes just the numbers and instructions for coding. The name of the client is not included; however, the identification number is. The client's version of the form is shown in Figure 6.6. It includes the client's name and center number (to facilitate access to records if a question should occur), the charge for services, the name of a referral (if any), the time of next appointment (if any), and the therapist's signature. These contact reports provide information useful for the management of a program.

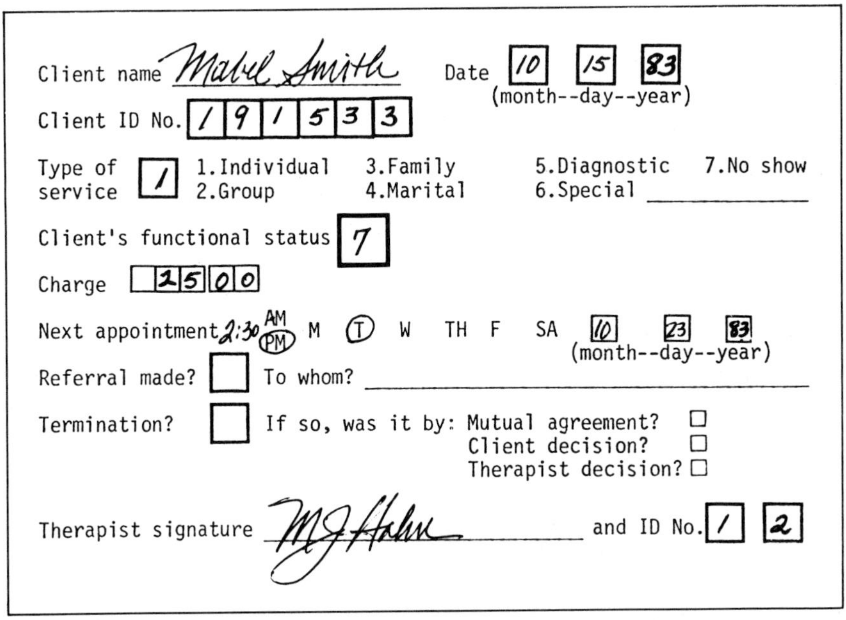

Client name Mabel Smith Date 10 15 83 (month--day--year)

Client ID No. 1 9 1 5 3 3

Type of service 1 — 1.Individual 2.Group 3.Family 4.Marital 5.Diagnostic 6.Special ______ 7.No show

Client's functional status 7

Charge 25 00

Next appointment 2:30 AM (PM) M (T) W TH F SA 10 23 83 (month--day--year)

Referral made? ☐ To whom? ______

Termination? ☐ If so, was it by: Mutual agreement? ☐ Client decision? ☐ Therapist decision? ☐

Therapist signature M J Hahn ______ and ID No. 1 2

FIGURE 6.4 An illustrative form for a therapist to use after each therapy session with a client. This copy would be kept by the center.

FIGURE 6.5 The way the information in Figure 6.4 would be transmitted to the person responsible for analyzing the information for future use.

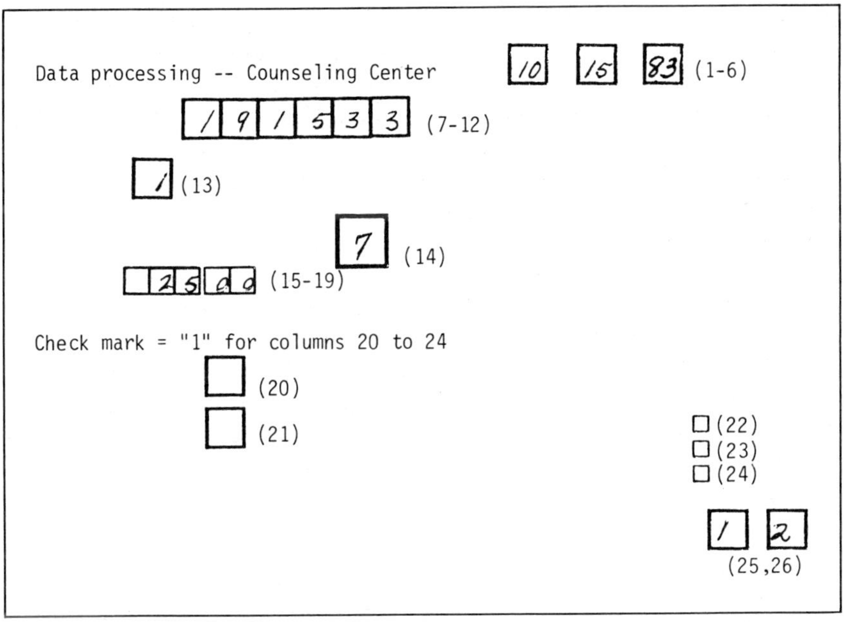

Data processing -- Counseling Center 10 15 83 (1-6)

1 9 1 5 3 3 (7-12)

1 (13)

7 (14)

25 00 (15-19)

Check mark = "1" for columns 20 to 24

☐ (20)

☐ (21)

☐ (22)
☐ (23)
☐ (24)

1 2 (25,26)

Client _Mabel Smith_ Date _10 – 15 – 83_

Your center no./ _9 1 5 3 3_

In case a question or a need to change your next appointment arises, our number is 887-7325. Please mention your center number when calling.

The charge for today's session is
$ _25.00_

Next appointment _2:30_ AM PM M (T) W TH F SA   _10 – 23 – 83_

Referral, if any, is to:

Therapist _____ _MJ Hahn_

FIGURE 6.6   The client's copy of the therapist's form illustrated in Figure 6.4 would contain the information shown above.

A monthly report of clients who have ended their association with the center could follow a format similar to that of Figure 6.7. Information about the amount and type of service received,[1] mean functional status at the beginning and at the end of therapy, amount of charges, number of referrals, and the type of termination occurring could be summarized and related to the demographic information previously obtained. Examining just the information in Figure 6.7, the director and staff can learn that about one-quarter of the clients apparently reject the services offered. This conclusion can be drawn from the facts that 24 percent of the clients accept two or less units of counseling and that 29 percent of the clients leave without the therapist's agreement. A director would probably seek to lower these proportions. The illustrative reports offer some clues about how to approach such a goal. The lower part of the report shows that older clients rejected therapy more frequently than younger clients did. Approaches to older clients could become a topic for in-service training at this center. Material presented later in this chapter will provide further suggestions for the director who seeks to lower the proportion of clients who receive little care at this center.

A monthly report can also be prepared for each therapist. Such reports

[1]A unit of service can be considered as one 50-minute period of individual psychotherapy or two 50-minute periods of group therapy. Other settings, of course, would require different units of service.

REPORT OF TERMINATED CLIENTS IN MAY 1984

CASES TERMINATED IN MAY: 84

TYPE OF TERMINATION	N	%
MUTUAL CONSENT	67	68
CLIENT DECISION	24	29
THERAPIST DECISION	3	4

UNITS OF SERVICE RENDERED	N	%
2 OR LESS	20	24
3 TO 6	14	17
7 TO 15	36	43
16 TO 30	13	15
OVER 30	1	1

RATINGS OF FUNCTIONAL STATUS

LEVEL	CLIENTS AT EACH FUNCTIONAL LEVEL WHEN THERAPY BEGAN	AT TERMINATION
DYSFUNCTIONAL: 1	0 (0%)	0 (0%)
DYSFUNCTIONAL: 2	0 (0%)	1 (1%)
DYSFUNCTIONAL: 3	2 (2%)	0 (0%)
DYSFUNCTIONAL: 4	25 (30%)	3 (4%)
FUNCTIONAL: 5	41 (49%)	2 (2%)
FUNCTIONAL: 6	8 (10%)	7 (8%)
FUNCTIONAL: 7	6 (7%)	4 (5%)
FUNCTIONAL: 8	2 (2%)	21 (25%)
FUNCTIONAL: 9	0 (0%)	46 (55%)
MEAN FUNCTIONAL STATUS	5.00	8.05

TYPE OF TERMINATION AND AGE OF CLIENT

	UNDER 29	30 AND OVER
MUTUAL CONSENT	25 (76%)	32 (63%)
CLIENT DECISION	6 (18%)	18 (35%)
THERAPIST DECISION	2 (6%)	1 (2%)
ALL	33 (100%)	51 (100%)

UNITS OF SERVICE AND AGE OF CLIENT

	UNDER 29	30 AND OVER
2 OR LESS	5 (15%)	15 (29%)
3 TO 6	7 (21%)	7 (14%)
7 TO 15	14 (42%)	22 (43%)
16 TO 30	6 (18%)	7 (14%)
OVER 30	1 (3%)	0 (0%)
ALL	33 (100%)	51 (100%)

FIGURE 6.7 A report on the clients terminated during one month, including characteristics of services rendered to these clients.

would provide the therapists with information about their work as compared to that of the other therapists as a group. People working in human services seldom have quantified information on how their work compares to that of others in their own field or institution. However, the value of feedback in improving one's performance has repeatedly been demonstrated. Seligman and Darley (1977), for example, showed that residential use of electricity could be reduced over 10 percent simply by providing consumers, on a weekly basis, with information on how much electricity was used. Other examples of the value of feedback were given in Chapter 1 of this text.

A report format that could provide information for the individual therapist is given in Figure 6.8. This example describes the therapist's caseload and the amount of service rendered during the month in question. Note that the therapist Helper has some problems. He had a higher proportion of clients drop out during the previous month than did the other therapists in the center. Of more importance, this hypothetical report shows that those who quit had received less service than was given to other clients before termination. This therapist also has a relatively large number of inactive clients, that is, clients who have not received any service for 90 days or more. The report politely requests that therapist Helper terminate these clients or see if they are still interested in continuing therapy. Last, there is a frequency table of ratings of psychological function of Helper's clients who officially ended their contact with the center during the last month.

Program changes or procedural changes can be planned to remedy any deficiencies found. What sorts of questions might therapist Helper want to discuss with his director? It seems that he is losing many clients after only one or two counseling sessions. Everyone has a string of bad luck once in a while. If Helper's record does not improve and he continues to lose clients prematurely, he should seek some assistance in improving his manner of relating to clients. Perhaps he is too judgmental; perhaps new clients need more direction during the first sessions. Ideally, noting undesirable characteristics early in a therapist's career should permit improvements in the therapist's techniques before poor practices are deeply ingrained. Also, it is to a therapist's advantage to learn of problems before hearsay and rumor define his or her therapy as below average in quality (House, 1976). Prue et al. (1980) described how feedback to staff improved the performance of workers at a state hospital. Feedback on treatment activities was a cost-effective method of improving service to the patients.

A Threatening Use of Process Evaluation

Gathering the type of information requested in Figures 6.1 and 6.4 permits the presentation of information in a way that can be very controversial. No one enjoys being evaluated. Nevertheless, so long as the process evaluation is only on a facilitywide basis, staff members may "grin and bear it." If the information available about an individual care giver is released only to that person, the controversy may concern merely the time and expense of the

	HELPER	OTHER THERAPISTS
TOTAL CASE LOAD ON JUNE 1, 1984	64	433
ACTIVE CASES	49(76%)	364(84%)
INACTIVE CASES	15(24%)	69(16%)
(NOT SERVED IN 90 DAYS)		

THE NAMES OF YOUR INACTIVE CLIENTS ARE:

ARCHIBALD, L	NORRIS, M M
BEST, B	OVERMAN, S
BOULDER, M M	PAKOWSKI, M M
ERNEST, G	RASMUSSEN, P
GRAND, K	THOMAS, A
HANSEN, M M	TRAVERSE, P
MORRISON, S	WILSON, G
NARWELL, B	

PLEASE FILE A TERMINATION NOTICE OR A REFERRAL NOTICE, OR HAVE AN APPOINTMENT WITH EACH OF THESE INACTIVE CLIENTS BY JULY 31, 1984.

	HELPER	OTHER THERAPISTS
TERMINATED CASES IN MAY		
TERMINATED BY MUTUAL CONSENT	10(48%)	47(75%)
TERMINATED BY CLIENT DECISION	9(43%)	15(24%)
TERMINATED BY THERAPIST	2(10%)	1(1%)
NUMBER OF THERAPY SESSIONS WITH CLIENTS TERMINATED IN MAY 1984 (MEDIAN)	4.0	7.5

RATINGS OF THE FUNCTIONAL STATUS OF TERMINATED CLIENTS WERE:

LEVEL	CLIENTS AT EACH FUNCTIONAL LEVEL	
	HELPER	OTHER THERAPISTS
DYSFUNCTIONAL: 1	0(0%)	0(0%)
DYSFUNCTIONAL: 2	0(0%)	1(1%)
DYSFUNCTIONAL: 3	0(0%)	0(0%)
DYSFUNCTIONAL: 4	2(10%)	1(1%)
FUNCTIONAL: 5	1(5%)	1(1%)
FUNCTIONAL: 6	1(5%)	6(10%)
FUNCTIONAL: 7	2(10%)	2(3%)
FUNCTIONAL: 8	4(20%)	17(27%)
FUNCTIONAL: 9	11(52%)	35(56%)

FIGURE 6.8 A possible format for feedback to individual therapists.

information system. However, the information generated by the methods just described permits numerical comparisons to be made among individual therapists. Most staff members dislike having their work compared to that of others in this way. Although such evaluations will be resisted, a manager needs objective comparative information. If staff members offer quite different services, obviously such comparative reports are more difficult to prepare. For example, crisis counselors, outpatient therapists, and inpatient group leaders cannot easily be compared to one another. However, when many individuals perform much the same tasks, contrasts among individuals become possible.

In general, information on individual staff members should never be released in a general report. Individuals can be given their own data, which they can compare to summary data from the whole facility; however, only the director has a right to information on each individual staff member.

In Figure 6.9 the work of each therapist is summarized in one line. Contrasts among the therapists are invited. Those with very low or very high caseloads and those with many inactive clients can be easily noted. If there are particular therapists who lose a disproportionate number of clients early in the course of counseling (and thus often deliver only a minimal service to these clients), they can be readily identified. See, for example, the information on Helper.

Therapist Helper has the largest proportion of inactive clients and loses more than anyone else before three counseling sessions. However, Helper rates his clients as functioning higher than all other therapists except Nelson. There are at least two interpretations of these findings. One, Helper has been assigned clients who do not really need counseling. He correctly sees them as generally functioning well and does not provide unnecessary counseling. Two, Helper is not providing counseling that is seen as helpful by the clients. Although they drop out, Helper rates their functioning "good" as a way of justifying his high rate of client loss. The first interpretation is tenable if the pattern does not continue. However, if clients are assigned at random or to whomever has an opening and the pattern continues, the second interpretation appears more likely. Such a negative evaluation does not mean that Helper should be dismissed. It may mean that Helper should have some in-service training; perhaps his approach in setting the stage for counseling is not appropriate to the population utilizing this center. Such possibilities should be explored and may resolve the situation. If so, Helper will be a better counselor and his clients will be better served.

Even though initial objections to process evaluation as presented in Figure 6.9 are likely to be numerous and intense, there are important advantages to preparing such materials. We believe that accurate information is better than impressionistic information of unknown accuracy. What is to be gained by giving the program director the sort of information in Figure 6.9? The director's chief responsibility is to facilitate the delivery of quality human services—psychotherapy in this example. If a therapist is performing markedly less well than others, clients are being shortchanged when they are assigned to that therapist. It would be best if therapists took the initiative in approaching the director for help in improving their work. However, if the individual does not approach the director, the director's job requires approaching the individual. The reason for providing this information frequently—once a month or once a quarter—is to encourage improvement before a situation becomes intolerable.

Figure 6.9 should be supplemented with an accounting of time spent on various activities. For example, if therapists Rudov and Williams are devoting much time to community work, to administration, or to in-service training, their rather low caseloads are readily understandable. As an exercise,

THERAPIST	CURRENT CASES AS OF JUNE 1, 1984						TERMINATED CASES IN MAY 1984			
	ACTIVE CASES			INACTIVE CASES						
	N	% OF CENTER CASES	FUNC- TIONAL STATUS (MEAN)	N	% OF CENTER CASES	FUNC- TIONAL STATUS (MEAN)	N	FUNC- TIONAL STATUS % ABOVE 7	% SEEN LESS THAN 3 TIMES	MEDIAN NUMBER OF VISITS
ABRAMS	39	11	6.5	4	7	6.3	6	100	33	6
COULDER	29	8	7.2	0	0	DNA	9	89	22	7
GREGORY	43	12	6.8	9	15	5.9	4	75	25	8
HELPER	49	13	6.7	15	25	6.7	21	71	48	4
MATTHEWS	28	8	6.5	1	2	6.0	6	50	17	9
NELSON	29	8	7.0	6	10	7.2	5	80	0	6
NICOLET	36	10	6.6	8	13	6.2	8	75	12	6
PETROVICH	38	10	6.2	10	17	5.9	5	80	0	7
RUDOV	19	5	7.1	1	2	5.0	4	100	0	9
VINCENT	35	10	6.5	4	7	6.3	10	80	20	7
WILLIAMS	20	5	5.9	2	3	6.5	6	100	17	8
ALL	365	100	6.6	60	100	5.4	84	80	24	7

FIGURE 6.9 A report permitting the center director to spot problems and to suggest ways to improve services given.

127

readers might try to prepare a form for therapists to use in accounting for their time. Categories of activities would include individual therapy, group therapy, administration, education, and community service. How might such report forms be designed? How might Figure 6.9 be extended to include this new information?

As with any type of information, a report such as Figure 6.9 can be misused. Critics fear that providing summaries of information usually hidden in files allows such data to be used in a vindictive manner. Most evaluators believe that providing more information will reduce the opportunities for directors to behave autocratically. Most unfair managers restrict information, just as despotic rulers control the media in the nations they govern. Nevertheless, certain precautions can be built into the system to circumvent some possible misuses of the information. For example, the system can be designed to minimize the possibility of acceptable variations in personal style appearing as deficiencies. Some therapists may encourage clients to leave therapy sooner than other therapists do. They may do this because of personal and theoretical convictions, not because of inadequate therapeutic skills. An information system should be planned in a way that does not confuse therapy designed to be short term with rejected therapy. In Figure 6.9 we sought to avoid this confusion by separately reporting the number of clients terminating after one or two counseling sessions. Even therapists who plan on short-term therapy expect to retain clients beyond two sessions.

Implementing an Information System

In 1976 Chapman concluded that a computer-based information system is not cost-effective in agencies or programs with 10 or fewer care givers serving 1000 or fewer people in a year. However, the development of personal computers and the extraordinary drop in the cost of computer memory (Toong and Gupta, 1982) has made such rules of thumb obsolete. The type of reports illustrated in this chapter can easily be produced by desk-top computers such as those manufactured by Apple and IBM (among others) that use database programs. The software for developing the tables illustrated in Figures 6.7, 6.8, and 6.9 is available for less than $300. Using such programs does not require any programming experience. (A computer, of course, could also be used to handle other aspects of managing an agency, such as billing, filing, or accounting.) The system described in this chapter is relatively simple.

If done poorly, monitoring services can be expensive, disruptive, and unpleasant experiences for all involved. If done well, such evaluations of effort can provide feedback on performance that often enhances growth. Kreitner (1977) has called such feedback *informational feedback*. There are other forms of feedback, such as *corrective feedback*, that are also useful in helping people to improve their performance. Although automated systems such as those described in this chapter provide very valuable sources of feedback, managers should not permit these and similar systems to be the only source of feedback given to staff members.

AVOIDING MAJOR PROBLEMS IN IMPLEMENTING
AN INFORMATION SYSTEM

Problems in implementing an information system may arise because people are naturally hesitant to try something new and suspect the motives of anyone gathering information that is feared to affect employment. In addition, the evaluator may fall into some traps that will make the task all the harder.

Avoid the Duplication of Records

Human service staffs will not happily cooperate with an information system that duplicates information already reported and stored elsewhere (Stull, 1977). Few agencies exist without any records. When introducing an information system, it would be undesirable simply to impose the system as an addition to the existing recording procedures. Instead, integrating the information required by the old system with the automation of the new system would be preferable.

It is likely that staff members may question the accuracy of an automated system. The fact that staff cannot describe the population they serve in quantitative terms may mean that they will at times be surprised at the content of the summaries of information gathered. Kivens and Bolin (1977) report that such surprises led some service providers to keep their own records for a time as a check on a new information system. If staff want to duplicate records for their own satisfaction, that is no problem. However, the evaluator should avoid requesting program staff to provide information for overlapping record systems.

Avoid Narrow-Minded Technology

Once a computerized system is considered, there is a temptation to concentrate on the technology of the system and to overlook the needs of the users. Lucas (1975) writes that information systems fail when user needs take a back seat to the technology of an information system. To avoid this problem, the users must be involved in the design of the system. The information that is needed, the manner of summarizing it, the frequency of reports, and other issues should all be determined with the people who will use the information. The evaluator may be enthusiastic about getting the system operating. However, learning what will be useful requires patient work with the staff and administrators. Although a completed information system is not chiseled in granite, it is expensive to change if someone thinks of a new bit of information after the system is operational. Involving users early and thoroughly will minimize the possibility of producing an expensive product that no one really wants.

Avoid Serving the Needs of Only One Group

People filling different roles in an organization will have different informational needs because their responsibilities are different (Patton, 1986). Hawkins, et al. (1978) described the diverse informational needs of judges, probation officers, and program planners in drug programs. In other settings evaluators should know that the needs of the accounting department differ from those of the billing department, which in turn differ from the needs of service delivery staff. By working closely with only one or two such groups, the evaluator runs the risk of providing information useful only to some groups. When that happens, the information system will be seen as irrelevant by those whose needs remain unmet; these people will resist giving information. The quality of information supplied can only be eroded when the system is not respected and valued. There is no substitute for understanding the organizational roles of all potential users.

SUMMARY

Human service agencies can begin an evaluation with a systematic description of their programs, the amount of service given, and the identity of those receiving the services. Such a process evaluation permits an accounting of how the agency's funds were expended and a comparison between the program as designed and the program as implemented. This sort of evaluation can be invaluable for showing what aspect of a program needs additional effort or why a program never had the impact intended. Also, the need to complete accrediting agency and government surveys can be met more easily if process evaluations are planned before the requests for information are made.

The two general approaches to program monitoring were illustrated: a summary of effort over a given time period and a systematized information system to permit repeated summaries of effort on a monthly or quarterly basis. The former requires a manual search through existing files that are often not designed with evaluation procedures in mind. If problems are found, even this kind of evaluation can lead to plans for improvement. When records are designed to facilitate evaluations, ongoing or repeated evaluations of effort are possible.

STUDY QUESTIONS

1. How does program monitoring fit into the schematic diagram in Figure 1.1.?
2. Explain the relationships between program monitoring and formative and summative evaluations.
3. People sometimes object to an evaluation of effort on the grounds that it reveals nothing about the quality of the service rendered. This statement is true. Why does this criticism not negate the reasons for doing the types of evaluations described in this chapter?
4. Suppose you managed a telephone sales office. Twenty people make telephone calls to potential buyers of educational films. If these potential buyers are interested in previewing a film, it is mailed to them. They either pay for it or return

it in seven days. How would you develop a monitoring system to keep track of what your employees are doing? How would you measure their success? What type of indexes of success would be important?

5. What are some of the evaluative questions that can be answered using a management information system? What are some of the questions that an MIS cannot answer? How do these two sets of evaluative questions differ?

FURTHER READING

BANK, A., AND WILLIAMS, R. C., eds. 1987. *Information systems and school improvement: Inventing the future.* New York: Teachers College Press.

HAGEDORN, H. J., et al. 1976. *A working manual of simple evaluation techniques for community mental health centers.* DHEW Publication No. (ADM) 76-404. Rockville, Md.: U.S. Department of Health, Education, and Welfare.

HARGREAVES, W. A., ATTKISSON, C. C., AND SORENSON, J. D., eds. 1977. *Resource materials for community mental health program evaluation.* 2nd ed. DHEW Publication No. (ADM) 77-328. Rockville, Md.: U.S. Department of Health, Education, and Welfare. See Part III for materials on management information systems.

part III

EVALUATION OF OUTCOME

Descriptions and illustrations of outcome evaluations make up a large portion of this book. A major purpose of these presentations is to encourage an understanding of the variety of forms an outcome evaluation can take. The selection among these methods is determined by the decisions evaluators and program managers make about the primary purpose of the evaluation.

The methods described in the following three chapters are appropriate whenever groups of people seek to gain similar benefits from programs. For example, students at any level of education share goals with their classmates, and health prevention programs are offered to many people who, it is hoped, will avoid certain illnesses. Chapters 7, 8, and 9 have been organized so that the simplest form of outcome evaluation is presented first.

A simple examination of the state of program participants after receiving a service will tell program managers and sponsors whether the participants leave a program with acceptable levels of achievement or health. If there are objective program goals that are widely accepted as valid, the simple evaluation designs described in Chapter 7 may be quite satisfactory.

When simple evaluation designs will not suffice, additional information must be gathered to improve the interpretability of the evaluation. Chapter 8 includes three approaches to improving the clarity of interpretations: observing the program participants more than twice; observing additional groups; and measuring additional dependent variables. Of course, these approaches can be combined to produce even better evaluation designs.

When the purpose of an evaluation is to ascertain beyond any doubt whether a program did or did not cause an observed change in the program participants, the methods of Chapter 7 will not be adequate. If the evaluation is carefully planned, the methods of Chapter 8 will often be quite satisfactory. All doubts about causality, however, are most easily eliminated if a true experiment is used to assess the outcome of a program. The advantages of true experiments and the precautions to follow to guarantee that an evaluation designed as an experiment remains an experiment when implemented are the topics of Chapter 9.

7

Nonexperimental
Approaches to Outcome
Evaluation

A neighborhood crime prevention program, a new way of admitting patients to a hospital, and a class for diabetic senior citizens are programs that have goals applying equally to all people using the program. Such programs are evaluated using information describing the average performance of a group of program participants. This section of the text focuses on the analysis of data gathered from groups for the purpose of evaluating the outcome of human service programs. The chapters begin with the simplest approaches and progress to the more complex and more scientifically rigorous. Each approach, regardless of its scientific rigor, has its place in program evaluation. However, the usefulness of a particular approach depends on the questions the evaluator seeks to answer. These chapters describe evaluative procedures that are more similar to standard educational and social science research procedures than the previous chapter or those in Part IV.

As indicated in the chapter titles, when evaluators are commissioned to learn if a program caused an outcome, they choose a more rigorous research design than when commissioned to document that clients leave a program at a certain level of competency or health. As these chapters progress, the questions each approach can address—as well as the misuses of each approach—will be described and illustrated. The reader should develop a sense of the purpose of careful experimental design and see how each level of control is introduced to increase the clarity of the interpretation of the data.

SINGLE-GROUP DESIGNS

One Set of Observations

When teachers, nurses, administrators, or judges inquire into the success of some social service program, they frequently use the simplest form of outcome evaluation. Basically, they want to know how the program participants are faring after the service has been provided. Do the members of a job-training group have jobs three months after receiving job skills training? What percentage of smoking clinic participants are in fact not smoking one month after the program? The first step in deciding if a program is useful is to learn if the participants finish the program with a level of achievement that matches the program's implicit or explicit goals. This simple form of evaluation requires that a set of systematic observations be made of one group at some specified time after completion of the program. This simple posttest-only assessment of outcome will show the staff and the evaluators whether the participants finish the program at a low, medium, or high level of achievement. For example, the rearrest rate for released first-time felons may be 5 percent, 15 percent, 30 percent, or 75 percent. If the program is to help ex-convicts avoid further trouble with the law, but nearly all fail to do so, then there may be no need to evaluate any further. Program improvements should precede any further outcome evaluation. On the other hand, if program graduates do have a low rate of recidivism, the staff *may* have an effective program, which should be studied more thoroughly. With this one-observation group design, evaluators would not know whether the program participants *improved* during the program. To learn whether people improved requires a more complex design.

One Group—Two Sets of Observations

The pretest-posttest design is used when the evaluators want to ascertain that the participants improved while being served by a program designed to help them. The program might have caused such an improvement; however, the pretest-posttest approach to data collection is not sufficient to permit such a conclusion. Case Studies 1 and 5 are both pretest-posttest designs.

The reasons why causal interpretations may not be permitted have been labeled "threats to internal validity" in the classic work by Campbell and Stanley (1963). *Internal validity* refers to being able to conclude that an independent variable (i.e., the program) caused a change in a dependent variable (i.e., the hoped-for outcome of the program). For example, showing that people who complete a reading program do indeed read well or, for that matter, better than they did a month before does not mean that the program itself led to the improvement. This caution is especially serious when only a small portion of those who began the program actually complete it. A plausible alternative interpretation is that the most motivated people learned, but the program is unsuccessful for most people. In order to evaluate the adequacy of various approaches to outcome evaluation, a detailed understanding of the threats to

NAME AND SYMBOLIZATION OF THE EVALUATION DESIGN[a]	QUESTIONS THAT CAN BE ANSWERED
Posttest only X O	How well are the participants functioning at the end of the program? Are minimum standards of outcome being achieved?
Pretest-posttest O X O	Both of the above questions. How much do participants change during their participation in the program?

[a]Throughout this text, the notation adopted by Campbell and Stanley (1963) will be used. The program is symbolized as X and an observation by O.

FIGURE 7.1 Single-group evaluation designs and the questions they can answer.

internal validity is critical. As the reader will see, the posttest-only and the pretest-posttest approaches are very deficient in terms of internal validity. As more complex designs are presented, various plausible alternative interpretations will be eliminated until finally the only plausible cause of change is the human service program itself.

The questions that can be answered by simple, nonexperimental approaches to outcome evaluations are summarized in Figure 7.1. This figure and others in the following chapters reflect the idea that the evaluation design should be based on the questions to be answered and on the resources involved with the program—not on *a priori* assumptions adopted from basic research practices (Cronbach, 1982). When programs are relatively inexpensive, not harmful to participants, and fairly standard, absolutely airtight evaluations are not needed (Smith, 1981). The bulk of this chapter is devoted to the appropriate uses of the pretest-posttest design and the reasons why care must be exercised when interpreting the results of pretest-posttest evaluations.

USES OF THE PRETEST-POSTTEST DESIGN

Did the Program Participants Change?

Statistical tests distinguish between random variation and systematic variation. In other words, statistical methods permit us to decide whether the observed improvement between pretest and posttest is large enough to indicate that some real change occurred in the participants, or whether the change is so small that it cannot be distinguished from such chance influences as the participants' health, mood, care in completing the forms, transient level of motivation, or liking for the interviewer. If unexplained chance variation is so large that one cannot be certain that participants did change, for whatever reason, there is no point in examining the data any further to learn whether the program could have affected the participants (Winch and Campbell, 1969). When statistical tests are discussed, the concern is not about internal validity, but merely about the reliability of the differences between two numbers, such as a pretest and a posttest mean. This is called a question of *conclusion validity* (Cook and Campbell, 1979).

Nonsignificant statistical results are not to be confused with having found that two means are equal. The lack of statistical significance can be due to many factors that reduce the sensitivity of statistical analyses; for example, small samples and unreliable measures of outcome. At times, low power to detect differences has been interpreted as meaning that the program had no effect. Freiman et al. (1978) showed that some clinical trials of experimental medications were not sufficiently sensitive for the researchers to be confident that even a 25 percent improvement would be detected. The studies examined used groups that were too small to permit the detection of clinically useful improvements. Nevertheless, the nonsignificant results were taken to mean that the studies showed that the medications studied were ineffective, an unwarranted conclusion. Since most evaluators in human service settings expect less than a 25 percent improvement in outcome variables, evaluators cautiously consider the possibility of Type II errors before concluding that participants were not affected by the program.

Did the Participants Change Enough?

If the change from pretest to posttest is statistically significant, evaluators face another issue: did participants change *enough* to demonstrate a real effect in their daily lives? Singh, Greer, and Hammond (1977) found that the outcome of a classroom program on civic responsibility was an increase of 3 points on a 92-point attitude test. The authors conclude that the amount of change, although statistically significant, was not large enough to have a practical impact on the children's behavior.

If evaluators want program evaluation findings to have an impact on decisions, they will be sensitive to the issue of meaningful change, not just statistically significant change. Many texts on statistics do not devote much attention to the question of actual size of the differences between two values. Consequently, many students feel their job is complete after they have performed a statistical test and found a statistically significant difference. Applied social scientists, however, cannot stop at the point of reporting a reliable finding. The sponsors of human services want to know if the participants are in any *practical* way better for having participated in the program. It is true that these questions are easier to raise than to answer. However, these are important questions, and they will be answered by someone—perhaps by a newspaper reporter. It's better if the evaluator and stakeholders themselves deal with the issue of the importance of the degree of the change.

For in-house evaluators performing a simple evaluation, the best approach to use in addressing the question of importance of the findings is consultation with the program's stakeholders after measures have been chosen but before data are collected. For example, would a job-training program be a success if only 10 percent of trainees found employment after three months? Would 25 percent be sufficient? Seventy-five percent? Would a mental health program be satisfied if depressed clients improved five percentile points relative to normative values? Or would a 15-point improvement be required to demonstrate that the improvement was satisfactory? In addition to the program staff, there are other groups who have an interest in the achievement of a program—for example, community groups, funding agencies, and program participants. The minimum amount of change necessary to define the outcome of a program as a success cannot be fully specified without considering the costs necessary to achieve that outcome. The relationship between the outcome and the costs of a program can be analyzed using the simple forms of cost-benefit and cost-effectiveness analyses discussed in Chapter 10.

Relating Change to Services and Participant Characteristics

The discussion of the pretest-posttest design to this point has concentrated on methods to use in documenting the possible improvement of program participants. Another approach to evaluation is to relate the amount of service received with the degree of improvement observed. Although such research may be open to the criticism that the results can be interpreted in various ways, it can be very useful in certain situations. For example, a very important study in the history of medical research followed the strategy of relating the patient's condition to the amount of treatment received. In 1835 Pierre Louis (Eisenberg, 1977) reported his study comparing the amount of blood drawn from patients with their progress in recovering from "inflammation" (pneumonia). Early nineteenth-century medical theory led to the expectation that the more blood drawn, the better the treatment and the more likely a recovery. Louis measured the volume of blood drawn from the patients. He then compared these values to the course of their illnesses. He found that a patient's prognosis was not related to volume of blood taken. This finding was an important influence on the medical practice of that time and contributed to the eventual discrediting of bloodletting as a form of medical treatment. Louis was unable to conclude anything about the cause or the proper treatment of pneumonia, but he did identify a useless treatment.

Another reason to do an evaluation even if it is unable to identify the cause of change is to search for characteristics of the participants that might be related to achieving program goals. Do men experience better outcomes than women? Do members of minority groups complete the program as frequently as majority-group clients? Is age related to outcome? These questions can be explored, tentatively to be sure, using a simple research design. If policy-relevant relationships are found between outcome and a characteristic of participants, that variable would be involved in any future studies. The findings may even have immediate impact if a program appears to have a good effect on some segments of the target population but little effect on other segments.

Although it is quite easy to discuss the idea that personal and service characteristics may be related to success in a program, the statistical method of relating improvement to other variables is often misunderstood. The most intuitive approach is to subtract pretest scores from posttest scores, label the difference "improvement," and correlate the improvement scores with age, number of units of service received, and any other variables of interest. This "obvious" method is not desirable. To understand this point fully requires more advanced statistical sophistication than readers of this book are assumed to have. The basic concept involved concerns the reason why improvement is more likely for some participants than for others. On the average, people who initially score low on a measure are more likely to improve than people who initially get high scores. Students know that it is generally harder to improve on a B+ than a C−. This observation is related to the concept of regression to the mean, which will be discussed shortly.

Nunnally (1975) comments that one should avoid using change scores because they are based on shaky statistical assumptions. Further, the complex methods suggested to deal with change scores are hard to explain to others and are controversial, even among experts. Nunnally makes one exception to this warning: when the evaluator is interested in relating change to some characteristic of the program participants, change scores may be used. For example, since the length of some human services, such as psychotherapy, is not standardized as is (for example) a school year, an evaluator might want to relate improvement to the amount of service received.

The best way to relate improvement or change to the amount of service received or to some characteristic of the program participant when information is available only from the group receiving the program is to use residualized change scores. Judd and Kenny (1981) call this approach *regression adjustment*. This approach is illustrated here because introductory texts do not cover the method. To calculate a residualized change score, it is necessary first to calculate a regression equation that uses the pretest to predict the posttest. Even though program participants improved on a variable, it is likely that those who were better off on the pretest will, on the average, be better off on the posttest. Thus, we usually expect a positive correlation between a pretest and posttest. Figure 7.2 includes hypothetical data which will be used to illustrate the calculation of residualized change scores. Imagine a job-training program consisting of 20 training sessions. The correlation between the pretest and the posttest given in this figure is 0.47. The goal of the evaluator is to correlate job skills improvement with amount of training received.

To do this analysis, the pretest is treated as the predictor, or independent variable (usually denoted as X in regression formulas), and the posttest is treated as the criterion, or dependent variable (usually denoted as Y in

PROGRAM PARTICIPANT	SKILL LEVEL			RESIDUAL AFTER	TRAINING SESSIONS	RESIDUAL SESSIONS
	BEFORE	AFTER	CHANGE			
1	24	26	2	−0.54	16	−2.26
2	23	29	6	3.12	18	−0.13
3	19	26	7	2.73	20	2.40
4	18	27	9	4.39	19	1.53
5	20	19	−1	4.92	16	−1.73
6	24	31	7	4.46	20	1.74
7	25	22	−3	−5.19	15	−3.39
8	24	25	1	−1.54	19	0.74
9	21	22	1	−2.58	19	1.14
10	14	16	2	−4.01	14	−2.94
11	14	26	12	5.99	20	3.06
12	21	30	9	5.42	19	1.14
13	18	22	4	−0.61	19	1.53
14	16	15	−1	−6.31	13	−4.20
15	23	26	3	0.12	19	0.87
16	14	13	−1	−7.01	17	0.06
17	23	26	3	0.12	19	0.87
18	19	29	10	5.73	20	2.40
19	17	28	11	6.04	19	1.67
20	16	27	11	5.69	18	0.80
21	14	15	1	−5.01	14	−2.94
22	22	21	−1	−4.23	19	1.00
23	25	26	1	−1.19	19	0.61
24	23	19	−4	−6.88	15	−3.13
25	21	27	6	2.42	17	−0.86
26	22	29	7	3.77	18	0.00

FIGURE 7.2 Hypothetical data illustrating how change can be correlated with amount of service, adjusting for differences among program participants at the start of a program.

regression formulas). The regression equation calculated to relate the two tests is

$$\text{Posttest}_i' = 10.86 + 0.65 \text{ Pretest}_i$$

The posttest score that is expected for each participant is calculated using the regression equation. For example, the value of the first person's pretest, 24, would lead one to expect a posttest score of 26.54. The difference between the actual posttest and the calculated posttest is the residualized change, −0.54. That is, on the basis of the relationship between the pretest and the posttest, person A showed a change 0.54 units lower than was expected.

To correlate residualized change with amount of service received, it is also necessary to use the pretest as a predictor of number of training sessions attended; that is, the service unit variable must also be adjusted for the individual differences in pretest score. In this phase of the analysis, the measure of service is treated as the dependent variable (the Y). Amounts of service received as predicted by the pretest is given by the equation

$$Service_i = 15.08 + .13\ Pretest_i$$

Expected service is calculated for each person. Then the difference between actual service and expected service is found. The residual of number of sessions has been adjusted to reflect the fact that there was a nonzero correlation between the pretest and the number of training sessions attended. (If the correlation between the pretest and the number of sessions had been zero, this step would have had no effect on the analysis.)

Finally, a correlation is found between residualized change and the residuals of units of service. The correlation between the two columns of residuals is 0.65. This indicates that more improvement was shown by those program participants who received more units of service, even when adjusted for differences in pretest scores. The same strategy can be used to correlate personality, education, or demographic information with improvements by substituting the variable of interest in place of the number of training sessions in this illustration.

This is an internal analysis for the purpose of learning something about differential improvement levels. In this hypothetical program we know that improvement occurred and that, on the average, the more sessions attended, the more improvement. However, the causes of improvement cannot be discerned on the basis of this analysis. The reasons for caution in interpreting the causes of improvement are described in the balance of this chapter.

THREATS TO INTERNAL VALIDITY

When a statistically significant improvement has been found that is large enough to be nontrivial, evaluators need to eliminate explanations of the change that are not due to the program. For example, sixth-grade children will do better on a task requiring precise eye-hand coordination than they did as second graders. Is this a result of primary school (the "program") or the result of maturation? Maturation is an alternative explanation that cannot be eliminated in this situation, and one that forbids attributing the cause of the change solely to the effect of grade school education. Such alternative explanations of research results are labeled "threats to internal validity" by Campbell and Stanley (1963). As mentioned above, the reasons why participants achieve or fail to achieve a certain level of outcome cannot be unambiguously attributed to the program when either a posttest-only or a pretest-posttest approach is used. However, it is important to know why these single-group approaches fail internal validity considerations. As this and the next two chapters progress, different methods will be described to eliminate plausible nonprogram explanations of change. Only when the nonprogram explanations are eliminated, can change be attributed to the program.

Actual but Nonprogram-Related Changes
in the Participants

Two threats to internal validity refer to *real* changes that occur in program participants due to influences not related to the program. *Maturation* refers to natural changes in people that can be expected solely due to the passage of time. The most obvious example is a child growing older. *History* refers to events happening in the community, society, or even the entire world that will change the behavior of the participants of a program. Events such as an election, a recession, or a war may all influence the measures of program success.

Maturation. Children can perform more complex tasks simply because they get older; people get more tired the longer they have gone without sleep; and there are predictable general patterns to the developmental processes of adults and elderly people. If an evaluation utilizes variables that can be expected to change merely with the passage of time, maturation could be a plausible explanation for the changes that occur between the time of the pretest and the time of the posttest. In other words, the evaluator may well have found that real change occurred during the course of a program; however, the reason for the change is that the program lasted x number of months and thus the participants are x months older and x months more experienced—not that the participants gained anything from the program.

The existence of maturation-based changes does not mean that maturation is the *only* explanation of the changes observed. Nor do plausible, alternative hypotheses mean that the program had no effect. Interpretations would be easier if the evaluator could learn how much of the change was due to maturation and how much was due to the program. Using the pretest-posttest design, this separation cannot be made. Methods to estimate the change due to maturation involve testing other groups of participants or potential participants as well as testing over a greater number of time periods as explained in the following chapter.

History. History refers to any specific event that occurs between the pretest and the posttest that affects the people in the program. For example, a recession may make even the most well-designed program to help people find jobs look like a dud. On the other hand, an economic recovery would make a similar but poorly run program look like a winner. These concurrent national economic changes are plausible alternative interpretations of any changes found among the participants of employment programs. All nonprogram events or series of events that affect the participants would provide plausible alternative explanations.

Some of the same approaches used to account for maturational effects can help isolate historical effects: test additional groups and test at additional times. However, maturation is more predictable and stable than is history. Unexpected events can occur at any time or may not occur at all during a given evaluation. Evaluators should be sensitive to societal or organizational changes that may affect an evaluation. In addition, Cook and Campbell (1979) discuss the influence of events occurring in a particular group under the term *local history*. Events such as staff being involved in personal feuds, the presence of a particularly influential individual in a program group, or a local community disaster cannot be accounted for by any evaluation research design unless the evaluation is replicated a number of times in different settings.

Who Was Observed

Three threats to internal validity must be considered when the participants in a program are not a random or representative sample of the people who might benefit. These three threats are called *selection, mortality,* and *regression*.

Selection. Participation in a human service program is voluntary. Even when prisoners or parolees are forced to participate, the level of meaningful participation is voluntary. Thus, the people obtaining a service are different from the typical member of the target population. In the posttest-only form of evaluation, the process of self-selection may mean that the participants were already relatively well off when they began the program. The fact that the posttest detects a desirable state tells the staff nothing about the effectiveness of the program because the staff's implicit standard of comparison may well be the typical member of the population for which the service was designed, not the typical person who selects him- or herself into the program. It is true that sometimes an evaluation of a program is based only on the end result for the people completing the program. Clearly, these individuals chose to complete the program and do not represent the effect of the program on all for whom the program was designed.

The pretest-posttest approach to evaluation is much stronger in controlling the unwanted effects of self-selection. By measuring the participants before the program, the possible change can be documented. Centra (1977) has reported that the college teachers most likely to be involved in faculty development programs are "good teachers who want to be better." After a faculty development program, most of these teachers, the program participants, will be quite good teachers. Their competence will tell us nothing about the quality of the program—these teachers were better than the typical teacher to start with. However, observations of their achievements before the program will permit an estimation of the amount of improvement.

Mortality. The posttest-only design is also inadequate when participant dropout (or attrition) is a problem. People differ in whether they will begin a program (selection), and they differ in whether they will complete a program (dropout). Campbell and Stanley (1963) use the term *mortality* to refer to dropping out of a program for whatever reason. Students drop courses they do not like or find too challenging; people in therapy quit when they learn that personal growth is hard; and in medical settings some patients in programs do actually die. The longer it takes to carry out an evaluation, the more attrition is likely to take place (Keating and Hirst, 1986).

The level of achievement observed at the end of a program may indicate how well the program functioned, how good the people were when they started, or how motivated the people were who stayed until the end. As a general rule, those who stay are more prepared for the program than are those who drop out. Failing students were more likely to drop a course than are those earning B's and A's. Patients who die were probably the least likely to benefit from a health care program. Without a pretest the evaluator will not know how much dropping out there was nor what sort of individuals dropped out. A director of a small drug-user program informally mentioned that his program had a 90 percent success rate. Upon inquiry, however, it was learned that only 10 percent of those who start the program are there at the end. Having success with 9 out of the 100 people who begin the program is markedly different from having a 90 percent success rate.

As with selection, the pretest-posttest design handles participant attrition fairly well. By pretesting, the evaluators know who has dropped out and how they compared to those who remained. The pretest-posttest design enables evaluators to know when preprogram achievement and participant dropout are not plausible explanations for the level of outcome observed at the end of the program.

Regression. The threat to internal validity labeled *regression to the mean* is one of the hardest threats to understand. This is true probably because some statistical thinking is required to understand this threat. However, as with most basic statistics, many people already understand regression to the mean at the conceptual level, even though they may not apply it consistently.

Kahneman and Tversky (1974) report that airplane pilot trainers have a practice that illustrates how people can be misled by the effects of regression. If you think carefully about the example, you will see what regression means and why its effects are often undetected. It is said that after a particularly good landing, the trainers do not compliment the trainee, because when such a compliment is given, the next landing is usually done less well. On the other hand, after a poor landing the trainers severely reprimand the trainee in order to elicit a better landing on the next try. It is clear that the empirical observations are true—complimented exceptionally good landings are often followed by less good ones, and reprimanded bad landings are often followed by better ones. However, let us see why the compliments and the reprimands have nothing to do with the quality of the following landing.

Imagine learning a complex task. Initially, performance level fluctuates—sometimes better, sometimes worse. What goes into the better performances? At least two things: the degree of skill achieved, and luck or chance. Flight trainees know they should touch the plane down with the nose up, but they do not yet sense the precise moment to lower the wing flaps and at the same time adjust the elevators to achieve the proper touch-down angle (Caidin, 1960). Sometimes they do it too soon and sometimes too late. Because these errors are largely due to chance, the likelihood of doing everything correctly at the precise second for two consecutive landings is low. Similarly, the likelihood of badly estimating the precise instant two times in a row is also low. Therefore, the likelihood of two consecutive good landings is low for pilot trainees. In other words, an observer (or a trainer) should *not* expect two consecutive good landings by a novice trainee, regardless of what is said or not said by the trainer.

The essentials of the effects of regression to the mean can be further illustrated with a rather silly but instructive example. Choose 20 pennies and flip each 6 times, recording the number of heads flipped for each penny. Select the penny that produced the most "excessive" heads (five or six heads can be considered excessive). Reprimand the penny for producing too many heads. Then flip that penny six more times to see if the reprimand had the desired effect. If the penny yields fewer heads than it did during the first set of six flips, the penny is behaving in the way it was urged to behave. On the average, the reprimand will appear to have been effective 98 percent of the time if the penny originally produced six out of six heads, and 89 percent of the time if the first result had been five out of six heads. The binomial distribution permits the calculation of these percentages (Hays, 1981).

In summary, regression to the mean warns that whenever a performance level is extreme, the next performance is likely to be less extreme. This principle applies to emotional adjustment as well as to learning to fly airplanes and flipping pennies. If the people who currently are the most depressed are included in a therapy group, it is very likely that in three months they will be as a group less depressed. This does not mean they will be at a healthy level of adjustment. Most likely, they will still be more depressed than the general population. However, some of the transient random events that caused the worst depression will have passed, and as a group the most depressed people will be less depressed than they were before.

Is regression a threat to the internal validity of the pretest-posttest evaluation design? Not necessarily, but it often is. If individuals who are representative of some intact group are tested before and after a program, then regression is not a problem for evaluations following this evaluation design. For example, if all children in a school are given a special reading curriculum, regression will not be a threat to internal validity. However, if only the children reading at the lowest levels on the pretest are included, regression will be a threat to the correct interpretation of the pretest-posttest change. The reasons why children are low in a single test include poor reading skills; but the reasons also include such chance things as poor guessing, breaking a pencil point, having a cold, misunderstanding directions, worrying about a sick sister, or planning recess games. A day, a week, or a semester later on a second test, these events will not be experienced by exactly the same individuals. Generally, these retest scores will be higher than those on the first test for the children who previously had scored the worst. Also, these retest scores will be lower for those who previously scored the best.

Regression is often a plausible alternative hypothesis for pretest-posttest change when human service programs are aimed at those people who are in need of help. Remedial programs are not prepared for everyone, but rather for those who have fallen behind: reading very poorly, earning a low income, feeling emotional distress, and so forth. Sometimes a screening test to select people for the program is also used as the pretest in an evaluation plan. For example, students reading the most poorly on a test are placed in a reading improvement program, and a second administration of the same test or of a parallel form is compared to the preprogram test scores. This is a poor practice; regression is a very plausible alternate explanation for at least part of the improvement. Improvement in such an evaluation cannot be interpreted. On the other hand, if poor readers or troubled clients get worse (that is, go down-hill when regression effects were likely to improve their level), then the evaluation can be interpreted. The correct interpretation is that the program has failed.

Methods of Obtaining Observations

There are two additional plausible hypotheses discussed by Campbell and Stanley (1963): *testing* and *instrumentation* effects. At times these can make the interpretations of outcome evaluations ambiguous. These threats to interpretation are generated by the evaluators themselves and by their observation methods.

Testing.   The effect of testing refers to changes in behavior due to the observation techniques. First, two administrations of a test or survey may differ simply as a function of the respondent's increased familiarity with the tool at the second administration. Ability scores increase reliably on the second administration for people unfamiliar with the test (Anastasi, 1982). People interviewing for jobs gain from the experience and can present themselves better on subsequent interviews.

A second aspect of the effects of testing is called *reactivity.* People behave differently when they know they are being observed, as compared to when there is no observer or when people are not aware of an observer. This concept was discussed in Chapter 3; however, it is worth recalling. Clients, patients, prisoners, schoolchildren, and so on will be affected when they know someone is recording their behavior, opinions, or feelings. Observation techniques vary in how reactive they are.

The pretest-posttest design is clearly weak in the control of testing effects. If program participants were unfamiliar with the observation procedures, scores might change on the second test. The direction of change that should be expected due to repeated testing does not seem clear except for ability and achievement tests, on which improvement is usually expected.

Instrumentation.   The last threat to internal validity to be discussed refers to the use of measurement procedures themselves. Most college instructors know they are not totally consistent when grading essay examinations. There is a real potential for standards to change as the instructor becomes familiar with written examinations. The standards may become higher or lower.[1] If a pretest-posttest design uses measures that are not thoroughly objective, it would be wise not to score the pretest until after the posttest is administered. Then shuffle the tests together and have them scored by someone who does not know which are pretests and which are posttests.

If the measures require observations that must be made before and after the program, the examiners may become more and more skilled as they gain experience. Thus, the posttests may go much more smoothly than the pretests. If so, a change in instrumentation becomes a viable alternative to concluding that the program had an effect. In such situations the examiner will be most effective if highly experienced before the pretest is administered.

Interactions of These Threats

Over and above the influences of these seven threats to internal validity, it is possible for our interpretations to be confused by the joint influence of two of these threats. For example, the parents who seek out special educational opportunities for their children (self-selection) may have children who are developing more rapidly than those of parents who do not seek special help for their children (different rates of maturation). This situation would be called a *selection-by-maturation interaction*. More will be said about this threat when more complex evaluation designs are discussed in later chapters.

The threats to internal validity refer to reasons why an observed change may not be caused by the program or human service that the group obtained between the pretest and the posttest. Internal validity is thus the most basic concern of evaluators who are examining whether a program was responsible for an observed improvement.[2] As noted above, obtaining strong evidence of causal relationships is not the sole reason for conducting an evaluation. However, if evidence for causality is needed, and if there are plausible explanations based on the types of influences just described, the evaluator may well avoid conducting an evaluation using these basic designs.

Internal Validity Threats Are Double-Edged Swords

When examining a comparison between means it is important to consider whether a significant effect could have been caused by an uncontrolled threat to internal validity serving to raise the value of the posttest. Although atten-

---

[1]One way to minimize these changes is to read all answers before assigning any grades. Only then are grades assigned. When there are a number of questions, there is a way to minimize the effect of the instrumentation change. Grade all answers to the first question, shuffle the papers and grade all answers to the second question, and so on. Even if standards change, the likelihood of individual total test scores being systematically affected is very low.

[2]If there is no "improvement," there usually is nothing to explain, except in rare circumstances where a loss of function is expected without intervention. A program for arthritic patients is an example of a service in which the goal is to avoid deterioration. Such programs hope at best to maintain abilities, not to cure.

tion is usually focused on threats to internal validity masquerading as a program effect, it is also quite possible for a threat to internal validity to hide a program effect. Therefore, the appearance of no program effect, when the samples are large and the measures reliable, could be due to an ineffective program or an uncontrolled threat to internal validity serving to reduce the value of the posttest. Examples of these effects include: an economic downturn, program participants being tired at the posttest, successful participants being unavailable for the posttest, initially good-scoring participants regressing to the mean, and more sensitive instruments detecting dysfunction that was missed by the less sensitive pretest.

CHANCE AND CREATIVITY IN SINGLE-GROUP DESIGNS

Threats to internal validity explain why some data collection procedures forbid interpretations of a causal connection between the program and the observed condition of those who received the program. The ways the data are analyzed can also create misinterpretations. Taking advantage of chance and developing creative interpretations can make an evaluation appear insightful when it is not. Because evaluators want to conduct valid research, being aware of these misleading practices is important.

Students and professionals not experienced in research methodology often engage in a practice that fosters inaccurate conclusions. This is the practice of "fishing" for statistically significant relationships among a large number of outcome variables and variables describing the people (such as sex, age, ethnic background). Fishing is often done by repeatedly subdividing the sample of program participants and comparing the ad hoc groups on the outcome measures. For example, if participants are repeatedly divided, first by gender, then by age, then by ethnic background, and so forth, some of the comparisons of the means of these groups will reveal differences that may indeed be significant, but just by chance. Finding significant differences just by chance is a Type I error. If a large number of relationships are studied, some will appear to be strong, just as flipping a large number of coins six times each will reveal that certain coins appear to be biased toward heads or tails. The same coins, if retested by flipping them six more times each, will be found to be unbiased. Unfortunately, when performing evaluations, new observations cannot be obtained as easily as flipping coins several additional times.

The second reason erroneous, chance relationships are not discovered is that *once the data are examined,* the evaluator or the program staff can usually make sense out of the results. Once a graduate student presented a senior professor with findings that seemed markedly at variance with the professor's own research.[3] The professor quickly interpreted the results in a

---

[3]The first author of this book was the student, but the senior professor must remain anonymous.

way that coincided nicely with the professor's work. A week later the student discovered that the computer program was malfunctioning and the initial results were meaningless. This anecdote has a happy ending: when the results were correctly analyzed, they were as originally expected, quite compatible with previous work. The point to remember is that reasonably creative people can make sense out of nearly any finding *once the information is presented.* This ability, coupled with the practice of gathering many variables and "fishing" for results, can lead to random findings that appear to be well thought out.

A nearly foolproof manner of discovering which results are simply Type I errors is to repeat the research. In controlled laboratory social science research, replication is not that difficult. However, because program evaluation often disrupts the service setting, it is seldom replicated at the same site. Replications at a variety of sites in different localities is very desirable (Cook, Leviton, and Shadish, 1985). When only one evaluation is going to be done, a practical approach involves collecting only the information that can be used and having rational or theoretical reasons for the planned analyses. In addition, unexpected findings are best treated as very tentative, especially if they are embedded in a large number of analyses that are statistically nonsignificant. Finally, evaluators are very suspicious of surprising findings that require a number of assumptions or elaborate theorizing to understand. The professor mentioned above was only able to interpret the computer-generated nonsense by making elaborate and novel, although plausible, assumptions.

USEFULNESS OF SINGLE-GROUP DESIGNS

When there are specified standards for the outcome of a human service program, and when the participants do not drop out, the pretest-posttest design may be sufficient to document the program's success. However, even when standards are not available, the reader should not gain the impression that these approaches do not have any legitimate uses. These single-group designs are less intrusive and less expensive than more ambitious designs and require far less effort to complete than the methods described in later chapters. Thus, these designs can serve very important functions in the evaluator's toolbox as first steps in planning rigorous program evaluations. Single group evaluations serve at least three purposes: (1) to assess the likely usefulness of more rigorous evaluations: (2) to search for promising variables related to success in the program: and (3) to "soften up" the facility for more rigorous evaluation in the future.

Assessing the Usefulness of Further Evaluations

Before embarking on a rigorous plan that will control for many plausible alternative interpretations, a single-group design would serve to show whether there is any improvement to interpret. If no program participants have jobs for which they were trained, it is likely that no further research is needed to evaluate a job-training program. The program failed, period. No statistical analyses are necessary. If participants finished at a good level, the pretest-posttest design may show that the people improved during the program. This finding may well satisfy some users of program evaluation reports. Also, the finding of reliable improvements may justify a more complex evaluation. Lenihan (1977) used a simple design as a first step in learning whether the use of the phone helped pretrial defendants to raise bond. Showing that 22 percent of the defendants who used a phone that was available on an experimental basis did raise bail suggested that a more rigorous evaluation could be worth the expense. Had only 2 or 3 percent been able to raise bail, the possible effect of the phone would have been very small, and no further study would have been done.

Correlating Improvement with Other Variables

The use of the pretest-posttest design and change scores permits improvement to be related to the amount of service obtained and to characteristics of the program participants. It may be that a program offered to a very needy population primarily benefits people who are relatively well-off. Thus, the good achievement found by a posttest design could be due to the already-competent people who selected themselves for the program. If so, further work is unnecessary. On the other hand, the good level at the end of the program may really indicate a general improvement in most participants. Perhaps the improvement is due to the impact of the program. Further work would be merited.

Preparing the Facility for Further Evaluation

A third reason for conducting an evaluation using only the program participants as respondents is to help staff accept the idea of evaluation. As described in earlier chapters, human service providers—from paraprofessional counselors, to teachers, to physicians—are beginning to recognize that their work can and will be evaluated. This realization does not come easily, because the quality of human services is hard to quantify. However, if evaluators begin their work with less threatening approaches, they have better chances of leading service providers to see the usefulness of evaluation and to value the contribution of evaluators.

The methods described in this and the previous chapters are among the least threatening. There is no possibility that the research could show that unserved people do as well as people who got the service—a very frightening possibility to staff members. There are studies indicating that in some situations people who receive counseling are not much better off than similar people not counseled (see Ellsworth, 1975, p. 242). However, evaluators who suggest that counseling does not work are not going to find that the counseling staff readily welcomes their services. Less threatening—but still an unwelcome possibility—is the finding that an alternative service is just as beneficial to program participants. If the alternative service is less expensive, a comparison of people in the two groups could create anxiety for the staff of the more expensive program. This anxiety will be manifested in roadblocks to the study, hostility, and general uncooperativeness.

Just this type of response occurred during an in-house evaluation of a hospital program. The director of the program was very cooperative in initiating and implementing a study of the patients in his program. He displayed considerable openness to evaluation, saying such things as, "Maybe we don't help people as much as we think we do—we should know that"; and "If a patient is institutionalized after leaving here, we have failed." However, when the evaluators proposed increasing the rigor of the evaluation by gathering data from a neighboring hospital without a similar program, the director seemed to change his position. Such a comparison could conceivably have shown that similar patients regained as much ability as those in the director's more expensive program. He now said, "The additional data is unnecessary since the value of these programs is well known and fully documented." The expanded study went on anyway. His negative attitudes dissolved when it became clear that the neighboring hospital had surprisingly few patients with the necessary diagnosis and that those who were available were much less severely ill than those served in the program. Because the two groups of patients were not comparable, the study could not threaten the program. Cooperativeness and cordial relations returned.

Rational use of resources requires that ultimately such cooperative studies be done. But they should not be done in a way that leaves the staff demoralized or bitter. In-house evaluators who try to force methodologically rigorous evaluations on staff and who are unable to see the value of approaches with less-than-precise experimental control will find their work undervalued and their influence on the program diminished. Beginning in a nonthreatening way permits evaluators to gain the confidence of staff members. We do not intend to devalue the more rigorous approaches. The point stressed here is that less rigorous studies can also be useful.

SUMMARY

This chapter emphasizes two major points. First, a careful understanding of the needs of the users of an evaluation may indicate that a simple research design is able to serve quite well to answer these needs at a particular time. Evaluators perform unnecessary work when they insist on giving users more than they want or can use. The second major idea concerns the conceptual tools useful to understand why simple single-group evaluation designs cannot answer certain questions often important to administrators and to those responsible for financial support of the program. These conceptual tools have been called threats to internal validity and have become part of the vocabulary of social scientists in recent decades. Evaluators can use this conceptual scheme to select the research design most appropriate to answer the questions put to them by those needing services and programs evaluated.

STUDY QUESTIONS

1. Not many years ago, when a child had frequent bouts of sore throat and earache, family doctors recommended removing the child's tonsils. Typically, the child's health improved afterwards. If parents and doctors attributed the improved health to the effects of the operation, what threats to internal validity were ignored?

2. Some 50 elementary school children witnessed a brutal murder on the way to school in a suburb of a large city. The school officials worked with a social worker, a school psychologist, and others in an attempt to help the children deal with their emotions, to avoid long-term ill effects, and to help parents with their children. A year after the tragedy, there appeared to be no serious after effects. What assumptions are necessary to call this program a success?

3. Politicians are notorious for attributing any improvements in government affairs to their own efforts and any deteriorating affairs to the policies of others. Find or recall examples. What threats to internal validity most typically operate in government affairs?

4. Why can a smoking control clinic be evaluated using a one-group pretest-posttest study? It is also possible to gather useful follow-up data to evaluate the program. What index of success could be used to summarize effectiveness if participants could be observed only after the program?

5. Prepare some examples of pretest-posttest evaluations that would appear favorable because of threats to internal validity. Also, prepare some hypothetical examples of evaluations of programs that appear ineffective because of threats to internal validity.

FURTHER READING

CAMPBELL, D. T., AND STANLEY, J. C. 1963. *Experimental and quasi-experimental designs for research*. Chicago: Rand-McNally.

COOK, T. D., AND CAMPBELL, D. T. 1979. *Quasi-experimentation: Design and analysis for field settings*. Chicago: Rand-McNally.

JUDD, C. M., AND KENNY, D. A., 1981. *Estimating the effects of social interventions*. New York: Cambridge University Press.

McCALL, R. B. 1986. *Fundamental statistics for the behavioral sciences*. 4th ed. New York: Harcourt Brace Jovanovich.

NUNNALLY, J. C. 1975. The study of change in evaluation research: Principles concerning measurement, experimental design, and analysis. In *Handbook of evaluation research*, vol. 1, ed. E. L. Struening and M. Guttentag. Beverly Hills, Calif.: Sage.

8

Quasi-Experimental Approaches to Outcome Evaluation

The previous chapter demonstrated how very simple research designs can answer important questions for the evaluator and for users of evaluations. However, early in that chapter it was stressed that these designs can seldom help evaluators identify the cause of changes in program participants. Whenever program administrators and governmental agencies commission evaluators to discover the cause of such changes, evaluations of greater complexity must be designed. In order to show that something causes something else, it is necessary to demonstrate (1) that the cause precedes the supposed effect in time; (2) that the cause covaries with the effect; and (3) that no other alternative explanations of the effect exist except the assumed cause. It is easy to satisfy the first criterion, and the second criterion is not that difficult to test either. Both can be demonstrated using the methods described in Chapter 7. The third, however, is much more difficult and is the focus of this and the following chapters.

In this chapter various methods are presented that possess greater internal validity than the simple methods described in Chapter 7. The validity of outcome evaluations seeking to demonstrate causal relationships can be increased by (1) observing the participants at additional times before and after the program; (2) observing additional people who have not received the program; and (3) using a variety of variables, some expected to be influenced by the program and others not expected to be affected. These methods have been labeled quasi-experiments by Campbell and Stanley (1963); although these methods do not achieve the airtight control of true experiments, quasi-experiments control for many biases and can thus yield highly interpretable evaluations—if carefully planned.

DISTINGUISHING CHANGE
FROM RANDOM FLUCTUATIONS

Increasing the number of observations across time is one approach to reducing the chances that an observed change was due to a nonprogram source. All behaviors show random variation over time. The number of crimes on a given day or week is not a constant, nor is it a uniformly decreasing or increasing variable. Although there are some predictable influences on the number of crimes committed (for example, cold weather inhibits crime, warmer weather seems to encourage it, see Anderson, 1987), the causes of most changes in the day-to-day crime rate are unknown. Nevertheless, the popular media often act as though such causes were known and effective remedial action well understood.

In July 1975, a few days after several thousand police officers were laid off in New York City, there were two days in which an abnormally high number of murders occurred: nine murders occurred on July 8, eight on July 9. These two high-crime days were contrasted with the average for the year—four per day. Were newspapers correct in attributing the cause of these additional murders to the reductions in the size of the police force (see Egelhof, 1975)?

The first criterion necessary for a causal conclusion was met: the police were laid off before the murders. However, it is not known if murder covaries with size of police force, and alternative interpretations of the observed number of murders were not even considered. Without some information about the normal variation from day to day, it is hard to know whether eight or nine murders is unusual on a summer day. No information was provided about the weather. It may have been unusually hot. Did the murder rate stay that high after July 9? Without this additional information it is impossible to draw even the most tentative conclusions about the effect, if any, of the reduction in number of police officers on murder rate. Ignoring these threats to internal validity can lead to quite erroneous interpretations of the causal relations between two events. As was mentioned before and will be stressed again, it is even possible that an effective program will look ineffective if possible explanations of change are ignored.

A second and frequently cited example of the possibility of misunderstanding a phenomenon when given limited information occurred in Connecticut during the 1950s (Campbell, 1969). In 1955 there were approximately 14.2 automobile accident fatalities per 100,000 residents. This was a record rate and was especially high compared to the 1954 rate. The governor initiated a crackdown on speeding during 1956. The fatality rate in 1956 dropped to about 12.2 per 100,000. Could the governor justifiably claim that the measures he took were responsible for the reduction in fatalities? Readers might stop for a moment to develop an answer to that question.

The way to decide if the governor could take credit for the drop requires information about fatalities before the crackdown year as well as after the crucial year. The number of fatalities before the record in 1955 may show that fatalities per year were systematically rising in response to the number of autos per resident on Connecticut roads and the number of miles driven per auto. Because accidents increase when the number of cars increases, a steady increase in fatalities, while undesirable, may be unavoidable in this situation. A program to reduce fatalities would be up against strong forces and could be expected to yield few results.

A second alternative would be to consider 1955 to be a very unusual year. Perhaps a few very tragic but fortunately infrequent multifatality accidents occurred during the same year. Or perhaps especially bad weather occurred just before or just after holidays when many drivers were on the road. Because consecutive years with such unusual patterns are unlikely, a remedy for the high fatality rate is quite likely to appear to succeed, regardless of how well or poorly conceived. The drop would then be due to regression to the mean, not due to any remedy implemented.

The actual fatality rates for the years before and after the Connecticut speeding crackdown were reported by Campbell (1969) and are given in Figure 8.1. The reader can see that the 1955 rate does appear to be a discrepant value, even though the magnitude of fluctuations from year to year is large. This example will be discussed in more detail later in this chapter. The point of interest here is that looking at accident rates over a number of time periods permits a much better informed conclusion than merely examining the rates just before and just after the introduction of the treatment.

A third example of the usefulness of examining information over a number of time intervals is provided by Rheinstein (1959), who examined the effects of tightening divorce laws in Germany in 1900. The divorce rate dropped dramatically after the change, and even dropped slightly the following year. A complex analysis revealed that the law had an impact; however, examining the divorce rate over a longer period (1902 to 1914) revealed that within four years the rate was equal to that in 1899, and by 1914 the rate was nearly double that of 1899. Mazur-Hart and Berman (1977) examined divorce in the context of a relaxation of legal requirements. They found that the introduction of no-fault divorce laws in a midwestern state also had no impact on divorce rate.

Time-Series Designs

In recent years considerable attention has been given to the use of information across many time intervals. These approaches have come to be called *time-series analyses*. Influences fostering this interest have come from economics at a macro level and from behavior analysis at a micro level. Economists have used information over long time periods, seeking to learn the ef-

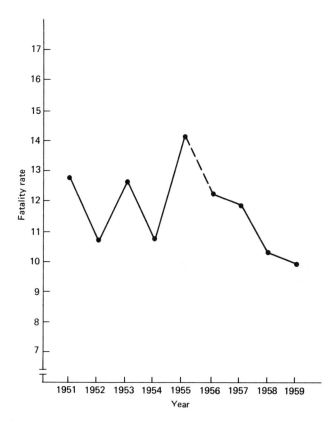

FIGURE 8.1 Automobile accident fatality rate for Connecticut by year, before and after the beginning of a crackdown on speeding drivers. (D. T. Campbell, Reforms as Experiments. *American Psychologist* 24 (1969): 419. Copyright 1969 by the American Psychological Association. Adapted by permission of the author.)

fects of policy changes on such variables as income level, industrial output, and employment. On a very different scale, behavior analysis research has utilized objective measurement of a single individual over many time periods, during which various interventions were begun and stopped. Once again, the unit of analysis—in this case a single person—is not appropriate for most evaluations; however, the importance the behavior analyst places on obtaining stable base-line measurements before an intervention and on documenting both change and the maintenance of change have become one of the concerns of program evaluators.

It is worth noting that the data of the economist and the behavior analyst are more similar to each other than might be supposed merely by considering the units of analysis used. Whether referring to a country or to a single child, the researcher obtains one value or makes one observation for each "subject" for each variable during each time interval studied. For example, for the economist there is only one unemployment level in the nation per time period, one GNP, and one inflation rate. For the behavior analyst there is only one index of a specific abnormal behavior per time period. Thus, writers can refer to "single subject" research in both cases.

Time-series designs as applied to program evaluation received strong encouragement from the work of Campbell and Stanley (1963), who gave them an important place among their quasi-experimental designs. Collecting data over many time periods is a way of satisfying some of the internal validity tests described in the previous chapter. Because maturation effects can be traced during the time periods before and after the intervention, the likelihood of confusing the program's effect with maturation effects is greatly reduced when using a time-series design rather than a pretest-posttest design. Similarly, the effects of history will be more easily detected using a time-series design than when an evaluation is performed using observations at only one or two time periods. By examining the reaction of the dependent variables to historical events, it is possible, at least at a qualitative level, to distinguish the effects of the program from the impact of major nonprogram influences.

A time-series approach to program evaluation minimally includes the following characteristics: (1) a single unit is defined, and (2) quantitative observations are made (3) over a number of time intervals (4) that precede and follow some controlled or natural intervention (Knapp, 1977). In the language of experimental design, the unit observed (person, group, or nation) serves as its own control.

Program evaluators, unlike economists, use time-series designs almost exclusively when a definite intervention has occurred at a specific time. The design is often called an *interrupted time series* (Caporaso, 1973); and the evaluator's job is to learn whether the interruption—that is, the human service intervention—had an impact. Figure 8.2 illustrates this design in symbols.

There are a number of possible outcomes observable in a graph of a program's outcome plotted over time intervals. Figure 8.3 illustrates some of

FIGURE 8.2 Simple quasi-experimental designs for program evaluation.

NAME AND SYMBOLIZATION	QUESTIONS THAT CAN BE ANSWERED USING THIS DESIGN FOR A PROGRAM EVALUATION
Interrupted time series O - O - ... O - X - O - ... - O - O	All the questions in Figure 7.1. Are there maturational trends that might explain an improvement? Do historical events cause the dependent variable to change?
Pretest-posttest with a nonequivalent control group O - X - O O - - O	All the questions in Figure 7.1. Is change more than the effect of history, maturation, testing, selection, or mortality?

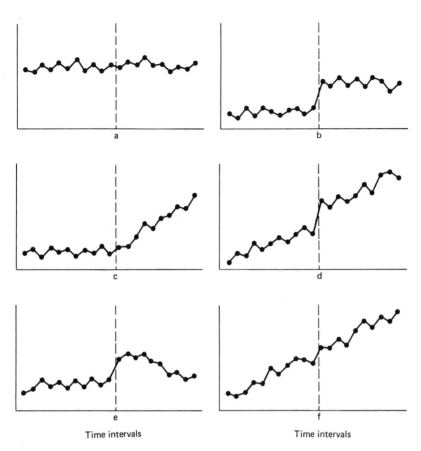

FIGURE 8.3 Some illustrative possible patterns of a criterion of program success plotted over time. Time of the program or intervention is indicated by the dashed vertical line.

these possibilities. Each part of the figure is plotted with time intervals along the abscissa, and magnitude of the outcome-dependent variable on the ordinate. Figure 8.3a illustrates no effect of the intervention: there appears to be no out-of-the-ordinary change in the observations after the program. In contrast, Figure 8.3b illustrates what is usually the most hoped for result of an interrupted time-series analysis. The graph shows a marked increase from a fairly stable level before the intervention, and the criterion remains fairly stable afterwards. One might expect this sort of result from an effective training program that increased the skills of employees or from the introduction of labor-saving devices. Clearly, the method can be used when the intervention is designed to lower variables as well as to raise them. Accident rates and failure rates are examples of variables one would like to see drop.

Figures 8.3c to 8.3f all show some sort of an increase after the intervention, but their interpretations are much less clear. Figure 8.3c shows an increase in slope after the intervention. The variable being measured began to increase over time after the intervention; however, there was no immediate impact as in 8.3b. An influence, such as television viewing or improved nutrition, whose impact is diffuse and cumulative might produce the result in Figure 8.3c. In 8.3d there is a localized increase apparently due to the intervention superimposed on a general increasing trend.

In Figure 8.3e there appears to be an effect due to the intervention; however, it seems to be temporary. Many new programs are introduced with much publicity, and the deeply involved staff members want the program to work. Perhaps extra staff effort is responsible for the immediate impact. However, once the program is part of the regular procedure and the extra effort is no longer extended, the outcome achieved returns to its former levels. Schnelle et al. (1978) showed that a helicopter patrol decreased crime in a high-crime area. However, the authors questioned whether the effect would hold up if the experiment was to be continued beyond the initial trial period. It is possible that although the *novelty* of the helicopter patrol served to frighten potential thieves and thus to lower crime for a short period, the airborne patrol's inherent effectiveness is not strong.

A possible pitfall for an evaluator could exist when a situation occurs such as that illustrated in Figure 8.3f. Here a steady increase over time is observed. A naive approach to the analysis would be to contrast the mean of the time periods before the intervention with the mean of the time periods after. This contrast may be statistically significant, but it does not help one understand the effect of the intervention.

Analysis of Time-Series Designs

Rigorous analysis of interrupted time-series design is beyond the scope of this book. The methods now accepted are described by McCleary and Hay (1980); however, advanced statistical sophistication is required to understand and use these methods. For readers of this book, some steps that fall short of the most correct and complete analysis may be taken that will help in interpreting time series data.

First, when the effects of the intervention are striking, statistical analyses may be unnecessary. Case Study 2, concerning the effectiveness of media, illustrates a situation in which the change in the dependent measure, the criterion of success, is so strong and so closely related to the intervention that one can conclude that the program had a positive effect. Similarly, McCarthy (1978) found a strong effect from a daily posting of the number of high bobbins in a textile plant. High bobbins lead to tangles and lost production time, but their incidence can be greatly reduced by additional employee care. The feedback and the workers' attempts to meet the posted goals resulted in a dramatically reduced rate of malfunction. A graph of the number of high bobbins showed a dramatic drop after feedback was initiated. Furthermore, when McCarthy temporarily removed the feedback procedure, the number of high bobbins began to climb. Reinstatement of the feedback brought the number back down again. It is hard to argue with the interpretation that the feedback caused the results.

There are other examples of time-series records that are not as easy to interpret. The literature on medical education shows that resident physicians on the average order more laboratory tests for hospital patients than do community physicians who have more experience (for example, Dixon and Laszlo, 1974). To learn whether this finding held for a specific community hospital, a plot of the number of laboratory tests per month was made beginning three years before a major expansion of the hospital's residency programs and one year after. Because neither the hospital's size nor its utilization rate changed systematically during the four-year period, the influence of these variables was ignored. The most striking observation was a steady increase in the average number of laboratory tests compared to the previous month. This increase of an average of an additional 500 tests per month was observed throughout the time period. However, the increase that occurred between the month before the program was expanded and the first month of the expanded program was about 10,000. Because the steady monthly increase resumed after this big jump—that is, the graph resembled Figure 8.3d—the evaluators felt safe in attributing the cause of the increase to the fact that young residents were now ordering the bulk of the laboratory tests.[1] The effect of the residents on laboratory tests seemed clear, and the interpretation fit published reports on the topic. However, the interpretation was not as compelling as the effect of feedback on high bobbins described above. The residency program could not be introduced, removed, and then reintroduced as McCarthy did in manipulating the high bobbin feedback.

Finally, there are situations in which there is a valid question about the interpretation of the results of a time-series design. Figure 8.1, showing the results of the crackdown on speeding, cannot be validly interpreted using the informal examination methods described here. Cook and Campbell (1979) report that recent analyses support the belief that the program had a reliable (that is, statistically significant) effect. The methods necessary to make that interpretation require mathematical skills beyond those assumed for readers of this text and beyond those possessed by most active evaluators. It is likely, however, that program evaluators will use these methods (for example, Gottman and Glass, 1978; McCleary and Hay, 1980) to a greater extent in the future.

One aid to visual inspection of a time-series graph has been provided by Tukey (1977). He suggests that the graph be smoothed by plotting the median of three adjacent points in place of each observation. Suppose that the following observations were made for a 15-month period: 30, 22, 40, 17, 35, 25, (Intervention), 45, 23, 55, 42, 35, 52, and 43. Plot these values. Now take the median of 30, 22, and 40. Plot 30 for month 2. Take the median of 22, 40, and 17. Plot 22 for month 3. Continue for the entire time series. When you are finished, you will see that the graph has been smoothed, so that the change that was caused by the intervention can be clearly seen. This tech-

---

[1]Partially on the basis of this sudden jump, the program director instituted procedures to reduce the excessive use of laboratory tests by residents.

nique is most useful when the intervention leads to a lasting, large change, but the change is masked by large random fluctuations among time intervals.

OBSERVING OTHER GROUPS

Nonequivalent Control Group Designs

The simple time-series design increases the interpretability of an evaluation by extending the periods of observations over time. Another approach is to increase the number of groups observed. If the pretest-posttest design could be duplicated with another group that did not receive the program, a potentially good research design would result. So long as the groups are comparable, nearly all the internal validity tests are satisfied by this design, called *nonequivalent control group design* (diagramed in Figure 8.2). Nonequivalent control groups may also be called comparison groups.

The evaluator expects to observe a larger improvement between pretest and posttest for the program group than for the comparison group, as illustrated in Figure 8.4. A statistical tool to analyze the data from such a design is the two groups by two time periods analysis of variance, with repeated measures over time periods (Kirk, 1982).[2] If the program was successful and the group means followed the pattern in Figure 8.4, the analysis of variance would reveal a significant interaction between group and testing period. Other analyses could also be used for this design. Reichardt (Cook and Campbell, 1979) showed how analysis of covariance can be used to compare the posttest means using the pretest to control for initial differences among students. He also showed that different analyses can bias the results in different directions depending on the pattern of data found. His discussion is beyond the level we can present in this book. It is important that readers realize that different approaches are available; none is always correct.

Including the comparison group permits a distinction to be made between the effects of the program and the several alternative plausible interpretations of change. Because the comparison group has been tested at the same time periods as the program group, both groups have had the same amount of time to mature. Historical forces have presumably affected the groups equally. Because both groups would have been tested twice, testing effects should be equivalent. Finally, the rates of participant loss between pretest and posttest can be examined to be sure they are similar. Nonequivalent control group designs are especially useful when part of an organization is exposed to the program while other parts are not. Since selection to the program is not in the hands of the participants, and since the participants' level of need does not determine eligibility, the comparability of the groups is quite good. Unfortunately, as will be shown below, these favorable conditions are not often met.

---

[2]Other names for this design are the split-plot factorial or mixed designs.

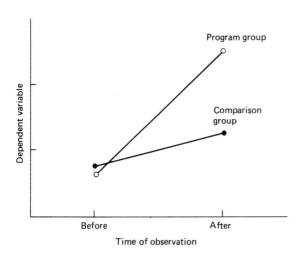

FIGURE 8.4 Hypothetical results of a nonequivalent control (comparison) group design.

Selecting Comparison Groups

Comparison groups are chosen according to the evaluation question to be studied. The no-treatment group suggested above would be used when one is seeking to learn if there is an effect of the program. At other times, stakeholders want to compare possible ways of offering the service. In such a case, variations in the program would be compared; a no-treatment group would not be an appropriate comparison group. If there is a suspicion that attention alone could affect that outcome, then the comparison group would be a placebo group, that is, a group which experiences a program, but not one that should affect the outcome measure used.

Weakness of the Design

Clearly, the major weakness in all nonequivalent control group designs is in selecting a comparison group not sufficiently similar to the program group to permit drawing valid interpretations. For example, it is possible that those who choose to be in the program may be maturing at a different rate than those in the comparison group. Parents who seek out special programs for their children may also be devoting more attention to the children at home than are parents who do not seek out special programs. Another problem will arise if the program participants are chosen because of extreme scores on the pretest, and the comparison group is selected from others with less extreme scores. If so, as mentioned in Chapter 7, the results may be distorted by regression effects.

    A way out of the problem caused by using a nonequivalent control group research design is often sought by matching the comparison groups with the program group—that is, people are chosen to form the comparison group because they resemble the program participants on income level, objective test score, rated adjustment, locality of residence, or other criteria. While matching is often used to select comparison groups for quasi-experiments, it is a controversial way to form such groups.

The widely cited evaluations of Head Start (Cicarelli, et al., 1969) has been criticized for its use of matching (Campbell and Erlebacher, 1970). Head Start, a program for disadvantaged children, is offered in the summer or during the year prior to beginning first grade. The program was designed for the preschool children most lacking in school-relevant skills and attitudes. In addition, nutritional and medical goals were involved in the program.

When Head Start was selected for evaluation, it was already widely accepted and offered in many communities (Datta, 1976b); therefore, the program could not be withheld from any group of children. The evaluation utilized a posttest-only design with national samples of children, some in Head Start programs and some matched samples not in Head Start. The evaluation compared achievement on standard tests of Head Start children in first, second, and third grades with similar non-Head Start children and concluded that Head Start was largely a failure. Critics attacked the methodology utilized in this evaluation on a number of grounds; however, the focus of the present discussion is on regression effects that likely lie behind the conclusions of the Head Start evaluation.

Because the population of children available for the non-Head Start comparison group was less disadvantaged than the children in the Head Start group, those children selected as matches could not be equivalent to the children in Head Start. In order to find children qualifying for Head Start who had cognitive achievement scores similar to those of children not qualifying, either or both of the following points had to have been true: (1) the comparison group was selected from among the less able children not qualified for Head Start; or (2) the experimental group was selected from among the more able children who attended Head Start.

To understand the effects of regression toward the mean, it is important to understand why the previous statement is true. Once a group is selected on the basis of need for a national program, there is no other group that can be found that is just like the people in the program. Thus, no perfect comparison group exists. However, on some variables (for example, family income, school grades, test scores) there will be overlap among the members of the two groups. Who will overlap? The people in the "needy" group who overlap with the "not needy" group *must* be among the relatively better-off among the "needy" people. Those in the "not needy" group who overlap with the "needy" children *must* be among the least well-off among the "not needy" people. Crano and Brewer (1986) include a numerical illustration of this principle.

Consider an artificial but illustrative example. Suppose a teacher wanted to provide a special spelling program for all the second graders. If the teacher wanted a comparison group, she could find some third graders who scored as low as the second graders. Are these groups equivalent? Probably not. These third graders would have been selected from the lower portion of a population that, in general, is more capable than the second-grade experimental group. What will happen upon retesting the groups in evaluation? Because no spelling test is completely reliable, the low-scoring third graders in the comparison group will look as though they improved, not only because they learned some new words but also because they are regressing toward the mean of third graders. This regression will make the second graders' improvement due to the program appear smaller and less impressive than it may actually have been.

In other words, the groups of children have different influences raising their scores. The program children will probably show an improvement because the new program has affected them and because they matured a bit. The comparison children will improve because of exposure to the regular spelling classes, added maturity, *and* regression. Campbell and Erlebacher (1970) assert that the Head Start evaluation was biased in just the way this hypothetical teacher's evaluation would be biased. Because human service programs typically produce small improvements, the size of the regression effects might even exceed the program's effect. In fact, Campbell and Erlebacher (1970) argue that regression artifacts may make compensatory education look harmful when, in fact, the programs may have had a small positive influence.[3] The moral is: the nonequivalent control group design is especially sensitive to regression effects when the groups are systematically different on some dimensions. In compensatory education evaluations a systematic pre-program difference between experimental and comparison groups is likely to be found.

The emphasis just placed on regression to the mean is not meant to imply that this is the only weakness of nonequivalent comparison group designs. Regression was stressed because some stakeholders may believe that selecting certain participants for inclusion in the evaluation can overcome the effects of preexisting differences between the pretest scores of the groups. There are, however, many other reasons why existing groups may differ from each other. One might compare neighboring classrooms in an attempt to learn if a novel teaching method used in one classroom is more effective. Although the children in two classrooms might seem equivalent, it might later be learned that the teacher of the non-treated class has been using methods of teaching that are similar to those used in the program. Or, when the patients of two physicians are used in an evaluation of a patient education brochure, it may turn out that the physician handing out the brochure has systematically encouraged her patients to read about their illnesses and treatments. Thus, her patients are more likely to read such material than are the patients of typical physicians. This pre-existing difference between patient groups may make the patient education program appear more effective than

---

[3]There is no controversy over whether regression occurred in this evaluation; however, the size of the likely regression effects is hotly disputed (see Cicarelli, 1970; Evans and Schiller, 1970).

would have been the case if patients of a different physician had been asked to distribute the experimental material.

It should be noted that if the program effect was massive and the program children improved markedly, the evaluation may reveal that the program was effective. Nonetheless, the size of the effect might still be over- or underestimated. On the other hand, when similar groups are available, the nonequivalent comparison group design is quite powerful and very useful.

REGRESSION-DISCONTINUITY DESIGN

There is one situation in which a comparison between nonequivalent groups can be made in a manner that is much more powerful than the methods presented so far. When eligibility for a service is based on a continuous variable, such as income, achievement, or level of disability, it may be possible to use the regression-discontinuity design. Suppose, for example, that 300 fifth grade children are tested for reading achievement in the fall. Those scoring the lowest are defined as those most in need of extra assistance. If the program has facilities for only 75 children, it seems reasonable and most fair to take the 75 children with the lowest scores into the program. This is simply a special case of the nonequivalent comparison group design; the strength of this design lies in the fact that the evaluator knows exactly how selection into program or comparison groups was made.

If all 300 are retested at the end of the school year, what would be expected? Before answering that question, note that we do not expect the 75 to outperform the 225 regular class students. We would expect comparisons between pre- and posttests to show that treatment and comparison children read better than in the fall since all children have been studying reading for the school year. If the program were effective, we would further expect that the treated children would have gained more than they would have had they stayed in regular classrooms.

The pattern of expected results given that the program is effective is given in the scatterplot in Figure 8.5 relating the pretest to the posttest. The hypothesized program effect is shown in the discontinuity in the regression line relating the pretest to the posttest at the point on pretest axis that divides the eligible children from the ineligible. If the special program was equivalent to the regular class, one would expect a continuous relationship between pre- and posttest. If the reading program was actually (heaven forbid!) worse than the regular reading classes, we would expect treated children to read less well than expected on the basis of the pretest. In such a situation the discontinuity would be the reverse of that in Figure 8.5.

Trochim (1984) describes a variety of methods to use to estimate the effect of the program depending on the way the evaluator believes the program affects the outcome variable, i.e., the posttest. The simplist alternative would be to use the posttest as the dependent variable in a regression analysis

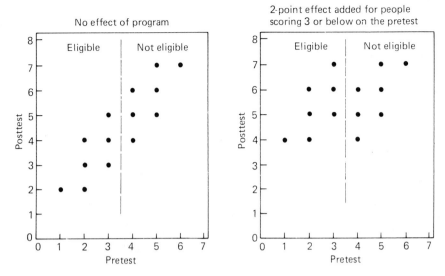

FIGURE 8.5 The relationship between pretest and posttest scores when people scoring 3 or below are eligible for special assistance to improve posttest performance. The graph on the left illustrates the case when the assistance was not effective; the graph on the right illustrates how the data would appear if the program enabled the eligible people to perform 2 points better than they would have without special assistance.

with two independent variables: (1) the pretest, and (2) a coded variable indicating whether the person was in the program or not in the program. For those in the program, this second independent variable could be coded "2," and for those not in the program, it could be coded "1." If the regression coefficient for this second independent variable was statistically significant, one can conclude that the program was effective; there is a discontinuity in the relationship between the pretest and the posttest. If a graph of the data before analysis suggests that the slope of the regression line to the left of the eligibility cutoff point seems different from the slope to the right of the cutoff point, one is advised to obtain Trochim's book and use a more complicated analysis than is suggested here.

OBSERVING OTHER DEPENDENT VARIABLES

At this point the methods described in Chapter 7 have been expanded to include observations of the program participants at many times and to include observations of groups other than the program participants. It is possible to increase the validity of interpretations by observing additional dependent variables that are not expected to be changed by the program, or at least are expected to be changed only marginally. Consider a remedial reading program offered during the summer vacation for children reading below their grade level. A pretest-posttest design would be markedly strengthened by testing the children before and after on arithmetic as well as vocabulary, grammar, and reading speed. All extraneous influences such as self-selection, history, and testing effects that may affect reading scores will also affect arithmetic scores. Thus, if scores on reading increase but those on arithmetic do not, the conclusion that the program is effective is fairly safe. Regression toward the mean could be a threat to internal validity. To minimize the effect of regression, the evaluators would make sure that children selected for the program were not chosen on the basis of their pretest.

There is a problem with this approach. The added dependent measures must be similar to the major dependent measure without being strongly influenced by the program. In the example above, if the children did read better, it might be expected that they will do better on a written, standardized arithmetic test than they did before the program. It is hard to imagine additional dependent measures that (1) would be affected by the same threats to internal validity as the outcome measure but (2) would not be affected by the program. Mark and Cook (1984) suggest that these difficulties mean that this "nonequivalent dependent variable" design is best used as an adjunct to other methods, not as the major evaluation design. Tyson (1985) found an applicable setting for this design when he evaluated the Medicaid-required second opinion on surgical procedures by comparing the percentage reductions for ten procedures requiring a second opinion with the reductions for nine procedures for which second opinions were not required.

COMBINING METHODS TO INCREASE INTERNAL VALIDITY

Time-Series and Nonequivalent Comparison Groups

The most interpretable quasi-experimental designs are those that combine the approaches mentioned above into one evaluation. If a group similar to the program participants can be found, the simple time-series design is considerably strengthened. The analysis of the Connecticut speeding crackdown mentioned earlier was made possible by examining the fatality rates of four neighboring states. Figure 8.6 contrasts the average of these four states' fatality figures with Connecticut's fatality rate. As can be seen in the figure, there seems to be a general trend toward a lower fatality rate in all five states; however, Connecticut's 1957–1959 rates are increasingly divergent from those of the neighboring states. Although regression toward the mean is a plausible alternative interpretation of the drop from 1955 to 1956, the continued favorable trend is hard to explain if the crackdown, which was kept in force during the following years, did not have an effect. Riecken and Boruch (1974) state that tests of significance are less important than a qualitative understanding of the various threats to the validity of causal conclusions about the impact

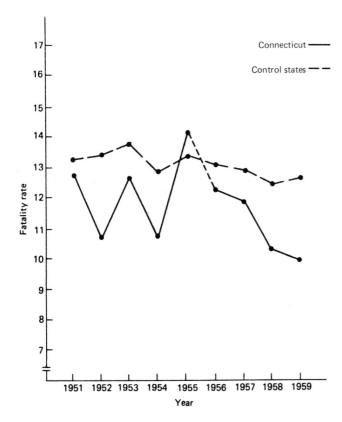

FIGURE 8.6 Automobile accident fatality rate for Connecticut and for comparable states (D. T. Campbell, "Reforms as experiments," *American Psychologist* 24 (1969): 419. Copyright 1969 by the American Psychological Association. Reprinted by permission of the author.)

of the intervention. However, methods to be used for precise analyses have been developed (see Abraham, 1980; McCleary and Hay, 1980).

A key to drawing valid interpretations from observations lies in being able to repeat the observations. If a study can be replicated, one can be much more sure of conclusions than if it cannot be. The time-series design with a comparison group that receives the same intervention as the experimental group but at a later time provides additional safeguards against validity threats. Figure 8.7 illustrates the ideal pattern of results from such a study. Cook and Campbell (1979) call this design an "interrupted time series with switching replications." If the observations fit the pattern in Figure 8.7, little in the way of statistical analysis needs to be done. Unfortunately, many societal changes are also occurring during the time of the observations, so that the dependent variables do not fall into an easily interpreted pattern. Case Study 2 is an example of a time-series design with switching replications in an evaluation of a media campaign.

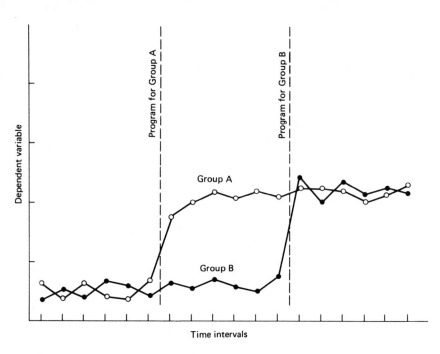

FIGURE 8.7 Hypothetical results of an interrupted time-series design with switching replications.

The Patch-Up Design

Cook and Campbell (1979) use the term *patch-up design* to describe a method that illustrates the essence of the quasi-experimental approach. Being aware of the threats to internal validity that are most likely to affect an evaluation, evaluators may decide to add comparison groups specifically designed to control for certain influences, until the most plausible competing interpretations are eliminated. With the use of advanced statistical procedures and an understanding of the validity of causal relationships, the patch-up design can be a powerful evaluation design (Cordray, 1986). The examples on the following pages illustrate relatively simple designs.

The dean of a college of arts and sciences in a medium-sized university requested an evaluation of a junior year abroad program sponsored and supervised by his college. The report was needed for a board of trustees meeting scheduled in six weeks. Clearly, there was no opportunity for a time-series design. (As mentioned in earlier chapters, it is not unusual for evaluators to work under considerable time pressure.) The research was planned around the obvious comparison—college seniors who studied abroad versus seniors who studied at the parent campus. In making this comparison, selection is one threat to internal validity that cannot be ignored. Students who decide to go abroad for a year are clearly different from those who remain at home.

An approach to estimating the preexisting differences between these two groups is to test individuals before they leave. A pretest-posttest design was impossible due to the short time allotted for the study. Because the decision to study abroad is costly and requires much planning, sophomore students sign up rather early for the program. By comparing seniors who have been abroad with sophomores arranging to go abroad, the self-selection threat is negated, because both groups have selected themselves to go abroad. However, now a second threat to internal validity becomes a problem. Sophomores are less mature than seniors. Two years in age may not be that critical for middle-aged or elderly people, but two years may make quite a difference in an evaluation of a program for college students. By adding one more group, sophomores who did not intend to study abroad, the major threats to the internal validity of this evaluation were covered.

The design is summarized in Figure 8.8. If self-selection was related to higher scores on the dependent measures, one would expect the groups in the upper row to have higher scores. If maturation led to higher scores, those in the right-hand column should have higher scores. If the program had an impact, then the upper-right-hand group, the self-selected seniors, should have especially high scores as illustrated. Unfortunately, the sophomores planning to spend the year abroad were very hard to find, and only three were tested. Therefore, the means in Figure 8.8 are hypothetical.

A more complicated patch-up design was described by Lawler and Hackman (1969). They wished to evaluate the success of having custodial employees design their own incentive plan to reduce absenteeism. The authors believed that an incentive plan would work only if the employees designed it themselves. The authors had to use intact, existing work groups; therefore, some form of the nonequivalent control group design had to be used. Three intact work teams making up the experimental group developed their plans

FIGURE 8.8 Hypothetical mean scores on a measure of international understanding for the students in the junior year and abroad evaluation. A program effect is indicated by these means.

		MATURATION LEVEL	
		SOPHOMORES	SENIORS
SELF-SELECTION	Students who will study or have studied abroad	50	65 (Treatment group)
	Students who have not studied or do not plan to study abroad	40	45

in consultation with the experimenters. The first comparison group had an incentive plan similar to that developed by the experimental group, but it was imposed upon them by management. Including this group enabled the evaluators to distinguish between the effect of an *employee*-designed incentive plan and the incentive itself. A second comparison group simply met with the experimenters to talk about the work and absenteeism. This group was necessary to show that any reduction in absenteeism would have been due more to the incentive plan than to the discussions with industrial psychologists. Finally, a comparison group with no incentive plan and no discussion was added.

The data were analyzed using a time-series analysis because (1) the rate of absenteeism may change slowly, and (2) absenteeism is recorded daily—whether or not there is a program. Comparing the level of absenteeism for the 12 weeks before the intervention with the level during the 12 weeks afterwards showed that the participant employees improved from 12 percent absent to 6 percent, while the rates for the other groups did not change. Note that without each of the control groups (just as in junior year abroad study), some alternative interpretation would have been plausible. The comparison groups were selected to counter specific, plausible interpretations of any improvement in the absenteeism rate of the experimental group.

There are other threats to internal validity with which the design does not deal because they were not plausible in this study. For example, instrumentation refers to possible changes in measures of outcome or success such as those that occur when staff become more vigilant or experienced because of interest in the evaluation. Because job absenteeism is a critical variable in work settings, the development of a program is unlikely to make any changes in the measurement of absenteeism.

SUMMARY

The use of quasi-experimental research designs in program evaluation is widespread. These approaches are often compatible with the need to minimize disruption in organizations and the need of evaluators to obtain sufficient information to permit the isolation of probable causes of changes in program participants. However, the use of quasi-experimental research designs is not straightforward; the evaluator needs to consider which specific threats to internal validity must be accounted for in each evaluation. Anticipating just which threats are likely to be problems can cause headaches for evaluators: there are no standard approaches to designing quasi-experimental evaluations. Often the correct statistical methods to use in analyzing a quasi-experimental evaluation are controversial. One of the most promising quasi-experimental methods, the interrupted time-series design, is receiving considerable theoretical study. New analytical methods are likely to become widely known in future years.

STUDY QUESTIONS

1. Explain which threats to internal validity are not covered by an evaluation of a parole program in which male parolees are tested before and after the program and are compared to a sample of men living in the same neighborhoods as the parolees.

2. Assume that reading levels in a school district were steadily declining over recent years and that a new reading program was implemented to counter this trend. After two years the reading levels continued to decline, but the superintendent announced that the program was a success because reading levels would have declined even more without the program. What would be necessary to evaluate the validity of such an announcement? Be sure to consider the cost of the information listed.

3. Suppose a new medical treatment were offered to residents of an upper-middle-class suburb. As a comparison group, similarly aged patients with the same diagnosis were found in a county hospital providing free care to welfare families. Evaluate this nonequivalent control group evaluation design.

4. A problem with quasi-experimental evaluations is that often a particular set of results can be interpreted, but a different set cannot. For example, assume a service to a disadvantaged group resulted in improved performance on some variable. If the postprogram performance of this disadvantaged group is better than that observed in the middle-class comparison group, the interpretation of the evaluation is clear. However, if postprogram performance of the disadvantaged group is lower than that of the middle-class comparison group, then there are many more possible interpretations. Explain these statements.

FURTHER READING

COOK, T. D., AND CAMPBELL, D. T. 1979. *Quasi-experimentation*. Chicago: Rand McNally.

MCCLEARY, R., AND HAY, R. A., JR. 1980. *Applied time series analysis for social sciences*. Beverly Hills, Calif.: Sage.

TROCHIM, W. M. K., ed. 1986. *Advances in quasi-experimental design and analysis*. San Francisco: Jossey-Bass.

9

Analysis of Causes
of Change

The previous chapter described various approaches to reducing the number of plausible interpretations of change observed in program participants. Such interpretations include many possible sources of bias as well as the desired positive effect of the program itself. These biases refer to the ideas summarized in the threats to internal validity—self-selection into the program by those who would benefit, general community or societal changes that overshadow all effects of the program, and the reactive effects of making observations, among other factors. The ways of separating these biases from program effects involved observing the participants at a number of time intervals and observing both the relevant dependent measures and dependent measures not likely to change due to the program. In addition, observations of intact groups not experiencing the program can improve interpretability if the groups studied are similar to the program participants. Even when carefully designed quasi-experimental evaluations are conducted, there usually remains a lingering doubt that some influence other than the program led to the improvement observed or masked a real program effect. Perhaps the people forming the nonequivalent control group were different from the experimental group in some way that was not considered in planning the evaluation. Perhaps the people in the nonequivalent control group were less motivated or reacted to the observations differently than the program participants.

A way to minimize these doubts is to adopt a research strategy that accounts for all the possible threats to internal validity. The easiest way to do this is to use the classic experimental design with random assignment of participants to the program or to a control group. This chapter reviews the need for experimentation as a tool in program evaluation, describes the most opportune times to introduce experimentation, and makes practical suggestions for meeting the problems of conducting experimental research in organizational settings.

EXPERIMENTATION IN PROGRAM EVALUATION

The Logic of Experimentation

Before discussing details of experimentation, a brief review of the logic of randomized experimental design may be useful. A true experimental evaluation refers to an evaluation based on observations of people who are randomly assigned to the program group or to some control group. In the previous chapter quasi-experimental methods were presented that are useful when evaluators do not have the administrative power to assign people to particular experiences. In such settings evaluators utilize preexisting intact groups; however, such intact groups were formed for reasons other than the need for an unambiguously interpreted evaluation. Because such groups exist of their own accord, it is very likely that the groups will differ on many variables.

Deniston and Rosenstock (1973) showed that neither a nonexperimental nor a quasi-experimental design validly estimated the effectiveness of a treatment program for rheumatoid arthritics. The cyclical nature of the severity of this illness creates large biases in any design other than an experimental one. In other words, threats to internal validity (particularly regression to the mean) could not be handled by a quasi-experiment when studying this population. No group can be used effectively as a nonequivalent control group for a study of the value of treatment for rheumatoid arthritis. Although this is an unusual population, Deniston and Rosenstock make the general point that even when evaluators recognize a potential source of bias, they may be unable to control for it—short of forming the groups themselves through random assignment. When done on a completely random basis, the treatment and control groups are comparable, since they do not differ systematically before the program begins.

Setting up truly equivalent experimental and control groups requires a nonbiased method of assigning the participants to the groups. Often evaluators believe that random assignment is impossible, when in fact it is a possibility, even within the strictures of functioning organizations. Carey (1979) evaluated the reorganization of a nursing service, taking advantage of a natural random assignment procedure. One of two medical floors of a large hospital was redesigned around a more personalized nursing concept. Assignment of new patients to rooms (and consequently to floors) was made on the basis of bed availability by admitting personnel who were unaware of the research and uninvolved in nursing organization. Because severity of illness and physician practice determine length of stay, the floor on which a bed is available in a hospital operating near capacity is a random factor. Thus, with no disruption of hospital routine, randomly assigned equivalent groups were obtained. Because the groups were not formed in a biased fashion (for example, physician preference for a floor, or assignment of the more severely ill to one of the floors), the results could be interpreted without concern for many of the threats to internal validity.

Boruch and Rindskopf (1977) liken a randomized experiment to an aspiring for evaluators; the evaluator is thereby relieved of the headaches involved in trying to identify and estimate the sizes of the biases that are present in nonrandomized evaluations such as the nonequivalent group design. The discussion of the patch-up design suggested that the evaluator introduce control groups to measure the impact of the identified biases. Although this is a good approach, there are times when the biases are recognized too late in the course of the evaluation. Further, there will be times when a comparison group needed to eliminate a particular threat to internal validity will be unavailable. Various statistical methods are used to remove the biases when randomization is not possible. However, the use of these methods is controversial and can lead to incorrect conclusions. Campbell and Erlebacher (1970) point out that evaluations using these statistical corrections might make a program look successful when it is not, or unsuccessful when it is successful. Boruch (1975) and others have shown that the statistical methods cannot correct for biases in basic evaluation designs whenever the variables describing group differences are imperfectly measured. Because measurements of academic achievement, emotional adjustment, criminal recidivism, productivity, and so forth are never perfectly reliable, the statistical adjustments fail to remove all biases.

Experimental Designs

Figure 9.1 includes diagrams of several experimental designs. Each of the groups in the research designs is formed by randomly assigning possible participants to receive the program (the experimental group) or not to receive it (the control group). The most simple form of the true experiment, diagramed in the top section of the figure, employs observations after the program is delivered, but uses no pretests. Because the groups are formed randomly, there is no theoretical necessity to use a pretest to show that the groups were equivalent before receiving the program. Such pretests are advisable, if not essential, when preexisting groups are used for an evaluation, as in the quasi-experimental, nonequivalent control group design. As pointed out in Chapter 8, without pretests the evaluator and the information users would never know if the program and the nonequivalent comparison groups were indeed comparable before the program group was influenced by the program. Although this is not an issue when true control groups are used, pretests also have other uses that will be discussed below.

At times a program can be divided into two parts that might be provided separately or together as a unit. In such a case the posttest design can be enlarged, as the second entry of Figure 9.1 shows. An evaluation using this design and the best method of analyzing it will be discussed later in this chapter.

FIGURE 9.1 Evaluation designs utilizing random assignment to groups, and the questions these designs can answer.

EXPERIMENTAL DESIGN	SYMBOLIC REPRESENTATION*	QUESTIONS THAT CAN BE ANSWERED
Posttest-only control group	X O O	Did the program cause a change in the program participants?
Two-by-two factorial	O X O Y O X Y O	Did either or both of the aspects of the program cause a change in the program participants? Is there something about having the two aspects of the program given together that creates an especially favorable climate for change? Or, do X and Y interfere with each other?
Solomon four group	O X O O O O X O	Did the program cause a change in the program participants? How much change occurred?
Time series with random assignment to groups	X O O O O O O X O O O O O O X O O O	Did the program cause a change in the program participants? Did the effect of the program hold up over time?

*The program is represented by X or Y; observations are represented by O.

A brief review of the threats to internal validity can illustrate the power of random assignment to distinguish between the effect of the program and nonprogram causes of participant change. There is no reason to believe that the groups differ in maturation rates or levels or that they experience different historical influences. The groups have not selected themselves into the program being evaluated. Since participants did not begin at different levels of health, adjustment, and so forth, regression to the mean is not a viable threat. Both groups have equivalent testing experiences. The possibility of instrumentation changes exist in evaluation projects, especially when observations are made over an extended period of time. The possibility of the meaning of scores changing as observers gain more experience with the research instruments or get tired of the project must also be considered. The potential problems caused by participant dropout after the evaluation has begun are no worse than with other designs.

In spite of the power of randomization to assure that the control and experimental groups will not be systematically different, some evaluators may feel more comfortable with pretests for both groups. Also, having pretests for experimental and control groups might help in communicating the findings to others who do not understand the advantages of randomization. For these reasons, the third design is given in the figure. The four-group design is not in any theoretical way better than the two-group design with posttests only. Flay and Best (1982), however, warn evaluators that randomization may fail in practice. If that happens, having pretest data can help to preserve the usefulness of the evaluation.

The use of pretests has a cost, however. Often the act of observation is reactive, especially in social settings. It is possible that the pretest may sensitize the program participants to the influences of the program, thus ensuring that the program will work only when the pretest is given. If this is true, then the pretest becomes part of the program. There is nothing at all wrong with including a pretest as part of any program; however, it is easy to forget that the pretest may cause the participants to react differently than they would have had the pretest not been given. In Campbell and Stanley's terminology (1963), adding pretests to the first design weakens its external validity because the pretest may have interacted with the program to cause the observed change. If testing is expensive, it is unlikely that program designers will want to incorporate the testing procedure into the program, even though the evaluation only showed that the pretest *and* the program lead to change—not that the program alone leads to change. The third design, using four groups, takes care of all these concerns.

An advantage of using pretests in experimental evaluation designs is illustrated in Case Study 3 (Majchrzak, 1986). By using pretests even though treatment and control groups were formed randomly and by monitoring program implementation, she was able to detect the effect of different levels of implementation. Pretest observations permitted an analysis of change that would have been impossible without pretests. A further advantage of pretests is that they allow the evaluator to adjust posttest scores for preexisting individual participant differences within each group. This can be done using just the two groups of the Solomon design that were pretested in an analysis of covariance. An analysis of covariance possesses great statistical power to detect differences between groups especially when the groups have been formed randomly. (See Hays (1981) for details.)

The advantages of time-series designs can be added to the experimental method by making repeated observations at regular intervals. In this way evaluators can learn whether the program's impact held up across time. The last design in Figure 9.1 is especially useful if follow-up assessments are desired and if the program is implemented on a staggered basis. The built-in replication provided by this design is a very attractive feature.

This discussion is not meant to imply that there are only four experimental designs. Many options are possible, depending on the needs of the evaluations. These four designs are described in order to illustrate some options that are available to the evaluator.

OBJECTIONS TO EXPERIMENTATION

When evaluators fail to use experimental methods, the reasons may be related to frequently voiced objections to experimental methodology. It is important for evaluators to be familiar with these objections, lest they encounter them for the first time while planning an evaluation or, even worse, after random assignment to programs has already begun.

Don't Experiment on Me!

People rightly are not anxious to have someone use them in a poorly thought out experiment. Unfortunately, experimentation has sometimes been unjustly associated with activities such as the CIA and Army "experiments" on the effects of hallucinogenic drugs (*Time*, August 4, 1975). The media do not use the word *experiment* in the careful way experimental design textbooks do. Consequently, it is not surprising when people not trained in social science methodology equate experiments to evaluate the effects of a social program or a medical treatment with the covert administration of dangerous drugs to unsuspecting people and other undisciplined attempts to learn about behavior. Evaluators planning an experiment will be careful to treat the question of experimentation with respect. The advantages of experimentation should be stressed. Furthermore, the fact that the program or service has been carefully planned by competent personnel should be clear to possible volunteers and committees overseeing the research.

Clinical Prerogatives

Often people are hesitant to become involved in experimentation because they want the best service available for their problem, be it a health, emotional, educational, or any other problem. They feel that because human service providers are trained and paid to choose the service most likely to help a person, random assignment to a control group means they are missing out on what they really need. In a similar fashion, service providers usually feel able to select the best care for a person in need or to select the people most likely to benefit from a service program. When they feel this way, the service provider is not likely to endorse an evaluation requiring random assignment to groups.

The fact of the matter is that in many ways people in need get a particular form of service on a fairly random basis. Different counselors follow various theories of counseling. Physicians do not follow set treatment patterns. Different cities draw up quite different welfare programs. Judges do not assign identical sentences to people convicted of the same crimes. The reasons why a particular person experiences a particular form of counseling, medical treatment, or job training are often unrelated to clinical insight.

It is quite natural for service staff to believe that they know best about the selection of treatments. The literature on clinical judgment and decision making also suggests that it is not unusual for staff to believe that the selection of a particular treatment is appropriate, when in fact it is worthless or even harmful to people (Gilbert, Light, and Mosteller, 1975). These misperceptions occur because we remember successes and fulfilled expectations; we often explain away and forget observations that do not fit our expectations (Chapman and Chapman, 1967, 1969). Highly prejudiced individuals remember incidents in which a minority member commits a social gaffe but quickly forget or sympathize with a person from a higher-status group committing a similar misstep (see Allport, 1954). Partisan fans see more rule infractions by opposing teams than by their own teams (Hastorf and Cantril, 1954).

It takes a considerable amount of tact to convince service providers that their clinical judgment may not always be valid. Providing examples of non-randomized studies that were later invalidated by randomized research may help service providers see the possibility of misperceptions and the advantages of unambiguous documentation of service effectiveness. In Chapter 2 we described the necessity of encouraging the development of an experimental orientation among program managers and staff. Campbell (1969) suggested that society should approach new human service programs as if they were experiments—treating a failure of a well-conceived program as an indication of our incomplete understanding of human nature, not as an indication of the low motivation or the incompetence of the staff. Admittedly, this philosophy is not practiced as often as it might be. Some human service providers act as though a negative evaluation means they are incompetent; and therefore they develop rationalizations whenever particular individuals do not seem to benefit from the service provided. Few teachers examine their own performance when a student does not pass an examination. By explaining away all failures, the program staff avoids the opportunity for growth that is provided by unfulfilled expectations. At these times evaluators feel the full force of the conflict between their skeptical role toward service programs and the providers' confidence in the effectiveness of the services given.

Time and Effort Involved

Anyone who has conducted research in an organization knows that research requires a commitment of time and effort. Evaluators should not agree to conduct a research project if they do not have the resources to carry it through promptly. Nevertheless, it takes only a little additional work to conduct an experiment rather than a noncontrolled evaluation. Planning and obtaining approval for an experiment requires more time and perseverance than a pretest-posttest single-group evaluation. However, once approval has been obtained, data collection, analysis, and presentation require the same amount of time, regardless of the quality of the evaluation design. Some care is required of the evaluator to be sure the experiment is not corrupted. These concerns will be discussed in the last section of the chapter.

THE COSTS OF *NOT* DOING AN EXPERIMENT

Performing a randomized experiment in a service delivery setting requires a lot of effort and tenacity on the part of the evaluator. In addition, the staff is inconvenienced because, at a minimum, additional forms must be completed. At worst, the staff may feel threatened and treat the evaluator with hostility. It is worth it? Gilbert, et al. (1975) point out that too often the costs of experimentation are not weighed properly. Instead of considering the costs in absolute terms, planners should compare them with the costs of *not* doing an experiment. Gilbert, et al. describe several medical procedures that became widely accepted on the basis of observational, nonexperimental studies. For example, in 1964 there were approximately 1000 treatment units being used to freeze duodenal ulcers in the United States for 10,000 patients. After a careful randomized experiment, the treatment was discarded. Although the study that finally showed the treatment to be worthless was expensive, the cost of the worthless treatment was expensive as well. The cost of bloodletting, previously mentioned, was also high. Patients in the latter case did not receive a worthless treatment, they received a harmful one. The cost of a small-scale experiment would have been minuscule compared to the cost of the mistreatment.

If a quasi-experimental study cannot be clearly interpreted, its cost is largely wasted. A number of writers have found that published, poorly controlled studies often favor a novel treatment. Although these studies may be a little less expensive than a well-controlled study, they actually cost more because of misinformation provided to readers who may seek to duplicate the results with their own clients, students, or patients. The proliferation of misinformation supporting an ineffective program means that people seeking help—who expect to receive the "best treatment"—may actually be poorly served. Even those who would have refused to be part of an experiment on the assumption that they would not be treated in the best way possible may end up with something worse than a recognized experimental program; they get a program that is only assumed to be effective.

Gilbert, et al. (1975) suggest that the alternative to careful clinical trials is "fooling around." A service provider trying an approach supported only by uncontrolled studies often does not inform the client/patient/trainee that the treatment is new and not thoroughly understood. Nor does the service provider seek to obtain informed consent as an evaluator would when conducting an experiment.

The costs of not doing an experiment, then, are many. Evaluations that seek to identify causes—but cannot—are totally wasteful. Evaluations that mistakenly purport to have found an effective program may encourage the use of ineffective programs. There are many reasons to initiate program evaluation. When the reason is to identify causal relationships between a human service (the independent variable) and outcome (the dependent variable), the cost of an experiment is surprisingly low when compared to the cost of not doing it.

THE MOST DESIRABLE TIMES TO CONDUCT EXPERIMENTS

It is the contention of this text that evaluation should be built into the daily operation of all organizations. Usually such evaluation procedures will not be experiments but rather the administrative-monitoring and performance-monitoring approaches described in Chapters 6 and 7. We agree with Lipsey et al. (1985) that the experimental paradigm is not the all-purpose program evaluation methodology. There are, however, circumstances that are best served by an understanding of cause-effect relationships and that are especially well-suited to experimentation, as the following sections illustrate.

When a New Program Is Introduced

When a new program is introduced, there are several conditions that are likely to increase staff and manager interest in an experimental evaluation: (1) responsible people are thinking about change; (2) if the control group receives the old program, it is hard to argue that its participants are being unfairly treated; (3) the program may take some time to implement, thus providing time for an evaluation; and (4) there is a need to document the program's success for internal requirements, as well as to show that it might work elsewhere.

One of the obstacles to good program evaluation is the fear people often have of change. It is only natural to become comfortable doing things in the same way year after year. Thus, an important variable that needs to be considered in planning evaluations is the staff's and administration's openness or readiness to change. Salasin and Davis (1979) have developed a scale to measure the beliefs of the staff about the likelihood that an evaluation (as well as other innovations) will be accepted and will have a positive effect on the organization. When the impetus for change comes from within the program in the form of a plan for a new service, the staff does not require prodding to consider change. Of course, the staff may need to be cautioned that most innovations, even when well planned, are not successful (Gilbert, et al., 1975).

When beginning a new program, the current form of service can be given to the control group. Whatever needs a group may have, its members receive help from somewhere. It may be from a previous program, from another agency, from family members, or from elsewhere. Because the service to be evaluated is new, it is hard to argue that randomly assigning people to continue receiving the service they have been getting is a deprivation. (People who believe deeply in the new program will raise the argument nonetheless.) The evaluator seeking to assign participants randomly will have an easier time defending the random assignment when a new program is introduced than when the program has been running for several years and is considered standard policy.

The fact that most new programs do not go into effect in all parts of the organization simultaneously is an advantage to evaluators. Human relations seminars for managers, for example, will not be given to all managers at one time. All that is necessary to conduct an experimental evaluation is to develop a random procedure to schedule the managers if there are several groups, each receiving the program at a different time. The essential aspects of this design were diagramed in the fourth entry of Figure 9.1. The delivery of the program at different times permits the formation of multiple control groups and the repeated replication of the experimental evaluation at times one through four. Furthermore, the possibility of follow-up assessment of success is possible. The most desirable outcome of the evaluation would be for the dependent variables to follow the pattern shown in Figure 9.2. If all five groups were to improve a similar amount after receiving the program, and if the groups maintained their posttraining level, alternative, nonprogram explanations of the results would be very hard to support.

In order to conduct this sort of evaluation, it is important for evaluators to have access to organizational plans. All too often evaluators' services are requested after the program is in place or after its implementation is planned. People untrained in social science methods seldom understand the evaluator's request for changes in implementation plans to accommodate the design needs of the evaluation. Because service personnel will have worked hard to gain approval for a new program, they will resist the idea of postponing implementation for the evaluator's sake. Whenever possible, it is far better to be involved in the planning stages than to ask for a change in plans.

A fourth reason why new programs may be evaluated is that there may be less anxiety over the possibility of failure, as compared to a program that is widely accepted in the organization. Less is at stake if the program does not look perfect, because fewer people have become committed to it.

A fifth reason to document the success of a new program concerns the favorable publicity generated among the general public and among organizations. Employees are likely to feel pride in being associated with an organiza-

FIGURE 9.2   The most desirable outcome for a three-group design with delayed program participation for Groups 2 and 3. Group 1 received the program before the first observations; Group 2, between the first and second observations; and Group 3, between the second and third observations.

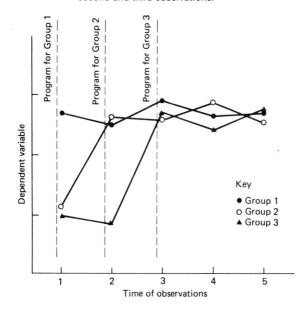

tion that has a reputation as an innovator. Referrals are more likely to be provided if human service personnel in other organizations have respect for an innovating agency.

When Resources Are Scarce

A second circumstance in which experimentation may be accepted is when resources are scarce. If the program cannot be offered to everyone who could possibly use it, some way must be found to decide who will get the program and who will not. The most desirable method—from the evaluator's point of view—is to use random selection to determine who can obtain the service. Riecken and Boruch (1974) report that the general public is remarkably willing to accept the idea of a lottery to determine who does and does not obtain a valuable service. In a real sense a lottery is more fair than a first-come, first-served policy; often those with "connections" are the ones who hear about the program first. Teenagers whose relatives are involved in city government will probably hear about a summer job program before those who must depend on newspapers or other sources for the announcement of application dates and eligibility criteria.

When resources are scarce, many service providers strive to give the program to those most in need. There is no question that such a strategy is in some ways just; however, it is also true that the ways of determining eligibility are not perfectly reliable. In fact, the way in which eligibility is determined is often quite unreliable, with different service providers coming to different conclusions. In cases where the most needy are to get the program, perhaps an agreement can be reached defining a category of uncertain eligibility. Program participants and controls could be selected randomly from this group, and an experiment performed utilizing just the people whose eligibility is uncertain (Crano and Brewer, 1986).

When There Is Controversy About Program Effectiveness

Evaluators who work with a program of uncertain worth enjoy some advantages and must adapt to some disadvantages. While this section stresses the advantages, we must also note the disadvantages.

If service providers disagree about a program, evaluation research will be viewed very critically; contending factions might each seek to recruit the evaluators to their side. The evaluators' behavior may be scrutinized for signs of favoritism. In such situations evaluators would do well to keep everyone informed of plans and to carry out plans in a careful, evenhanded manner. Although such scrutiny may make program evaluation somewhat more stressful for the evaluator, the final products may actually be of higher quality—unless evaluators refuse to draw any conclusions from the research. More will be said about handling controversial conclusions in Chapters 13 and 14.

Controversy provides an advantage to evaluators, because controversy over programs can be directed to support an experiment. If some influential people in an organization do not believe in the program, they will not be moved by arguments that it is unjust to deprive a control group of a particular service. If there are others who strongly support the program, it is possible that there will be an institutional battle. In such a case the question of offering the program may be decided on political grounds. If, on the other hand, both sides could agree on what they would accept as evidence of the program's success, the setting for an experiment could well be excellent.

For example, various forms of welfare reform have both proponents and detractors. A number of experiments have been conducted to test whether income supplements would enhance or reduce the willingness of people to seek employment (Kershaw, 1972). Some welfare recipients were randomly assigned to participate in various forms of income maintenance programs or to remain in current programs. Liberal legislators may argue that the people in the control group were being treated unfairly, while conservative legislators might argue that the new program was a giveaway. If program evaluation can supply social science observations to both groups, evaluation will fill a useful role in society. Whether or not welfare is ever designed on the basis of the findings of this research, the level of debate will be raised—and the validity of arguments used will be increased—on the basis of good research (Abt, 1977).

There has been controversy over the question of whether nutritional supplements to malnourished children in tropical areas would have long-term effects on cognitive development (McKay et al., 1978). McKay et al. randomly assigned malnourished children of low socioeconomic status of Cali, Colombia, to receive food supplements beginning at four different times before they reached school age. The four groups received the supplement for periods of 45, 34, 26, or 10 months before starting school. The authors found that the sooner a nutritional supplement was begun, the more impact there was on cognitive development. However, for all groups there was a positive impact lasting at least one year after the supplements were no longer given. By use of an experiment, the cause of improvement was shown to be due to the nutrition, not to self-selection, regression to the mean, testing effects, or any other nonprogram effects. (This particular experiment was strengthened through the use of two additional untreated groups, one high and one low in socioeconomic status, that were not made up of randomly assigned children.)

When Change Is Desired

Program evaluation utilizing experimental methodology is useful when there is widespread dissatisfaction with current conditions but no consensus about what changes should be instituted. Income maintenance evaluations (Kershaw, 1972) are examples of experiments conducted in response to a desire for change in welfare policies accompanied by uncertainty about what to do. In the late 1960s the desire to prevent, or at least to reduce, the rate of school failure of disadvantaged rural and urban children led to a series of experiments with Head Start, a preschool program aimed at improving cognitive skills, health, and nutrition (Datta, 1976b). On a facility level Carey (1976) took advantage of dissatisfaction with a mandatory counseling requirement for couples seeking sterilization to conduct a randomized experiment in a general hospital. Experimentation as a conscious, rational approach to selecting among alternatives is the prime example of Campbell's concept of the "experimenting society" (1969), in which government and public alike agree to submit proposed changes in human services to experimentation, recognizing that although most innovations do not live up to expectations, the best way to choose among various possibilities is through careful program evaluation. This is especially important when government policy choices will affect thousands, even millions of people. When evaluations do have policy implications, evaluators consider how similar the program participants are to the people who would experience the program at other sites. The more the people observed in the evaluation are like the potential participants, the more confident one can be about the external validity of the evaluation and about making policy recommendations.

PRESERVING AN EXPERIMENTAL DESIGN

Up to this point this chapter has emphasized (1) the advantages of experiments over other approaches as methods to show that a program caused a change in behavior; and (2) the situations that are likely to lead to the acceptance of random assignment to experimental and control groups. As unfortunate as it seems, evaluators cannot rest after planning and getting approval for an experimental design. Once begun, experiments have a way of breaking down without careful shepherding. There are some precautions that can be taken to maximize the integrity of the evaluation so that it will remain an interpretable experiment (Rezmovic, et al., 1981).

Precautions Before Data Collection Begins

One of the problems with evaluations is that participants drop out of various groups. If the experimental group is receiving a service, its members are likely to be more easily followed than the control people, who have nothing to gain by staying in contact with the evaluator. It is also possible that participants will drop out of the experimental group if the program makes rigorous demands on participants. Harris and Bruner (1971) sought to measure the impact of a contract weight reduction program involving a cash deposit that would be refunded at a rate of $1.00 or $.50 per pound lost in a given week. In the first experiment 58 percent of the program participants dropped out after random assignment. In the second experiment *all* participants dropped out after random assignment to the program. The evaluation was not without any utility; the dropout rate clearly showed that a program requiring a cash deposit was not acceptable to these overweight people! If the dropout rate is high and dropout is different from group to group, even the most well-planned experiments will become uninterpretable.

Perhaps one of the most thorough attempts to minimize treatment-related dropout was carried out in the selection of participants for the New Jersey Income Maintenance Study. Riecken and Boruch (1974) report that in order to minimize treatment-related dropout, the evaluators explained to possible participants all the levels of income supplement involved in the study and described the information that would be needed from them. Only those people who agreed to provide the information regardless of the group to which they were assigned were retained and randomly assigned to groups.

Few advantages are gained without some accompanying cost. Postponing random assignment until some attrition has occurred, perhaps during pretesting, introduces the possibility that the participants no longer represent the population for whom the program was designed. The people who dropped out because they would not agree to provide information regardless of the group they were in are likely to be different from the people who agreed to all the conditions. It is most likely that those who dropped out included some irresponsible or transient people. It is also possible that some of the most motivated obtained jobs during the initial negotiations and thus were no longer interested in the program. Income maintenance programs, if incorporated into the welfare system, would be provided to all who qualified through low incomes—not only to those who would agree to cooperate in an experiment on income maintenance. If a large proportion of possible participants refused to cooperate with the research, those who refused may have been quite different from those who agreed to cooperate. If so, then conclusions drawn from the experiment may not apply to more than a fraction of the population. What appears to be a successful program may only be successful with some. Sound experiments whose results cannot be applied to other locations or populations are said to lack external validity (Campbell and Stanley, 1963).

A way to counter this threat to generalization is to compare those who refuse to participate with those who do participate. When evaluating a welfare program, a considerable amount of information is available about those who do and do not cooperate. If such variables as age, income, or education do indeed differ between the groups, the usefulness of the evaluation is reduced. If, on the other hand, the groups do not differ on such variables and the proportion of dropouts is small, the conclusions drawn from the experiment can be trusted.

Precautions While the Experiment Is Occurring

Even after the experiment has begun, evaluators must remain close to the data-gathering procedure in order to be sure that agreed-upon procedures are being followed. Cook and Campbell (1979) described additional threats to internal validity (not presented in Chapter 7) that can occur after an experiment has been designed and begun; each of the five serves to reduce the interpretability of an experiment.

First, *diffusion or imitation of the program* can occur when the controls learn about the program and, in effect, administer it to themselves. Straw

(1978) described a weight reduction program in general terms to all volunteers before random assignment. One person who was subsequently randomly placed in the control group (i.e., scheduled for the program later) used the brief oral description to design her own weight reduction program. By imitating the program, she achieved a greater weight reduction than any of the people in the experimental group.

Second, *attempts to compensate the control group* occur when staff or managers seek to give the members of the control group some special service to make up for their not being in the experimental group receiving the program. Posavac (1974) was evaluating an information/counseling program for postcoronary inpatients. Part way through the evaluation, he learned that nurses were distributing a short book to control patients who were the most insistent about getting more information. The nurses had difficulty accepting the requirements that controls not be given the program textbook until after the predischarge assessment of knowledge and attitudes. Successful compensation of control groups will result in a negative evaluation, because compensation will tend to make the experimental and control groups equivalent on the outcome measures. A way to discourage such compensation is to point out that compensating the controls can serve to reduce the likelihood of finding support for the program and, consequently, reduce the probability of the program being offered in the future. Thus, if the program is actually effective, compensation of the controls could result in the loss of a worthwhile service for people who need it.

Third, control groups sometimes feel a *rivalry with the experimental group*. Rahe (1978) experienced this problem in an evaluation of an exercise program for Navy fliers. The program was designed to increase the fitness of the fliers in an attempt to lower physiological stress reactions when landing on an aircraft carrier. Because the groups were all aboard a single ship, some of the controls heard about the program and were observed working out on the exercycles in order to "score" as well on the physiological outcome measures as the pilots in the experimental group.

A threat whose effects are opposite to rivalry is *resentful demoralization* of those not in the program group. It is possible that people in a control group will learn that there is a group receiving what they may consider is a valuable service. One can easily imagine an experimental job skills program offered to some applicants for welfare. Those without the program may feel that the others have an unfair advantage in obtaining work and, consequently, reduce their job-hunting efforts. If they did react this way, the demoralization alone could make it appear that the program was effective.

The first three threats serve to make the experimental and control groups similar. The fourth may lead to greater differences between groups. *Local history* is a threat that can have either effect. Local history refers to events that occur to members of one group in an experiment. This may be a threat when participants are tested in groups, even though randomly assigned individually to control or experimental conditions. The possibility exists that one member of the group may affect the others in a way that will either enhance or reduce group differences. One member of an elementary school class may act out during testing and affect the scores of the other children. If the class is part of the experimental group, group differences could be reduced. If the class belongs to the control group, the controls might appear even less accomplished due to this one student. Thus, local history could bias the evaluation to favor the control group or the experimental group. The way to avoid the effect of local history is to deliver the program and assess its effectiveness to many small groups (or even to individuals), not just to a small number of large groups.

There is no substitute for an evaluator keeping close track of the data-gathering process. Although close personal attention is time consuming, the delegation of duties to program staff or to people not really involved with the evaluation process may lead to situations that destroy the usefulness of the evaluation. Competent data collection requires commitment to the task. Data gathered by people hired just for data collection have been falsified even by well-trained individuals (Rezmovic, et al., 1981). There is no substitute for careful supervision of data collectors.

These four threats to internal validity in the context of an experimental evaluation suggest an additional concern for the evaluator to worry about. The best evaluators recognize that outcome data do not reveal much about the day-to-day functioning of the program. Thus, outcome evaluations are most effective when carried out in conjunction with program monitoring (Chapter 6) in order to judge the degree the program has been implemented. Furthermore, quantitative information, even when gathered in thoroughly valid ways, cannot substitute for a detailed understanding of (1) the quality of the interaction between the staff and program participants, (2) the degree the program meets the needs of the participants, and (3) how the program fits into the overall organization sponsoring the program and the community in which the program is offered. Such issues are best addressed by using qualitative methods (described in Chapter 12) to supplement the methods and evaluation designs presented so far.

SUMMARY

Whenever program evaluations are designed to determine whether or not a human service program caused any change in the people served, an experimental research design should be considered. It should not, however, be forced on a program or facility that does not support the requirements of experimental research. When implemented, program evaluations based on experimental research designs are easier to interpret and to analyze than are the less well controlled evaluations described in Chapter 8. Recall the comment that experimental designs are like aspirins; they reduce the number of headaches experienced by evaluators—reduce, but not eliminate. The most carefully designed evaluations will not be interpretable if they are not carried out as planned. Evaluator recognize that many human service professionals will not fully understand the advantages of the experimental approach and could in all innocence nullify the evaluator's plans. As with all forms of evaluation, someone will need to exercise close supervision over the way the data are collected and the way individuals are assigned to research groups.

STUDY QUESTIONS

1. If more program participants than members of the control group drop out of an experimental evaluation, what can be concluded from the evaluation? (Note: The answer "nothing" is incorrect.)
2. List the advantages and disadvantages of experimental and quasi-experimental evaluation designs. Use parallel columns so that when you are finished with the list, you have a concise way to compare these two approaches.
3. Using language that can be understood by someone without training in statistics and research methods, explain the advantages of experimentation, including random assignment to groups. Imagine you are addressing an elementary school teacher, a nurse, a police officer, or a similar human service staff person. The adequacy of your answer depends on its technical correctness and its appropriateness to the intended audience.
4. Suppose that after an experiment is described (as in question 3 above), someone asks: "If the new program is worth experimenting on, and if the staff feels that the program is good, how can you justify not letting the controls reap the benefits of the program?" What would be an appropriate answer?

FURTHER READING

BORUCH, R. F., AND CORDRAY, D. S. 1982. *An appraisal of educational program evaluations: Federal, state, and local agencies.* New York: Cambridge University Press.
CAMPBELL, D. T., AND STANLEY, J. C. 1963. *Experimental and quasi-experimental designs for research.* Chicago: Rand-McNally.
COOK, T. D., AND CAMPBELL, D. T. 1979. *Quasi-experimentation: Design and analysis issues in field settings.* Chicago: Rand-McNally.
GILBERT, J. P.; LIGHT, R. J.; AND MOSTELLER, F. 1975. Assessing social innovations: An empirical base for policy. In *Evaluation and experiment,* eds. A. R. Lumsdaine and C. A. Bennett. New York: Academic Press.

part IV

ADDITIONAL APPROACHES TO PROGRAM EVALUATION

Approaches to outcome evaluation that emphasize experimental control as discussed in Chapters 7, 8, and 9 have many advantages. However, these approaches cannot be applied in all evaluation settings nor can they be used to answer many important evaluative questions.

Some evaluations focus on the efficiency of program delivery. Knowing that a program achieves what it sets out to do is essential, but it is also helpful to compare program costs to the outcomes achieved. It is important that the achievements of a program be worth the funds expended on it. However, even if a program can show results that are worth more than the resources expended, it is possible that more efficient programs could be instituted. Such questions are treated in Chapter 10 on analyzing costs and relating costs to outcomes.

At times goals must be tailored to individuals. Therapeutic settings ideally structure services to meet particular client needs. Similarly, business settings develop plans for increasing productivity that require the specification of unique goals for each manager. Although this latter approach to goal setting can be used as part of individual performance assessment, it has so much in common with program evaluation that it has been included in Chapter 11 on individual goal attainment.

Programs providing unusual services to individuals or groups and programs containing many interrelated elements may be very hard to evaluate using quantitative research approaches. If one is unable to draw up surveys and interviews to estimate need and monitor implementation, if staff find it hard to describe the process by which the program helps its participants, or if it seems very difficult to imagine quantified outcome measures to use with all aspects of a program, adopting a qualitative approach as described in Chapter 12 may be advisable. Be sure to note, however, that although few complex statistics are needed for qualitative evaluation, this approach is probably the most complex described in this text.

10

Analysis of Costs and Outcomes

The outcomes of human service programs can be fully evaluated only when their costs are considered. Most service providers do not have training in cost accounting and thus often begin work remarkably naive about costs. However, Demone and Harshbarger (1973) assert that recommendations for programs whose costs are not estimated are simply statements of philosophy that will not be taken very seriously. Similarly, conclusions about the outcome of a program are not really complete unless the evaluator has discussed the costs of obtaining the outcome. Even an evaluation accounting for all threats to internal validity and finding a highly significant degree of improvement may be a negative evaluation if the costs of obtaining the outcome are prohibitive, or if the outcome could be achieved less expensively using a different program. Being able to relate evaluation activities to cost accounting is becoming a more important aspect of the role of the evaluator (Becker et al., 1982).

Cost analysis is not a new idea to commercial people and business analysts. The local hardware store manager counts receipts every evening and periodically records costs. By converting transactions into dollars, business people can compare input costs (salaries, inventory, and building costs) with cash receipts. A comparison of these two values tells managers whether they are going into debt or making money. Bookkeeping, of course, is not this simple in practice; however, the principle is straightforward and the unit of analysis, a dollar, is widely accepted. In human service settings the principles are less clear, and the benefits are usually hard to convert into dollars.

Cost analyses are done both after a program has been evaluated and in the planning stage. The topic is presented at this point in order to illustrate how outcomes are related to program costs. When cost analyses are used in planning, costs are estimated and probable levels of outcome are projected on the basis of previous evaluations of similar programs. Conducting cost analyses in the planning stage of program development helps planners to select the programs that are likely to provide the best return on investments.

COST ANALYSES

The first step in a cost analysis, whether the program is already functioning or planned, is to divide program costs into categories. It is impossible to estimate the costs of a program as a whole without this breakdown. Popham (1975) presents several ways of conceptualizing costs. His categories of costs include variable versus fixed, incremental versus sunk, recurring versus non-recurring, and hidden versus obvious.

Variable versus Fixed Costs

All human service facilities must be housed somewhere. If the service requires special equipment, as do medical and dental care and vocational training, the facility cannot easily be used for any other purposes. Also, it is necessary in such services to have a complete set of equipment before treating the first patient or training the first student. Thus, the costs of the facilities and equipment are *fixed costs*. Because of the fixed costs of getting started, there probably is some optimal number of people to serve in order to minimize the fixed costs per person served.

Variable costs are those that will change with the size of the program. The supplies used by the individuals served clearly vary with the size of the program. The costs of maintenance, postage, custodial services, and secretarial assistance are examples of costs that will grow as the program grows to its optimal size.

Incremental versus Sunk Costs

Incremental costs are those that occur as the program continues; *sunk costs* are those that have already been expended. Thus, the distinction is useful only for decisions about continuing or terminating a program; there are no sunk costs for a planned program.

In 1978 the General Accounting Office suggested that it might make financial sense for the Postal Service to abandon its two-year-old billion-dollar automated system for sorting packages (*Chicago Tribune*, June 14, 1978). It may seem foolish to abandon a billion-dollar system after only two years. However, the decision to continue or abandon it should be made on the basis of the cost of running the system as compared to alternative systems. The money already invested (a sunk cost) is irrelevant to the new decision. Writing off the expensive system may be a big waste; however, it is cheaper than continuing to lose even more money. The GAO concluded that the incremental costs of the automated package system exceeded the benefits received; the sunk costs were not considered. Such a decision reflects the popular wisdom that there comes a point at which people seek to "cut their losses" because these losses may simply grow in the future.

Recurring versus Nonrecurring Costs

Recurring costs, as the name suggests, are those that will be due at regular intervals, such as salaries, rents, and utilities. The cost of purchasing equipment is a *nonrecurring cost* if the equipment is expected to last a number of years before wearing out.

Hidden versus Obvious Costs

In estimating the costs of a new building, no one will forget to include the costs of construction; less obvious costs include furniture, custodial service, lighting, heating, and maintenance. In estimating the costs of expanding staff, salaries will certainly be considered; somewhat hidden but just as real are fringe benefits and liability insurance.

An Example

Figure 10.1 gives the budget of a small Equal Opportunity Program for minority college students. The proposal writers assumed that a small office could be found with furniture in an existing building. The writers did not include maintenance, custodial services, or insurance costs, because these would be the same regardless of what program the university decided to adopt and house in that space. Thus, the budget is for the cost of this program operating

Director (half-time)	$14,800*
Tutors (graduate student teaching assistants) 3 @ $5,200	15,600
Secretary (half-time)	7,490*
Work-study tutors 3 @ $1,400 (university contribution, 20%; state contribution, 80%)	4,200
	$42,090
Supplies	$ 1,750
Word processor/computer	2,100
File cabinets	500
Copying	800
Phone	900
	$ 6,050
*Fringe benefits @ 15%	$ 3,344
	$51,484[a]

[a]All costs are in 1988 dollars.

FIGURE 10.1   Proposed first-year budget for an Equal Opportunity Program serving 25 college students.

in the space available. Note that some costs are recurring (salaries and phone), and others are nonrecurring (word processor). To make a decision on this proposal, the college administrators must compare this budget with a similar budget from alternative programs, in light of the college's values, goals, and expected benefit from the program.

Direct versus Indirect Costs

Although the terms above—adapted from Popham (1975)—are very helpful for conceptualizing the cost involved in programs, another set of terms is also frequently employed. The distinction between direct and indirect costs is important in understanding the costs of human services (Carter and Newman, 1976). *Direct costs* are those that are incurred in providing services for specific clients. *Indirect costs* are those that cannot be associated with specific clients. For example, the time a social worker spends helping a family obtain assistance from city agencies is a factor in direct costs. The wages (including all fringe benefits) make up the direct cost of the service. The salary of the secretary in the social welfare office who makes the social workers' appointments cannot be related to specific clients. Thus, the cost of secretarial assistance, as crucial as it is in maintaining a service, is not a direct cost but an indirect cost. The facility administrator's salary, telephone bills, amount paid for custodial service, and so forth are all indirect costs. In providing a service program, both direct and indirect costs (also called *overhead*) are incurred, and both must be considered. These costs must then be related to the amount of service given.

The Necessity of Examining Costs

At times agencies supported by public funds have ignored the task of calculating costs per unit of service. Mitlying (1975–76) participated in a cost analysis of a publicly funded alcoholism treatment facility. The agency discovered that the cost (including direct and indirect costs) for each hour of service was $60. (Taking inflation into account, this figure is equivalent to about $150 in 1988 dollars.) This figure, which was more than anyone in the agency had expected, was unacceptably high. Regardless of a facility's source of funding, costs should be found and should be divided into direct and indirect costs.

The exact way specific costs are labeled is not standard (Carter and Newman, 1976); however, the distinction is necessary to permit rational decisions about the amount of charges that should be allotted to given clients. Although the college students in the minority program (see Figure 10.1) will not be billed over and above their tuition, the budget items can be divided into direct and indirect costs. Direct costs include all the tutors' time and probably part of the director's time, because he or she will certainly also be directly involved with the students. Part of the director's time, however, will be spent for indirect services, such as handling correspondence, organizing and supervising the tutors, and finding space for the tutors. Secretarial and office expenses will be indirect costs.

At this point you should have begun to appreciate the basic fact that costs must be considered in planning a program. The discussion should not suggest that estimating costs is easy. Many estimates have been grossly in error. Congress passed a bill to support kidney dialysis for people suffering kidney failure and unable to obtain a kidney transplant (Culliton, 1978). When the bill was approved in 1973, the costs were estimated to be in the low millions. In 1978 the cost was $1 billion, which was half the entire budget for the National Institute of Health. By 1983 the Federal government was paying $1.8 billion per year for dialysis (Wallis, 1983). And, in 1987 the total came to $2.4 billion (Colburn, 1987). The failure to provide an accurate estimate of costs led to an unexpectedly large cost to the taxpayer and made it impossible to implement other programs dealing with pressing health concerns such as preventive care for poor pregnant women. Not addressing such other concerns raises important ethical questions for some observers (see Moskop, 1987).

Further, more detailed presentations of cost analysis can be found in Hagedorn et al. (1976) and Carter and Newman (1976). Although the work by Hagedorn et al. is directed to community mental health center evaluators, the methods presented apply to all human service settings. In addition, this work includes estimates of the time required to carry out the analyses described. Evaluators with limited training in accounting procedures can benefit from this material.

COMPARING OUTCOMES TO COSTS

Once costs are calculated or estimated, the next step in a cost-benefit analysis is to develop an approach to estimating the benefits of a program. Benefits occur when goals are achieved. Surgeons save lives when they remove diseased appendixes. Because their patients lead normally productive lives afterward, there are considerable benefits to this and many other surgical procedures. Another example of a cost-effective program was a federal attempt to reduce the number of government forms. The commission set up to do this is reported to have saved 350 times as much money as the cost of the commission (Abelson, 1977). A number of cost-benefit analyses have shown the worth of education after high school. Sussna and Heinemann (1972) concluded that the benefits of two-year training in health services were such that the increased earnings were equivalent to putting the cost of education into a bank and obtaining 34 percent interest per year for nursing students and 21 percent interest for laboratory technician students. Clearly, education was a better investment for these students; no savings account can rival such rates of return.

The Essence of Cost-Benefit Analysis

The essential characteristics of cost-benefit analyses illustrated are in a study conducted by Schnelle et al. (1978). They sought to evaluate the effectiveness of a helicopter patrol in reducing burglary in a high-crime area. Increasing the number of patrol cars seems to do little to reduce crime (Kelling et al., 1976; Schnelle et al., 1977). However, there was some speculation that a helicopter patrol with its inherently better surveillance ability might reduce burglary. In the city in which the project was done, most burglaries occur during daylight hours and are perpetrated by local youths. Because helicopters can repeatedly observe large areas (in daylight hours), the patrol was expected to frighten off potential burglars.

Schnelle et al. used a strategy developed in the field of behavior modification to test the effectiveness of the helicopter. The experiment was divided into five parts. First, a base-line rate of burglaries in the target area was obtained during 21 days. Second, the helicopter was introduced for 12 days. The pilot was shown the area and asked to fly low enough to be able to observe suspicious activity. Third, for 16 days the helicopter did not patrol. Fourth, the helicopter was used again for 12 days. Last, there was no helicopter patrol for 18 days. Regular car patrol continued during all phases of the experiment.

The burglary rate during the 9 A.M. to 5 P.M. shift was the outcome measure of interest. The experiment was a success in the sense that an average of 1.02 burglaries per day were committed during the periods of regular car patrols (base line) in contrast to an average of only 0.33 burglaries per day when the helicopter patrol was on duty. However, these data alone did not form a complete evaluation, because the helicopter patrol added to the police department's costs.

Because the helicopter pilot and hangar were already part of the police department, these costs were not considered. However, the costs of additional fuel and maintenance were calculated. These costs were compared to the benefits of lowered amount of goods stolen. Figure 10.2 summarizes the calculation of the benefit-to-cost ratio. The cost of using the helicopter was easy to calculate. The cost of the burglaries was estimated from insurance company material. The fact that the benefit-to-cost ratio was 2.6 indicates that

	TOTAL	PER DAY
Cost of the program (24 days)	$ 3,032	$126
Cost of the burglaries during no-helicopter patrol periods (55 days)	$27,171	$494
Cost of burglaries during helicopter patrol periods (24 days)*	$ 3,853	$161
Benefits (for 24-day program)	$ 8,004	$333
Benefit/cost ratio	-------	$333/126 = 2.6

*The burglary cost figures were not supplied by Schnelle et al. (1978); however, these costs could be approximated from their report.

FIGURE 10.2 The calculation of the benefit-to-cost ratio of the helicopter patrol.

the program was a success. The helicopter patrol did lower crime in an efficient manner.

Several costs and benefits were not considered. Citizen's feelings of security may have increased (a benefit), but feelings of decreased privacy and irritation at the increased noise may also have occurred (costs). The benefit of lowered court costs, which occurred because it was necessary to try fewer burglars, was ignored. Also ignored was the fact that fewer burglaries permitted police officers to devote more time to other crime-preventive and investigative work (an additional benefit). Ignoring these benefits and the psychic costs of loss of privacy and of increased noise illustrates an important principle for applied social scientists. Evaluators seek to answer practical questions directed to them in an efficient manner; once the essential question can be answered, they collect no more data. For Schnelle et al., the essential question could be answered using costs and benefits that were fairly easy to estimate. Therefore, the evaluators did not concern themselves with the very difficult task of pricing additional benefits. If they had, the benefit-to-cost ratio would have simply increased above 2.6. If the ratio had been less, say 1.1, then the additional benefits of reducing court use and freeing police time might have been priced. Because it was not necessary, it was not done. A theoretical social scientist may want to estimate the "real" benefit-to-cost ratio; an applied social scientist requires only enough information on which to base a practical decision. Case Study 4 also illustrates the use of estimates to determine benefits of a program and the practice of selecting benefits to "price" outcomes without trying to specify all the benefits.

Although Schnelle et al. chose to use costs and benefits that were fairly easy to convert into dollars, many cost-benefit studies have found it necessary to quantify costs and benefits that are hard to price. The Army Corps of Engineers has routinely used the recreational value of water projects to help justify construction plans. The dollar benefits of human services are even harder to estimate. If a service prolongs the working life of an employee, some benefits can be calculated. If a job-training program permits some to leave welfare rolls, certain savings can be quantified. But what is the dollar value of better mental health? Of reduced anxiety among cancer patients? Of a 5 percent gain on a standardized reading achievement test for sixth graders? Of increased levels of art and music appreciation? Clearly, these outcomes are worthwhile. But how much they are worth is subject to considerable disagreement.

Military planning provides an even more striking example of the limitations of cost-benefit analysis. How are the "benefits" of a bomb to be calculated? Clearly, the bomb destroys. Benefits, if there are any, accrue to a nation if a war is won or averted. However, the net outcome of a war is negative, not positive, even for the victor. Instead of calculating cost-benefit ratios, one can ask how *effective* the bomb is in fulfilling its purpose. In oversimplified terms, the bigger the hole, the more effective the bomb. Thus, the concept of *cost effectiveness* was developed to use in situations in which the dollar values of benefits are very difficult to quantify.

The Essence of Cost-Effectiveness Analysis

A bomb could be rated in terms of the size of the hole it makes (expressed in cubic yards) divided by the dollar cost of the bomb. There is no way of deciding if the cubic yard/$ figure is good or bad until it is compared to the effectiveness-to-cost ratio of a second bomb. By comparing the two ratios, military planners can choose the bomb providing the bigger bang per buck. This same approach can be utilized in human service agencies whenever improvement can be quantified. If two or more programs effect an improvement on the same variable, the amount of improvement per dollar can be found for each program, and a cost-effectiveness evaluation can be made.

Cost-effectiveness analyses are also important in measuring the productivity of businesses. For example, a plant in Ohio that produces titanium routinely calculates three indexes based on effectiveness divided by cost measures. First, pounds of titanium produced divided by number of employees is calculated; second, pounds of titanium are divided by the total assets of the plant; and third, since energy use is so high in the production of titanium, pounds of titanium are divided by the BTU's used in production (Day, 1981). The second of these three indexes is the traditional measure of cost effectiveness; however, the other two indexes help the managers find the aspect of the plant's operation that is responsible for good or poor performance. This example illustrates that evaluators can adapt cost analyses to the needs of the particular organization in which they are working. The measures of outcome and costs will differ from organization to organization.

Peterson (1986) describes three approaches to using cost-effectiveness analysis in planning decisions. First, if the amount to be spent is set, an analysis can be done to see which alternative will achieve the best outcome for a specific cost. For example, one could seek to reduce highway fatalities by increasing the number of police patrols, by increasing seat-belt use through education, or by eliminating some dangerous highway curves in rural highways. Second, the costs of achieving a specified outcome can be compared for various possible approaches to a program. A school district wishing to raise the average percentage of students in class from 87 percent to 92 percent could consider a number of approaches ranging from lotteries for students with perfect monthly attendance records through a redesigned curriculum. Third, using a specified approach to a problem, the cost effectiveness of different levels of one type of program could be found. A city council, for example, might ask to what degree coronary deaths would be reduced by spending one half, one, or two million dollars on paramedics and intensive care ambulances.

When Outcome Cannot Be Quantified

The size of a bomb crater can be measured directly. Quantification of improved mental health is hard, but measuring improvements in perceived environmental quality is even harder. Measuring increased art appreciation may be impossible. In these instances another approach can be used. Methods that incorporate the subjective value of the decision maker, funders, and the consumers of a program are called *cost-utility analyses* (Levin, 1975). In this case the subjective values and the costs of two or more programs are compared, and the one appearing to offer the most utility per dollar is chosen. The proposed Equal Opportunity Program (Figure 10.1) would be compared to other proposals in terms of subjective utility, not in terms of quantified effectiveness or benefits. The MAUT procedure described in Chapter 5 is an example of using a subjective utility analysis to choose among alternative programs.

SOME DETAILS OF COST ANALYSIS

There are a number of issues to examine when conducting an analysis of costs, which can affect the conclusions of cost-benefit and cost-effectiveness analyses. Although some of these points are details subordinate to the major ideas presented above, these issues are extremely important, both when preparing cost analyses and when evaluating them. We present these points as issues of concern because there are no widely accepted formulas for a cost analysis in the human services.

Units of Analysis

The units of the cost analysis should be compatible with the goals of the program. Binner (1977) illustrated how use of two different units can make quite a difference in a cost analysis of inpatient psychiatric treatment. The most obvious approach might seem to be to calculate the cost per day. If there are an average of 100 patients in a facility and the cost for the year is $912,500, then the cost per patient per day would be $25. Is cost per patient-day a reasonable unit? The way to answer that question is to reflect on the reasons for institutionalizing a person. The goal is to aid patients to function in society, not simply to house them. A better unit than cost per patient-day would be cost per healthy, discharged patient. (For the moment, assume that each patient discharged is able to adjust to society and to earn a living.) The use of cost per patient-day actually encourages a departure from the true goals of institutionalization. Whatever can be done to lower the cost per patient-day will be encouraged, using this unit of analysis. The term *warehouse for people* was coined to describe the practice of developing the cheapest means of keeping people alive. On the other hand, the unit cost per patient discharged alive encourages a return to the real reason for institutionalization.

Note how the unit chosen affects the conclusion drawn from the cost-effectiveness analysis in the following example. Binner cites a state hospital that could house and feed a patient in 1901 for $2.38 per day (corrected to 1974 dollars). The cost per discharged patient in 1901 was $10,309 (1974 dollars). Comparing this hospital to 1974 averages, we find evidence for a 1300 percent increase as well as evidence for a 50 percent decrease in costs since 1901. Can both figures be true? Yes. In 1974 the average cost per patient-day was $30.86 (the 1300 percent increase), and the average cost per alive discharged patient was $5,513 (the 50 percent decrease). Should we be heartened by the decrease or alarmed at the increase? If the goals of the treatment focus on restoring patients to the community, then we should be heartened by the decrease. A comparison of these figures reflects the fact that restoring the ability to live in society requires therapy, community contacts, and medical treatment, among other things. Providing these services raises cost per day but lowers cost per discharged patient; patients are now more likely to return to the community than they were in 1901.

In recent years some nursing homes for disabled elderly people have been the subject of intense criticism for inadequate treatment—poor food, little medical care, few recreational opportunities, limited privacy. Such conditions would be encouraged by the cost per patient-day approach. Although it would not be easy to implement, relating a cost analysis of such facilities to measures of the patients' level of functioning could encourage the facility to help the patients stay healthy and alert (see Kane and Kane, 1978).

There is another complication related to the units of analysis used. At times the meaning of improvement on the variable of interest may change, depending on what level of the variable is involved. For example, it is not necessarily true that an improvement in work skills that leads to an increase in income from $0 to $6,000 is equivalent to an increase from $2,000 to $8,000. The amount of change of motivation and upgrading of skills related to these numerically equal benefits are probably markedly unequal: changing a person from being unable to hold a job to being able to hold one is probably harder than simply improving a person's skills.

Alternative Uses of Investments

A mistake often made by people informally considering costs is to ignore the component of costs called *opportunity costs*. The most expensive aspect of college education is not the tuition, even at the most exclusive private schools. The cost of tuition is less than the income students could have earned had they been employed rather than attending college. This lost opportunity is a cost of college and should be considered by potential students. Ignoring the cultural, intellectual, and social growth available to college students, people evaluating a college education on the basis of cost alone will ask whether the salaries available to college graduates sufficiently exceed those of high school graduates to allow the college graduate to make up for this initial deficit of four years' wages. Economists interested in education report that college education in simple dollar terms is more cost effective than simply going to work after high school, although the advantage has eroded in recent years (Freeman and Hollomon, 1975). Further, if people value the conceptual, intellectual, and cultural values of college, these hard-to-quantify benefits add to the advantage of a college education.

A person's time is part of the cost of all human services. However, the time an individual spends waiting for a human service is often not considered a cost of the service, although it should be. Medical care that is ostensibly free is not free if waits of three or more hours are required to obtain it. If people in need of medical care do not have any employment, perhaps the oversight is understandable. However, even then, time spent waiting cannot be devoted to rearing children, preparing meals, or looking for work.

Future Costs and Benefits

A sophisticated cost analysis will include benefits occurring at times in the future. Successful rehabilitation or therapy will enable a person to live with less need of special services in future years. Improvements in work skills, psychological adjustment, and physical health may well have benefits for the children of people served or cared for. The worth of these long-term benefits is, not surprisingly, hard to estimate. Viewing the human services recipient as a member of a family system and a community system is a way to become sensitive to possible secondary benefits of human services. What are some of these secondary benefits? Drug rehabilitation should lead to less crime, because addicts frequently support their habit through theft. If crime is reduced, commercial activity may be encouraged since people might now be more willing to venture into the central business district. Also, the lower the crime rate, the lower the amount the community needs to spend on detection, prosecution, and punishment of criminals.

The noneconomist faces a problem in comparing programs requiring funds and providing benefits at different times in the lives of the program. This is true because the money needed and the benefits available in the future are worth less than the same amount of money and benefits available now. This principle makes perfectly good sense when you ask yourself whether you would rather have $100 now or in 12 months. Ignoring for the moment our normal preference for instant gratification, it makes economic sense to have the money now, because if it is put into a savings account, it will be worth $106 in 12 months. On the basis of this observation, some have criticized state lotteries that spread out $1 million grand prizes over 20 years. The state has the use of some of the money during those years, not the prize winner, so in a real sense, the prize is not worth as much as the promotions promise. The present value of the twentieth $50,000 payment of the million-dollar grand prize is only $10,730, because that sum invested in a readily available 8 percent savings account will yield $50,000 after 20 years. There are some tax advantages in spreading out the awards; however, the basic point remains true.

This text cannot go into the methods used to calculate the current worth of a benefit projected to occur in 20 years. The point to remember is that the cost of programs should include what could be obtained by an alternate use of resources. For example, is it worth spending $100 now in order to receive a benefit of $200 ten years from now? The answer depends entirely on the assumed rate of return for an alternative use of the $100. The amount one could obtain from this other use is the *opportunity cost*. If the rate of return for the latter were 3 percent, the answer to the question above would be yes, because $100 invested at 3 percent will be worth only $131 in ten years. The opportunity cost is less than the benefit. If the rate of return were 8 percent or more, the answer would be no, because $100 invested for ten years at 8 percent will equal $216. It would be better to put the money into an 8 percent savings account than to seek the $200 future benefit.

The interest rate assumed should be realistic. Critics of the cost-benefit analyses provided by the proponents of large-scale water resource projects have asserted that the rates of interest selected are unrealistically low (for example, Hanke and Walker, 1974). If so, the cost of the project would appear lower and the benefit-to-cost ratio would appear higher than they really are. For example, the opportunity cost of a $200 benefit that is ten years away would be $134 if an interest rate of 3 percent were chosen, but it would be $179 if a more realistic figure, 6 percent, were used. It is probably obvious to the reader that fluctuating interest rates greatly complicate these analyses.

Who Bears the Costs and Who Reaps the Benefits?

Many programs are sponsored and paid for by people who do not obtain the benefits. Clearly, the costs of primary education are borne by the whole community, while only the teachers and the children (and their parents) benefit. The community indirectly benefits by gaining a reputation for good schools that attract and hold residents. The value of homes remains high, and good employees are not likely to move away. A tax increase referendum is more likely to pass if residents believe they benefit at least indirectly by having good schools in their community. Public transit systems are often criticized by people who are required to support the systems through taxes but who never expect to benefit personally from them.

Another example of this problem is seen in the development of outpatient surgery procedures. Hospitals are under intense pressure from insurance companies and from the federal and state governments to lower costs or at least limit increases in costs. One response to this pressure is to develop outpatient surgical centers. A patient needing relatively minor surgery does not stay in the hospital overnight. The cost of providing the surgery is markedly lower than traditional practices. However, neither the patient nor the hospital benefits from these savings—Medicare, Medicaid, and insurance companies experience the savings (Evans and Robinson, 1980). In the long run, it was hoped that society, in general, would pay lower costs for medical insurance when the costs of surgery were minimized. However, recent evidence suggests that surgeons have raised their fees for surgery done outside of hospitals (Millenson, 1987). This negative side effect was not an outcome that planners had in mind when outpatient surgery clinics were developed.

Evaluators conducting a thorough analysis of costs and benefits will point out the problems in program implementation that will be associated with a discrepancy between who benefits and who pays the costs of programs. Whenever the benefits are enjoyed by people other than those paying for the program, special problems may exist in mobilizing political action to initiate and to maintain the program. However, it is important to note that people voluntarily enter into many contracts from which they hope to receive no dollar benefits. All insurance policies—home, life, health, and car—are designed to provide fairly large amounts of money to those in need after an illness or accident. Clearly, the costs are borne by the majority, who benefit little in terms of dollars. The year-to-year benefit is primarily the peace of mind created by knowing that large expenses will be covered if a misfortune occurs. Most policy holders are satisfied with such assurances and would be delighted never to need to receive a tangible financial benefit from their insurance.

Using Cost-Benefit and Cost-Effectiveness Analyses

If the benefits of a program can be priced in dollars and a cost-benefit analysis can be done, one approach to program selection is simply to adopt the program having the largest benefit-to-cost ratio. Often, of course, outcomes cannot be valued in dollars. Furthermore, Nagel (1983a) has shown that many decisions involve far more than simply giving or withholding support for a program. Because governmental agencies have predetermined budgets, agency managers are not free to choose a program with the highest benefit-to-cost ratio if the cost exceeds the allotted budget. Instead, managers ideally should seek to obtain the most benefits for the resources they have available. Given the costs of the various programs and the size of the budget, the best program to select might not be the most efficient, *when considered one at a time.*

If the benefits are expressed in different units, stakeholders and managers can still use analyses relating costs with outcomes to select which programs should be maintained or expanded. The crucial technique is to list all possible courses of action and compare them to each other, taking two at a time. For example, suppose that a program to train 3,000 unskilled workers per year to fill maintenance positions could be funded for 10 years for the same cost as a road improvement project that is expected to save 5 accidental deaths and 20 injuries during the same 10 years. If—according to past research and evaluations—both outcomes are equally likely, which course of action should a state legislature chose? This selection can be made without estimating the value of jobs or averted deaths and injuries; however, the selection will reflect the relative importance of the two outcomes in the eyes of the majority of the legislators. Next, a third program could be compared to this selection. Thus, even when cost-benefit or cost-effectiveness analyses cannot be done, relating costs to outcomes will illuminate the debate and allow the various stakeholders to see the options more clearly than they could without such analyses. At a time when limitations on the financial resources of governments and other organizations are crucially important, analyses that help decision makers understand the impact of their decisions seem worthwhile.

Major Criticisms of Cost Analyses

There are a number of major criticisms of both cost-benefit and cost-effectiveness analyses. Users of these approaches will profit by being aware of these criticisms, which point up limitations of these useful methods.

Psychic benefits.   As mentioned above, improved emotional health is hard enough to price. But what about clean air? Clean streams? An unlittered park? Access to quiet places to walk? One approach would be to study what people are willing to pay to escape environmental deterioration. Another approach is to calculate what must be paid to induce workers to accept employment in dirty, dusty, noisy, or dangerous occupations. These approaches are indirect and probably will never be completely satisfactory.

The value of lives.   A second major criticism concerns the approach to valuing lives. Strictly economic analyses based on current or projected earning power place low values on the lives of children and the aged. The present economic value of young children is very low, because children cannot earn anything until 10 to 15 years into the future. However, people clearly do not act as though children are to be evaluated on the basis of economic value. Nor are our moral values determined by dollar values. Considerable resources are expended on all children, and especially sick children. Very ill, premature babies may be hospitalized for months at a cost in the tens of thousands of dollars. In a somewhat similar way, economic analysis fails as an approach to determine the value of the elderly. Those who are unlikely to have a job in the future would have a negative dollar value. Because elderly people also have emotional value to others, this economic value does not reflect the feelings or predict the behavior of others toward the elderly.

An alternative approach to estimating the value of lives is an indirect way, similar to the approaches suggested for pricing the benefits of clean air. An examination of court settlements involving accidental deaths and the amount of money the community will spend to save lives will suggest the dollar values of lives. Abt (1977) reported that in spite of widely discussed large court-determined damage awards, American society placed a $10,000 to $20,000 price tag on a year of human life.

Degrades life.   Critics respond to an observation such as Abt's by saying that cost-benefit analysis degrades life by putting a price tag on the priceless: no amount of money can be worth a life, and attempts to put a price on life are inhumane. Social scientists often respond by saying—as Abt did—that reporting what people do does not endorse what is reported. The reporter's views, whatever they are, did not cause the courts' decisions. If people believe that society's actions are wrong and that lives should be worth more, then those feelings will become part of the political process.

The amount that is spent on saving lives can vary markedly even within one country. Okrent (1980) cites reports that the French spent $30,000 per life saved through highway accident prevention programs, but $1 million per life saved through airplane accident prevention. Expenditures in Great Britain to save lives varied from $10,000 for agricultural workers through $20 million per life for high-rise apartment occupants. Cost-effectiveness analyses are tools to demonstrate these inequities. What is done about the inequities is part of the political process.

Requires many assumptions and estimates. Whenever cost-benefit analyses are conducted, the analyst must make assumptions about future conditions and must approximate some costs and the values of benefits. Since there is a great latitude in making these assumptions and approximations, it is not surprising that cost-benefit and cost-effectiveness analyses can be used to support predetermined opinions (Joglekar, 1984). Being open about assumptions and giving reasons behind approximations enables others to assess the validity of the analyses. Furthermore, adopting different assumptions may permit one to bracket the most likely ratios. Many evaluators would argue that having a range of cost-benefit ratios would be preferable to not having any comparisons of the cost of the program with its benefits.

Not complete. Sometimes cost analyses are criticized for being incomplete. This criticism was implied in material already discussed. All benefits cannot be properly priced. Those that cannot should not be assigned an arbitrary or purely speculative price (Levin, 1975). Meaningless values lead to disguised error. Such errors are bigger problems than those caused by incomplete pricing. This incompleteness need not be viewed as a failure of the approach. Cost-benefit analyses are but one aspect of the evaluation of programs and only a portion of the information evaluated by managers and community representatives.

Nevertheless, costs must be considered; regardless of our values, there are limitations on our resources. Communities must make choices among the various human services that could be offered. Some services will be offered regardless of what a cost-benefit analysis would show: the value assigned to the life of a child transcends the child's economic value. However, many other decisions and choices may be more closely related to dollar benefits. For these decisions and choices, cost analyses will take on more importance, but they still will not be the only inputs considered. And this is as it should be.

SUMMARY

Cost accounting is a necessary aspect of operating an organization in either the public or the private sectors. Efficient use of resources requires that costs be categorized as an aid to management and as an aid to making decisions about launching, maintaining, or terminating a service or other organizational activities. The distinctions of variable versus fixed, incremental versus sunk, recurring versus one-time, hidden versus obvious, and direct versus indirect costs all aid evaluators in conceptualizing and describing costs. Being able to measure the results of programs enables evaluators to calculate cost-benefit and cost-effective indexes. To use costs in organizational and governmental decisions it is not necessary to be able to place a price on the results of programs; however, it is necessary to be able to describe the expected results of the expenditure of resources. Stakeholders can then select among the possible uses of governmental or organizational resources. The chapter also included a discussion of several potential problems in the use of costs in program evaluation: using appropriate units of analysis, recognizing opportunity costs, and distinguishing between people who benefit versus those who pay are important issues for anyone using cost-benefit or cost effectiveness in evaluation.

STUDY QUESTIONS

1. Pretend you are involved in planning a storefront legal aid program. Draw up a budget for the first year. Take educated guesses as to costs of salaries, rent, supplies, and so on. Label each entry as to whether it is a recurring, fixed, hidden, or some other type of cost. (Some costs will have more than one label.) Then group the costs into two categories—one for direct costs and one for indirect costs.

2. Compare the following two reading programs using cost-effectiveness analysis. Program A costs $6,000 and results in an average of a six-month reading level increase. Program B costs $13,000 and results in an average gain of eight-months reading achievement. Suppose Program A serves 100 children and Program B serves 300. Which of the two programs is more efficient? (Assume that the children are randomly assigned to programs.)

3. Compare cost-benefit analysis with cost-effectiveness analysis. Think of the different types of decisions that can be made and the kind of information needed to do the analyses. Summarize your comparisons in two columns.

4. The state of medical technology is such that ill or injured people can be unable to do anything—see, hear, talk, read, walk, groom, or dress—but yet be considered alive because their hearts are still beating. While the families of such patients face very large bills, they do not really have their loved one. This problem has ethical, legal, and cost implications. What would a cost-benefit approach have to say about this problem? Think about psychic costs and benefits, opportunity costs, and alternative services to other ill patients before beginning your answer.

FURTHER READING

LEVIN, H. M. 1983. *Cost-effectiveness: A primer.* Beverly Hills, Calif.: Sage.
THOMPSON, M. S. 1980. *Benefit-cost analysis for program evaluation.* Beverly Hills, Calif.: Sage.

11

Assessing the Achievement of Individualized Goals

Chapter 6 discussed methods used in administrative monitoring. Such methods are frequently quite useful in helping one to understand a program. Nevertheless, the most effective use of information gathered through monitoring procedures requires that comparison be made between the data found and some standard of effectiveness. Poister (1982) called this approach *performance monitoring*. Without standards of care or service, monitoring can find only, for example, that X units of care were given, or that one staff member sees more clients than another member. Therefore, the question of whether the amount of work done or whether the effort of any staff member is satisfactory cannot be answered using the methods described so far.

Society sets many standards. There are fairly clear and objective fire safety standards, such as: the halls of public buildings must be so many feet wide; exit doors must open out; and furniture must not be placed in exit routes. In schools a specified number of square feet must be provided for children of various grade levels. In counseling settings there may be standards about how many hours of direct service each counselor must offer per week.

More important than standards describing physical structures or effort expended, however, are standards of quality of outcome. This would be especially true in human service settings; professionals seldom really know what does and what does not reliably work to help people learn, to help them improve emotional health, to help them hold a job, and so on. This chapter focuses on methods that assess the achievement of individualized goals, that is, goals that are prepared for specific individuals or for a specific category of people. This individual-focused approach to evaluation is quite different from evaluations focused on the average outcome for a group of people whether the group is a community, a class, or all people receiving therapy during some time period.

The task of evaluating success in meeting a goal would be relatively easy if the parties involved could agree on objective goals. When such agreement exists, a program can be evaluated simply by observing the group of people experiencing the program. Foxx and Azrin (1973) have described a method of toilet training based on the behaviorist principles of shaping and reward. The goal or criterion of success was the time required to train the child to use a child-sized toilet. Because the goal set for the program—one day—was so much shorter than the time most parents require, there was ready agreement with the goals of the program. For parents who have worked for months to achieve that goal, there is no need to ask whether such an outcome would indicate that the program was successful.[1] A program that far exceeds typical levels of outcome is not difficult to evaluate, especially if a wide consensus endorses the level of outcome achieved. Stanley (1982) made a similar point in a discussion of a program to aid gifted teenagers. He maintained that since very, very few fourteen- and fifteen-year-olds started college, the high college-entry rate of such students in a summer math/science program argued for its positive impact. An evaluation did not require a sophisticated design such as those described in earlier chapters.

However, few outcomes are as striking as those in Foxx and Azrin's and Stanley's programs, and seldom is consensus so easily achieved. Outcomes are not striking because longstanding behavior is hard to change; change is usually small, even after an effective program (Rossi, 1972). Consensus on ideal outcomes is not likely—people with different viewpoints desire different outcomes. In Chapter 3 the different expectations of the client, the therapist, and the community were described for the case of psychotherapy. Ideal outcomes are also hard to specify because people enter program with different levels of abilities and, therefore, are likely to complete programs at different levels.

In order to assess the degree to which programs achieve their goals, methods are needed that help the evaluator develop standards and assess whether those standards or objectives were achieved. This chapter focuses on several techniques used when there is a need to evaluate the degree to which the service approaches predetermined standards of effective work. There are three general methods illustrated: Goal Attainment Scaling, management by objectives, and peer review. These evaluation techniques have been found useful in a variety of settings, and they illustrate a number of important principles.

DEVELOPING OUTCOME GOALS

There are a number of reasons why it is extremely important to have performance goals for human services. In the first place, specifying a goal forces people to become more realistic in their aims. It is very easy to set ambitious

---

[1]For those new parents among the readers, Foxx and Azrin did succeed. The mean time required to toilet train the children was 3.9 hours.

but vague goals that are seldom achieved by anyone (House et al., 1978). Often, in perhaps a sincere attempt to persuade decision makers, people describe what *could* be achieved by someone accepting counseling, therapy, job training, or some other human service. When the therapy or training is over and these very optimistic goals have not been achieved, it is fairly easy to rationalize why these goals were not met. It is important to be optimistic, but it is also important to be realistic. Spelling out the specific goals to be achieved is a discipline that helps human service professionals look very carefully and critically at their plans.

A second reason why specified goals are important is that it is hard to know just when a human service should stop. When helping a person learn social skills, write more effectively, or develop marketable job skills, it is possible to see additional room for further improvement, regardless of positive changes that have occurred. Having specific goals prepared ahead of time makes it easier to decide when the service can end.

Third, when goals are specified, the client, other staff members, and third parties such as insurance companies or employers can participate in setting and evaluating the achievement of goals and human services. Psychotherapists, for example, often have been criticized for having private goals and for being the only judge of whether those goals were achieved. Frequently these criticisms are valid. Preparing specific goals and discussing them with the client, with other staff members, and at certain times with employers ensures that many individuals participate in this process.

A fourth reason to set specific goals is that clear goals are in themselves motivating. People work more efficiently when they know what is expected of them. Industrial psychologists have found that difficult but specific goals lead to better performance than do nonspecific goals (such as "Do the best you can"), easy goals, or no goals at all (Locke, 1968; Yukl and Latham, 1978). McCarthy (1978) used goals to reduce carelessness in a textile plant. Dicken (1978) writes that goal setting is a motivator for patients recovering from serious illnesses. Burns (1977) found that setting goals was effective in improving the performance of school principals. Most workers and students are happier, more productive, and more satisfied when they know what is expected of them. Realistic but challenging goals can provide human service personnel with considerable help in their work.

Finally, goals are important because managers need to monitor performance. Lohr et al. (1980) comment on the widely differing levels of quality of care provided by physicians, even when the procedures involve elementary medical care. Moeller (1982) makes a similar observation, blaming poor performance on lapses of attention, carelessness, and poor follow-through—not on lack of knowledge.

Problems in Setting Performance Goals

There are certainly many problems in setting goals for any human service facility. One of the major problems students raise when goal setting is first described to them is: what is to keep people from setting very low goals, therefore guaranteeing that they will always achieve and often exceed those goals? If the mere achievement of goals was all that was important, this would be a damning criticism of this approach to program evaluation. However, just as athletes cannot set unrealistic goals that they can easily achieve, neither can human service care givers. In both cases other people are involved in evaluating the validity of the goals. Counselors whose only goal is to prevent clients from committing suicide would probably achieve that goal with more than 99.9 percent of their clients; if, however, therapists must share these goals with other staff members and with the client, then this very minimal goal will be challenged and rejected as meaningless for the vast majority of clients seeking counseling. It is likely that if clients and other staff members share in the development of human service goals, a balance will be found between the ambition to achieve overly challenging goals and the temptation to set easy-to-achieve goals.

A second problem that people raise when they first consider explicit goal setting is that it renders the care giver's job harder to do. Very often in health care settings, if therapists or nurses are asked what their goals are, they usually say to provide good medical care so that people can get better. Colleges set goals such as training educated and cultured men and women. Such goals cannot be challenged. However, they are so general that it is impossible to know to what extent the goal is ever achieved. Setting explicit goals will make the care giver's job somewhat harder. However, if human service agencies hope to be perceived as helpful and expect to be paid for their efforts, they will have to show that they are planning services or curricula carefully, that they usually achieve what they expect, and finally that what they expect is accepted as worthwhile by patients, trainees, clients, and the institutions or individuals paying for the service.

Finally, goals are also very hard to specify when program planners and staff members have not developed an impact model. When planners are not clear on why a given service is expected to change behavior, it is very hard to list what level of improvement is likely. In contrast, using behavior theory and their experience working with children, Foxx and Azrin (1973) were able to predict that their training approach would lead toddlers to learn to use toilets in less than one day of training. Given the complexity of counseling, education, and medical care it is hard to fault staff members when they do not have a complete impact model and are unable to specify the level of expected program success in quantitative terms. In such cases, the evaluation methods described in Chapters 7, 8, and 9 are to be preferred over the methods described in the current chapter.

The Approaches to Be Presented

This text will explicitly discuss two approaches to goal construction. One of these approaches is that developed by Kiresuk, called Goal Attainment Scaling (Lund and Kiresuk, 1979; Kiresuk and Sherman, 1968). The second approach discussed is called *management by objectives* (McConkey, 1983). Goal Attainment Scaling (GAS) and management by objectives (MBO) are actually quite similar; however, the person whose behavior is described in the goals is different for the two approaches. MBO concentrates on the manager's behavior, whereas GAS concentrates on the behavior of a client of a human service facility. There are other forms of goal setting for clients, patients, and managers. GAS and MBO, however, are widely used and well known and are good illustrations of the value of an individualized goal-setting approach to evaluation. Finally, peer review, a method of monitoring quality of work popular in health care settings, will be described.

INDIVIDUAL TREATMENT GOALS

Constructing individual treatment goals is important as a discipline, as an evaluation strategy, and as a means of encouraging communication between client and therapist. Explicitly recording goals requires much more discipline and thought from the therapist than simply saying, "We'll do the best we can." As an evaluation strategy, the preparation of explicit goals is important because the quality of intended care and actual care can then be compared among various approaches or organizations. Finally, sensitive care givers realize that their goals may not be the same as those held by the client. For example, a couple seeking marital counseling may, by chance, select a counselor who concludes that divorce is the only option and directs the counseling toward having the couple accept divorce and carry it out as smoothly as possible. Another couple with the same level of difficulties may select a counselor, just by chance, whose goal is to avoid a divorce at all costs. It seems important that clients and therapists discuss goals ahead of time so that all concerned understand each other's assumptions. Communication is also to be encouraged between client and therapist so that time is not wasted on minor problems or on repeatedly following the whims of client or therapist while forgetting the major problems.

What is required in the construction of individual outcome goals? First, goals must be explicit, and they must be recorded. Second, they must be realistic yet ambitious. The balance between realism and ambition is likely to be achieved when the goals are constructed in cooperation with the client and in consultation with other staff members. Third, the goals must be reviewed; as therapy progresses, the client may become dissatisfied with the original goals and wish to revise them. On the other hand, the client may become satisfied in having achieved the goals and desire to end therapy. Or the client may realize that those goals have been achieved and may wish to construct new goals that would have seemed overly ambitious when therapy began.

Goal Attainment Scaling

Goal Attainment Scaling goes beyond what has been discussed in the preceding paragraphs: it permits measurement of the *degree* of attainment of the outcomes desired, regardless of the unique needs of an individual client. Making such measurements requires some ingenuity, because human service goals are often difficult to quantify. However, obtaining a quantified index of success is an advantage, since comparisons among treatments and institutions then become possible.

In selecting the goals for a therapy relationship, the initial discussion with clients must center on why they have requested therapy and what they would like to get out of it. Therapists will at the same time discuss what they feel can be expected and, if all goes well, what might be possible. In the initial one or two interviews, clients and therapists should be able to agree on some outcome goals for the therapy.

It is possible that the therapist may have some additional goals that would be important for a client to achieve but that the client would not be prepared to accept as legitimate goals during the early stages of counseling. One can easily imagine a psychotherapist being struck by the abrasiveness or the manipulating manner of a new client. Few people enter therapy because they are dissatisfied with their own abrasiveness or manipulative approach to social relations. It may be possible as counseling progresses that clients might begin to sense that some of their own characteristics are involved in the problems that brought them to counseling. At that time they may wish to include it as a goal in their therapy. Thus, there is a place for goals that the therapist may not wish to share immediately with the client. However, having made this point, the reader considering the use of GAS should remember that GAS goals must be shared to obtain the method's full usefulness.

After the goals have been stated and recorded, GAS requires that each goal be weighted by its relative importance. In general, the client is to cooperate with the therapist in rating the importance of these goals. One of the easier procedures to use in rating the importance is to assign some arbitrary value to the least important goal. A value of 10 is easy to work with. The therapist and client must then decide how much more important the next goal is. Perhaps that goal would have a weight or value of 20 because they agreed it was twice as important as the least important goal. In this way numerical values can be applied to the goals that therapist and client agree are central to a therapeutic relationship. (This weighting process is identical to that described for use with the MAUT model in Chapter 5.)

An Example of the Use of GAS

If a school counselor was going to begin a counseling relationship with a student in academic and disciplinary trouble, several school-related goals might be set up to guide the counseling. Perhaps the student wants to achieve higher grades, to be sent less frequently to the principal's office for discipline, and to improve his or her reading speed.

Once the dimensions have been specified, the next step is to describe what the student is expected to achieve by the end of some time period, if counseling goes normally. Then the most unfavorable and the most favorable outcomes are described. The dimensions and the descriptions are the basis

LEVEL OF OUTCOME	VALUE OF OUTCOME	SCALE 1: SCHOOL GRADES WEIGHT: 15	SCALE 2: READING SPEED WEIGHT: 10	SCALE 3: TRIPS TO PRINCIPAL WEIGHT: 20
Most unfavorable	−2	D− or F	75 wpm✓	7+
Less than expected	−1	D✓	100 wpm	4–7✓
Expected level	0	C− or C*	150 wpm*	2–3
More than expected	+1	C+ or B−	200 wpm	1*
Most favorable	+2	B or A	250+wpm	0

Check marks refer to levels at the beginning of counseling. $T = 33.53$
Asterisks refer to levels at the end of counseling. $T = 52.99$

FIGURE 11.1   Examples of a goal attainment grid using objective individualized levels of goal attainment. (Adapted from Garwick, 1973.)

of the GAS grid. For example, a D student may be expected to improve to a C level: the worst outcome would be to fail; the most favorable outcome would be to obtain B's and A's. In terms of improving reading speed, the worst outcome would be to stay the same, since it seems unlikely that reading speed would drop during the following several months. On the basis of standard test scores, the counselor feels that the student could double his or her reading speed if real effort were expended. Finally, suppose that the student was being sent to the principal's office an average of six times a month when counseling began. The worst outcome would be even more discipline problems; the most favorable outcome would be no discipline problems. These scales and descriptions are shown in Figure 11.1.

The values recorded to the right of the various outcome levels are equivalent to z-scores.[2] The expected outcome is valued at 0 because the mean of a set of numbers has a z-score of 0. The most favorable outcome is expected to occur only 5 times out of 100, so it has a z-score of 2. Finally, the least favorable outcome, also expected 5 times out of 100, is valued at −2. The two less extreme outcomes are assigned z-scores of +1 and −1.

To take full advantage of the method would require assigning importance weights to the three scales. If we assume that the student was in danger of being expelled for behavioral problems, scale 3 would be weighted most heavily, and reading speed would be least important. The counselor assigned reading speed a weight of 10. Grades were felt to be 50 percent more important, so scale 2 was weighted 15. Finally, fewer trips to the principal was weighted 20. These weights do not add up to any set value, since only their relative values are important.

[2]Standard scores such as z-scores are described in any statistics textbook.

The beginning level of the student is checked on the grid. After counseling, an asterisk was added to record what the student achieved during counseling. Numerical values can be calculated using the weights and the scale attainment levels associated with each level of outcome. The formula given by Kiresuk to calculate a standard (T) score analogous to the standard scores on personality tests is

$$T = 50 + \frac{10\Sigma\,w_i\,x_i}{\sqrt{(1 - \rho)\Sigma w_i^2 + \rho(\Sigma w_i)^2}}$$

In the formula, w_i is the weight assigned to the scales, x_i is the attainment levels on the scales, and ρ refers to the average scale intercorrelation, which is assumed to be 0.30. For our hypothetical student, the initial value of T was found by substituting the attainment levels before counseling as follows:

$$T = 50 + \frac{10[15(-1) + 10(-2) + 20(-1)]}{\sqrt{(1 - .30)(15^2 + 10^2 + 20^2) + .30(15 + 10 + 20)^2}}$$

Carrying out the calculations, we find that the student began at a level of 33.53.

If the student remains in counseling and tries to adjust more successfully to school, the student is expected to improve to 50. Any better achievement will result in a score above 50. Assume that the asterisks in Figure 11.1 indicate the level of the student at the end of the school year. If the counselor calculates the goal attainment level after counseling, a value of 52.99 would be found. Thus, the student did a bit better than was expected and is functioning quite a bit better than at the start of counseling.

The use of GAS is a valuable discipline for counselors. Although calculating the T-values for a single client provides little useful information not already available from the grid itself, comparisons of outcomes among programs or types of approaches to counseling can be made if GAS is used routinely. When GAS is used, individual therapists receive their GAS results plus a summary of the overall average attainment levels of the rest of the staff. In this way therapists learn how effective they are in comparison with other therapists, without the possible embarrassment caused by general release of each therapist's average attainment level.

The question of who does the final outcome rating is critical. In the example of a junior high school student, the outcomes are objective and very easy to access. The question of outcome assessment is far more difficult when outcomes are stated in terms of less dependence or less manipulativeness. An example grid for counseling requiring such scales is given in Figure 11.2. In such situations periodic follow-up by raters other than the therapist is probably required to use GAS in order to contrast treatment types or to evaluate the competence of individual therapists.

Check whether or not the scale has been mutually negotiated between patient and CIC interviewer. SCALE ATTAINMENT LEVELS	SCALE HEADINGS AND SCALE WEIGHTS				
	Yes __ No X SCALE 1: Education (w_1=20)	Yes __ No X SCALE 2: Suicide (w_2=30)	Yes __ No X SCALE 3: Manipulation (w_3=25)	Yes X No __ SCALE 4: Drug Abuse (w_4=30)	Yes X No __ SCALE 5: Dependency on CIC (w_5=10)
a. most unfavorable treatment outcome thought likely (-2)	Patient has made no attempt to enroll in high school. ✓	Patient has committed suicide.	Patient makes rounds of community service agencies demanding medication, and refuses other forms of treatment ✓	Patient reports addiction to "hard narcotics" (heroin, morphine).	Patient has contacted CIC by telephone or in person at least seven times since his first visit.
b. less than expected success with treatment (-1)	Patient is enrolled in high school, but at time of follow-up has dropped out.	Patient has acted on at least one suicidal impulse since her first contact with the CIC, but has not succeeded. ✓	Patient no longer visits CIC with demands for medication but continues with other community agencies and still refuses other forms of treatment.	Patient has used "hard narcotics," but is not addicted, and/or uses hallucinogens (LSD, Pot) more than four times a month. ✓	Patient has contacted CIC 5-6 times since intake.
c. expected level of treatment success (0)	Patient is enrolled, and is in school at follow-up, but is attending class sporadically (misses an average of more than a third of her classes during a week).	Patient reports she has had at least four suicidal impulses since her first contact with the CIC but has not acted on any of them.	Patient no longer attempts to manipulate for drugs at community service agencies, but will not accept another form of treatment.	Patient has not used "hard narcotics" during follow-up period, and uses hallucinogens between 1-4 times a month. *	Patient has contacted CIC 3-4 times since intake.
d. more than expected success with treatment (+1)	Patient is enrolled, is in school at follow-up, and is attending classes consistently, but has no vocational goals. *		Patient accepts non-medication treatment at some community agency. *	Patient uses hallucinogens less than once a month.	
e. best anticipated success with treatment (+2)	Patient is enrolled, is in school at follow-up, is attending classes consistently, and has some vocational goal.	Patient reports she has had no suicidal impulses since her first contact with the CIC.	Patient accepts non-medication treatment, and by own report shows signs of improvement.	At time of follow-up, patient is not using any illegal drugs.	Patient has not contacted CIC since intake. *

FIGURE 11.2 An example of goal attainment scaling when outcomes are hard to quantify. The level at intake is marked with a check and yields a value of 29.4. The level at follow-up is marked with an asterisk and yields a value of 62.2. The difference between these values is the Goal Attainment Change Score of 32.8. (Reprinted with permission from T.J. Kiresuk, "Goal Attainment Scaling at a County Mental Health Service," *Evaluation*, Monograph No. 1, 1973, p. 15. Copyright 1973, The Program Evaluation Project.)

MANAGEMENT BY OBJECTIVES

One approach to management that is applied in many human service facilities is management by objectives (often abbreviated MBO) (Gerstenfeld, 1977). The approach used in MBO was first suggested in the mid-1950s by Drucker (1954) and McGregor (1960). Their approaches stressed the following three points: (1) organizational goals must be clearly established and communicated to all managers in the organization; (2) the managers of the organization are to set individual goals that conform to the intent of the organization's goals; and (3) periodic review of the degree to which managers are achieving their objectives is necessary.

This is not a book on management; therefore, we cannot go into management procedures in great detail. However, the program evaluator should have some familiarity with this well-known and widely used management technique.

The initiation of MBO requires commitment of the whole organization to the MBO approach. Top levels of management set their own goals; however, it is important to notice that in the MBO approach, all managers are involved in some way in the goal setting. Goals are not imposed on anyone but are developed jointly by managers and their supervisors.

Performance must be reviewed or, in our terms, evaluated. Managers must receive feedback and evaluation on the degree to which they are meeting their goals. Such evaluation assumes that all managers have some freedom in developing their approaches to achieving the goals of their units. If the managers had no freedom to choose how to approach meeting the goals, then one could hardly hold them accountable for the success or failure of their own unit.

In one study managers said that the most important advantage of MBO was that it improved the planning and organization of work. The second most important advantage was in helping managers understand the goals of the organization and their responsibilities in meeting those goals (Sloan and Schrieber, 1971). Moore and Staton (1981) reported similar findings with city managers who said that MBO was effective in clarifying their goals.

Like all management and all evaluation procedures, MBO has some disadvantages as well. A repeated objection to MBO concerns the amount of time consumed in completing the paperwork and in developing the goals themselves. It is likely, however, with any systematic procedure of keeping records and developing goals, that the time commitments will decrease as people become familiar with the system.

Preparing MBO Goals

The central step in developing a workable MBO plan is the statement of goals, or objectives. Such objectives must refer to observable organizational behavior and be compatible with the organization's overall objectives, regardless of the level of management preparing them. Some examples can be based on a study of alcoholism treatment for native Alaskans (Miller et al., 1975). There were a number of problems in assessing severity of alcoholism, in treatment planning, and in follow-up procedures. For example, in only 283 out of 775 cases of alcoholism did the therapist assess the severity of the problem although assessment of severity was thought to be crucial.

Objectives that could be written following the search of records include:

- The severity of the alcoholic problem of every client is to be assessed by the care giver before a treatment plan is developed.
- A review of the client's related problems must be made during intake procedures.
- Assessment of treatment effectiveness must be attempted.
- When follow-up proves that the treatment did not result in improvement, alternative treatment plans should be used.

The achievement of these goals by the staff should be strongly encouraged. Every staff member whose performance on these goals will be monitored must have participated in planning them and must know that management will be directed by these goals. A casual presentation of goals is insufficient to assure a wide understanding of them. Perhaps care givers could have the importance of these goals discussed with them individually. A minimal requirement would be that each manager discuss the importance of these goals with the staff.

Institutionalizing MBO Goals

One way to institutionalize these goals would be to develop some formal procedures that incorporate them. If these goals were incorporated into a record form that was used at all institutions, the communication of these goals would be carried out. Although it may seem that a new form is a minimal response to these clear needs, using a form that requests information about the client's condition, the planned treatment, and the timing of follow-up may be sufficient to change the care giver's behavior to meet the goals we have suggested above.

Figure 11.3 is the form that was developed by the Alaskan Native Health Board as a first step in improving care for people needing alcoholism treatment. Persons gathering intake data from new clients would be required to assess the severity of the problem by completing the form. Because the form requires a description of the plan for treatment, one cannot complete the form unless there is a plan for treatment. There is also a section of the intake form that is filled in after treatment, when follow-up is attempted. One cannot require therapists to contact all clients after treatment; however, one can require documentation of an attempt to contact the client. If care givers fill in this form completely and accurately, they will have achieved the objectives described above.

The Native Health Board also had a long-range goal in mind in developing this form. They discovered in their process evaluation that it was impossi-

SYMPTOMS – DISABILITY INDEX

INSTRUCTIONS: STAGES REFER TO FACTORS PRESENT IN LAST THREE MONTHS ONLY. CHECK APPROPRIATE BOXES. WRITE ADDITIONAL INFORMATION ON REVERSE SIDE.

FACTORS WHICH MAY INDICATE SEVERITY OF DRINKING PROBLEM		STAGE 0	STAGE 1	STAGE 2	STAGE 3	STAGE 4	STAGE 5
PHYSICAL	APPARENT INTOXICATION & ADDICTION	None	Alcohol abuse averages less than once per month	Alcohol abuse averages more than once per month	Evidence of addiction Can't go more than one day without drinking and/or DT's		
PHYSICAL	INJURIES DUE TO INTOXICATION	None	Only one alcohol related injury in the past 3 months that required medical att'n.	More than one injury in the past 3 months that required medical attention.			
PHYSICAL	PATHOLOGIC CHANGES (This section may be completed by a physician)	None	None	Preclinical target organ damage	Symptomatic target organ damage	Irreversible liver damage	Irreversible brain damage
SOCIAL	FAMILY RELATIONSHIPS	No problems related to alcohol abuse	Some quarrels related to alcohol abuse (with spouse, parents, etc.)		Breakage of family ties because of alcohol abuse (divorce, drinker leaves home, etc.)		
SOCIAL	NON-FAMILY RELATIONSHIPS	Usually does not associate with alcohol abusers		Usually associates with alcohol abusers	Only associates with alcohol abusers		
ECON.	EDUCATIONAL/ VOCATIONAL	No problems with school, job, or employability related to alcohol abuse	Some problems with school, job or employ-ability related to alcohol abuse.	Threatened with expulsion from school or loss of job because of alcohol abuse.	Out of school or unem-ployed because of alcohol abuse.		

PERSONAL DATA

NAME_____
  Last   First   Initial

Individual's Agency Number_____

Social Security Number_____

Birthdate _____ / _____ / _____ Sex: Male_____ Female_____
           month   day   year

Race: White_____   Indian_____   Other_____
       Black_____   Oriental_____ Unknown_____

Marital Status: Married_____   Widowed_____   Divorced_____
                 Single_____   Separated_____ Unknown_____

INFORMATION ABOUT THIS CONTACT

Ambulatory care ☐ or Institutional care ☐

First contact_____ Recontact_____

Appointment_____ Walk-in_____ Home Visit_____

Referral from_____

Who is seen

Individual with drinking problem_____

Family members or others (name-relationships) ·

PROBLEMS WHICH MAY CONTRIBUTE TO ALCOHOL ABUSE

	Yes	No	Plan For: Past Three Months	Today and/or Future
1. Physical Disabilities	—	—	_____	_____
2. Psychiatric Problems	—	—	_____	_____
Social Problems				
3. Vocational/Educational	—	—	_____	_____
4. Family	—	—	_____	_____
5. Housing	—	—	_____	_____
6. Legal	—	—	_____	_____
7. Financial				
8. Other (specify)	—	—	_____	_____

Physical / Psychiatric Diagnoses
_____
_____
_____

TREATMENT PLAN FOR ALCOHOL ABUSE

Counselling

		Plan For: Past Three Months	Today and/or Future
20. Individual	- Insight	_____	_____
	Supportive	_____	_____
21. Group	Insight	_____	_____
	Supportive	_____	_____
22. Family Therapy		_____	_____
23. Behavior Therapy		_____	_____
24. Alcoholics Anonymous		_____	_____
25. Counseling for family members		_____	_____
26. Other (specify)		_____	_____

Institutional Admission

	Plan For: Past Three Months	Today and/or Future
9. Sleep-off Ctr.	_____	_____
10. Halfway House	_____	_____
11. Jail	_____	_____
12. Med. Hospital	_____	_____
13. Psych. Hosp.	_____	_____
14. Nursing Home	_____	_____
15. Other (specify)	_____	_____

Medical Treatment of Alcohol Abuse

16. Antabuse	_____	_____
17. Tranquilizer	_____	_____
18. Detoxification	_____	_____
19. Other (specify)	_____	_____

FUTURE CARE

Follow-up at this Agency
1. None _____
2. or_____visits a month here
Referred to other Agencies
Names of Agencies_____

Agency_____

Signature of Therapist and Job Description_____

Today's date _____ / _____ / _____
              month   day   year

NO TREATMENT PLANNED

27. Individual refuses care	_____
28. Individuals' family refuses care for themselves	_____
29. Care deferred until next visit	_____
30. Other (specify)	_____

CASE CLOSED ON THIS VISIT

31. Planned_____ or Unplanned_____
Closure by:
32. Individual _____
33. Therapist _____   34. Both_____

FIGURE 11.3 A form to promote better treatment for alcoholism. [Reprinted with permission from E. Helmick et al., "A Monitoring and Evaluation Plan for Alcoholism Programs," *British Journal of Addictions* 70 (1975):371. Copyright 1975, Longman Group, LTD.]

ble to compare the effectiveness of any one institution with another; records of the clients' needs for treatment and the outcome of treatment were not available—or else the records were so different from one another that comparisons were impossible. The use of this standard form in all alcoholism treatment facilities in the state made possible comparisons among facilities. In addition, the use of a common form made it easier for a client to move from one facility to another. A common problem that human service givers face is the number of clients who drop out of treatment. Many clients change homes or for personal reasons wish to seek service at a different facility. The use of a common form permits the facilities to keep track of transient clients. Such long-range goals may conceivably be developed by the health board for the whole state. Of course evaluators and managers do not confuse checkmarks on a form as equivalent to quality of care. Other procedures are needed to examine the actual practices of care givers.

PEER REVIEW

The methods described so far have focused on monitoring the organization's procedures (Chapter 6) and on the success of the organization's service (GAS and MBO). However, neither approach is primarily designed to examine the skill or judgment of the care givers or managers in achieving desired outcomes. Neither approach can directly isolate inadequate work nor provide clues to guide the improvement of work. In both medical and psychotherapeutic settings, the trend is toward requiring some sort of outcome review that can document patterns of good and poor care (Drude and Nelson, 1982; Jacobs et al., 1976; Markson and Allen, 1976).

Peer review refers to any system whereby peers of care givers (physicians or psychotherapists) examine the techniques used and outcome produced in treating patients or clients. Sometimes these systems are called quality assurance, quality control, or utilization reviews. Without acceptable peer reviews, hospitals risk the loss of their accreditation.

Peer reviews can serve different purposes and can vary in their thoroughness and the degree to which they intrude into the care giver's behavior. The least thorough and least intrusive peer reviews may simply consist of a staff meeting at which therapists voluntarily describe cases and their plans for treatment. The comments of other staff members fill an educational function and serve as a way to help the care giver obtain new points of view. If the procedure is voluntary, and if the advice does not have to be followed, the reviews may be done only infrequently, and they may have limited impact on the behavior of the care giver.

Newman and Luft (1974) described how a community mental health center met the problem of unacceptably high costs for psychotherapy through a peer review process. The center's administrators did not want to develop a harsh, conflict-generating system to control costs, but they did feel costs were out of control. The most direct cause of high costs was the amount of therapy hours provided. It was decided to introduce peer review panels whose approval was necessary if therapists intended to provide tax-supported counseling for more than six sessions. To obtain such approval, the therapist was required to make a case presentation to a three-member panel justifying the longer therapy. In order to minimize the perception of coercion, the reviews were organized so as to increase the potential educational benefits of the review. Note that this approach was not threatening to the therapists, because the only information the panel obtains was provided by the therapists themselves.

How well does the system seem to work, and how well were the reviews received by the therapists? Luft (1979) reported that the review system resulted in fewer treatment sessions per patient and that clients spent fewer months as active patients of the center. The most striking effect was the reduction in the number of very long-term patients.

Many therapists report that they came to value the assistance they received from the review panels. (In fact, Luft found that that system was received far more favorably than the administration had expected.) The therapists believed that only a few patients required more therapy than they received, and a survey of patients revealed a high level of agreement between therapists and patients about improvement and about whether there was a need for additional therapy. Most patients and therapists agreed that sufficient therapy had been obtained.

Overall, the therapists felt that the review procedure has been an aid to their professional growth. Those who most frequently utilized the panels seemed to be influenced in their nonreviewed cases as well. Only a small proportion of therapists felt that the review procedure has interfered with their work.

A more thorough review procedure would require an examination of the actual content of the therapy sessions or the medical care given. Psychotherapy peer review can be based on tape recordings of counseling sessions. Experienced clinicians report that most clients do not appear to be disturbed by the tape or cassette recorder. A major difficulty with reviewing tapes is the time involved. A less desirable alternative would be to review the counselor's notes on a case. Unfortunately, a counselor's notes are subjective, and reviewing them would also require much time. There probably is no good *and* practical way to review the content of more than a small proportion of counseling sessions; however, the educational value of reviews of even some sessions may well lead to improved therapist skills.

SUMMARY

The common thread tying together the methods in this chapter is that criteria describing desirable individual outcomes of human services can be developed. Services can be evaluated by comparing the actual outcome observed with standards of good outcome. The outcome-oriented methods in this chapter differ from those in the previous chapters in that the methods presented here can be applied only when outcome is assessed on an individual basis; these methods do not require data based on group trends. Because of this individual emphasis, these methods are applicable in settings in which an individual's ideal behavior can be described. Thus, these methods are useful in counseling, rehabilitation, and medical facilities in which the client's or patient's outcome is assessed, as well as in all management settings in which the manager's achievement is of interest.

STUDY QUESTIONS

1. Construct a GAS Grid (Figure 11.1) for a college student who wants help in learning to study more effectively. Imagine a student who is not doing well in school. What are some things he or she might do differently? Make up specific goals that student could follow in trying to improve study habits.
2. Discuss the problem of maintaining confidentiality of records when peer review procedures are used in mental health settings.
3. Most of the following objectives are too vague for use in performance monitoring. Make them more objective. One objective is too ambitious. Make it more realistic.
   a. Improve the level of community mental health.
   b. Conduct in-service training workshops.
   c. Reduce the waiting time for new clients seeking care.
   d. Have all people referred to a second agency actually make contact with that second agency.
4. Answer this objection to GAS: "The method forces me to harden my treatment plans, but I think I should remain flexible. In fact, my clinical experience indicates that the flexible clinician is far more helpful than one who makes hard-and-fast plans or sets inflexible goals for therapy."
5. Among the goals that a university wished its graduates to achieve were
   a. reflection and critical judgment
   b. passion for justice
   c. enjoyment of life in its highest forms
   On the basis of what was presented in this chapter, what would a program evaluator say about these goals? How could an evaluator go about learning whether these goals were achieved?

FURTHER READING

MAGER, R. F. 1972. *Goal analysis.* Belmont, Calif.: Fearon.
McCONKEY, D. D. 1983. *How to manage by results,* 4th ed. New York: AMACON.
SECHREST, L. B. 1987. Research on quality assurance. *Professional Psychology: Research and Practice,* 18, 113–116.

12

Qualitative Evaluation of Need, Process, and Outcome

"We were just about to begin collecting data on our NSF project, but Marcia and Jose tell me that they will be leaving the graduate program at the end of the semester," Dr. Lamont complained to Dr. Montrose, the Chemistry Department chairman. "There are so many graduate students dropping out that we are in danger of losing our grant," she continued.

"Perhaps we should reevaluate our admissions decision process," Dr. Montrose suggested, "There is a university research office that might help with the job."

"I'm a little suspicious of those social science types," Dr. Lamont said, "but we need to try something."

Dr. Montrose spoke with the Graduate School Dean and together they contacted Al Gomez of the Institutional Research Office. They told Al that one-half of the new students drop out within the first two years of their graduate study. In a time of scarce resources for supporting graduate students, the faculty felt that this dropout rate was much too high. Faculty effort was wasted because just about the time students are ready to conduct their own research many leave, student assistantship money is wasted, and the students themselves experience frustration. They asked Al if his office could evaluate the procedure that they used in selecting students for admission from the large number of applicants.

Al is a recent graduate from a well-known and respected graduate research methodology program. His professors were very successful in obtaining sizable grants to evaluate federal and state welfare and education demonstration projects. Their practice was to conduct careful experiments as described in Chapter 9. Having participated as part of the evaluation team in some of these projects, Al had become proficient at designing and organizing the efforts to conduct such evaluations. His first suggestion to the department chair was that the best 100 applicants be identified using grades and Graduate Record Examination scores. These 100 would then be randomly divided into two groups of 50. Ten students from one group would be randomly chosen for admission. Ten students would be chosen from the other group of 50 using the methods the faculty had been using to select the best students (i.e., letters of recommendation and interviews). Al wanted to follow the academic success of both groups of ten in order to learn if faculty selection procedures were any more valid than using the simple numerical indexes of grades and GREs.

The faculty members were shocked by this suggestion. "Accept students randomly?" they asked. They were nearly insulting toward Al. The chairman pointed out that it would take years before anything was learned using this approach. The department and the dean wanted a report in four months. Dr. Lamont said that she always felt social science types could not be trusted with important jobs. As a back-up plan Al suggested that the records of the selection decisions of the past ten years be examined to try to detect the way the faculty admission committee had made their selections. This would be impossible, he was told, because there were no records other than who was accepted and who was rejected. The selections were made by weighting the applicants' grades, GRE scores, the strength of the letters of recommendation (with an eye on the academic standing of the person who wrote the letter), and their general feeling for the applicant after the interview. These pieces of information were discussed, but no records of the deliberations were made beyond the accept-or-reject decision.

Reporting back to the Dean, Al said that the admission procedure could not be evaluated because the faculty would not let him change the procedure to approximate valid experimental procedures nor were records available to go back to look at previous decisions. The Dean explained again how much resources, time, and money were lost due to the drop-out of graduate students. She described the loss of faculty productivity as the faculty worked with students who never became proficient at conducting research. Al repeated that he understood the need, but the admission procedure could not be evaluated. The Dean looked incredulous. "Surely, it can be evaluated!" she insisted.

The program can be evaluated, but not by using the methods described in the previous chapters. These methods do not apply because the admissions procedure is not based on a clearly defined policy, the decision rules of the admissions committee are not known by anyone, and the evaluative question itself may not be fully developed. Something different has to be done to conduct an evaluation in this setting. The strategies outlined in this chapter are necessary when working in an evaluative setting similar to that faced by Al. These methods have become more popular in recent years as evaluators have come to recognize that some programs cannot be studied using the methods developed to conduct quantitative social science research. This does not mean that the evaluation is not to be done rigorously; it does mean that it will be done quite differently from what has been described to this point.

EVALUATION SETTINGS BEST SERVED
BY QUALITATIVE EVALUATIONS

The emphasis of this text has been on traditional evaluation methods that depend on programs having identifiable goals that can be specified and measured quantitatively. Evaluators have been encouraged to develop methods to quantify the degree to which objectives have been achieved. Furthermore, the assumption has been made that with enough care the evaluator could discover if the influence of the program did or did not cause changes in the participants. Finding positive program effects after conducting a proper evaluation was assumed to suggest that the program could be implemented in a similar setting with some degree of confidence that the program would succeed again.

Experienced evaluators often find that they are asked to conduct evaluations when these assumptions cannot be made. First, in order to develop political support for a program, the goals may purposely be left vague (Cook et al., 1985). Vague goals permit different stakeholder groups to read their own goals into the program's objectives. Uncritically following the suggestions of Chapter 4 would lead the evaluator to decline to conduct the evaluation. This may not be the most advisable course of action. Vague goals have sometimes resulted in criticism about the evaluator's choice of the program outcomes to observe or the way to measure the outcomes observed. Evaluators who believed that they made careful choices among possible outcomes to observe, and that the most objective methods of measuring these outcomes were used, have been accused of stacking the deck in favor of (or against) finding positive findings. It is also true that programs favorably evaluated in one setting were not received favorably in another setting or agency.

What do these experiences mean? Are evaluations impossible? On the contrary, evaluation is possible and needed; however, the methods outlined in the last several chapters are not applicable in all settings. There are evaluation questions and settings that require a radically different form of evaluation. Proponents of qualitative evaluation methods do not assume that program goals will be stated clearly, and they recognize that totally objective measurement is extraordinarily difficult, if not theoretically impossible (Guba and Lincoln, 1981; Patton, 1980). Qualitative evaluators, furthermore, insist that programs are highly sensitive to the specific context in which they are offered; a program working in one setting may not work elsewhere. Therefore, great care must be taken to understand the setting of the program.

This chapter outlines qualitative evaluation approaches that will be helpful when the evaluation setting is very complex or when the questions addressed by the evaluator cannot be answered by evaluation approaches based on clear goals and agreed-upon quantitative measures of outcome. Evaluating the graduate admissions procedure is a situation that cannot be approached using only the methods of Chapters 7 through 9 and still meet the needs of the stakeholders. The following paragraphs describe some aspects of program situations for which qualitative evaluations are particularly useful.

Admission Procedure with Subjective Decision Rules

Vague goals. Although most university faculty members can identify a good graduate student when they see one, it is very hard to specify how to select the best potential students from the applicants. Graduate school performance is multifaceted, requiring ambition, creativity, a good memory, endurance, independence, as well as intelligence. It is not surprising that it would be hard to select the most promising applicants from a number of applicants all of whom did well as undergraduates.

Contentious, value-laden atmosphere. It would not be surprising to find that faculty members disagree over the characteristics suggesting that an applicant would develop into a good graduate student. Some faculty members on the admissions committee will depend almost totally on standard test scores, others will stress actual undergraduate performance in classes, while others will weigh letters of recommendation most heavily.

Rich program context. Graduate school performance occurs in a very complex context. Some students will not do well because they are concerned about uncertain future job prospects. Some will not be able to adapt to the degree of independent, self-initiated work required of a graduate student. Furthermore, the criteria of success of graduate students are far more complicated than those for undergraduate students who merely need to accumulate passing grades in a sufficient number of properly chosen courses. To further complicate the evaluator's job, grades cannot be easily used as a measure of successful performance since range of course grades is not very wide among the graduate students of a department.

Dissatisfaction with a Library Collection

Two additional examples may make the need for qualitative evaluative methods even more compelling. Although these examples have been prepared for this text, just as the admission procedure scenario was, the points they illustrate are not unusual. Imagine that a community library began to receive many complaints about the books that have been added to the collection during the last several years. The library board was confused about the criticisms. The board members knew that something had to be done to meet these criticisms since a referendum was about to be put to the voters in order to raise funds needed to carry out extensive and necessary remodeling. Board members were afraid that if vocal critics did not feel that their concerns were being addressed, the referendum would fail and library services would have to be severely limited. After some debate the board decided to evaluate its acquisitions department. Evaluating library functions in order to find areas for short-run improvements cannot be done using experimentation.

Complex goals and potentially conflicting goals. Should the library seek to get the best, critically acclaimed books? Or, should the bulk of the collection match the intellectual level of the community? How much should be spent on meeting the needs of school children? Is the library being asked to meet school needs that the school districts should meet?

Conflicts among stakeholders. Several church groups have complained about the moral tone of some of the novels that have been purchased in recent years. They have presented a list of "inspiring" material from little-known publishers. Junior and senior high school students have requested that more than one copy of frequently used reference material be available. Residents of a local retirement community have actually picketed the library and board meetings over the unwillingness of the acquisitions department to buy more than a minimum number of large print books which many elderly people need in order to read. And then there was the bitter letter from the music society attacking the board for letting the library purchase rock albums for the music department. "How can we satisfy everyone?," the board members asked each other.

A Political Campaign

Imagine a politician in a state-wide campaign who becomes dissatisfied with the voter's reaction to his campaign. Not surprisingly, he would not turn to a professional program evaluator for an experiment. Like other examples in the previous paragraphs, a political campaign is a diffuse, complicated endeavor. Although the ultimate goal of a political campaign is very objective and quantitative, votes cast is not a useful index of campaign effectiveness if one wants to improve the campaign. An approach is needed that will provide conclusions that can be put to use very quickly.

The problem faced by this hypothetical politician is not unlike many other situations in which policy must be evaluated, but one cannot wait for the ultimate outcome index in order to conduct an objective evaluation. Major, expensive evaluations of programs have been criticized because it took too long for the results to become available; when the evaluation was completed, it was no longer relevant to the needs of policy makers. When, for example, the findings of the evaluation of the experimental alternative welfare system (called the "negative income tax") were published, Congress and the White House were no longer in the mood to even consider an innovative welfare reform regardless of the outcome of the evaluation (Cook et al., 1985; Haveman and Watts, 1976).

These three examples, graduate student selection procedures, library acquisitions, and political campaigns, are presented to show some types of situations that need evaluation approaches quite unlike the designs presented so far in this text. Crucial characteristics of these situations include (a) a longer cycle between program input and outcome than is expected for class lessons, medical treatments, or job training; (b) success indexes that are based on the whole program rather than individual variables such as lab tests or ratings of improvement; (c) a need for results in a fairly short time; (d) multiple stakeholders perhaps with conflicting values; and (e) a request for suggestions for improvement rather than just an evaluation of outcome. Every qualitative evaluation is not conducted in settings having all of these characteristics, but some of these issues will be associated with every qualitative evaluation.

This chapter is divided into a section treating methods of gathering qualitative information and a section treating the validity of qualitative evaluation. The data-gathering processes include making observations of the operation of a program and conducting interviews with people involved with the program in some way. The observation can be made while actually carrying out a role in the program (called "participant observation") or by simply being present for the sole purpose of gathering data (called "nonparticipant observation"). In the first part of this chapter, we make the strongest argument that we can in support of qualitative evaluations. Our preference, however, is for a judicious combination of qualitative and quantitative evaluation methods as the latter part of this chapter illustrates.

GATHERING QUALITATIVE DATA

Before we provide an overview of observation and interview techniques, the importance of the evaluator in gathering data personally must be stressed.

The Central Importance of the Data Gatherer

The single most distinctive aspect of qualitative data as contrasted with the type of measures described so far is the personal involvement of the evaluator in the process of gathering data. Usually measurement procedures are designed to dissociate the evaluator from the data-gathering methods. This is often done by using written measures of the achievement of objectively defined goals. The criteria of program success are defined before the evaluation is begun. Measurement instruments are administered, perhaps with little involvement of the evaluation team except to verify that the data are coming in. When this degree of automated data collection is achieved, a form of objectivity is gained. Proponents of qualitative program evaluation, however, would argue that something very important has been lost.

What is lost is the opportunity of the evaluator to respond to the data as it is gathered. In a very real sense, the qualitative evaluator is viewed as the measurement instrument. The evaluator is intimately involved in qualitative data collection so that he or she can react to the observations made. Such reactions may involve adjusting the focus of the evaluation. For example, it may become evident very early in the process of observation that the staff's expectations are very incorrect. Or, the program sponsor's goals might be quite different from the goals of the program participants. An inflexible evaluation plan that had been planned around a misconception will yield a useless report.

Some evaluators object to qualitative evaluations fearing the possibility that evaluations will become very subjective. The loss of the credibility of the evaluation process would be disastrous for evaluators who have strived to show the utility of systematic, objective evaluation for organizations. Qualitative evaluation can be rigorous; however, the meaning of research rigor in qualitative evaluation is not the same as the criteria of valid designs as described in previous chapters. It should be made clear at this point that qualitative evaluations based on direct observations and interviews using the evaluator as the instrument does not mean that anything goes when conducting an evaluation. Alexander (1986) stresses that while qualitative evaluators recognize the difficulty, even the impossibility, of finding one correct point of view about the program, this does not imply that all interpretations are equally legitimate.

The tests of validity that are used in qualitative evaluation will be described throughout this chapter. At this point consider the tests of the validity of information that are used in daily life. In a mystery story you can correctly conclude that "the butler murdered the horse trainer" by gathering data from different sources and carefully combining the information in a qualitative manner. Even when a perfectly credible eyewitness is not available, defendants can be found guilty when caught in a web of evidence. Many court decisions stand on a qualitative synthesis of a great number of observations. The tests of validity of court decisions are similar to the tests of the validity of qualitative evaluations. Such tests involve corroboration of evidence from multiple, independent sources, a sense of the correctness of the conclusions, and confirmation of the conclusions by people involved in the program.

This chapter includes more information on the validity of qualitative information. At this point we turn to the methods used to gather qualitative information for evaluations.

Observational Methods

Nonparticipant observers.   Since the goal of qualitative evaluation is to understand the program, procedure, or policy being studied, it is essential for the evaluator personally to observe the entity being evaluated. Observers who are personally present, but who serve no role in the administration or delivery of the program are called "nonparticipant observers." Case Study 5 shows the importance of nonparticipant observers in an evaluation of an educational program.

Using nonparticipant observers to gather evaluative data is quite practical when evaluators can be sure that their presence would not change the social system of the program. The presence of observers can lead the program staff to act in very guarded ways in order to look as though they really are doing their jobs effectively. Observers may make the staff nervous. The authors of this text have inadvertently distressed some staff members who had not been given sufficient warning that observations were going to be made. Defensiveness is likely to be a problem if the observation period is brief and not part of regular procedures. When observation becomes part of normal operating procedures, staff members become surprisingly relaxed to the point of doing things in front of a nonparticipant observer that could have resulted in suspension if observed by a supervisor (Licht, 1979). The settings in which nonparticipant observations would be most feasible include ones in which activities are relatively public, such as schools, libraries, many aspects of businesses, and even graduate school admissions committee meetings.

What are qualitative evaluators looking for during such evaluations? It is impossible to specify precisely what will be seen as important before the evaluation begins. If it were possible to list all the things one would be looking for, qualitative evaluation would not be necessary. The general goals include being able to understand the critical issues in the setting and to learn how the program operates in practice. If the graduate student admission procedure can be improved, the evaluator needs to learn the weaknesses of the current method. Given that few people can clearly describe their own decision processes (Simon, 1976), having an evaluator present seems essential. It may be that some useful variables are not considered. Or, the qualitative evaluator may discover that there is nothing wrong with the admission procedures, but that the way first-year graduate students are treated is responsible for the high dropout rate. Avoiding mental blinders and remaining open to many possible points of view is an important contribution of the qualitative evaluator.

Participant observation. When the services of a program are too private to permit a nonparticipant observer to be present or when the staff members are so defensive that they would not be able to carry out their duties, then it may be necessary for a participant observer to enter the system. A participant observer is one with a legitimate role in the program. Being a nurse in an emergency room would permit one to obtain detailed information about an emergency room. Serving as a secretary in a personnel office or as a police officer in a local police force could yield rich data about the effectiveness and the problems of the service being evaluated.

The problem with such an approach to evaluation is probably evident to the reader. Discovering that one member of the team has provided evaluative information without the agreement of the staff could be very disruptive if such a person were seen as a "management spy." Certainly such an underhanded approach to evaluation is also incompatible with the philosophy of evaluation espoused on the pages of this text. Approaching evaluation without the agreement of the people whose work is being evaluated would violate the spirit of mutual trust felt to be important in effectively functioning agencies. Participant observation could, of course, be done with the agreement of members of the program staff. This might be a good approach in settings in which the program participants would find the presence of observers unsettling. Medical patients undergoing painful or embarrassing treatments might be offended by the presence of an unnecessary person, but knowing that research on the quality of medical care is being conducted might even be a comfort to the patient.

A variant of participant observation involves a pseudo-participant to go through the system. The treatment and medication practices of mental hospitals were evaluated by Rosenhan (1973) by having people feign emotional illness thereby gaining admission to a mental hospital. Once admitted the pseudo-patients stopped reporting any symptoms and simply participated in the ward activities. Rosenhan and his qualitative evaluators were able to provide a compelling critique of the way patients are treated by the medical and nursing staffs of the hospitals. These observations implied that the slow improvement shown by psychiatric patients may be partially attributed to the way they are treated by the members of the staff of supposedly therapeutic settings.

Examining program traces. Chapter 3 listed program records as a valuable, nonreactive, and fairly inexpensive data source for evaluation. The term *traces* refers to a wide variety of physical remains and outcomes of the program or policy being evaluated; records are one type of trace. In a school setting a qualitative evaluator might examine these traces: graded homework, teacher lesson plans, tests, litter in hallways, graffiti on walls, student club projects, student newspapers and yearbooks, damage to desks and lockers, etc. In evaluating a neighborhood improvement program one might examine repairs to and painting of buildings, discarded appliances and furniture in yards and vacant lots, litter and broken glass in front yards and alleys, cars parking in front of fire hydrants, abandoned cars, yards with carefully maintained lawns and flower beds, etc. These traces can be observed without the cooperation of anyone in the community or anyone associated with the program. One might take pictures of the neighborhood before and after the program to use in an evaluation report.

The important point to recognize in a discussion of the uses of physical traces in evaluations is the degree of understanding that is gained by examining these items. Physical traces add a dimension to an evaluation that is hard to gain in some other way. Someone conducting an evaluation of a school program or a community improvement program would gain considerable understanding of the school or community by systematically examining the traces suggested above. This understanding could not be gained without the personal presence of the evaluator or members of the evaluation team.

The meaning of any one physical trace is nearly impossible to understand. It is the accumulation of evidence from many traces that leads one to a conclusion. Furthermore, tentative interpretations are checked with information obtained through interviews and observations of behaviors. By seeking various forms of data as well as various data sources and then triangulating to interpretations infuses qualitative evaluations with power to explain and evaluate programs.

Interviewing to Obtain Qualitative Data

Qualitative interviewing is different from simply administering a written survey orally. A structured survey given orally is still a structured survey. Although structured surveys can be used in qualitative evaluations, they are usually used only after many observations and unstructured interviews have revealed detailed information to the evaluator. When the evaluator wants to verify tentative interpretations near the end of data collection, structured interviews may well be appropriate. However, the value of qualitative evaluation is in expanding knowledge of the program and its impact. Thus, the interviewer remains open to new information and follows leads to viewpoints that had not been considered before data collection began. Interviewers seek to help interviewees to use their own words, thought patterns, and values when responding to the questions.

Recording answers. Lincoln and Guba (1985) review the advantages of recording the interview versus taking written notes. The advantages include having complete records and having the statement in the interviewee's own words in case a dispute occurs later. But, Lincoln and Guba strongly recommend written notes instead of cassette recordings for the following reasons: writing is less threatening to the interviewee, taking notes keeps the interviewer involved, technical problems with equipment can be avoided, the interviewer can record his or her own thoughts during the interview, and written notes are far more easy to work with than tapes are.

Preparing for the interview. Before conducting interviews evaluators take pains to be sure that the interviewee understands the purpose of the interview and has consented to be interviewed. There is no point in trying to mislead the individual as to the purpose of the interview. Such unethical behavior may well lead to controversy when the report is prepared and discredit the evaluation. It is a good idea to confirm the appointment for an interview a day or two beforehand. The interviewer should be on time, even early. One will have better rapport if the interviewer dresses according to the norms of the organization. One need not dress in a three-piece designer suit to interview an executive, but one had better not show in up faded jeans and a torn sweatshirt.

Developing rapport. Interviewees will usually be guarded as the interview begins. Even well-established, secure people will not trust the interviewer at first. A personal relationship is needed to establish rapport and a degree of trust between the interviewer and interviewee. Rapport can be fostered by asking some orientation questions and showing acceptance and friendly reactions to the interviewees. Starting out asking, "How did you first become a librarian?" gives a librarian a chance to talk and relax.

Asking questions. One of the most critical points in developing and asking questions is to avoid using questions that can be answered "Yes" or "No." Patton (1978) presents several sets of questions that could produce little information unless the interviewee spontaneously went beyond the actual question. Figure 12.1 was inspired by Patton's suggestions. As the questions in the figure show, qualitative interviewers use questions that encourage the respondent to talk and elaborate. The best questions will begin with phrases such as "What is it like when ... ?," "How do employees react when ... ?," "Please tell me how ... ," or "What goes through your mind when ... ?" Clearly, someone can refuse to answer the questions completely or may provide misleading answers; however, the format of the questions has encouraged the informant to provide answers revealing important information.

Probing for more information. A major value of taking the time to conduct a qualitative interview is the opportunity for the evaluator to react to the information. Sometimes the evaluator senses that there is something more to be said, or the interviewee has not understood the point. At these times the interviewer can probe by simply asking, "Can you tell me more about ... ?"

QUESTIONS NOT LIKELY TO ELICIT USEFUL INFORMATION FROM AN INTERVIEWEE	OPEN-ENDED INTERVIEW QUESTIONS THAT WILL ENCOURAGE THE INTERVIEWEE TO PROVIDE INFORMATION
Is this a social psychology graduate program?	What is the name of this graduate program?
Are you the director?	What is your role in this program?
Is the emphasis on applications of social psychology?	Please characterize the emphasis of the program.
Do the students enter the program with interests in applications?	What are the interests of the applicants to the program?
Do the courses have an applied orientation?	How do the courses relate to the emphasis of the program?
Do the students like the applied orientation?	How do the students react to the applied orientation?
Are the theses and dissertations related to the theme?	How do the theses and dissertations fit into the program's theme?
Do the students seek teaching positions after graduation?	What type of positions do the graduates seek?
Do the graduates get good positions?	How do graduates use the skills learned from the program?

FIGURE 12.1 Two possible sets of questions for a director of an Applied Social Psychology graduate program. The contrasts between the two columns are the important points of this figure. Do note, however, that the qualitative interviewer would not have an inflexible set of questions ready to use. One would have the issues clearly in mind, but the actual questions asked would develop as the interview progressed.

Or, the interviewer may want to check on an interpretation of what was said by asking, "Let's see, if I understand you, you said that. . . . If that is correct, can you tell me why that happens?" The interviewer will seek to give encouragement to the interviewee regardless of the degree of agreement between the interviewer and the source. Such signs of encouragement can be seen during televised interviews as the journalist keeps nodding while the newsmaker talks. Obviously such a behavior can become artificial and counterproductive; the goal, however, is to show the interviewee that the evaluator is listening and wants to hear more.

Ending the qualitative interview. A structured interview will end with the last prepared question. A qualitative interview, in contrast, could go on and on. When the scheduled appointment is nearly over, when the participants are fatigued, or when the information being discussed has become redundant, the time to quit has arrived. It is usually wise for interviewers to summarize the major points that have been made in the interview. One might say, "Here is how I understand your views. You have said that (a) . . . , (b) . . ., and (c) . . . ." The advantages of summarizing include getting a chance to check on interpretations before leaving, permitting the respondent to expand on some point now that he or she has had a chance to think about it, and having the person on record as having made those points. Finally, interviewers thank the respondent for his or her attention and thoughtful answers to the questions. One might ask if it would be possible to check back for clarification if necessary.

Plan of Naturalistic Evaluations

Although naturalistic evaluations require more involvement and creativity on the part of the evaluator than do traditional evaluation methods using surveys and checklists, the essential plan of a qualitative evaluation is quite similar to the careful procedures one would use to learn about anything. We present the plan of the evaluation in phases; however, we will have erred if readers view these phases like a step-by-step recipe. The phases overlap and later phases provide feedback to earlier phases, possibly causing the evaluator to revise initial conclusions. Nevertheless, different activities predominate at different times during the preparation of an evaluation.

Phase one: unrestricted observation. In the first stages of a qualitative evaluation one would first examine the most crucial program events, settings, and documents and observe the most important activities of the program. If the program is part of an educational setting, one would begin by observing the structured and unstructured interactions between teachers and students as well as interactions among teachers and among students. The school setting, assignments, buildings, and student products would be examined. The important stakeholders, including children, teachers, administrators, parents, and school board would be interviewed. Qualitative evaluators do not seek to interview or observe a random selection of teachers or students. Instead they would seek those who are likely to know more or are able to provide more information. Although the interviews and observations are unrestricted, the experience of the evaluator will direct the observations to those things that are most likely to be important. Thus, school program evaluators probably will not examine the school furnace or the roof. The important point, however, is that the observations in this phase are to be unrestricted so that the qualitative evaluator can gather a wide range of impressions. Both observations and interpretations are recorded in extensive field notes.

Phase two: digest initial data. The second phase, which actually begins with the first observation, is to digest the impressions that were formed during this unrestricted observation period. From these impressions evaluators develop some specific ideas about how the teachers provide the program, how the students respond to it, how parents feel about the program, and so forth. Observations and interviews again are conducted in order to check on the accuracy of these impressions. With this additional qualitative information the evaluator refines the initial impressions. When additional observations no longer change the impressions, the major part of the data-gathering phases are completed.

Phase three: sharing interpretations. As impressions are formed, qualitative evaluators share their views with stakeholders and other evaluators. The qualitative evaluation approach has been misunderstood as subjectivity running wild. As a check on this possibility, impressions are formed and then presented to others who either know the program and have a stake in it or understand evaluation methodology. People intimately familiar with the program can correct misinterpretations by providing additional data that were overlooked by the evaluator. Experienced but uninvolved evaluators can offer suggestions based on their experiences with programs from other settings.

Phase four: preparing the report. Once checks with stakeholders and colleagues verify the impressions that have been formed, the evaluator is able to present the descriptions of the program and to draw evaluative conclusions about the program. The report will be lengthy. One of the central goals of qualitative evaluation is to provide detailed descriptions of programs through the eyes of the stakeholders along with the insights of the evaluator. The place of the evaluator is to integrate the views of many stakeholders providing feedback on those views so that everyone understands the program better than before.

This description will not be presented as a final version of the truth since different information can come to light later, conditions may change, and the membership of the stakeholder groups will not remain the same. It is easy to imagine how a school can change when the students change, when a school board mandates changes, or when a loss of revenue forces the teachers to work with larger classes and fewer resources. The report can be used in other settings to the extent that the other settings are similar to the one evaluated. Since qualitative evaluators are sensitive to the many specific factors that can affect program success, generalizing to other settings is done only with extreme care.

It would not be surprising if many readers reacted to this presentation with concern about the subjectivity of the process. Two comments are offered in response to such concerns. First, many years ago the first author had a conversation about research methods with a more experienced psychologist. The question concerned the issue of this chapter—traditional quantitative research procedures compared to more qualitative personal observations. I asked the following question: "If you wanted to learn about a group you know nothing about, would you go there and live among them or would you develop and send surveys and questionnaires?" The more senior professor responded, "Go and live there." Although we both would have preferred personal involvement as the mode of personal learning, we both continued to use the standard social psychological approaches to measure the variables in our research. Qualitative methodology is an attempt to obtain a better understanding of programs and people than can usually be obtained through predetermined surveys and checklists.

It is undoubtedly true that in an effort to be objective and to minimize bias, evaluators have planned and conducted evaluations at too great a distance from the program being evaluated. At times, evaluations that simply did not reflect the richness or important nature of the program have been conducted. Program stakeholders have rejected evaluations not only because they felt threatened by some negative feedback, but also because they did not recognize the program presented in the report as their own. Only through close contact with the program can the evaluator come to understand it. When evaluators understand programs fully, evaluations will have a greater likelihood of having impact.

The second response to the concern about the subjectivity of qualitative evaluations centers on the question of just how much objectivity quantitative evaluations possess. The subjectivity of quantitative evaluation is not found in the scoring of surveys or in the analyses of program records. However, the presuppositions that determine the choice of outcome variables to be measured and the decisions to ignore the less quantifiable program effects can inadvertently direct an evaluation toward certain conclusions. Although the sources of subjectivity may be different for qualitative and quantitative evaluations, evaluators must be equally wary of unexamined assumptions regardless of the form of the evaluation.

ESTABLISHING TRUST IN QUALITATIVE DATA

Approaches to establishing trust in traditional social science evaluation methods as developed in Chapters 7, 8, and 9 are fairly well known. The criteria of construct validity, internal validity, statistical conclusion validity, and external

validity have been used by many evaluators to judge the quality of the evaluation designs and sources of information. These criteria cannot be applied in
a direct manner to evaluations based on qualitative procedures. This might
lead one to feel that qualitative data gathering procedures are more likely to
fall short of acceptable standards needed for program evaluations than are
traditionally designed program evaluations. Lincoln and Guba (1985) argue
that few if any quantitative evaluations meet the rigorous criteria listed by
Cook and Campbell (1979). Kytle and Millman (1986) describe their experience in which the funding source wanted the proper form of evaluation, but
not an actual evaluation. The use of quantitative, but superficial, procedures
resulted in an evaluation containing no challenging information to disturb
the program's sponsors. Although quantitative procedures are not necessarily
superficial, evaluators who use qualitative procedures (e.g., Patton, 1980) believe that naturalistic approaches to describing programs are more likely to
reach below surface appearances than many less than thorough quantitative
evaluations. Lincoln and Guba (1985) have begun to develop the criteria by
which the trustworthiness of qualitative evaluation procedures can be judged.

Because quantitative procedures have been frequently described, this
discussion will seek to show how the trustworthiness criteria of qualitative
procedures relate to these standards of social science research. It should be
noted that proponents of qualitative evaluation methods argue that judging
qualitative procedures by the criteria of quasi-experimental and experimental
designs is like evaluating the qualities of a cat by criteria originally developed
for evaluating a dog. Dogs and cats have different qualities; a good dog will
not possess the characteristics of a good cat even though both may make
wonderful pets. After examining the parallels between the criteria of good
measurement and valid research designs used with qualitative methods and
those used with traditional approaches, an additional criterion of good evaluations developed out of qualitative approaches will be presented.

Criteria of Trustworthy Measurement Procedures

Reliability and dependability. As described in Chapter 3, measurement is reliable if a variable made up of several items measures one dimension
(see Split-Half Reliability) or if different people find similar levels of a rated
characteristic (see Inter-rater Reliability). Qualitative assessment, based on
the evaluator's personal observations, can be trusted to the extent that other
evaluators describe the situation in similar ways. However, since no two qualitative evaluators are likely to have exactly the same experiences, Lincoln and
Guba (1985) suggest that observers keep detailed field notes and record their
interpretations of the observations frequently. A disinterested, but trained
person should be able to review these materials and make the same interpretations as the original observer. This procedure is a bit like inter-rater reliability;
Lincoln and Guba call this "dependability."

Validity and credibility. Traditional measurement approaches judge measurement instruments on the basis of whether they correlate with some behavior of interest. Thus, college entrance tests should correlate with college grades, measures of psychological adjustment should correlate with ratings of adjustment made by family members or therapists, and checklists of neighborhood quality should correlate with ratings by residents or experts. One cannot correlate qualitative observations with other measures; however, the concept of construct validity can be used with qualitative observations.

Construct validity refers to whether the instrument measures some variable that fits into a network of meaningful relations with other variables. Although qualitative observations cannot be placed into a quantitatively verified network, the observations gain credibility when they fit into an interlocking pattern of meaning with multiple checks on interpretations. Credibility thus resembles traditional definitions of construct validity. Credibility is enhanced by prolonged presence at the program site(s), by the use of a variety of sources of information, and by checking interpretations with other evaluators and participants of the setting being evaluated.

Objectivity and confirmability. Traditional measurement approaches were considered to be good if they were very objective. Attempts to achieve objectivity have resulted in sterile and misunderstood data according to critics (e.g., Patton, 1986). Qualitative evaluators would seek to establish that their interpretations can be confirmed by other disinterested evaluators after examining the original field notes and records of judgment processes. This approach to demonstrating trustworthiness is similar to that described for dependability.

Criteria of Trustworthy Evaluation Designs

Internal validity and credibility. As readers of Chapter 7 will recall, threats to internal validity have become classic topics in the study of research design. Controlling for viable alternative interpretations of the differences between pretests and posttests are the signs of internally valid evaluation designs. As qualitative evaluators make their observations, they will be aware of these alternative interpretations, such as a general economic upturn masquerading as the positive effect of a job training program on the employment rate of trainees. Qualitative evaluators, however, do not seek to control for such a threat by designing a controlled experimental evaluation. Instead, by making varied, detailed observations and by carefully documenting their interpretations, they would expect that their overall interpretation would have credibility such as a legal case would have when made by a good detective. Qualitative evaluators would argue that their on-site observations and interviews would be more likely to detect the many influences on the program participants than would a traditional hands-off approach that depends on the research design to guarantee the internal validity of the evaluation.

Statistical conclusion validity and dependability. In order to distinguish random error from differences among groups that result from the impact of the program, most evaluators will use statistical significance tests. To use statistical techniques the observations must be quantified in some way. Qualitative data, thus, are unsuitable for statistical tests; however, the question of whether the information being interpreted can be trusted or is just the product of random events must still be addressed. In order to discover trends qualitative evaluators depend on the examination of detailed field notes made by independent evaluators who base their notes and interpretations on multiple sources. One can think of this independent analysis as serving a function similar to that provided by statistical tests used with quantitative data.

External validity and transferability. External validity refers to the extent that the conclusions of an evaluation can be applied to other groups of people not in the specific groups studied. The question of external validity is very important when a demonstration program is funded and evaluated for the primary purpose of learning whether it is successful and, thus, worth funding more widely. Traditional evaluators have depended on evaluating the program in a number of different settings (e.g., northern cities, West Coast cities, and southern rural sites) in order to develop confidence that the evaluation has external validity and, therefore, the program can be instituted elsewhere. Qualitative evaluators depend on detailed observations and descriptions to show what it is about the program, the participants, and the setting that permitted the program to work effectively. Such "thick" description will permit readers to learn whether the program is likely to work elsewhere since readers can determine whether proposed settings and projected participants are similar to those studied.

This brief overview cannot do justice to the detailed presentation of Lincoln and Guba (1985); however, you should have developed a sense of the different ways that the trustworthiness is established using the two different approaches to gathering data and describing a program.

Authenticity of Evaluation

In addition to trustworthiness, qualitative evaluators wish to apply another criterion of quality to evaluations. The criterion of authenticity is developed from the nature of qualitative research methods; it has not been applied to traditional evaluation designs. Evaluations occur in organizational contexts that are laced with stress, fear, hope, sometimes greed, at least some conflict, and lots of uncertainty. Since evaluations occur in such contexts, not in controlled laboratory settings, evaluations can be held to standards not used with laboratory research. Aspects of authentic evaluation include: (a) concerns for fairness; (b) increasing the understanding of all stakeholders about their own and other stakeholders' needs and values; (c) putting theory into action; and (d) involving all stakeholders in the evaluation so that they are empowered through the evaluation.

Lincoln and Guba (1985) do not claim to have the characteristics of authentic evaluation fully developed. Their point is that program evaluations involve important issues for the program staff, those who pay for it, and those who receive services through the program. The best evaluations, they say, will treat all stakeholders and their values with respect and will serve to enlarge their understanding of themselves, the program, and the other stakeholders. According to Lincoln and Guba qualitative evaluation based on intimate knowledge of the program and its stakeholders has the best chance of meeting these authenticity criteria. It is important to note that such aims go very far beyond the goals of even well-funded, ambitious evaluations.

Many quantitative evaluations, we are told, are managed in such a way that some stakeholders are barred from participating in the evaluation and that frequently the findings of evaluations are not put into practice. One must ask whether these failings are due to the very nature of quantitative evaluations, as some assert, or whether quantitative evaluations can be carried out in ways that are fair, educative, sensitive to values, able to be applied, and empowering. Cook et al. (1985) support this latter position. They argue that evaluators can and should use a range of types of data and that the characteristics of authentic evaluations can indeed be met through evaluation designs Lincoln and Guba would reject. The present text, although in the quantitative, Cook-and-Campbell tradition, has espoused many of the concepts said to flow only from a qualitative approach to evaluation.

The difference of opinion seems to center on the way stakeholder concerns, empowerment of less powerful groups, and fairness have been presented. Lincoln and Guba (1985) are correct in saying that such issues have not been viewed as central in traditional evaluation research designs. Instead, most evaluators have treated such concerns as important aspects of evaluation planning, data analysis, and follow-through after the evaluation report has been completed; that is, as independent from the internal validity of the evaluation. Nevertheless, these concerns have been viewed as important by quantitative evaluators. For example, in their evaluation of the children's television program, "Sesame Street," Cook et al. (1975) displayed many of the values said to be associated with qualitative evaluations when they pointed out that although the program was initially funded to help lower economic class children, upper economic class children were more likely to watch and benefit from it. Cook et al., although using quantitative methods, were clearly concerned about the issues of empowerment and values. One contribution of qualitative evaluations has been to put the issues of fairness and conflicts among values into the focus of the evaluation design. Some observers imply that aspects of authenticity, such as empowering all stakeholders, is often not possible in the context of an evaluation (Greene, 1987; Mark and Shotland, 1985). It may be that Lincoln and Guba urge evaluators to do more than evaluations are able to do. One need not accept all of the rationale used to support qualitative evaluations in order to appreciate this contribution to the science and art of program evaluation.

MIXING QUALITATIVE AND QUANTITATIVE METHODS

Although purists from both camps would object, the best approach is to mix qualitative and quantitative evaluation methods (Cook and Reichardt, 1979; Maxwell, 1985; Rossman and Wilson, 1985). Depending on the setting and the evaluation questions addressed to the evaluator, the mix of methods will vary. Light and Pillemer (1984) write: "The pursuit of good science should transcend personal preferences for numbers or narrative" (p. 143).

The Setting

As the examples in the beginning of this chapter were meant to illustrate, there are reasonable and important evaluative questions that cannot be handled using traditional evaluation methods. In contrast, someone evaluating a new medication will use quantitative measures of health improvement rather than depending only on qualitative approaches. However, it would be important for evaluators involved in medical research to keep asking questions about quality of life for the patients who may be undergoing painful treatments. It is not unknown for physicians to concentrate on the length of life and to pay minimal attention to questions about the quality of life (Illich, 1976).

Switching Between Approaches

In addition to combining methods in a single evaluation, it is quite possible for an evaluation planned as a quantitative evaluation to become a qualitative evaluation when unexpected, negative side effects are suddenly noticed. Carefully planned strictly quantitative evaluations are blind to side effects since unexpected bad effects (or good ones, for that matter) cannot be included in the planned evaluation. Evaluation procedures also change when plans for comparison and control groups cannot be carried out. In order to make any interpretations of available data it may be necessary to change to a more qualitative approach.

In a similar fashion a qualitative evaluation can become more quantitative as the evaluation questions become focused and clear. Once qualitative impressions are well developed, it might be possible to form hypotheses about the expected pattern of some quantitative measures of program outcome. In this way evaluators can verify some aspects of their conclusions. Qualitative evaluators argue that one cannot verify hypotheses without first becoming very knowledgeable about the details of the program.

The Evaluation Question

Evaluations have been classified as evaluations of need, process, outcome, and cost effectiveness. It is hard to conduct a cost-effectiveness evaluation using qualitative methods. Certain questions are more likely to require an emphasis on one or the other form of evaluation. However, most evaluations have multiple purposes. Implementation must occur before one can expect outcomes to be affected. Evaluating implementation can be treated in a quantitative fashion. For example, "How many sessions are held? How many people are served? What is the average income of participants?" are quantitative questions. But one might also like to know how participant questions are handled, how healthy the staff-participant interpersonal relationships are, and how the participant families make personal decisions. Fry and Miller (1975) showed that an innovative, cooperative public-private effort to assist alcoholics was so badly flawed in conception and implementation that it resulted in acrimonious interpersonal staff relationships that, in turn, led to decreased help for alcoholics, not improved care. In the area of social and health services such issues are very important in deciding how to improve programs.

Since there are so many, complex evaluative questions, it seems quite reasonable to believe that evaluations combining aspects of both qualitative and quantitative approaches would be better than methods focusing on one or the other approach.

Cost of Evaluation

How do costs of qualitative evaluations compare to traditional approaches? The extensive, on-site involvement of the evaluator can become quite expensive. The time involved created problems for some naturalistic evaluators (see, Barzansky et al., 1985). The additional expense is compounded by the open-ended design of qualitative approaches. The stakeholder paying the evaluator may want to know what is going to come out of the evaluation before agreeing to support it. Lincoln and Guba (1985) agree that more trust is needed on the part of those who commission a qualitative evaluation compared to those potential funders who are given a clear description of just what variables are going to be measured and how the information is going to be presented before agreeing to support the evaluation. Since trust in the evaluator is required if any evaluation is going to be used, the difference in the methods may be more apparent than real. However, it is true that it is harder to estimate the cost of a qualitative evaluation than it is to estimate what it will cost to construct a survey, to administer it to 100 people, and to analyze it.

SUMMARY

There are settings in which evaluators cannot follow traditional social science research methods that emphasize experimental control. Some complex programs requiring an evaluation in a fairly short time cannot be approached using strictly quantitative methods. At times direct observations are required to fully understand the program and quantitative information. Furthermore, a thorough understanding of the program is necessary if the evaluator's recommendations are to be taken seriously. Qualitative methods, while appearing simple (e.g., talking, watching, and drawing conclusions), are more complicated and harder to work with than most quantitative procedures. The internal and statistical conclusion validity tests used with quantitative evaluations are not easy to translate into forms useful in qualitative work. Nevertheless, the use of qualitative methods in conjunction with quantitative procedures strengthens program evaluation.

STUDY QUESTIONS

1. Referring to Chapter 3 on measurement, what qualitative questions could be asked instead of the structured survey items given in Figure 3.4?
2. Draw up a series of interview questions that could be used for a qualitative evaluation of the program described in Case Study 1 in this book.
3. Construct a paragraph statement explaining the value of qualitative evaluation directed to someone who feels that a report of an evaluation must include tables of numbers.
4. Some larger human services facilities have program evaluation specialists on their own staff. Many observers worry that in-house evaluators may be under pressure to produce overly positive evaluations of services provided by their own organizations. Why would it be especially important to have external consultants available when conducting naturalistic evaluations that might be used with community stakeholders?

FURTHER READING

COOK, T. D., AND REICHARDT, C. S., eds. 1979. *Qualitative and quantitative methods in evaluation research*. Beverly Hills, Calif.: Sage.
LINCOLN, Y. S., AND GUBA, E. G. 1985. *Naturalistic inquiry*. Beverly Hills, Calif.: Sage.
MILES, M. B., AND HUBERMAN, A. M. 1984. *Analyzing qualitative data: A source book for new methods*. Beverly Hills, Calif.: Sage.
YIN, R. K. 1984. *Case study research: Design and methods*. Beverly Hills, Calif.: Sage.

part V

EFFECTIVE APPLICATION OF FINDINGS

"Do you think that they read our report?"

"Well, if they read it, they ignored our recommendations!"

A frequent complaint of evaluators who feel that they conducted a sound evaluation of a program and made concrete and useful suggestions is that decision makers ignore the report and recommendations. At least one young evaluator quit her job in order to call public attention to her findings and recommendations concerning prison conditions (Solomon, 1975).

Although devising an effective and appropriate design and writing a clear and meaningful report give evaluators satisfaction, nothing fosters the feeling of psychological success as much as seeing the report effectively utilized. On the other hand, it is disheartening and deflating when a report with substantial and meaningful findings remains in a file drawer, neglected and unused. The final payoff for the professional evaluator is not receiving the check for services rendered, but rather knowing that the evaluation will have an effect on policy and program improvement. The skills involved in bringing about effective application are partly technical, partly psychological, and partly political.

The final two chapters in this book deal with the effective application of findings. When findings are not effectively utilized, it is often difficult to pinpoint the precise reason. The problem could lie with the manner in which the report was written, the way in which the report was presented, the climate in which the report was presented, or any combination of the above.

Chapter 13 contains a discussion of how to write and present an evaluation report in a way that increases the probability that it will be read. Methods that will contribute to a climate conducive to the effective use of evaluation findings are presented in Chapter 14.

13

The Evaluation Report: How to Get It Read

Without effective communication, carefully prepared technical reports are apt to gather dust on agency shelves—never to be read by policy makers or implemented by program administrators. The need for effective communication strategies has received increased attention in recent years (Smith, 1982). A clear, concise, and attractive report enhances the possibilities of effective impact and represents the first step in having findings effectively utilized. After the data have been collected and analyzed, the results must be communicated to multiple audiences, such as program sponsors, program managers, program personnel, program recipients, other researchers, and the public at large. Because not all groups have equivalent needs or equal rights to know all the results, a single version of the report will ordinarily not be appropriate for all readers. Therefore, the quality and quantity of material, as well as the style of presentation, are best tailored to the group addressed. In this chapter suggestions are made about effective writing and presentation of an evaluation report, including the content and style of a report, pitfalls to avoid in reporting, and the manner of report distribution.

THE CONTENT OF A REPORT

The introduction of an evaluation report should describe the setting and nature of the evaluation project. First, the author should describe the program being evaluated, answering such questions as: What is the nature of the program? Who is supervising or delivering program services? How long has the program been in operation? What are the major characteristics of the physical setting in which the intervention takes place?

Second, reports should describe the type of evaluation undertaken. Have the evaluators conducted a needs, process, outcome, or cost-effectiveness study? If the evaluation has a primary and secondary focus, what are they? For example, is the primary focus on outcome evaluation, with secondary attention to cost effectiveness? If the program has a number of aspects, which aspect is being evaluated?

Third, why was the evaluation commissioned? The general purposes can be described. The evaluation may have been undertaken to maintain accreditation, to improve participant satisfaction, to justify funding, to choose between educational organizations, or to improve public relations.

Fourth, have similar evaluations been undertaken? If so, how does the present evaluation project fit into the literature? What inadequacies (if any) does the evaluator see in previous attempts to evaluate similar programs?

Consider how the above principles are observed in the following excerpt from an in-house report entitled, "Cancer Care Center—An Evaluation of Support to Patients and Relatives," conducted for a large metropolitan teaching hospital (Carey and Posavac, 1977a). The introduction reads as follows:

> On September 1, 1976, the Cancer Care Center of Lutheran General Hospital began accepting patients. The center is a 20-bed unit designed to treat advanced cancer patients utilizing a team approach. Patients are actively treated with the hope of arresting the illness. However, regardless of whether the illness is arrested, the center's overall goal is to help patients cope with their condition and thus to live more effectively than they could otherwise.
>
> The specialized unit was developed because it is believed that cancer patients have needs unlike those of patients with illnesses that are less frightening and less serious than cancer. Further, it is believed that medical care personnel who are particularly interested in the needs of such patients would be better able to help them compared to personnel with no particular interest in cancer care. In order to help patients retain an effective and satisfying lifestyle, the center staff includes a social worker, a chaplain, a nutritionist, and other personnel in addition to physicians and specially selected nurses.
>
> Although most observers would agree that the center's goals are laudable, it is necessary to document the success of the center in meeting its goals. The project described in this report was designed to assess the success of the center in meeting the emotional and personal needs of patients and their relatives. To assess the center's success in improving the various aspects of physical care requires Quality Assurance studies. Quality of medical care is not discussed in this report.

The above introduction contains a brief description of the cancer care program, when it began, various personnel included on the staff, the type of evaluation, and the focus of the study. The review of literature was not mentioned because at the time of the evaluation, no reports of similar programs could be found. As will be mentioned in the next section, on the style of the report, an effort is made to keep the introduction brief for an in-house report, since readers are fairly familiar with the program. However, for the article that was later submitted for journal publication, the introduction was considerably expanded. A more extended description of the cancer care program and the need for such a program were provided for journal readers. Similarly, reports submitted to agencies responsible for funding the program will also contain more details. Funding agencies like to see detailed information about how the program is carried out.

Who Were the Participants?

The section of an evaluation report following the introduction should deal with methodology. This section should contain both information on program participants and details about the procedure employed. The part dealing with participants should include a description of the target population, the nature of the sampling method used, pertinent demographic material on the sample, and the degree of cooperation obtained from the target population. If the percentages of participants who failed to return surveys or who dropped out of the program are fairly large, some effort should be made to explain their lack of participation.

Consider the following paragraphs from the methods section of the cancer care study:

> *Patients studied.* There were three groups of patients studied in preparing this report. A pre-unit comparison group ($N = 67$) was surveyed before the center was opened. After the center was opened two more groups were surveyed. A sample of patients ($N = 52$) who were treated in the specialized center and a group of patients ($N = 53$) with similar diagnoses but treated in regular medical units of the hospital were studied.
>
> Not all cancer patients in the hospital were candidates for the research; however, the same selection procedures were used with all three groups. An experienced nurse examined the chart of every patient discharged with a diagnosis of cancer. Only those patients who were admitted with a diagnosis of cancer could be part of the study. Those admitted without a diagnosis of cancer were eliminated because they could not have been part of the center's program. The following criteria were used to eliminate patients who would have difficulty responding to a survey because they were too sick:
>
> 1. The chart indicated the patient was close to death,
> 2. The patient was described as disoriented (i.e., suffering metastasis to brain),
> 3. The patient was discharged to a nursing home.
>
> In addition, patients over 70 were eliminated because it was expected that many of these patients would find the surveys difficult to complete and might also be suffering from other physical ailments. [Figure 13.1] includes a demographic description of the patients who responded to the surveys in the three groups. Overall, the groups were quite comparable in terms of age, sexual composition, marital status, etc. The one possible difference is found in the different death rates among the patients who were telephoned to inquire about nonreturned surveys. The rate (4%) for the post-unit comparison patients contrasts with the higher values (13%) found for both the Center patients and the pre-unit comparison patients.

		PATIENT GROUP	
VARIABLE	CENTER	PRE-UNIT COMPARISON	POST-UNIT COMPARISON
Number of surveys mailed	52	67	53
Number of usable surveys returned (% return rate)	29 (56%)	38 (57%)	31 (58%)
Age (means)	54.4	54.4	60.2
Sex: Males	31%	45%	36%
Females	69%	55%	64%
Marital status (% married)	62%	84%	81%
Self-reported diagnosis:			
Cancer	90%	90%	67%
Other	10%	10%	33%
Median stay (days)	12	10	13
Number of patients who died before follow-up telephone calls (%)	7 (13%)	9 (13%)	2 (4%)

FIGURE 13.1   Descriptions of the patients in the three cancer treatment groups.

Notice that the program patients are carefully described, along with the patients in the two comparison groups. No sampling method was used in this study. However, certain types of patients were eliminated from the study for methodological and humanitarian reasons. Although mention of the two comparison groups introduces the question of evaluation design before the procedure section, this was done to establish the comparability of the groups on the same table that described the patients.

How Was the Evaluation Conducted?

The procedure part of the methodology section contains material on the evaluation design, methods of data collection, and the operational measures of the dependent variables under investigation. In this section discussion can focus on the details of the experimental or quasi-experimental design chosen, possible biases in data collection and how they were controlled, and the validity and reliability of measures designed specifically for the evaluation. A description of the plan for statistical analysis can either be included in the procedure section or in the beginning of the results section. If a fairly complicated analysis has been selected, then it is advisable to explain the details either in a footnote or in an appendix, especially for an in-house presentation. Comments may be made about the tests for significance or for the degree of association, and about the power of the tests chosen. The amount of detail presented on these items will depend on whether the author is writing a journal article, an in-house report, or a report to a governmental or foundation funding agency. More will be said about this in the section on the style of the report.

In the evaluation we have been describing, the authors chose to place a description of statistical analysis in an appendix so that the flow of the report would not be broken for in-house readers. Read the following paragraph, taken from the appendix, and see whether you agree with that decision.

> Without very sizable numbers of patients in each group, it is not possible to detect small differences among the answers of the three groups tested. With sizes of the groups available, differences among groups would have to have been at least 20 percentage points to be "significant" using standard statistical procedures. For example, if pre-unit care was rated at 72% favorable, the center's care would have to be rated at least at 92% for the statistical test to detect the improvement. Clearly, an improvement of 20% over an already high 72% may be too much to hope for. Because of the problems with such an item-by-item analysis, the data in this study are analyzed on a *set*-of-items basis. The statistical tests used answer the question of whether a set of items has shown *overall* improvement, not whether any given item has shown improvement. The result of this form of analysis is that the reader should *not* view the results of any single item as worthy of particular attention. This is true whether the individual comparison is favorable to the center or unfavorable.

What Was Observed?

In the results sections of short reports the data can be presented without lengthy interpretation or discussion. The author seeks to answer the questions: What happened? What findings appeared? Editorial comments are usually saved until the discussion part of the report. In longer reports, however, it is often more convenient to interpret findings as they are presented. Our illustrations are taken from evaluations that required only brief reports of 10 to 15 pages.

Tables and figures should be brief and simple. All the results for the Cancer Care Center evaluation were presented in three easy-to-read tables (Figures 13.2, 13.3, and 13.4). Notice that in the report's second table (Figure 13.2), containing questions relevant to the evaluation of process, the appropriate comparisons were percentages. In the third table (Figure 13.3) the three groups of patients were compared on the basis of mean scores; percentages were again used to evaluate the attitude of relatives in the fourth table (Figure 13.4). In all three tables the most favorable value among the three groups was underlined to facilitate reading.

The text describing the results can be presented very succinctly, as the following example illustrates:

> *Patients' reactions to hospital care.* Before closely examining the results, a few points must be noted. Whenever patients make generally favorable comments about their treatment, innovations of any sort are not likely to greatly improve the patients' ratings of the care received. This fact, called the "ceiling effect," should be borne in mind whenever innovative programs are introduced into a setting that is already well-received. The ceiling effect is often a problem in detecting the positive impact of an innovation here because most patients already view the hospital quite favorably.
>
> The percentages of patients in the three groups who responded favorably to the survey items are summarized in [Figure 13.2]. In no unit did patients evalu-

	PATIENT GROUP		
QUESTIONNAIRE ITEMS	CENTER	PRE-UNIT COMPARISON	POST-UNIT COMPARISON
1. Were you admitted to your hospital nursing unit in a respectful manner?	96[a]	95	93
2. Were disgnostic tests clearly explained?	82	74	80
3. Were questions about your illness answered to your satisfaction?	82	74	90
4. Were possible side effects of treatments explained before you received the treatments?	92	71	75
.	.	.	.
.	.	.	.
.	.	.	.
8. Did you receive assistance with your diet?	87	75	68
9. Was someone available when you wanted to talk?	92	88	85
10. Did you share in the planning of your care?	68	50	50
11. Were your family members encouraged to be involved with your day-to-day care?	91	72	68
12. Did you feel the staff was interested in helping you?	100	90	90
.	.	.	.
.	.	.	.
.	.	.	.
15. Was the ministry of the chaplain of value to you?	88	61	64
16. In your opinion did the hospital staff communicate well with each other?	89	89	90
17. Was the general atmosphere of your nursing unit depressing?	7	10	3

[a]The most favorable percentage among the three groups is underlined.

FIGURE 13.2   Percentage of patients answering "Yes" to some of the questions concerning hospital care.

ate their care in unfavorable terms. In spite of the problem of the ceiling effect, the center's patients described their care in more favorable terms, as compared to the patients in the other two groups. The center's care was evaluated more favorably than the care given the pre-unit group on 15 characteristics, while the reverse occurred only once. The center's care thus was reliably evaluated as better than that obtained before the unit was opened ($\chi^2 = 12.25$, $df = 1$, $p < .001$). In comparing the center's patients with those treated at the same time but on different units; the center's care is again evaluated more favorably on 12 out of 16 characteristics ($\chi^2 = 4.00$, $df = 1$, $p < .0025$). A note about the method of analysis is in the Appendix.

PROFILE OF MOOD STATES (POMS) SCALE	PATIENT GROUP		
	CENTER	PRE-UNIT COMPARISON	POST-UNIT COMPARISON
Tension-anxiety	11.08	11.76	<u>8.84[a]</u>
Depression	7.80	10.03	<u>7.84</u>
Anger-hostility	<u>3.40</u>	6.24	<u>3.24</u>
Vigor	12.80	12.47	<u>14.00</u>
Fatigue	10.60	11.65	<u>8.60</u>
Confusion	6.68	7.18	<u>5.68</u>

[a]The most favorable value among the three groups is underlined.

FIGURE 13.3 Means of the patients' self-described psychological moods (mean scores).

	PATIENT GROUP		
	CENTER	PRE-UNIT COMPARISON	POST-UNIT COMPARISONS
Description			
Sex of relative: % Male	48	43	56
% Female	52	57	44
Relationship: % Spouse	55	79	68
How much help did you receive from the following personnel?	% reporting having received GREAT help		
Physicians	50	<u>65[a]</u>	58
Nurses	<u>74</u>	51	56
Social workers	<u>39</u>	24	31
Chaplains	<u>38</u>	29	19
Nutritionists (diet counselor)	<u>35</u>	10	27
Physical therapists	<u>44</u>	13	27
Were you disappointed in any of the same hospital personnel?	% reporting disappointment (% YES)		
Physicians	4	6	<u>0</u>
Nurses	<u>0</u>	8	4
Social workers	<u>0</u>	6	4
Chaplains	<u>0</u>	12	4
Nutritionists (diet counselor)	<u>0</u>	10	4
Physical therapists	<u>0</u>	0	<u>0</u>

[a]The most favorable value among the three groups is underlined.

FIGURE 13.4 Responses about medical care personnel by the relatives of the cancer treatment patients.

The patients' moods. The mean values for the patients' moods are presented in [Figure 13.3]. On this set of measures center patients were better off than the pre-unit group; however, the post-unit group described themselves as the best off of all. Finding the post-unit group to be the best off was a surprising finding. It may be that this finding is related to the death rate found as a result of calling discharged patients to ask them about the nonreturn of surveys. If the proportion of patients dying within four weeks of going home is an index of seriousness of illness, then it may be that the post-unit group is the most healthy. If so, then their higher values on the POMS may be due to their generally better state of health. This reasoning is supported by the center staff's belief that they treat patients who are in more advanced stages of cancer than other units in the hospital.

Relatives' views of medical care personnel. The relatives' reports of how much help various medical care personnel gave them personally are summarized in [Figure 13.4]. Also in this table are the proportions of relatives who reported disappointment in the various medical care personnel. As in [Figure 13.2], no group of relatives contained a large proportion of disappointed people. The most favorable ratings were given by relatives of the center's patients on nine out of the eleven items ($\chi^2 = 4.45$, $df = 1$, $p < .0025$).

If a program's effects are given as means, it is helpful to include the standard deviations in an appendix. Merely to report that a treatment group differed from the comparison group at a given level of statistical significance does not provide the reader with enough information to evaluate the practical importance of the difference. For example, if an evaluation finds that program and comparison groups averaged 8.55 and 8.19, respectively—but that the pooled standard deviation was 3.92—readers can conclude that the improvement was of little practical use. That is, in most settings staff members would probably not recognize a difference among the groups. Furthermore, if the new program is costly, there is little reason to support it, even if the findings are statistically significant. If, on the other hand, the mean scores had been 11.55 and 8.19, the difference would have been important, since the improvement is over three-fourths of a standard deviation, a fairly respectable improvement (Smith and Glass, 1977; Wortman, 1983).

While it is always crucial to examine the amount of improvement, we cannot overemphasize the importance of evaluating the amount of improvement with regard to the variable being measured. Rosenthal and Rubin (1982) have shown how misleading common statistical indexes can be when the evaluator does not interpret such indexes in the light of the variable being examined and the number of people potentially affected. If the variable is objective and intrinsically valuable (such as survival rate or unemployment), even small improvements can be very valuable. Furthermore, a slight improvement in a program that is experienced by many people (for example, a small reduction in the cost of immunizations or a slightly more efficient automobile engine) can be valuable when the benefits to society are added together.

What Action Should Be Considered?

The discussion section interprets and comments on the results. In the case of a needs evaluation, how strong are the arguments for establishing the given program? In a summative evaluation, what are the arguments for and against continuing the given program? In a formative evaluation, what steps should be taken to improve the program? Is further evaluation indicated? What recommendations are appropriate in light of the results? It is not always easy to say whether the benefits of a given program justify the cost, although the fixed and variable costs of a program can be enumerated. In a cost-effectiveness evaluation the author should indicate whether the findings suggest that the same results could be obtained more economically by a different program.

Consider excerpts from the discussion section of the Cancer Care Center evaluation:

> The overall impact of the Cancer Care Center is positive. Patients and relatives alike view the program in more favorable terms than the care provided in other units of the hospital. The results of the study are unambiguous except for the POMS variables. Previous research has shown that the more discomfort and pain people suffer, the more depressed and, in general, less well-adjusted they seem (Carey, 1974). If the center's patients are indeed in more advanced stages of cancer, the less pleasant moods can be readily understood. To evaluate the impact of the center on patients' moods requires a group of patients just as ill. If the death rates in [Figure 13.1] do reflect the health of patients, then the center patients ought to be compared with the pre-unit group only. If that comparison is made, then the center was successful on all three sets of variables used in this study.
>
> This study has shown that the emotional and educational needs of cancer patients are better met by the program in the Cancer Care Center than by nonspecialized units. The study does not address the question of whether medical care is better in the center than in other units. Such a question can be addressed by a quality assurance study done before the center's organization, contrasted to one with patients only from the center.

Notice that a long discussion section is unnecessary. A cost-effectiveness analysis was not included, because it was not requested by the decision makers. The discussion section also makes clear what is not evaluated—namely, the quality of the medical care offered to patients in the Cancer Care Center.

The discussion may also include consideration of the adequacy of the program. Is the program sufficiently extensive to serve the people who need it? Is the program sufficiently intensive to deal with the degree of need shown by the people who seek the service (or should be served by it)? Some critics assert that most governmental programs are not funded at levels that can realistically be expected to enable people to resolve their problems (Sechrest et al., 1979). For example, people who cannot hold jobs often need job skill training, emotional counseling, social support, educational services, health services, and so forth for a fairly lengthy period of time. Piecemeal programs providing one of these services will probably have little lasting effect.

Report Outline

It is recommended that evaluators begin the preparation of a report by outlining the points to be covered and the order in which they are to be addressed.

The outline can be modified as the report takes final form, and can then be used as a table of contents. Figure 13.5 illustrates a report outline that might be used to present the findings of an evaluation of the institutional effects of a physician residency program. Notice that the summary is presented first, not last, as is usually done in a journal article. Program personnel will usually read an evaluation report in its entirety. However, policy makers often want a quick overview before deciding how much time they need to invest in reading a report. If the evaluation detects significant problems, policy makers may decide to study the report carefully in order to evaluate possible approaches to follow in making program improvements. Otherwise, some policy makers may need to read only the summary. Note that a summary is longer and more detailed than an abstract often used in journals reporting basic research. Some students write summaries that end with a statement about the proce-

---

Evaluation of the Impact of the Physician Residency Program on General Medical Hospital

I. Summary
II. Introduction
    A. Background of the program
    B. Residency program created important changes in care
    C. Problems in conducting the evaluation
III. Procedure and Method
    A. Data collection
    B. Respondents
    C. Content of the interviews
VI. Results
    A. How respondents evaluate the teaching function of the hospital
        1. Attending physicians' reactions
        2. Nonphysician hospital staff evaluations
        3. Residents' views of their programs
    B. Perceptions of the quality of care provided by the residents
        1. Perceptions of technical skills
        2. Interpersonal skills
            a. Staff rapport with residents
            b. Patient rapport with residents
            c. Care of dying patients
            d. Use of hospital nonmedical resource personnel
    C. Organizational changes brought about by the development of the residency program
        1. Increase in number of hospital-based physicians
        2. Development of new outpatient care unit
        3. Conflicts among residents in different specializations
        4. Effects of the program on the cost of medical care
V. Conclusions and Recommendations
    A. Overall comments
    B. Seven recommendations

References
Appendix A. Growth of residency programs at the hospital
Appendix B. Interview forms used with nurses

FIGURE 13.5 Sample in-house evaluation report outline.

dure and a comment that "various recommendations are made in the report." A summary is to be a real summary; a list of major findings and recommendations should be included.

THE STYLE OF REPORTS

In-House Reports versus Journal Articles

As we mentioned above, in-house reports and journal articles differ to some extent on style and emphasis. An in-house report deemphasizes the introduction and methodology sections and emphasizes the discussion and results sections. The reason for this is that in-house readers are familiar with the elements of the program and have no need to know elaborate details of methodology that would enable them to replicate the study. Therefore, they have less interest in the review of the literature, program design, and methodology. In-house readers are most interested in a general overview of the results of the evaluation and the recommendations made. For these reasons, the authors of this text suggest putting a 200- to 500-word summary of the salient findings and recommendations at the beginning of an in-house report of 10 to 20 pages. The needs of many readers will be met by this summary. Clearly, the summary will be longer for evaluations of wider scope and greater length.

In journal articles, on the other hand, it is appropriate to put considerable emphasis on the introduction and methodology sections. Journal readers, and especially other evaluators, are likely to be interested in theoretical issues, the value of the present evaluation to the particular field of study, and the possibility of replicating the study. These readers would be less interested in the implications for the specific institution where the evaluation was conducted. For these reasons, more details on the experimental design and the statistical analysis of results are appropriate.

Where evaluators have undertaken an ambitious and well-funded evaluation for some large institution, it may be necessary to write a single report for multiple audiences. In this case the report may be written in two volumes. The first volume will be a short, easy-to-read text listing the main findings and explaining the conclusions and suggestions for action. This volume would be intended for executive use in decision making. The second and more lengthy volume would contain copies of the correspondence that set up the goals, conditions, and financial agreements of the study, as well as extensive methodological details and specialized charts that would have interest only for those needing more detailed information. The evaluation of New York State's drug law illustrates the use of a multivolume report. There were actually three published reports of this evaluation: (1) a 33-page conclusion section that would be read by those interested in the overall findings; (2) a 115-page section providing the supporting data for the conclusions; and (3) a 322-page report providing more detailed backup analyses (*The Nation's Toughest Drug Law: Evaluating the New York Experience*, 1978; *Staff Working Papers of the Drug Law Evaluation Project*, 1978).

Quantitative versus Qualitative Style

A *quantitative style* of evaluation puts heavy emphasis on the collection of hard data that can be analyzed statistically; a *qualitative style* emphasizes observations either by participants or by outside observers. Both the quantitative and qualitative approaches have their strengths and weaknesses. The quantitative approach is traditionally considered to be more objective and less liable to be influenced by the bias of data collectors. As pointed out in Chapter 12, quantitative methods limit what can be studied and thus may introduce a bias of omission. However, trained observers and interviewers can capture behaviors that often elude quantitative forms of data.

Ideally, both the quantitative and qualitative approaches can be integrated into an evaluation and into the final report. In the evaluation of an outdoor survival program (Smith et al., 1976), the writers first presented a quantitative analysis and then included the diary of one of the participants who experienced the program. The first part of the report is rather dry reading, but it documents the extent to which the program achieved stated goals with quantitative operational measures. The second part of the report is a fascinating description of one participant's experience that helps explain the meaning of the statistics in the quantitative analysis.

Another example is the report that integrated quantitative and qualitative findings of the Kansas City preventive patrol experiment (Kelling et al., 1976). The study evaluated the widespread belief that the presence or potential presence of police officers on patrol severely inhibits criminal activity. The report is divided into seven parts. Part one contains the introduction to the study and major findings. The next three parts of the report describe the quantitative analysis and contain a description of the police patrol experiment, data sources, and the experimental findings. The next two parts of the report contain qualitative observations by police officers regarding police use of time when they have no special assignment and the attitudes of police officers toward the patrol. The final part presents the observations and conclusions of the authors.

The Importance of Attractive Packaging

Whether writing an in-house report or a journal article, it is important to package a report attractively if you want it to be read. First, use a composition style that is marked by clarity, succinctness, and cohesiveness. It helps a great deal if each paragraph is introduced by a topic sentence that summarizes the main idea of the paragraph. Second, good typing increases attractiveness. Readability can be enhanced by the layout of material, proper underlining, and arrangement of tables and figures. A report that has typing errors makes the reader wonder whether the authors were as careless in collecting data as they were in proofreading their manuscript. Third, the report should be as brief as possible. It is hard to state an absolute length in words or pages for any section of a report; the length will obviously depend on the scope of a project. However, the shorter a report, the more likely it is to be read and used. Reports are also more likely to be read when the authors do not try to present every peripheral finding in the study but rather exercise discretion in satisfying the needs of a particular audience. Fourth, color coding various sections of the in-house report can make it more appealing to the eye and can make it easier for the reader to locate material of special interest. Color coding is ordinarily not needed with a short report, but in more extensive presentations it can be of great assistance. For example, if there are a number of appendixes or a series of tables added at the end of a report, these might be printed on different-colored stock than the main body of the text. This would make it easy for the reader to thumb through the report and locate the section where the tables are printed. Finally, if a report is packaged with an attractive cover, it is more likely that readers will pick up the report and read it with interest. Twenty pages of single-spaced type on white bond paper stapled in the left corner are much less attractive to the eye than the same report bound in yellow firm-paper cover with an attractive design on the front. The authors of this text have made it a practice to use a cover that identifies the report as coming from the Office of Evaluation and Research and leaves space for the title of the evaluation, the authors, and the date. Adding an institutional logo to the cover adds to the attractiveness of the report.

PITFALLS IN REPORTING

Overgeneralization from Inadequate Sampling or Return Rate

The first pitfall to avoid in reporting findings is overgeneralization based on inadequate sampling of the total population or inadequate return rate on a survey. For example, if evaluators chose to take a 10 percent sample of a population, some evidence should be presented that this was done in a manner adequate to test the hypotheses or answer the questions posed by the evaluation. Stratified random sampling (that is, sampling that assures that various subgroups of the population will be proportionately represented) is a stronger procedure than mere random sampling. However, let us suppose that only approximately one-third of a random sample completed a program being evaluated. If the data show that the participants who actually did complete the program are much improved compared to a control group who did not receive the program, the evaluator has to be very careful about interpreting the results. It is not legitimate to conclude that the dropouts would have profited as much as those who actually did complete the program.

It is not unusual for newspaper reporters to overinterpret surveys received from only a small fraction of the people approached for information; it's even worse when the evaluator does. In one study questionnaires were sent to 39,097 American Catholic priests, but just 16.3 percent (6,414) responded. An article quoted the study director as saying: "The survey results are extremely valid in view of the number of respondents and the general consistency of the respondents across the country." If the director was quoted accurately, he overgeneralized from proportion of priests who returned the survey. A response rate of 16.3 percent does not permit one to conclude much of anything about any group, regardless of the sample size. As pointed out in Chapter 2, the important issue is the representativeness of a sample, not its size.

Conclusions That Are Too Strong for Modest Differences

Once an organization has invested a great deal of time and effort into an evaluation, there is a strong desire to demonstrate that the work was useful to the program. Sometimes, especially for in-house evaluators, this results in a temptation to read more into their findings than is actually there. In the long run the reputation of evaluators will be enhanced by interpreting findings cautiously. Modest differences between program and control groups should be interpreted as "some evidence" in support of the program, and should not be seen as "demonstrating" that a program is valuable to the organization sponsoring it.

For example, a health screening clinic wanted to increase the number of people who responded to a mailed announcement of its services. The message on the announcement was changed from a neutral tone to either a threatening ("Your health may be bad") or a positive ("We can help you stay healthy") message. An evaluation of the changes revealed that the threatening message led to fewer responses, while the positive message led to more responses. However, the percentage of people who made appointments only increased from 32 percent to 36 percent (Kirscht et al., 1975)—certainly not a strong effect. If such an innovation had been expensive, it probably would not have been worth doing. It is a fact that many programs have only small effects (Light, 1983). One role of the evaluator is to be sure that people recognize that small effects are likely and that statistically significant effects might be found for programs that are of no practical importance.

Ignoring the Possibility of Type II Errors

Some evaluators feel that if results do not reach the level of statistical significance, they should be ignored; however, the costs involved in gathering data makes them too expensive to be recklessly ignored (Cronbach, 1975). This is especially true when the sample sizes that are available are so small that detecting statistically significant findings is unlikely. One response to this situation is to observe a larger number of program participants. If this can be done, it is the solution of choice. However, to detect a 5 percent increase over a pretest level of 80 percent favorable with a 10 percent chance of a Type II error (missing a real effect) at a significant level of 0.05 would require 1,066 observations in each of the comparison and innovative program groups. If the evaluator could tolerate a probability of a Type II error of 0.50, the required sample sizes drop to 388 (Fleiss, 1973). Obtaining this many respondents is obviously an impossible task for most in-house evaluators. Nevertheless, when evaluating an existing and costly program, evaluators should be reluctant to describe the program as a failure when the probability of not detecting a real improvement is large. (Recall the ethical questions discussed in Chapter 4.) If the evaluator had anticipated this result, the evaluation should not have been undertaken. However, there are many surprises when working in an action setting. For example, the number of people available for testing is often lower than program personnel expected when the evaluation was being planned.

Being cautious about Type II errors is not the same as saying that every nonsignificant statistical test must be seen as a "trend." However, when one is guided by strong prior knowledge, nonsignificant findings can at times be justifiably considered a trend. For example, when a relationship has been predicted on the basis of solid theory or previous evaluations, then the evaluators are more justified in giving serious attention to trends supporting this relationship, even when statistical tests do not yield traditional levels of statistical significance. Trends without such strong *a priori* support should not be given serious attention until replicated.

Analyzing Specific Rather Than Total Effects of a Program

When an index of the success of a human service program approaches the maximum possible, detecting a statistically significant improvement on individual criteria is a difficult task. For example, this problem would be experienced by evaluators working with a well-run program. In such a program, satisfaction would be highly skewed, with the bulk of responses toward the favorable end of the satisfaction continuum. With respondents answering 80 to 90 percent favorable on individual items, innovative programs designed to provide higher quality or more convenient service, and so on, can seldom raise the level of satisfaction by more than a few percentage points.

In instances such as this, the people responsible for the innovative program are usually more concerned with answering the question of whether their new program has an overall positive effect than with knowing whether it was successful on every single criterion. If, indeed, a single criterion was so important that the program would not be a success if it were not achieved, then the researchers must evaluate that program on this single criterion. However, this is often not the case.

One approach to dealing with small effects is to evaluate the program *as a whole*, rather than on a goal-by-goal basis. In this case, rather than evaluating the success of a program by examining each individual standard of success, the evaluators look at the total effect of the program. This was the approach that Carey and Posavac (1979) used in evaluating the Cancer Care Center. (A description of the statistical approach was put in the appendix of the report and was mentioned earlier in this chapter.) Analysis revealed that patients reported better results on 13 of the proposed 17 specific goals than either of the two comparison groups. Although the program was not significantly superior to the comparison groups on any individual criterion, the program taken as a whole was demonstrated to be successful. In effect, the evaluators traded evaluative specificity for statistical power (Posavac and Carey, 1978).

Being Honest to the Point of Being Tactless

The final pitfalls in reporting is to present the findings in such a blunt fashion that the feelings of the program personnel are injured. It is possible to be honest to the point of being tactless. Negative findings must be presented in a manner that demonstrates a humane concern for the dignity and feelings of people connected with a given program.

For example, in an evaluation of presterilization interviewing conducted by chaplains at a religiously oriented hospital, the findings clearly showed that mandatory pastoral interviewing before sterilization operations did not have great value for most couples in the study (Carey, 1976). However, for many years the chaplains had put a great deal of time and effort into this service. It was important to couch the findings in language that would convey the message but still not place the entire blame for the lack of effect on their skills or efforts. Indeed, lack of skill or effort was not responsible for the negative finding. The evaluator tried to put the findings and focus in a tactful way, as the following excerpt from the discussion section demonstrates:

> Follow-up interviews suggested that the failure to find value in the interviews may have been due to the manner in which they were structured and conducted. First, some couples quoted their physician as telling them, "The interview is only a formality," in a tone and manner that indicated that it was a waste of time. The interviews might have been viewed differently if the physician had set the stage for the interview by recommending it as worthwhile and outlining its purpose and nature. Second, some chaplains dislike mandatory interviews. They feel that couples have made up their minds and that nothing is gained in the interview. Chaplains who feel they are conducting a useless interview are likely to communicate this feeling. Finally, the time assigned (15 to 30 minutes) seems inadequate to cover the issues involved.
>
> However, a few couples were clearly in need of help. One of the original 100 couples canceled the operation because they obtained a divorce. Another woman admitted to extreme guilt that she was not handling well. Five spouses said their marriages were unhappy and their sexual relationships were unsatisfying.
>
> In addition, nearly half of the wives reported some degree of anxiety, although this was not necessarily connected with the operation. There is no indication that adequate counseling will be provided by physicians. Only 13 percent of the responding couples saw a physician for counseling, and less than half of these found his counseling of great value. Therefore, in spite of the findings of this study, one should not hastily conclude that mandatory interviews should be dropped without providing an adequate substitute (Carey, 1976, p. 494).

Notice that in this example the evaluator considered the role of the physician in making presterilization interviewing a success, as well as the attitudes of the patients who came in for interviewing. The evaluator also pointed out that some patients, indeed, were in need of counseling, and that the interviews should not be hastily dropped without providing some substitute. As it turned out, this report was well received by the Division of Pastoral Care in the hospital, and hospital policy was modified to make counseling mandatory only for those couples under 30 years of age. This change in policy seemed to concentrate the efforts of the chaplains on the age group where most difficulties and feelings of ambivalence were likely to occur. Also, the physicians were urged to make greater efforts to prepare the patients for a more meaningful interview.

MANNER OF DISTRIBUTION

Respecting Both Sponsors and Program Personnel

The manner in which a report is released is almost as important as the quality of the research design and the composition of the report itself. If evaluators wish to see action taken on the basis of their report findings, it is critical to maintain the good will and support of decision makers and of those who wield power in an organization. Consider a situation in which several people feel they have the right to obtain the evaluation report first. Program personnel, the program director, and program sponsors (administration or the funding agency) may be eager to see the results and may be somewhat anxious about the effects the report could have on their work situation. The problem the evaluator faces is how to be sure that none of these groups feels slighted because it was not the first to see the report.

The authors of this text have found it helpful to distinguish between the *final draft* and the *final report*. It seems best to give those who are in immediate operational control of a program the first peek at the findings. This is done by letting them know that they are going to see the final draft on a confidential basis and that their suggestions for clarifying or elaborating on points that are made in the report will be accepted. This preview, however, should not result in the censorship of valid interpretations. This look at the final draft usually has the effect of allaying the anxiety of program directors who are often hoping for the best but expecting the worst. It also gives them a chance to reflect on any surprises that might be in the report.

After meeting with the operational directors of the program and obtaining their comments, the evaluators can incorporate whatever modifications are necessary in assembling the final report. The final report, then, is presented first to the top administration of the organization or institution, who may have funded or at least sponsored the program and the evaluation research. It is important that they are made to feel that they are special people and the first to see what is potentially sensitive information. The failure to do this may mean that the evaluators will lose the administration's support, which is necessary for future evaluation projects, or perhaps not even be invited to conduct further evaluations in the organization.

After presenting the report to the top administration, the order of further release depends largely on the importance of the report and the sensitivity of its contents. Evaluators must be guided by administration with respect to the order and time sequence of distribution. It is possible that administrators can abuse this authority and try to keep the report from being distributed any further, but this is not the ordinary situation in a well-run organization.

Personal Presentation to Key Persons

In presenting both the final draft and the final report, it is strongly suggested that evaluators resist the temptation to simply mail a copy of the report to program personnel or administration. It is recommended that evaluators set up a personal appointment with the key people who will be seeing the draft or report and distribute a copy to them marked "CONFIDENTIAL" soon enough for them to be able to read it before the meeting—but not so far ahead that there is danger of the report being leaked to other people within the organization. The purpose of the personal presentation is to give the evaluator first-hand knowledge of which sections of the report need further clarification, of the specific reactions of key persons, and of the likelihood that the latter will take some concrete actions in light of the recommendations. This information, which can be obtained only in a face-to-face meeting, will guide the evaluators in the manner in which they will release the information to other people in the organization and also to those outside the organization. They will know which parts of their report can be shortened, strengthened, or clarified.

Interim Reports

Interim reports are those that are given in the course of an evaluation project before the final report is ready to be released. They are usually unofficial communications about the progress of the evaluation project, the problems being experienced, and, when appropriate, the findings that are beginning to emerge. Interim reports are especially useful in evaluation projects that last a year or more. They help to maintain the interest and enthusiasm of program personnel who focus their attention on the delivery of program services, not on the evaluation. Program personnel can also be thanked for their crucial assistance to date and can be advised about how they might further help data collection.

Distribution Outside an Organization

Neither program personnel nor sponsors are always enthusiastic about having an evaluation report published outside the confines of their organization or institution. Few evaluations will be entirely positive, and program personnel are as anxious to have outsiders believe only the best about their programs as parents are to have others see only the good aspects of their children. On occasion, program personnel want to be the first ones to write about their program, and they resent being upstaged by a researcher who publishes before they do.

Evaluators can also be faced with the sensitive situation of balancing their obligation of confidentiality against the obligation to share findings with those who have a need or a right to know. In the case of evaluations that are funded by the government, this will rarely be a difficulty, because part of the grant money will be earmarked for publication of results. However, in privately funded evaluations it would be helpful to agree beforehand on ownership of the data and rights of publication. Many private institutions have a research and publication committee or its equivalent that claims the right of censorship over articles published about institutional operations. It is good to clarify the limitations on the rights of the evaluator before the evaluation begins.

If the evaluation is of such a nature that local community or civic groups might be interested in the results, the public relations department of an organization can often be of great help to the evaluators. Public relations personnel are usually eager to release summaries of reports to local newspapers; just be sure that the public relations writer understands what was learned.

Evaluators will also wish to share their work with the professional community. This involves choosing an appropriate journal for the evaluation report. In writing a journal article, it is important to keep the audience in mind. Some journals are read mainly by program personnel, the people who actually deliver the services; others are read mainly by university teachers and researchers; still other journals appeal to a mixed audience. In any event, it is helpful for evaluators to know the editorial policies, type of audience, and level of professional acceptance of the journals relevant to the field in which they are working.

In addition to the printed media, evaluators may wish to contact others through a presentation to their professional organization. There is a good deal of value in doing this. First, evaluators can keep in touch with professionals of similar interests and promote the sharing of their work. These presentations help others to keep current, because it usually takes over a year before journal articles are published. Second, some evaluators are in the position of having their expenses paid to a meeting only on the condition that they make a presentation. Finally, it may help evaluators to have an additional item on their résumés, demonstrating that they are active and productive. Evaluations are presented at the meetings of many organizations that have a human service emphasis. Educational, psychological, sociological, criminology, and health organization meetings as well as those of the American Evaluation Association consider papers and posters on evaluation. Such presentations are more useful to others if the findings provide some lesson or conclusion that goes beyond the recommendation for the specific service evaluated.

FEEDBACK TO PARTICIPANTS

In addition to distributing the evaluation report to key personnel within the institution and also to those who have a right or interest in knowing about the findings outside the institution, it is important to keep in mind the obligation of providing feedback to participants. The program would not have existed, nor would the evaluation have been conducted, without the help and cooperation of those people who received the program. In many cases they have a desire to know something about the results of the evaluation, and at times they have a right to know. If evaluators promised participants they would obtain some information on the results of the program, then evaluators should fulfill their pledges. This does not mean the evaluators have to send a complete report to everybody who took part in the program. However, they can give a brief summary to the findings with information on where more details can be obtained.

The manner and time of release of this information to program participants should be approved by the administration or program sponsors. Once again, depending on the nature and sensitivity of the findings, administrators may see potential political problems that have to be addressed in light of the findings. They need time to prepare to address these potential problems before information is released on a wide scale. Releasing the report in a proper fashion provides them with the opportunity and time needed to prepare themselves.

Providing summarized feedback to participants does not have to be an expensive undertaking. Also, it is possible in the course of data collection to sort out the participants who wish to receive some information on the final study from those who do not. For example, in doing survey research the evaluators might ask respondents to include a stamped self-addressed envelope together with their return questionnaire if they wish to receive a copy of the results. In this manner the evaluators can respond to the interest of the participants without unduly increasing the cost of disseminating the report.

SUMMARY

A report will be read when its contents are pertinent; when it is not unnecessarily detailed; when the style is readable and thought-provoking, but not tactless; and when it is distributed in a manner that respects the authority and sensitivities of the organization and its personnel. A well-written report will not necessarily be utilized, but unless it is written well, it has no possibility of having an impact on policy. Creating a climate conducive to effective utilization is the subject of the next chapter.

STUDY QUESTIONS

1. Examine the following means, standard deviations, and group sizes. Comment on the relative practical importance of each finding. (The actual importance will depend on program cost, the value of the outcome, and the alternate uses of the resources expended for the program.)

EVALUATION REPORT	COMPARISON GROUP			PROGRAM GROUP		
	MEAN	S.D.	N	MEAN	S.D.	N
A	51.2	10.6	30	58.7	11.5	30
B	51.2	10.6	10	58.7	11.5	10
C	51.2	22.5	100	58.7	20.5	100
D	5.1	4.0	5	8.6	4.2	5

Calculate a *t*-test for each evaluation. How does statistical significance compare to relative importance?

2. Now, suppose that the variable in Report C is number right on a job-related achievement test and that the variable in Report A is the score on a self-report psychological mood test. How might this affect your interpretation of the results of A and C in Question 1?

3. Under what circumstances do results that fail to reach the level of statistical significance deserve serious attention? When should they be ignored? What is the danger involved in being too permissive toward Type II errors?

4. Explain why the representativeness of a sample is more important than its size.

5. Discuss the merits of the quantitative and qualitative style in reporting evaluation findings.

6. Consider the various stakeholders in a university course-evaluation procedure. List their rights to information as well as possible problems in providing the information.

FURTHER READING

BECKER, H. S. 1986. *Writing for social scientists*. Chicago: The University of Chicago Press.

SMITH, N. L., ed. 1982. *Communication strategies in evaluation*. Beverly Hills, Calif.: Sage.

14

A Favorable
Evaluation Climate:
How to Encourage
Utilization

The first step in having findings utilized effectively was discussed in the last chapter—namely, writing and presenting a report in a manner that will get it read. In this chapter attention is given to fostering a climate that is conducive to having the report implemented aggressively. This subject is discussed under five headings: (1) encouraging the proper attitude among program staff and policy makers; (2) dealing with negative findings in a constructive fashion; (3) dealing with mixed results; (4) overcoming the obstacles to effective utilization of findings; and (5) improving evaluations.

ENCOURAGING PROPER ATTITUDE IN STAFF AND POLICY MAKERS

Some Innovations Will Not Succeed

The realization that not every innovation or creative idea will be a success is the first element of a productive attitude that will contribute to the effective utilization of evaluation findings. Program directors and staff must feel free to innovate; but they must also recognize failure and learn from failures. Accepting the possibility of failure enables individuals to read an evaluation report with relaxed and open minds rather than with defensive attitudes that prompt them to reject an entire report at the first sign of criticism. It also enables people to set aside less productive ideas and procedures when the evidence is not sufficiently strong to support a certain approach to a problem. Freedom to fail also enables staff to experiment with other approaches to achieve program goals.

The effects of the fear of failure in organizational development (OD) is illustrated in the study by Mirvis and Berg (1977). Organizational development is a relatively new and developing behavioral science that aims at assisting organizations in their efforts at self-improvement. Sometimes this involves introducing complex programs designed to change the structure of an organization, its social climate, or the day-to-day behaviors of specific individuals within the organization. Because of the complexity of the situations addressed by OD programs, mistakes are unavoidable. However, because of pressure to succeed, many failures in OD efforts are ignored or denied, or remain unrecognized. When failures are covered up, it becomes impossible to learn from them. Problems common to OD efforts in many organizations are considered unique because they have not been publicly described. As a result, some prevailing OD practices go unquestioned and are not improved. Errors in nonroutine situations such as those faced frequently in complex and rapidly changing organizations are neither shameful nor completely avoidable, and patience and persistence may eventually be viewed as the only "right" answers in organizational development. The more fruitful approach is to measure competence not by skill in avoiding errors but by skill in detecting them and acting on the information openly. We must learn to reward those who recognize the risks involved in creating change, and yet still choose to risk, persist, and learn from their errors.

While an atmosphere that respects the freedom to fail is essential for the effective use of findings, it will often be beyond the power of evaluators to foster such an atmosphere where it does not already exist. The attitude of top administration will usually determine whether an organization or program is characterized by a desperate need to make a program work or whether there is a realistic attitude toward the possibility of failure. In healthy organizations administrators understand that innovation entails the possibility that even well-designed and implemented programs may fail. Where a healthy attitude toward innovation already exists, evaluators can make the most of it and use every opportunity to underscore and publicize the enlightened attitude of the administration. Where the atmosphere is not entirely receptive toward the risk of failure of promising innovations, evaluators may be able to foster a healthy attitude toward failure by requesting top administration to make some explicit statement to allay the anxiety of timid or insecure program personnel. In those organizations where the need of success is paramount and the fear of failure is rampant, evaluators will very likely be able to do little to bring about a change in attitude that will enable a research report to be received in a productive manner. However, evaluators will rarely be faced with this situation; organizations with a strong fear of failure will not be inclined to sponsor evaluation research in the first place.

Innovations Can Be Improved

A second element of a productive attitude involves helping personnel to expect suggestions about new ways of developing and improving existing programs rather than a bare presentation of "good news" or "bad news." It is relatively rare that an existing program will be terminated or continued solely on the basis of an evaluation report. In fact, evaluators are pleased when their report produces any noticeable modification in policy and procedures. However, program personnel tend to be highly involved in their program and are occasionally unduly worried about the continuation of the program in the face of a critical report. As a result, they often look for a one-line answer to the question: Does the evaluation support our program or not? In other words: Does the evaluation bring good news or bad news? Evaluators will have a better opportunity of seeing their findings utilized effectively in those instances in which program personnel understand that every evaluation report brings some good news and some bad news, and that the more important question is: What concrete improvements are suggested by the evaluation report that are feasible for implementation? Evaluators must encourage program personnel to see evaluation as a way to help them improve and modify their program—not as a means to enshrine it or destroy it.

For example, in conducting the evaluation of the physical medicine and rehabilitation unit in a community hospital, the health care delivery team understood from the beginning that the rehabilitation unit was going to stay intact regardless of the outcome of the evaluation. However, they were interested in finding out just how much progress the stroke patients were making during their stay in the unit, and also whether those who had improved during their hospitalization continued to improve, or at least maintained their improvement, after they left the hospital. The results of the study showed that during their hospitalization the stroke patients improved their physical skills (walking, eating, dressing) more than their cognitive skills (speaking, remembering). This information focused the attention of the health care delivery team on improving their efforts to restore cognitive skills. The results also showed that the majority of patients who made progress during their hospitalization maintained their improvement after they left the hospital. The information gave the rehabilitation team a more exact picture of the percentage of those who did not maintain their improvement and enabled them to evaluate whether a follow-up program geared to these patients was needed.

Applications May Be Broader Than Expected

The third way evaluators can promote healthy attitudes is to help program managers be aware of the connection between the findings of the report and their own specific needs. On some occasions program managers fail to see the full value and implications of the report. For example, the chairman of a large department of pastoral care at a religiously oriented hospital commissioned an evaluation of the department in the hope of learning what the patients, nurses, and physicians expected from chaplains and the extent to which patient and staff needs were being met by the chaplains (Carey, 1972). The immediate value of the research was to enable the chaplains to get a clear picture of the differences in expectation among patients of different religious denominations, ages, and marital situations. It also revealed that physicians and nurses had slightly different role expectations for the chaplains than did the patients. Furthermore, many chaplains were surprised to learn that the physicians and nurses placed a higher value on the assistance chaplains gave them in their work than the patients did on the more traditional role of the chaplains. This latter finding was largely due to the very active role the chaplains play at this hospital in assisting the staff to care for patients and family in a time of serious illness and death.

These secondary findings with respect to physicians and nurses turned out to be more valuable than originally expected when later that year representatives from Medicare and certain insurance companies refused to reimburse the hospital for the one dollar a day per patient that was set aside to pay for the care from chaplains. The representatives took the position that these expenses should be disallowed, and the cost of the chaplaincy should be underwritten by the religious organization sponsoring the hospital. They took this position because they assumed that the role of the chaplains was primarily to provide emotional support to a minority of patients who had religious needs. However, the president of the hospital was alert enough to see the application of the evaluation to defend the financing of the chaplaincy program out of patient room costs. The evaluation reported that 87 percent of the nurses and 76 percent of the physicians had said they found chaplains to be of great help to them personally in their work with patients. Because this was true, it could not be argued that chaplains were assigned primarily to serve a minority of the patient population. The hospital's viewpoint prevailed, largely on the force of the evaluation report. In this instance hospital administrators saw implications of the evaluation report not recognized by the director of the pastoral care program. The most effective evaluators are alert to practical issues that may be peripheral to the original intent of the evaluation. If they fail to do so, the full implications may go unappreciated—even program managers cannot always be relied upon to see all the values of the evaluation findings.

Findings Are Working Hypotheses

A final aspect of engendering a proper attitude for a productive use of findings is to phrase conclusions as working hypotheses rather than as definitive generalizations. It would be very satisfying to be able to summarize a report with a clear, succinct statement that settles a question or solves a problem once and for all. When much time, effort, and money are spent on a report, one would like to have something solid to show for the results. However, those who look to an evaluation report to provide definitive conclusions are almost always disappointed.

One of the reasons why conclusions are best seen as working hypotheses is that local conditions do not allow for a generalization that can be applied to every situation. For example, Cronbach (1975) explains that those using personnel tests have long known of the danger in generalizing about how widely specific personnel tests can predict job success. This is true because test validity varies with the particular applicants taking the tests, the conditions of the specific job, and the criteria of job success. To select sales people on the basis of a test found valid in *other* firms is unacceptable in the absence of solid knowledge about how aptitudes interact with the dimensions along which sales jobs vary. For the same reasons, positive results obtained with a new educational program in one community warrant another community trying it; but instead of trusting that those results apply, the next community needs its own local evaluation. Of course, there comes a point when a generalization can be made; then the focus of evaluation can turn from documenting successful outcomes to documenting adequate implementation of the program.

Definitive conclusions are equally hard to arrive at, even in those instances in which a strict experimental design is used. Even with true experiments, program personnel should not be allowed to entertain unrealistically high hopes for a critical experiment. For example, Sloane et al. (1975) conducted one of the best evaluations of psychotherapy ever designed. Groups who received behavior therapy and psychoanalytically oriented psychotherapy were compared with each other and with a control group. The results showed that the target symptoms of all three groups improved significantly, but the two treated groups improved equally well and significantly more than those on a waiting list. However, one year and two years after the initial assessment, all groups were found to be equally and significantly improved. These researchers tried to move beyond the basic question of whether psychotherapy is effective to the question of what type of therapy would be most productive with what kind of patients. Even with an excellent experimental design, the study fell short of giving definitive answers to this question. Nevertheless, the study is a model for future work. More important, it provided new hypotheses for future investigations that enabled researchers to fine-tune their research designs.

DEALING WITH NEGATIVE FINDINGS CONSTRUCTIVELY

There Are Many Reasons to Continue a Program

Negative findings are disappointing. The temptation is to try to rationalize one's way out of the situation by saying, for example, that the program was never fully implemented or that a number of special and unusual cases in the sample affected the outcome. There are more productive ways of dealing with negative findings. One productive approach is to focus on the arguments for continuing a human service program—even if the findings are not supportive—if there are good reasons for continuing the program other than those originally proposed. For example, Waldo and Chiricos (1977) caused some consternation for policy makers who supported growth of a work-release program for prisoners. An analysis to determine whether members of work-release programs and those in a control group differed in recidivism showed that the programs provided no advantage on measures of rehabilitative success. In analyzing and discussing the results, the authors speculated that the work-release program had become an established policy in the absence of empirical justification because it saved money and because it appealed to the common sense of legislators and policy makers. The research, in fact, showed that the program led to no harm. The authors did not argue for the elimination of work-release programs, because such programs might be justified on humanitarian and economic grounds. However, they concluded that policy makers should not attempt to "sell" work release on the basis of its rehabilitative merits but should be prepared to discard it when better programs are demonstrated. The researchers concluded that in the long run legislators (and consequently correctional administrators) are most concerned with economic utility—even in those fields where "changing people" is the presumed mission of the organization.

Common Sense Supports Some Innovations

Common-sense plausibility is another reason for continuing a program in the face of negative findings. When there is considerable agreement on the plausibility of a hypothesis, nonsupportive findings argue for an intensification of research rather than an abandonment of it. Ross (1975) argued in this manner after the evaluation of the Scandinavian laws on drinking and driving failed to support the hypothesis that drunken driving would be deterred by strict laws. According to the deterrence hypothesis, an interrupted time-series analysis of motor vehicles casualty data from Sweden and Norway should have showed change as a result of the initiation of the legal reforms in question. The expectations were not fulfilled. Ross concluded:

> Failure to find support for the deterrence hypothesis does not disprove the hypothesis, which has the merit of common-sense plausibility, but it indicates that the current widespread faith is without firm grounding. From the practical standpoint, it is suggested that the continuation of current policy in Sweden and Norway and its adoption elsewhere, should be more tentative and subjected to more scrutiny and critical evaluation than has been the case to date (p. 286).

Seligman and Hutton (1981) also provide an example of where common-sense plausibility and prior research overrode a no-effect finding. They report an evaluation of the use of a feedback meter to motivate consumers to conserve energy. While the evaluation did not provide any evidence that households with the feedback meter used less energy than households without one, the idea of providing feedback to homeowners through instrumentation is still being promoted. The most obvious reason is that earlier research showed that feedback was effective. Indeed, the prior research was an experimental field study that supported common sense and a theoretical understanding of conservation behaviors.

Some Elements of a Program May Be Valuable

Another approach to dealing constructively with negative findings is to use no-difference findings to eliminate costly elements of a program. For example, consider the evaluation of presterilization interviewing that was discussed in the previous chapter (Carey, 1976). The policy of the hospital board of trustees was that mandatory interviewing by chaplains or by the local clergy was required before any sterilization operation at that hospital. An evaluation of presterilization interviewing was done by randomly assigning couples who applied for tubal ligations or vasectomies to an interview group and a control group. Results showed no difference in level of anxiety, guilt feelings, or marital adjustment between the interviewed group and the control group. In fact, in some cases hostility was generated in couples who either had a large number of children or who were near the end of their childbearing years and had made a very firm and well thought out decision not to have any more children. The chaplains themselves felt that mandatory interviewing in these circumstances was counterproductive. As a result of the evaluation, the hospital policy on mandatory interviewing was limited to those instances in which the person to be sterilized was under 30 years of age. This change in policy saved a good deal of time and money and at the same time preserved the purpose of the regulation, which was to discourage younger couples from making a hasty decision in regard to sterilization.

No-difference findings have also been used productively in evaluating methods of law enforcement and criminal correction. For example, one innovation after another has been tried, but crime and recidivism rates have not been affected. Glass (1976) comments:

> These no-difference findings, the bane of the experimental scientists, are grist for the evaluator's mill. If cutting reformatory sentences in half does not produce increased recidivism, then shorter sentences are 100 percent more cost-effective [all other things being equal]. . . . Doing as well as in the past but doing it more cheaply is a gain in value as surely as is doing better at a great cost (p. 11).

Using no-difference findings in this manner to eliminate costly aspects of a program must be done carefully. It is crucial that the evaluators demonstrate that they used a good research design, had adequate sampling procedures, and used valid measures of program success. It is possible that no-difference findings can result from a poor design, from inadequate number in treatment and control groups, or from inadequate measurement (Lipsey et al., 1985). Nevertheless, with these precautions, a negative finding can lead to a more efficient use of resources.

Finally, even disappointing results can lead to worthwhile changes and improvement in a program, when evaluation efforts are closely linked to the decision-making behavior of program planners and administrators. For example, Smith (1975) evaluated the outcome effectiveness of a new clinical care program for seriously disturbed patients of traditional state hospitals. Outcomes were assessed in terms of social competence and economic cost to the patients and society. The results were very disappointing. Although the increased staff, the increased expenditures, and the community orientation of the new center represented a clear advance in the humanitarian care of the mentally ill, no evidence was found that this new approach substantially altered the social outcome of serious mental disorders or of the disability associated with them. Examination of other outcome studies did not uncover any strong evidence contrary to the negative findings of Smith's investigation. The result of Smith's study was that the center substantially shifted its resources from traditional management techniques (drugs, group psychotherapy) to rehabilitation techniques (teaching useful job skills, skills in daily living, homemaking). Staff were assigned to upgrade community placement facilities and to establish community rehabilitation centers at key locations throughout the region. These new programs were scheduled for another round of evaluation. Unless evaluation had been strongly linked to program planning and administration, as it was at this community mental health center, such shifts in emphasis might not have taken place.

Even in cases in which results are not negative, experience has proven that a strong link between program evaluators and policy makers is essential if results are to be utilized effectively. This link may take the form of liaison individuals or linking situations that translate the needs of policy makers into evaluation research, and evaluation research into practice. Liaison persons are the bridges that give research results maximum impact for nonresearchers. For example, in the field of agriculture, extension agents act as intermediaries between the experimental agriculture stations and farmers. The agricultural extension agents are among the earliest examples of liaison persons who translate research results to the ultimate users. To make effective applications of rapidly developing technology also requires sources of information for potential uses. Public Technology, Inc., headquartered in Washington, D.C., transfers research knowledge to such users as urban government, agencies, and organizations who seek to use technology to solve urban problems.

DEALING WITH MIXED RESULTS

The problem of dealing with mixed results—that is, with some findings that support a program and others that do not—is different from dealing with negative findings, when analysis of the data overwhelmingly indicates that the program or treatment under investigation had no practical effects. When there are mixed results, proponents of a program focus attention on those findings that support the program, and those who would like to see the program terminated focus attention on the negative aspects of the evaluation report. The problem of dealing with mixed results is accentuated when politics are involved, when a large number of jobs hangs in the balance, or when many people are rallied to opposing causes. Four approaches for dealing with mixed results and an assessment of the appropriateness of each are presented here.

Allowing Others to Interpret Mixed Results

First, evaluators can report the findings and leave the interpretation to the readers—that is, to policy makers, administrators, or program staff. This can be accomplished by avoiding extended interpretation and discussion of the results in the written report and identifying the difficulties of interpretation only in the oral report, if at all. This approach may be appropriate in those instances in which an evaluator had an explicit agreement with the sponsors of the research to keep the interpretation of findings to a minimum, and when the role of the evaluator was not to deal with the implementation of the recommendations.

However, as we have argued elsewhere, evaluators will ideally have a significant role in program planning. In addition, program personnel correctly expect evaluators to take a position in their analysis and discussion of the mixed results. Evaluators should seldom try to let the numbers "speak for themselves." Data will be interpreted: if the evaluator does not do the interpreting, others with less objectivity will. Scriven (1980) argues that evaluators are commissioned to show whether a program has merit and worth. The failure of evaluators to draw interpretations and to make clear recommendations suggests incompetence or lack of courage.

The Easy Way Out

Evaluators can choose the interpretation they feel is more favorable to the program and emphasize the results in the study that support the favorable interpretation. Where hypotheses in the study were not confirmed, or where the effect was weak, evaluators can tone down unfavorable results by (1) alleging that the outcome measures were unreliable, insensitive, or inappropriate; (2) attributing the lack of statistical significance to the sample; (3) suggesting that implementation of the program was inadequate due to lack of time, complexity, lack of funds, and so forth; or (4) putting great weight on measures of consumer satisfaction, which is often surprisingly favorable even when more objective results are marginal.

Choosing the more favorable interpretation may be defended in some instances—for example, when the positive findings concern the more critical issues and there is hope that the program personnel will support a follow-up study to clarify the mixed results if they do not lose confidence in the evaluators. However, to espouse the more favorable position out of fear of being criticized by program sponsors, to avoid hurting feelings, or merely to obtain further evaluation funding is not defensible.

The Adversary Approach

Two other approaches to handling mixed results are more professionally responsible and in the long run more valuable, both to the evaluators and to program personnel. The evaluators can use an adversary approach to interpret the results. They can first argue one position and gather all the results in the data that support this interpretation, and they can then take the opposite viewpoint and present the data that support that view. The evaluators can then clearly state which side, if either, they think has the strongest case. If the evaluators cannot decide, they can point this out, along with their suggestions for follow-up research to clarify the ambiguity of the present study.

Another form of the adversary style of presentation would be to ask two independent researchers who had not been connected with the report to study the design and the data collected and then write a position paper supporting each side of the issue. These reviews by researchers representing different viewpoints can then be bound with interpretations of the independent experts and conclude with their own summary and position. The adversary approach has been suggested by some writers (for example, Braithwaite, et al., 1982; Datta, 1976a; Levine, et al., 1978); however, this approach is likely to be relatively expensive, making it unrealistic for the evaluator working in an institution or government office.

Using the Evaluation to Improve the Program

Perhaps the best way to deal with mixed results is to emphasize that the purpose of the evaluation was not to terminate the program or provide performance appraisals of program managers but rather to help managers and staff improve the program or their conceptualization of the program. In keeping with this line of thought, Nagel (1983b) and Leviton and Boruch (1983) suggest that utilization is often viewed simplistically because evaluators have not thought through what *might be* utilized from the study. Focusing only on a simple outcome study, utilization can only be a continuation of a good program or a discontinuation of one with weak outcomes. There are other uses of evaluations, however. By thinking through alternatives and basing recommendations on those, there are many degrees of utilization. When the use of evaluations is defined broadly and sufficient time is permitted for knowledge to be used, Leviton and Boruch (1983) find that evaluations are used constructively.

One type of evaluation that is almost guaranteed to produce mixed results, as well as hostility, is an employee work attitudes survey. Among other things, such surveys help managers identify and prioritize problems and monitor the effectiveness of changes and interventions introduced by management. Because there are few units in any organization that do not have some problems and shortcomings, it is not surprising that an employee attitude survey highlights some of these shortcomings for the management team. Some department managers may be hurt and perhaps resentful of what they view as unfair employee criticism. Indeed, they may also resent the evaluators who prepared the employee attitude survey report for having brought them what they consider to be bad news.

To diffuse the possible negative attitudes on the part of managers and program staff, we have found a useful analogy from the medical field. Managers are asked to view evaluators in the same way physicians view laboratory and other support personnel in a hospital. Physicians have the responsibility for the welfare of their patients and for developing medical care plans to address their patients' illnesses. However, before developing a medical care plan, physicians will have their patients undergo a series of laboratory tests, urine analyses, X-rays, or other diagnostic procedures. In studying the results of these tests, physicians develop a better perspective on the strengths of their patients as well as the underlying causes of their symptoms.

After prescribing a medical regimen for their patients, physicians will once again have their patients undergo a similar series of medical tests to evaluate the effectiveness of their medical care plans. If the results of these posttests do not show that the patient improved, physicians do not interpret the disappointing laboratory findings as attacks on their competence, nor will they harbor resentment toward the laboratory personnel for the negative evaluation reports. Rather, they will conclude that the problem is difficult to diagnose and treat or does not respond quickly to treatment. After studying the implications of the reports, physicians develop alternative treatment plans to address the unrelieved symptoms of their patients. In like manner, managers and program staff can work with evaluators as partners in trying to understand the relative strengths and weaknesses of their work units or programs. Using this approach, evaluators can be viewed as auxiliary members of the management team, rather than as adversaries.

OBSTACLES TO EFFECTIVE UTILIZATION OF FINDINGS

In this section four of the more common obstacles to the implementation of findings are discussed. Evaluators will not always be in a position to remove these blocks to the effective use of their findings, but at least they can be aware of their existence and try to work around them where possible.

Value Conflicts among Evaluators

Evaluations and policy research cannot be insulated from personal values. Research methods are used to minimize such influences; however, choice of topic and variables as well as sampling procedures can affect the results of the research. When conclusions of studies of the same policy differ, one can seek out the reasons for the differences or the proponents of contrasting views could attack the motivation and common sense of those drawing opposing conclusions. Unfortunately, the latter course of action has been followed. For example, after initially supporting school busing to achieve racial integration, Coleman concluded that school busing was leading to renewed segregation as people fled urban school districts (Coleman et al., 1966; Coleman, 1976). This change of conclusions resulted in a heated exchange between Pettigrew and Green (1977) on one hand and Coleman on the other. Coleman accused Pettigrew of being "blind to reality" while Pettigrew accused Coleman of conducting incompetent research. There were real differences in the values of the camps, and these values affected how the same information was interpreted. Campbell and Erlebacher (1970) disagreed with Cicarelli et al. (1969) on the evaluation of Head Start as mentioned in Chapter 7; however, the debate was kept civil.

The Weight of Nonempirical Influences

The second obstacle to the effective utilization of findings is the weight of other influences and pressures that compete with the impact of the information in an evaluation report. At times it may seem to evaluators that decision makers are not disposed to give their attention to a report and do not wish to reexamine the policy decisions in view of new information received. However, decision makers may receive a report with an open mind—even with eagerness—and yet find themselves unable to act because they are constrained by economic realities and political pressures.

Bigelow and Ciralo (1975) studied the question of what value there was in collecting information and presenting it to human service administrators. Would information improve their decisions? They studied this question in a large community health center that had 30 management and supervisory personnel. They used three different strategies to try to learn how management was using evaluation feedback. First, they conducted interviews with managers using the Information Use and Decision-Making Questionnaire. Second, they interviewed supervisors when a substantial program modification had been made within their jurisdiction. Third, they introduced a body of data bearing on a program management issue during a meeting of supervisors and then tried to trace the effects over a two-week period. They concluded that managers were disposed to use information, that it affected their intentions to modify programs, and that it resulted in further exploration of a particular management question. The study did not demonstrate that the information resulted in improved performance for the organization. Nevertheless, in the specific instances in which information had, in fact, been introduced, the relative impact of information was appreciable. However, the conclusion that information does have an impact on management had to be qualified by the Heisenberg principle: the very decision making may have resulted in part from participation in the investigation rather than from the input of the feedback data.

Another instance of how other influences and pressures can have a great influence on decision makers is in the issue of guaranteed income as a form of welfare reform (Haveman and Watts, 1976). From the awarding of the original grant for this welfare experiment to submission of the final report in late 1973, a total of six and one-half years elapsed. The 4 years of the operating phase of the experiment were sandwiched between 14 months of planning and design and 16 months of data analyses. The experiment cost about $8 million, about one-third of which went for payments to participating families. In spite of this massive effort, there has been no national movement to modify the present income tax regulation to accommodate a guaranteed income provision. Frankly, no one should have expected a guaranteed income program to develop from the experiment. Public sentiment would have been so overwhelmingly opposed to the idea that legislators would have voted against such a change in the law, even if they were convinced of the merits of the innovation. However, even though public policy has not been changed, the evaluation did alter future debate and discussion of the issue of guaranteed income. Although most economists and politicians would have predicted that even the limited form of guaranteed income used in the study would result in massive malingering and a loss of motivation to work, these theories were not supported. As a result, the loss-of-work-incentives argument was eliminated from the discussion of income maintenance policy. Thus, although the evaluation did not change income tax law, it did change the form of the debate.

Preexisting Polarization of Interested Parties

A third block to the effective utilization of findings occurs when opposing factions have been strongly polarized before an evaluation takes place. Recommendations fall on deaf ears when administrators and public representatives have already chosen their position, regardless of the results of an evaluation. As a consequence, they miss important nuances in the findings. A clear example of the effect of polarization can be seen in the interpretations of the evaluation research conducted by Zimring (1975) on the impact of the Federal Gun Control Act of 1968. Gun control legislation is a highly emotional issue. It was unlikely from the beginning that any evaluation would materially change the opinions of many of those aligned on both sides of the issue. Zimring comments on this at the beginning of his report.

> The study will be of little use to the most fervent friends and foes of gun control legislation. It provides data they do not need. Each group uses the Act's presumed failure to confirm views already strongly held. Enthusiasts for strict federal controls see the failure of the law as proof that stricter laws are needed, while opponents see it as evidence that no controls will work. The picture that emerges from available data is more equivocal. There is evidence that the approach adopted by the Act can aid state efforts at strict firearms control, although other resources necessary to achieve this end have never been provided by Congress. There is also reason to believe that the potential impact of the Act is quite limited when measured against the problems it sought to alleviate (p. 133).

Another emotional issue on which some have already decided their position prior to research is the abortion issue. On one hand, proabortionists place the freedom of the mother above all other values and will not modify this position regardless of the demonstration of harmful effects on society caused by the ready availability of abortion. On the other hand, those who belong to the so-called Right to Life movement place the life of an unborn fetus above all other values and are not about to change this position, even though research shows the harmful effects of back-alley abortions.

The abortion issue is also an example of an issue where other influences and pressures influence decision makers. It is hard for legislators to objectively weigh the evidence of the studies when they are bombarded by letters and public protests on both sides of the issue. In fact, legislators are doing the correct thing in not allowing themselves to be guided merely by the results of sociological or psychological investigations. Policy makers must be alert to the input from the legal profession, philosophers, and medical experts, as well as input from social science studies.

Misapplied Methodology

Evaluators have tried to learn more than their resources would permit. In their review of published evaluations, Lipsey et al. (1985) showed that although many outcome evaluations were planned to investigate the causal effects of the program on the outcome, only a minority of the evaluations were designed in ways that permitted the evaluation to find a causal relationship. The evaluator and the stakeholders are often disappointed when this occurs. This tragic result can occur when too few program participants are observed, threats to internal validity are not controlled satisfactorily, the outcome variables were not measured with enough reliability or validity, among other reasons.

Evaluator incompetence is not the usual cause of misapplied methodology. Instead, limits on resources in the context of overly ambitious or confused evaluation requests makes valid experimental and quasi-experimental evaluation impossible. Frequently, people not trained in evaluation methods do not appreciate the challenge of conducting valid research in service settings. A program evaluation that cannot be interpreted validly damages the reputation of the discipline. Experimentation to isolate causes is to be reserved for situations that require an unambiguous understanding of causes. Since this is seldom the need of the program, evaluation can better help the stakeholders by providing valid information on implementation or by helping the staff to develop clearer ideas about why the program is expected to influence people. Evaluators who give stakeholders a correct understanding of the benefits and limits of program evaluation have a better chance of meeting the stakeholders' needs.

METAEVALUATION

Another way to increase the impact of evaluation is to improve the evaluations themselves. Evaluators will be more likely to see their studies effectively utilized when they demonstrate that their work can stand the test of careful analysis and that they themselves are open to growth through constructive criticism. These goals can be realized in part by the practice of evaluating evaluations, or what has been termed *metaevaluation*.

Various authors have given slightly different meanings to the term *metaevaluation* and have suggested different ways to carry it out. For example, Stufflebeam (1978) distinguishes formative metaevaluation from summative metaevaluation. Formative metaevaluation is conducted before an evaluation takes place and is intended as a guide to help evaluators effectively carry out their project by improving the evaluation plan. For example, Stufflebeam described an ambitious formative metaevaluation by a National Institute of Education (NIE) project designed to develop a system for NIE's use in evaluating research and development institutions. The NIE project had two teams prepare alternative evaluation plans and then had a third team evaluate the two plans. Summative metaevaluations are studies of the merits of a completed evaluation. Both formative and summative metaevaluations assess the extent to which an evaluation is technically adequate, useful in guiding decisions, ethical in dealing with people in organizations, and practical in the use of resources. Stufflebeam suggests 34 standards as dependent variables for judging the merit of completed evaluations and presents 68 guidelines as procedural suggestions to help evaluators meet the standards. His work provides a detailed outlined for those who wish to conduct a metaevaluation of their own work or someone else's work.

Cook and Gruder (1978) use the term *metaevaluation* in a slightly different sense than Stufflebeam. They use the term to refer only to the evaluation of empirical evaluations—that is, studies in which data are being, or have been, collected. They exclude from consideration the evaluation of proposed evaluation plans, an activity that Stufflebeam called formative metaevaluation.

Cook and Gruder discuss seven different models of metaevaluation: four that are subsequent to the initial evaluation and three that are simultaneous with it. The three simultaneous models are more complicated and costly, and they are beyond the scope of the present discussion. However, the four models of metaevaluation that can be used subsequent to the primary evaluation are less costly, more practical, and within the consideration of most evaluators. Overviews of three of their models are presented below.

An Essay Review

An essay review can be based on the evaluation report alone or on the proposal and interim progress reports. To facilitate such a metaevaluation, evaluators will keep careful records of their procedures and decisions made in the course of the evaluation. As the chapter on qualitative methods pointed out, this form of review is essential to support the conclusions of qualitative evaluations.

At times a metaevaluator, although approving of the data collection and analyses of the original evaluator, may draw a different conclusion than initially presented. Pettigrew, et al. (1973) disagreed with Armor's (1972) evaluation of the effects of busing to reduce school segregation. Armor judged busing to be a failure because the gap between the achievement levels of racial groups was not reduced; Pettigrew et al. judged busing to be a success because the absolute achievement level of bused minority children increased.

Another form of essay review occurs when a draft of the report is sent to people with technical skills and substantive knowledge or to individuals with different orientations toward the program. Since people with different skills or viewpoints will interpret reports in ways that are different from the intentions of the authors and since others can supplement the insights of the authors, such a review will strengthen the report. Sometimes while making a final report, trivial factual errors or controversial, but secondary, points in a report can become the focus of discussion rather than the evaluation's main points. Anticipating such problems before submitting a final report can improve the chances that an evaluation will have an impact.

Secondary Analysis

A metaevaluation that is based on a reanalysis of the data from the original evaluation is called a *secondary analysis*. Mosteller and Moynihan (1972) reanalyzed the Coleman (1976) report on the effects of busing students to reduce school segregation. Cook et al. (1975) reanalyzed the evaluation of "Sesame Street," the children's television show. Such metaevaluations are better than essay reviews since quantitative analyses incorporate values and assumptions that are often implicit. Another evaluator may spot such values and assumptions more readily than the initial evaluator. (Of course, metaevaluators may also hold implicit or explicit values that could affect the evaluations.) While empirical reevaluations can shed light on important issues of public policy, they seldom can be conducted in time for organizational decisions. Whenever evaluators make their original data available to others, the evaluation has enhanced credibility. Secondary analyses are seldom conducted on the data gathered for an in-house evaluation. Major, policy-relevant evaluations, however, can be reanalyzed to examine additional evaluation questions or to explore the effect of different statistical procedures.

Quantitative Integration

The approach to metaevaluation that utilizes a quantitative integration of a number of evaluation reports is called *meta-analysis* (Glass, et al., 1981). This approach statistically combines the results of evaluations of similar programs in order to draw overall conclusions about the effectiveness of a given type of program. A meta-analysis is an appropriate form of metaevaluation when a topic has been studied repeatedly in a number of settings. For example, Smith and Glass (1977) conducted a meta-analysis of psychotherapy outcome evaluations. They coded and integrated the findings of nearly 400 controlled evaluations of psychotherapy. There are a number of ways to combine the data from different studies (see, for example, Rosenthal, 1984). Smith and

Glass calculated an effect size for each study by subtracting the mean of the control group from the treated group and dividing the difference by the standard deviation of the control group. In essence, this approach yields a z-score for the mean of the treated people with respect to the distribution of the untreated people.

As you may remember from your statistics class, z-scores do not have units. Since these effect sizes do not have units, the mean of effect sizes can be found for a group of similar evaluations. If the distribution of effect sizes can be assumed to approximate a normal curve, the mean effect size can be converted to a percentile. Smith and Glass found that after psychotherapy the average treated patient was better off than 75 percent of the untreated patients. This kind of conclusion is simply impossible using the traditional qualitative integration of a set of studies.

Meta-analysts not only code the outcomes of evaluations; they can also code any characteristic of the evaluations that are important in understanding the outcomes of the programs. For example, since Smith and Glass coded the theoretical orientations of the psychotherapists, they could contrast the effect sizes of different forms of psychotherapy. Posavac et al. (1985) coded different approaches used to motivate patients to comply with medical treatments. The literature showed that helping patients to fit the medication schedule into their daily routine was more effective than telling patients about the medical reasons for taking their pills. These meta-analysts also coded type of medical treatment recommended by their physicians. It was concluded that patients are much more likely to be influenced to take their pills faithfully than they can be influenced to show up for follow-up appointments or to lose weight. Meta-analytic procedures discourage the simple-minded approach to review involving the mere counting of the number of statistically significant findings in a body of evaluation reports, a procedure that has been criticized for many years (see Light and Smith, 1971).

Light (1983) suggests that meta-analyses will make important contributions to improving evaluation methodology. Wortman (1983) agrees, but he points out that the methodology of meta-analysis itself is still in the developmental stage. In summary, metaevaluation will increase the probability of findings being utilized effectively, because metaevaluation research is a means of improving the quality of evaluation methodology and indirectly testing whether program evaluation delivers what it promises. Light and Pillemer (1984) have authored a quite readable text on the nature and uses of meta-analysis. They illustrate many creative approaches to examining a set of related studies to detect patterns in research or evaluation findings that could not be examined in any other way.

SUMMARY

Evaluators have become increasingly concerned about the utilization of the information that they provide to organizations and stakeholder groups. When presenting reports, one can improve the chances of information being utilized by encouraging a healthy attitude toward evaluation and developing ways of handling negative and mixed evaluations that will lead to program improvements. The desire to have evaluations lead to program improvement is more likely to be achieved when evaluators are routinely involved with the program in the planning stage (see Chapter 2), all the way through discussions of reactions to completed evaluations, than when evaluators are seen only as technicians who supply data when requested to do so.

STUDY QUESTIONS

1. Discuss some of the negative attitudes that can block the effective utilization of well-conducted evaluations.
2. Should an evaluator argue for the termination of an existing program when an evaluation is predominantly negative? Describe the conditions under which one would so argue, and the conditions under which one would advocate further study.
3. Give an example of how political or economic factors might block the effective utilization of an evaluation report.
4. Explain some of the different meanings that the term *metaevaluation* can have, and give an example of each. What is the value of metaevaluation?

FURTHER READING

EGAN, G. 1985. *Change-agent skills for the helping and human service professions.* Belmont, Calif.: Wadsworth.
HAKEL, M. D. et al. 1980. *Making it happen: Designing research with implementation in mind.* Beverly Hills, Calif.: Sage.
LIGHT, R. J., AND PILLEMER, D. B. 1984. *Summing up: The science of reviewing research.* Cambridge, Mass.: Harvard University Press.

part VI
CASE STUDIES

These case studies of evaluations illustrate different styles of program evaluations. Examining these five cases studies will reveal some of the forms that evaluation can take as evaluators tailor their plans to the questions that concern stakeholders.

Each case is based on a published report of an evaluation. The articles were rewritten to approximate the form that a report to a stakeholder would follow. In order to get to the heart of the points to be illustrated, many details of each report were omitted. Furthermore, a summary was written for each report that did not appear in the original.

A variety of types of programs are represented in the topics of these cases. Case Study 1 concerns the improvement of the work environment that was marked by a high level of stress threatening the quality of the performance of the staff. Although it was in a hospital setting, the principles employed can be used in any work setting. Case Study 2 measured the effect of a media campaign. It was conducted in a university setting; however, the need to show that a media campaign can get the attention of a target population is relevant to many settings. Case Study 3, carried out in an armed services base, concerned a program to improve management style and effective goal setting in organizations. Case Study 4 sought to answer the question of whether a welfare program was worth the tax money being spent on it. Last, Case Study 5 examined if an educational program was implemented in a way that fulfilled the objectives of the program. The methods used and the findings of this study can be applied in many evaluations.

A quick reading of all five case studies after reading Chapter 1 will help readers get a flavor for the field of program evaluation. Then each case study can be read carefully after reading the chapter on the evaluation method illustrated in the case study. Case Study 1 shows the usefulness and the limitations of a pretest-posttest design. In addition, it shows how a program developed out of a work-environment problem. Case Study 2 illustrates the use of quasi-experimental designs in evaluation as well as the value of measuring multiple outcomes. An experimental design is illustrated in Case Study 3. This evaluation also shows how important it is for evaluators to monitor the degree that program plans are actually carried out. The crucial steps in carrying out a cost-benefit analysis are illustrated in Case Study 4. Assumptions about benefits must be made when conducting a cost-benefit evaluation; some readers may well dispute the assumptions of the evaluators who conducted the fourth case study. Last, Case Study 5 demonstrates how direct evaluative questions addressed to program participants might not provide an accurate evaluation of the program. Conclusions drawn from in-person observations by these evaluators seem to be more accurate and more useful in improving the program.

Readers may benefit from examining the process of identifying the stakeholders and the evaluators' attempts to meet the stakeholders' needs. The fact that stakeholder groups will differ on what they think is important in evaluating a program can create difficulties for the evaluator and can lead to continued controversy after the evaluation is completed. Note the importance that the choice of stakeholder groups makes in Case Studies 4 and 5.

CASE STUDY 1

When human service work is very stressful, staff members can experience emotional burnout, which may result in a loss of concern about the quality of the service given. The staff of a hospital burn unit began to sense that the emotional environment on the unit was threatening to hinder the delivery of higher quality medical care to the patients on the unit. Notice that the need for the intervention is discussed early in the evaluation. This evaluation illustrates the evaluative attitude that we have stressed in this text. Instead of simply intervening in a way that seemed reasonable, the designers of the intervention sought to show that change did occur.

In a project prepared for a single work unit, one cannot conduct an experiment. Thus, the approach to improving the unit was evaluated using a simple pretest-posttest design. Consider which threats to internal validity might be considered important in the interpretation of this evaluation. There would be a variety of ways that one could examine the possible effects of such threats, some involving unacceptable commitments from the people of the organization.

Finally, notice that the intervention did not resolve all problems that staff of the unit were experiencing. Experienced evaluators and staff recognize that evaluations will not show interventions to be cure-alls.

AN EVALUATION OF AN INTERVENTION
TO CHANGE A WORK ENVIRONMENT:
AN EXAMPLE OF A BURN UNIT[1]

Summary

Staff members of a burn unit seemed to be experiencing high levels of work-related stress. The head nurse invited a hospital-based psychiatrist to explore solutions to problems affecting staff morale and patient care. The approach taken involved assessing morale levels using the Work Environment Survey, providing feedback to

[1]Based on Koran, L. M.; Moos, R. H.; Moos, B.; and Zasslow, M. 1983. Changing hospital work environments: An example of a burn unit. *General Hospital Psychiatry, 5,* 7–13. Copyright Elsevier Science Publishing Co., Inc., 1983.

the staff from that assessment, assisting in staff planning and implementing changes in the unit, and reassessing the work environment. After an initial staff meeting but before the intervention, there were large differences between the staff's view of the ideal work-setting and their actual work-setting. During the 11 subsequent meetings staff members could discuss their feelings about individual patients, staff communication gaps, and conflicts among staff and between staff and physicians. Efforts at problem solving focused on reducing tendencies toward rigid perfectionism, planning for change, and clarifying expectations for nurses, burn technicians, and physicians. Private meetings with the head nurse and medical director addressed staff-physician cooperation. Requests for help with individual patients were honored with a view to teaching additional skills in the nature and treatment of pain.

After the intervention, the readministration of the Work Environment Survey showed that staff perceptions of the unit's environment had improved; the ratings on seven of the ten dimensions had improved. Two scales improved reliably ($p = .05$) and one marginally ($p < .06$). The differences between real and ideal ratings were reduced for nine of the ten ratings. Reductions were reliable ($p < .05$ or $.01$) for the three scales. Although there was still room for improvement, the process of assessment, feedback, planning, and implementation, and reassessment was associated with positive changes in the rated work environment.

Problem Addressed by the Intervention

Work-related stress has been linked to impaired performance and high rates of turnover and absenteeism among nursing and other health center staff. Responsibility for acutely ill patients and the tense emotional climate associated with serious illness can lead to high levels of emotional stress and the loss of motivation. Staff of burn units run the risk of exceptional stress due to the nature of the patients' problems and the intense pain involved in burn treatments. Understandably, unlike many other patients, burn patients cannot express appreciation for the care they receive from nurses and technicians. Relatives of patients frequently place impossible demands on the staff. Last, work on a burn unit, like other intensive care settings, involves hard work requiring lifting of patients, exposure to severely damaged patients, and guilt feelings when patients die.

On this particular burn unit the staff felt that communication patterns had broken down. The staff felt that they had difficulty cooperating on matters of patient care and felt only minimal support from supervisors and resident physicians who seemed to be unavailable to help with decisions involving patient care. Many felt frustrated in dealing with hostile patients and relatives.

Brief Description of the Intervention

The intervention took place in the burn unit of a 425-bed county general hospital affiliated with a medical school. The full- and part-time staff consisted of 18 nurses, 3 burn technicians, 11 attendants/orderlies, and 2 unit clerks caring for 5 acute patients and 6 patients recovering from plastic and reconstructive surgery. Physical therapy, dietary, and social work services were available on a consultative basis. The average length of hospital stay was about 20 days, although some patients stay more than 60 days.

The head nurse contacted a hospital psychiatrist whose job entailed assisting with psychosocial problems interfering with quality of patient care. The intervention was based on (a) a systematic assessment of the work environment; (b) feedback to staff emphasizing differences in real versus ideal work settings; (c) planning and instituting specific changes; and (d) a reassessment of the work environment. The psychiatrist agreed to meet with the staff for an hour every other week to attempt to resolve issues affecting the quality of care. Such issues could include problem patients, insufficient support from physicians, and personal conflicts affecting patient care. Personal conflicts could be discussed only if all parties to the conflict were present. It was believed that if staff could air these sources of stress, morale would improve. Furthermore, the problem-solving process and the solutions developed were expected to create a more healthy work environment that would result in the maintenance of good patient care.

The intervention was delivered in eight group meetings held at the time of the change between day and evening shifts, two group meetings during the day shift, and two group meetings during the night shift. In addition, requests to assist with particular problem patients were honored. These consultations centered on dealing with acute and chronic pain, management plans for patients with personality disorders, and the management of severe depression. Such patient-specific training and several teaching lectures were designed to raise the level of staff competence, increase independence of staff, decrease pressure and time urgency, and promote innovation in patient care.

Plan of the Evaluation

The Work Environment Scale (WES) was administered before the beginning of the intervention and six months afterwards. Assurances of confidentiality for individual answers were given. The WES consists of ten dimensions of the social environments of work settings. These ten dimensions fall into three general categories: (1) *relationship* dimensions—how involved people feel in their work and the support they give their coworkers; (2) *goal orientation* dimensions—how much autonomy people have, the emphasis on planning and efficiency, and how much time pressure there is; and (3) *system maintenance and change* dimensions—clarity of expectations, the extent rules are used to control behavior, the degree innovation is encouraged, and the pleasantness of the physical setting. There are two forms of the WES, real and ideal. Differences in the ratings of both forms from the mean ratings of norms are indicated in the feedback of the ratings.

It was expected that at the pretest there would be sizable differences between the real and the ideal work environments. In addition, it was expected that the real ratings would be less favorable than the norm values. A successful intervention was expected to show decreased differences between the real and ideal rated work environments as well as real ratings that were closer to the mean norm values.

Evaluation Findings

Preintervention Work Environment Ratings

The preintervention WES real and ideal ratings are summarized in Figure C1.1a and the postintervention ratings in Figure C1.1b. The ratings were converted to standard scores with 50 equaling the mean of the norm population and 60 equaling a rating one standard deviation above the mean of the norms. Before the intervention the problems described by the staff were reflected in the WES ratings. The preintervention survey was completed by 72 percent of the nurses and 75 percent of the other members of the unit staff. Poor communication patterns were seen in the large differences between real and ideal ratings of *Peer Cohesion*. Supervisor support also was said to be needed. A very sizable discrepancy was observed between ideal and real levels of the *Clarity* (of rules and policies) dimensions.

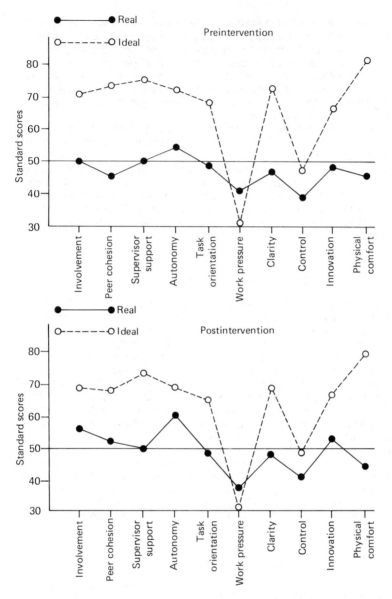

FIGURE C1.1 Preintervention and postintervention WES profiles for burn unit staff.

Postintervention Work Environment Ratings

The response rates for the WES administration after the intervention was 72 percent for nurses and 94 percent for other staff members. The postintervention work environment survey is shown in Figure C1.1b. The figure reveals somewhat smaller discrepancies between real and ideal ratings compared to the preintervention ratings. There are several ways the two halves of Figure C1.1 can be compared. It is of interest, first, to learn whether the staff's views of the quality of the work environment improved. Second, since discrepancies between ideal and real ratings would indicate that staff members were stressed by their work, the discrepancies between the preintervention and the postintervention ratings were examined.

Comparing ratings of actual work environment. Of the ten WES scales, seven of the real environment ratings changed in a favorable direction. Two did not change and *Physical Comfort* changed for the worse. The increase in *Autonomy* was statistically significant ($t(47) = 2.17, p < .05$)[2] while the increases in *Involvement* ($t(47) = 1.65, p < .06$) and *Peer Cohesion* ($t(47) = 1.68, p = .05$) were marginally significant.

Comparing real and ideal ratings. Real and ideal discrepancies were reduced in nine of the ten WES scales; there was no change in *Physical Comfort*. The real-ideal discrepancies decreased significantly for *Involvement* ($t(47) = 2.17, p < .05$), *Peer Cohesion* ($t(47) = 2.79, p < .01$), and *Autonomy* ($t(47) = 3.85, p < .01$).

Conclusions

The favorable changes in the ratings of the work evaluation matched the perception of the head nurse and the medical director that morale on the burn unit had improved during the intervention. Although there still was room for improvement and although it would be helpful to clarify how an improved work environment affects patient care, the intervention was accompanied by positive changes in the burn unit. Benefits of the assessment, feedback, consultation, and reassessment process included:

1. Staff members were encouraged to think about many dimensions of the work setting, not just high or low stress.
2. Important, but often overlooked qualities of work-setting, such as clarity of expectations, became explicit.
3. Involvement was increased simply because staff members were working together to change the work setting.
4. Staff members were given a chance to expand their concerns from care for individual patients to considering the impact of the setting on all the patients and the staff as well. Being considered competent to participate in program planning was a boost to their morale.

Since these changes accompanying the intervention were positive, it seems advisable to recommend similar work with other hospital units whose staff members are reporting high levels of work stress.

[2]All *t*-tests were directional.

CASE STUDY 2

Members of industrialized societies are bombarded with nearly countless messages encouraging us to buy something, do something, believe something. These messages come over the radio and television, are printed in newspapers and magazines, appear on billboards, and seem to generate spontaneously in our mailboxes. It is not surprising that most people try to ignore ads and slogans. Anyone trying to get the attention of a population will consider whether the message is likely to get through. This evaluation sought to answer the question of whether messages encouraging college students to use alcohol wisely would be noticed. Regardless of how noble the cause is, messages that are ignored cannot influence people for good.

Note how the program designers explored the need for the program before implementing a program. This evaluation illustrates the use of an interrupted time series design with switching replications, a particularly powerful quasi-experimental design. Note percentages of students claiming to have seen the media messages before the campaign began. These students could have been mistaken, could have seen a similar message off-campus, or could have just been saying what they thought the interviewer wanted to hear. Regardless of the reason, evaluators seek to use research designs that permit the effect of the program to be found in spite of such a source of error.

RESPONSIBLE ALCOHOL USE MEDIA CAMPAIGN: CAN WE GET COLLEGE STUDENTS' ATTENTION?[1]

Summary

Responsible alcohol use was encouraged by a program sponsored by the Alcohol Education Project at Southern Illinois University. A needs assessment showed that students endorsed moderate drinking, but believed that their friends expected them to do more heavy drinking. The experiences of the Alcohol Education Project (AEP) staff suggested that another problem on campus was drinking and driving. A cam-

[1]Based on McKillip, J.; Lockhart, D. C.; Eckert, P. S.; and Phillips, J. 1985. Evaluation of a responsible alcohol use media campaign on a college campus. *Journal of Alcohol & Drug Education* 30, 88–97. Copyright 1985 by the *Journal of Alcohol & Drug Education*.

paign was planned to encourage students to (a) resist peer pressure to drink heavily and (b) stop friends from driving while drunk. Posters, newspaper ads, an information booth, and a radio call-in show were used by the AEP staff to stress these two themes. There is evidence that students still forming their drinking habits can be influenced by appropriate information; however, information will not be received if the media used to provide the information do not attract the attention of the target audience.

Since the effectiveness of posters, ads, etc. in attracting student attention was not known, an evaluation was conducted during a ten-week period. A two-week baseline period (with no AEP posters or ads in place) was followed by a two-week period emphasis on resisting peer pressure to drink. A second two-week baseline period was followed by a two-week emphasis on keeping friends from drinking while drunk. The evaluation ended with a third two-week baseline period. During the two intervention periods, posters, ads, and a radio show stressed one of the themes. For the first four periods (i.e., eight weeks) the information table was set up in the student union on Thursdays during the lunch hour. No AEP materials were available during the last two-week period.

Interviews during the ten-week evaluation showed that students were aware of the campaign and its themes since student recognition of theme one increased abruptly during week three, but the level of recognition of theme two did not change. When theme two materials were available (during weeks seven and eight), recognition of theme two increased abruptly. The conclusion that students were aware of the messages was also supported by the numbers and types of material taken from the information table during the weeks of the campaign. Last, a mailed survey during weeks nine and ten showed that the two themes targeted by the campaign were recognized more frequently than the other AEP themes not stressed in this media program.

It was concluded that the media campaign was effective in attracting student attention. Although getting student attention is merely a first step in a chain that is hoped to result in responsible alcohol use, it is an essential step. Student services staff members can be confident that using well-placed posters and providing alcohol-related information is an effective use of educational resources.

Needs to be Met by the Program

Widespread evidence indicates that the rate of abuse of alcoholic beverages on U.S. college campuses is a current problem with implications for the future health of students. Informal observations suggested that alcohol abuse is also a problem at Southern Illinois University as well. In addition, answers to mailed surveys to students indicated that although the majority of SIU students viewed moderate drinking as desirable, they believed that their peers expected them to drink heavily. It seemed important for students to be encouraged to hold to their belief in moderate drinking by helping them to resist peer pressures to abuse alcohol. Drinking and driving was also found to be a frequently encountered alcohol-related problem on campus. On the basis of this needs assessment, the SIU Alcohol Education Project staff designed a media-based education program to address alcohol use as related to peer pressure and driving.

Program Description

Target Population

SIU students, approximately 18,700 undergraduates and 3,300 graduate students, made up the target population of a multimedia campaign to encourage responsible alcohol use.

Intervention

Previous research (Ray, 1973; Rothchild, 1979) has implied that students who are not heavily involved in alcohol abuse, those just forming their alcohol-related attitudes, can be influenced by material strengthening inclinations toward responsible alcohol use. Therefore, the staff of the Alcohol Education Project (AEP) expected that a media-based education project could have positive effects. (Heavy drinkers and those whose drinking patterns are well practiced would probably not be influenced by this approach.)

The two themes for the intervention were selected on the basis of the needs assessment. Theme one was: "It's not rude to refuse a drink." Theme two was: "Friends don't let friends drive drunk."

The program sought to increase student awareness of these themes by (a) putting posters in public places throughout the campus (307 were used for the first theme and 203 for the second); (b) placing half-page ads identical to the posters in the Tuesday and Thursday issues of the campus newspaper; (c) creating a 9.8 ft^2 window display in the student union concerning the theme being publicized; (d) having an AEP staff member on a radio call-in show during the first week each of the themes was stressed; and (e) providing an information table in the student union during the noon hours of each Thursday stocked with written material on responsible alcohol use with an AEP staff member available to answer questions.

Evaluation Questions

The materials could be ignored or they could be attended to by students. Thus, the evaluation sought to assess the degree that the media campaign attracted student attention. As will be described, interviews, surveys, and behavioral measures were used to judge whether students were aware of the campaign.

Evaluation Design

To permit an evaluation of the program, the campaign was divided into five two-week periods as shown in Table C2–1. The five periods included:

1. A two-week baseline period that only involved the informational table in the student union.
2. A two-week period, weeks three and four, during which the first theme was emphasized using posters, newspaper ads, the window display, and the radio call-in show.
3. A two-week baseline period during which all materials for the first theme had been removed except for the materials at the information table.
4. A two-week period, weeks seven and eight, during which the second theme was emphasized in the same ways used with the first theme.
5. A two-week baseline period in which all campaign materials were removed including the information table.

The use of baseline periods is frequently used in some forms of psychotherapy in order to show that the treatment had an effect. If the present program had an effect, one would expect students to be more aware of the themes of the campaign after the posters, ads, etc. were put in place compared to the weeks before. The use of two interventions permitted a replication of the design. That is, if any apparent effects of the first theme of the program were detected by comparing the first period with the second, the pattern could be verified by comparing the first six weeks of the program with the fourth period, i.e., weeks seven and eight, using

TABLE C2-1. Time-line for Media Campaign and Evaluation Activities

	WEEK OF SEMESTER									
	1	2	3	4	5	6	7	8	9	10
Media[a]:										
Theme 1	O	O	X	X	O	O	O	O	O	O
Theme 2	O	O	O	O	O	O	X	X	O	O
Measurements:										
Interviews	+	+	+	+	+	+	+	+	+	+
Mailed Survey	a	a	a	a	a	a	a	a	+	+
Media Booth	a	+	+	+	+	+	+	+	a	+

[a]Includes posters, newspaper advertisements, window displays and radio appearance.
NOTE: "O" indicates that media related to the theme were not available and "X" indicates that media were available, "+" indicates measurements were taken and an "a" indicates that measurements were not taken. All measurements were relevant to both campaign themes.

student reactions to the second theme. If the patterns were very similar, one could confidently conclude that the AEP media campaign was responsible for student awareness of the themes. Possible alternative interpretations based on national news reports or alcohol industry ads could be rejected as implausible.

Evaluation Findings

Interviews

Over the ten weeks 371 students were interviewed, 60 percent were male and 40 percent were female, approximating the composition of the student body. No student was interviewed more than once. During each of the ten weeks approximately 40 students were selected at random during the lunch hour from students at the library, a student union cafeteria, and busy outdoor walkway. AEP staff members interviewed students concerning the recall of the poster and the newspaper ad. Respondents were shown a facsimile of the newspaper ad/poster for both campaign themes and were asked if they had seen them in the university newspaper or as a poster.

Figure C2.1 includes the percentage of students reporting that they recalled seeing the poster and the newspaper ad for each of the ten weeks of the campaign. The upper panel of the figure shows the pronounced jump in awareness for the first theme in week three. Note that the lower panel shows that the second theme was not recognized by as many students during weeks three and four as was the first theme. Since only the first theme was being publicized, these patterns support the interpretation that the campaign was effective in attracting student attention. The difference in the students' reactions to the two themes shows that students were not simply saying that they saw the posters/ad because they thought that is what the interviewer wanted them to say.

In week seven the materials for the second theme appeared. As expected, awareness of having seen theme two material increased abruptly. Recall of theme one material did not drop to the baseline level since students could remember having seen theme one material earlier. This replication gave credibililty to the interpretation that the multimedia campaign was responsible for student awareness of the program's themes.

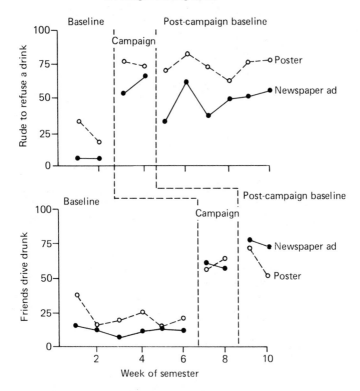

FIGURE C2.1   Record of percentage of students interviewed reporting recall of poster and newspaper ad containing media campaign themes. *Baseline*—period before theme's posters or ads were introduced. *Campaign*—two weeks period in which posters and ads for particular theme were displayed about campus and published in campus newspaper. *Post-theme baseline*—period following campaign, ads for theme were not published and posters for them were taken down.

Mailed Survey

During the final two-week period, a 12-page survey concerning alcohol use was mailed to a random sample of 1,113 students. Usable questionnaires were received from 56.7 percent of this sample. Answers to demographic questions indicated that the respondents accurately reflected the characteristics of the student body.

In addition to questions about alcohol consumption, students were asked which of the seven AEP posters, two from the campaign themes and five not used in this campaign, they had seen. All posters were identified only by their textual content and had been available from AEP since the spring semester prior to this fall semester study. The percentage of respondents who recalled having seen each of the posters "more than once" was the measure of program effectiveness. Theme one was recalled by 62 percent of the respondents and theme two by 83 percent. In contrast, the other five AEP (noncampaign) posters was recalled by from 12 to 48 percent of the respondents. The difference between the campaign themes and the other messages was statistically reliable (p < .05). The level of recall was not related to respondent gender, reported college class, or self-described level of alcohol consumption.

Media Information Table

During weeks one through eight the information table was maintained during the Thursday lunch hours in the student union. An AEP staff member answered questions and seven different posters (two campaign theme posters and five others) as well as other materials were available for student use. Overall, more responsible alcohol-use literature was taken during the weeks of the campaign compared to baseline weeks. During the campaign weeks (i.e., weeks three, four, seven, and eight) an average of 13.00 campaign theme posters were taken per day compared to an average of 5.33 during the baseline weeks ($t(14) = 2.38, p < .025$, one-tailed). Furthermore, during the four weeks of the campaign an average of 75 pieces of material were taken compared to 51 pieces during the baseline weeks. This difference is in the direction that one would expect if the campaign had been successful; however, the difference was not reliable.

Conclusions and Implications

These findings support the use of media, especially multiple media, to publicize responsible alcohol use. Attracting student attention is the essential first step in providing information that may be internalized and may, in turn, result in the development of responsible alcohol use habits. The staff of the Alcohol Education Project can feel confident that media programs are effective uses of educational resources.

References

RAY, M. 1973. Marketing communication and the hierarchy of effects. In P. Clarke (ed.), *New models for mass communication research.* Beverly Hills, CA: Sage.

ROTHSCHILD, M. L. 1979. Advertising strategies for high and low involvement situations, In J. Maloney and B. Silverman (eds.), *Attitude research plays for high stakes.* New York: American Marketing Association.

CASE STUDY 3

Employers in many sectors of American society complain about absenteeism. It may be a surprise, but absenteeism is also a problem in the American Armed Services. A social science research firm was asked to examine the problem of absenteeism in the Marine Corps and to develop an approach to reduce the extent of the problem. Preliminary studies suggested that absenteeism problems were due in large part to leader actions, that leaders rarely monitored absenteeism over periods of time, and that rewards for units achieving low absenteeism were infrequently and arbitrarily administered.

There are three particular points that are illustrated in this case. First, this case study clearly shows how the program was developed on the basis of organizational theory rather than on implicit, atheoretical ideas about the process of bringing about the needed change in behavior. Unfortunately, the use of explicit conceptualization is still rather rare in the design of organizational interventions. Second, note that the setting and the number of the individuals available for the program permitted the use of true experimental design. Third, the value of careful monitoring of the implementation of the program illustrates how the planned analysis had to be adjusted to reflect the varying degrees to which the program was implemented.

KEEPING THE MARINES IN THE FIELD[1]

Summary

Unauthorized absences (UAs) of Marines creates problems for unit effectiveness and morale. Preliminary analysis showed that the most common reason for UA was an attempt by the Marine to deal with a problem that the chain of command did not handle well. A study of the practices of Marine commanders showed that rate of UAs was related to leadership practices. A program to deal with UA was developed on the basis of these preliminary studies and research on the behavior of effective leaders.

[1]Based on Majchrzak, A. 1986. Keeping the Marines in the field: Results of a field experiment. *Evaluation and Program Planning* 9, 253–265. Copyright 1986 Pergamon Journals Ltd.

The program consisted of (a) setting UA objectives at the company level rather than at the battalion level; (b) developing a method to monitor and graph UA rates; (c) clarifying and communicating the battalion policies to company commanders; (d) discussing UA trends in sessions that also served to clarify policies; and (e) rewarding platoons for meeting UA objectives. This program was thought to affect UA rate, commander behavior regarding UA, and individual Marine's understanding of UA policies.

Eight battalions were randomly divided into a treatment group and a control group of 20 companies each. The degree of implementation of the UA program was carefully monitored by the evaluators. A randomly selected group of Marines answered a pretest while a second randomly selected group answered a posttest six months later. An average of 78 Marines from each company answered the pretest or the posttest. Differential degrees of the use of the program suggested that the 20 treatment companies should be divided into 10 companies in a strong treatment group and 10 in a weak treatment group.

The program did not seem to affect commander behavior. Marine attitudes, on the other hand, did differ across levels of treatment; however, not always in the ways expected. UA in the control companies seemed to get worse while it remained relatively stable in the treatment groups. The higher levels of Marine turnover in the control companies indicated that length of time in the Marine Corps needed to be considered in the analysis. An examination of the degree to which changes in UA policies were noticed by Marines in the treatment companies showed differences between companies. In those companies whose members did not report a change, UA actually went up. Among the companies whose members noticed the most change, the UA rate dropped from being higher than the control companies at the beginning of the program to being below the control companies at the posttest. Although the findings do not permit one to specify which of several possible processes accounted for the program's effectiveness, a 50 percent reduction was obtained when the program was implemented and communicated to the Marines. This reduction occurred with only minimal changes in commander behavior.

Needs Assessment and the Specification of the Problem

Although all members of the Marine Corps are expected to be present for duty every day, illness, personal problems, and cases of maladjustment can result in cases of Unauthorized Absences (UAs). Some studies have shown that the rate of UA has been over 10 percent in some units. Absences occur for different reasons. Nicholson (1977) suggested three types of absenteeism for industry in general: a rational decision involving a weighting of the sanctions against personal preferences; second, an impulsive pain avoidance reaction by those who cannot cope with the stresses of the military; and, third, a way to resolve a problem that is not handled well by the military commanders.

Distinguishing among these possible causes for UA is important since an approach addressing one reason may not be appropriate to deal with a different one. For example, if UA is due to individual maladjustment to the military, the approach most likely to reduce rates of UA will center on selection of volunteers for the Corps. There would be little that officers could do once the UA-prone person was in the Corps.

Interviews with 34 Marines, some with UAs and some without, suggested that Nicolson's third possible cause of UAs was the most frequent: going UA was a method of handling a problem that the Marine felt was not being handled well by the chain of command. For example, if a Marine private was not given time off to take his sick child to the doctor, he might go UA especially if he was aware of other Marines being given time off for less pressing reasons.

These interviews also suggested that the commander's actions may be related to UA behavior. To verify this impression, surveys with 267 commanders (i.e., battalion and company commanders in the U.S.) were conducted to learn about their attitudes, actions, and policies concerning UAs. Comparing the survey rates with the actual battalion-level UA rates showed that leadership activities were indeed correlated with UA. Taking both sources of data together suggested that a program focusing on leadership behavior might reduce the rate of UAs.

UA Prevention Program

Previous research on leadership behavior yielded five tentative conclusions about the behavior of effective leaders. According to Bass (1981) effective leaders clarify the purposes and objectives of performance, spell out the criteria of evaluation, explain how to meet the criteria, provide feedback about the degree the objectives are being met, and allocate rewards contingent on meeting the objectives. A program was designed to assist Marine officers to follow these principles in dealing with UAs.

To develop a program for use in the Marine Corps it was necessary to integrate the program into the existing chain of command. A battalion, the largest Marine fighting unit, ranges in size from 600 to 1000 members. Battalions are divided into five companies (for infantry units) or five batteries (for artillery units). Daily activities generally occur among members of the same companies or batteries. Thus, although company and battery commanders report to the battalion commander, they have a fair amount of discretion in the ways in which they supervise. Any polices toward UA had to be carried out at the company or battery level while simultaneously being compatible with the policies of the battalion commander.

Setting Objectives

The first part of the program involved setting objectives. In the past, UA objectives had been set; however, they were typically unattainable since a goal of 0% UA was usually set. The criterion was also flawed in that individual company commanders deal with UA policy but the 0% UA objective referred to the larger battalion level. To correct these problems, commanders were taught how to set realistic objectives. New monthly UA objectives were to be based on the previous month's UA rate, subordinate commanders were to be involved with setting objectives, and methods to monitor false reports were mentioned. [Note: The term *company* will be used to refer both to companies and batteries for the rest of this report.]

Monitoring UA Rates

UA had been reported daily; however, no methods had been used to track trends of UA rates. The UA Prevention Program (UAPP) provided forms and graphs so that each unit could calculate and post UA rates with comparisons to unit objectives. Individual Marines could monitor the progress of their own units in meeting objectives.

Clarifying and Communicating Commanders' Policies

Clarifying policies was approached by having battalion commanders examine issues that seemed to be related to an individual's propensity to go UA. The battalion commander reported what UA policies were acceptable. The commander could indicate that from 30 minutes to one-half day time off for each of 16 personal situations was acceptable in the battalion. The commander was then to write a two-sentence description of a situation in which the policy would be appropriate. After the commander described acceptable UA policies, these policies were communicated to the company commanders in the battalion. The company commanders were responsible for communicating the policies to the Marines in each company.

Monitoring Command Actions

By using the trend graphs, the written policies, and example cases in weekly discussions among commanders and between commanders and Marines, policies were clarified and communicated and command actions were monitored.

Providing Small Units with Rewards

Performance-contingent rewards were included in the UAPP. A period of time off was to be awarded to the members of any platoon, the smallest unit in a battalion, that had no cases of UA in a month.

Implementing the Use of UAPP

Throughout the development of the program, field commanders were consulted about all decisions of the program planners. To assist further in implementation, a handbook was developed to help commanders use the five parts of the UAPP. The handbook dealt very specifically with the five phases of the program and the battalion and company commander activities. The contrast between this approach and standard management training is worth noting: most management training consists of generalized management training apart from the actual management setting while this program dealt with specific activities and very clearly defined problems.

UAPP was pilot tested for six weeks with a battalion that was scheduled to be deployed overseas before the actual evaluation of the program. This battalion was used for the pilot test so that members of the other battalions were less likely to learn of the program before it was implemented in their own battalions.

Evaluation Design

Eight battalions were used in the evaluation design. Three pairs of battalions were matched on variables that could affect UA, for example, tenure of commander. Matched battalions were randomly assigned either to the UAPP or control. Two unmatched battalions were also randomly assigned to treatments. This approach resulted in 20 treated companies in the program and 20 control companies.

Although the Divisional Commanding General wrote all 20 treatment company commanders strongly supporting the program, individual company commanders did not have to adopt the UAPP. Thus, careful implementation checks were built into the design. Site visits by the evaluators, checklists of UA activities, and a survey of Marines were all used to check on implementation. These checks showed that some commanders needed clarification of the instructions while some others were hostile toward attempts to encourage the adoption of the program.

Outcome Variables

Three types of effects were expected if UAPP had been fully implemented: effects on commanders, on unit members, and on UA rates.

UA rates. The UA rate among the first-term Marines for each of the 40 companies was obtained using a specially designed procedure for capturing each unit's UA individuals without the unit's knowledge. Since reports of UA for longer than 24 hours are reported more reliably than shorter UA periods, the former were from the focus of this report. The rates were computed as the number of different individuals going UA in a month divided by the number of first-term Marines in each company averaged across each day of the month.

Commander variables. If the commander used the UAPP materials, it was anticipated that the UA standards for unit members would become more clear. Increased consistency in the battalion's chain of command was expected to follow, and the commander was expected to have better information about UA rates.

First-term Marines. Increased knowledge among Marines of the commander's expectations was a third anticipated result of UAPP. Clearer policies were expected to change the way Marines learn about UA policies. Instead of grapevine and other informal sources, UAPP was expected to lead to more announcements of policy and the perception that UA policies were more equitable in the treatment compared to the control battalions. Finally, the use of UAPP procedures was expected to lead to more commander attempts to solve the problems that lead to Marines going UA.

Effects on commanders and Marines were assessed using questionnaires. These questionnaires were given to 48 commanders and random samples of Marines prior to the program and at the termination of the 6-month program. On the average, 39 marines per company answered the questionnaire for the pretest or for the posttest. A random sample of Marines were chosen to answer the pretest. An independent sample was chosen to answer the posttest since few Marines stayed in the same company for more than the 6-month period.

Evaluation Findings

The observations of the degree to which UAPP was implemented revealed that the 20 companies in the treatment group should be divided into strong treatment (10 companies) and weak treatment (10 companies) groups. Without the efforts to learn how company commanders implemented the program, these differences in the degree of implementation would not have been recognized.

Effects on Commanders

Although there were some differences among the three groups of commanders, UAPP did not produce the expected changes in the behavior and knowledge of the commanders. [Note: The description of the analysis of the commanders' surveys have been omitted from this condensation to save space.]

Effects on Marines

The pretest and posttest samples were compared on various demographics to assess their equivalence. Posttest Marines had spent less time in their units than pretest Marines ($t(1783) = 3.72$, $p < .001$). This difference accurately mirrored changes among the Marines at the base. Furthermore, the turnover rate was higher in control group than in the treatment group. These differences made it important to statistically control unit tenure by using analyses of covariance.

Marines were asked to name UA policies in their company. On the average they were able to name 2.14 ($sd = 1.17$) out of 4 policies. The means for the three groups are given in Table C3–1. The number of policies rated as fair was a second variable, the overall mean was 1.08 ($sd = 1.27$). Since UAPP was designed to enable commanders to reduce UA rate, Marines were asked for their own level of agreement with the statement: "The chain of command can do little to prevent a Marine from going UA." Also, they were asked how much they thought their com-

TABLE C3-1. Effects of UAPP on Unit Marines

EXPECTED EFFECTS	STRONG TREATMENT		WEAK TREATMENT		CONTROL	
	$\overline{X}(SD)_{Pre}$	$\overline{X}(SD)_{Post}$	$\overline{X}(SD)_{Pre}$	$\overline{X}(SD)_{Post}$	$\overline{X}(SD)_{Pre}$	$\overline{X}(SD)_{Post}$
1. Number of policies known (Range: 0–4)*	2.15(1.6)	2.20(1.5)	2.14(1.1)	2.19(1.2)	2.18(1.2)	2.03(1.1)
2. Number of policies unfair (Range: 0–4)	0.89(1.2)	1.02(1.3)	1.14(1.3)	1.17(1.3)	1.03(1.2)	1.17(1.3)
3. Own attitudes about leaders preventing UA (Range: 1–5; 5 = most positive)	2.97(1.5)	2.89(1.5)	2.65(1.5)	2.78(1.5)	3.06(1.5)	2.97(1.5)
4. Perceived attitudes of leaders (Range: 1–5; 5 = most positive)**	3.00(1.5)	3.30(1.5)	3.00(1.5)	3.21(1.5)	3.13(1.5)	3.14(1.5)
5. Number of formal methods to learn policies (Range: 0–3)†	0.83(0.9)	0.75(0.9)	0.69(0.9)	0.81(0.9)	0.74(0.9)	0.64(0.9)
6. Frequency of discussions with leaders about problems‡	2.56(1.5)	2.45(1.5)	2.59(1.4)	2.60(1.6)	2.52(1.5)	2.16(1.3)

* $F_{(2,3096)} = 4.2, p < .01$
** $F_{(2,2747)} = 2.8, p = .06$
† $F_{(2,3096)} = 4.5, p < .01$
‡ $F_{(2,2746)} = 3.1, p < .05$

manders would agree with the statement. Both ratings averaged close to the scale midpoint (2.90 (*sd* = 1.51) out of 5) for Marine attitudes and 3.14 (*sd* = 1.47) for perceived commander attitudes. Marines were asked to indicate the number of formal methods they used to learn about UA policies. The maximum possible was three. The overall mean was 0.73 (*sd* = 0.93). Last, Marines were to indicate how frequently they discussed personal problems with their leaders; one indicated "1 or 2 times per month" while six indicated "nearly every day." A grand mean of 2.4 (*sd* = 1.47) was found.

If UAPP was effective, the treatment groups (strong and weak) were expected to show changes between the pretest and the posttest, but the control battalions were expected to show no systematic change. Table C3–1 contains the means and standard deviations for the three groups at the pretest and the posttest for the five variables. Each dependent variable was analyzed using a two (pretest vs. posttest) by three (strong, weak, control) analysis of covariance using time in unit as the covariate. Support for the expectations for the program would be reflected in interactions between time of test and type of treatment.

As the table shows, four variables showed the expected interaction; however, not in the form that had been expected. Instead of showing no change, the control group showed a decrement in good UA management from the pretest to the posttest, while the treatment groups showed more stability or slight improvement. For example, examine the means of "discussing problems with leader." Marines reported that discussion frequency dropped in the strong treatment condition, stayed the same in the weak treatment condition, but dropped markedly in the control battalions. It is possible that the high turnover among the Marines made it impossible for them to notice improvement. It seemed that the impact of UAPP was to counteract the deleterious effects attributable to being in the unit a short period of time.

Effects on UA

Table C3–2 contains two sets of mean UA rates. When divided by the three groups, UA rate went down in both the strong and weak treatment battalions, but increased in the control battalions. Although this pattern of changes was supportive of the program, the results were not statistically significant, and the weak treatment battalions had higher UA rates than the control battalions.

The lower part of Table C3–2 divides the battalions on the basis of number of changes in UA policies as perceived by Marines. The data in Table C3–2 were reanalyzed for each battalion separately. The seven treatment battalions whose data produced no statistically significant changes were grouped together. The six treatment battalions showing one significant change from pretest to posttest were grouped together. Seven treatment battalions showed two or more statistically significant changes. Preprogram and postprogram UA rates were calculated for each of these three groups. As shown in the lower part of Table C3–2 the greatest decrease in UA rate occurred in the battalions whose members detected the greatest number of positive changes. Those treatment battalions in which no change was detected actually showed an increase in UA. Furthermore, in spite of beginning the program with UA rates higher than the control battalions, the battalions in which change was detected showed lower UA rates after the program. Several approaches to the analysis of the lower half of Table C3–2 to rule out such alternative interpretations as regression to the mean [omitted from this condensation] showed that only the battalions whose members detected changes showed reductions in UA rates. The reduction in UA rates was approximately 50 percent.

In summary, the UAPP seemed effective in its overall goal of reducing UA rates. However, the process of changing UA rates is not clear. Several of the expected changes in leaders' behaviors were not found. It appears that the rates were reduced in those units whose members experienced a greater opportunity to learn

TABLE C3-2. Effects of UAPP on Unit UA Rates

A. UNITS GROUPED BY IMPLEMENTATION

STRONG TREATMENT (N = 10)		WEAK TREATMENT (N = 10)		CONTROL (N = 20)	
$\overline{X}(SD)_{Pre}$	$\overline{X}(SD)_{Post}$	$\overline{X}(SD)_{Pre}$	$\overline{X}(SD)_{Post}$	$\overline{X}(SD)_{Pre}$	$\overline{X}(SD)_{Post}$
2.59(.7)	˙1.86(1.4)	3.04(1.4)	2.23(1.4)	1.89(1.2)	2.09(1.2)

B. UNITS GROUPED BY CHANGES TO MARINES

TREATMENT: ≥ 2 CHANGES (N = 7)		TREATMENT: 1 CHANGE (N = 6)		TREATMENT: NO CHANGE (N = 7)		CONTROL (N = 20)	
$\overline{X}(SD)_{Pre}$	$\overline{X}(SD)_{Post}$	$\overline{X}(SD)_{Pre}$	$\overline{X}(SD)_{Post}$	$\overline{X}(SD)_{Pre}$	$\overline{X}(SD)_{Post}$	$\overline{X}(SD)_{Pre}$	$\overline{X}(SD)_{Post}$
3.10(1.6)	1.57(1.1)	2.52(.7)	1.27(.8)	2.78(.8)	3.19(1.3)	1.89(1.2)	2.09(1.2)

about the commander's policies, were able to test those policies through discussions, and had the policies periodically reviewed. Since the unit members knew that a policy existed, punishment for UA would not be unexpected. Even though the Marines were not less likely to view the policies as fair, knowing about the policies made it more likely that they would be obeyed. An important point is that the 50 percent reduction in UA was achieved with relatively minimal changes on the part of the commanders who agreed that the changes were "good management practices."

References

BASS, B. M. 1981. *Stodgill's handbook of leadership.* New York: The Free Press.
NICHOLSON, N. 1977. Absence behavior and attendance motivation: A conceptual synthesis. *The Journal of Management Studies* 14, 231–252.

CASE STUDY 4

Welfare policies continue to be a source of controversy. Some people say that welfare is essential in a complex, humane society. Others argue that welfare is misused and encourages passive, unproductive behavior. The provision of family planning services is particularly controversial. An evaluation cannot resolve disagreements over philosophical and value-related issues. However, one could ask if public tax money is being spent in a way that achieves the short-run goals of the program. And, in the case of welfare services designed to prevent future problems, one could ask if the probable cost of the prevented problems exceeds the cost of the preventive welfare services.

Case Study 4 sought to answer whether publicity funded family planning services were saving tax dollars by estimating what the welfare costs of users of the services would have received if the family planning service had been unavailable. Estimating what did not occur is a problem for an evaluation of any preventive service whether in a medical, criminal justice, or education setting. Note how the evaluators made estimates of what could have been expected if the services had not been available. They then converted these estimates into estimated additional welfare costs and compared them to the costs of the preventive program.

THE COSTS AND BENEFITS OF TITLE XX FUNDING
FOR FAMILY PLANNING SERVICES IN TEXAS[1]

Summary

Through the Title XX program the Texas Department of Human Resources funded family planning services for 227,253 women in Fiscal Year 1981. A cost-benefit analysis of the program was conducted to learn whether this use of state funds was effective. The outcomes of a program designed to prevent something from occurring are especially difficult to determine. The approach chosen was based on making estimates of births that would have occurred among the women served by this

[1]Based on Malitz, D. 1984. The costs and benefits of Title XX and Title XIX family planning services in Texas. *Evaluation Review* 8, 519–536. Copyright, 1984, Sage Publications, Inc. This condensation omits references to Title XIX programs, which were included in the original.

program in its absence. These estimates were made by using national data giving the typical effectiveness rates of the various contraceptive methods used by the women who sought services from the 78 providers funded by Title XX. Information on the contraceptive methods used before entering the program and after receiving services were gathered from the providers for randomly selected samples of 1606 adolescents (< 20 years old) and 1605 adults (> 19 years old). Information was provided by 65 of the 78 providers yielding rates of 78.0 percent of the adolescent sample and 79.9 percent of the adult sample. The biggest changes were in the percentages of women changing from "no method" to using the pill. The number of births that would have been expected in the next 12 months were compared with similar estimates of the number of births expected during the 12 months after the women received the services of the funded centers. These estimates were converted into the number of births averted through the services funded by Title XX. On the average, 99 births were estimated to have been averted for each 1000 patients served.

Estimates were then made for the welfare costs that the state would have incurred during the next 12-month period. Hospital care for mothers and infants eligible for Aid to Families of Dependent Children (AFDC) would have averaged $2111 per birth. Welfare maintenance for 12 months would have averaged $2038 for AFDC-eligible mothers. Last, additional food stamp allotments would have totaled $475 for 12 months. These total $4624 saved for each birth to a family that would have qualified for AFDC. Using state-wide data it was estimated that 30.4 percent of the women served would have qualified for AFDC. The 69.6 percent of the patients who would not have qualified for AFDC would have received an additional $82 in food stamps if a child had been born. Combining these projected costs with the percentage of AFDC-eligible families yielded an average saving to the Department of $1,463 per birth averted. Since 99 births per 1000 women were averted, the average savings per client patient was $145. Cost per woman served was $75, yielding a cost-to-benefit ratio for the 12 months after treatment in the funded clinics of 1 to 1.93. In other words, the department saved nearly $2 for each dollar spent within the first year. The report describes the estimation methods and divides the patients by adolescents and adults.

Program Being Evaluated

Family planning services funded by the State of Texas (Title XX) are administered by 78 providers throughout the state. In Fiscal Year 1981 227,253 women were served by these programs. Many of the women served and their children would be qualified to receive welfare support including Aid to Families of Dependent Children (AFDC), Food Stamps, and Medicaid.

The Evaluation Question

All government-funded programs face the issue of relating their costs to their benefits. Welfare programs are especially scrutinized since the beneficiaries of the programs do not pay for the services provided. Services purchased directly by consumers are not subject to a similar scrutiny since the purchaser and the consumer are identical, and consumers are presumably doing their own evaluations. The present report focused on the question of the costs and benefits of family planning services funded by the Texas Department of Human Resources (TDHR) for women qualified for public assistance. The costs of the programs funded by Title XX are easy to ascertain; however, the benefits are much more difficult to determine. Conducting a cost-benefit study is especially difficult when the program is preventive in nature. It is necessary to estimate the frequency of what would have happened had the program not been available.

Evaluation Method

To conduct a cost-benefit analysis it is necessary to define what benefits will be included in the analysis and which benefits will be ignored. It was decided to limit the benefits analyzed to the cost savings to TDHR due to lower demands on AFDC, Food Stamp, and Medicare programs in the year following contact with a supported family planning agency. There are other benefits from Title XX that were not considered. Some women benefited from health screening, which is part of Title XX services. Some patients benefited by avoiding the adverse effects of adolescent pregnancy; however, these benefits were not considered either. Last, limiting births may have helped some of the patients to avoid long-term welfare dependency, a benefit to the women and TDHR. The difficulty of estimating the value of such a benefit suggested that it not be used. By ignoring these benefits, the value of Title XX services was underestimated. However, by focusing on more objective outcomes, cost-benefit analyses are less controversial as long as benefits exceed costs. If the analysis were going to be used to argue that the program was inefficient and should be curtailed, then it would be important to search for every possible benefit.

Calculating the amount saved in welfare costs required an estimate of the number of births averted through Title XX. To estimate the number of births that were averted, the proportions of patients using various contraceptive methods before they entered the program (premethod) were compared to the proportions using various methods at their last visit (postmethod). The degree to which the patients began to use more effective methods would indicate the degree of program effectiveness. Use-effectiveness rates are available for methods of contraception. The number of pregnancies expected during the 12 months following entry into the program could be calculated using these use-effectiveness rates. It was assumed that without the program, the women's choices of contraception methods would not have changed. Similarly, the pregnancies expected for the 12 months following the last visit were also estimated from the use-effectiveness rates. The difference between these two estimates is the number of pregnancies averted through the services of Title XX.

Data Collection

Patients were stratified by provider and age: adolescents (19 years and younger) and adults (20 years and older). Based on this stratification and expected rate of return from providers, random samples of 1606 adolescents (about 2.5 percent of the Title XX adolescent population) and 1605 adults (1.0 percent of the adult patients) were defined. Surveys were prepared for each of the women sampled and sent to the appropriate providers. These surveys asked the provider to report the date when the patient first came to the center, the date of the last visit, and the methods of contraception used at both times. Staff were assured that patient confidentiality would be respected. In fact, the forms were designed in a way that permitted the names of the patients to be readily removed.

Results

Pregnancies, Births, Abortions, and Miscarriages Averted

Contraceptive method and averted pregnancies. Survey forms were returned by 65 of the 78 providers. Overall, 1252 complete and usable survey forms for adolescents (78.0 percent) and 1283 for adults (79.9 percent) were returned.

Table C4–1 summarizes the contraceptive use rates for adolescents and adults. When the surveys indicated that a patient used multiple methods, the most effective

TABLE C4-1. **Contraceptive Method Use Patterns and Expected Number of Pregnancies Averted Among Title XX Patients Served**

CONTRACEPTIVE METHOD	EXPECTED NUMBER OF ANNUAL PREGNANCIES PER 1,000 WOMEN	PERCENT USING EACH METHOD BEFORE FIRST VISIT AND AFTER LAST VISIT TO PROGRAM			
		ADOLESCENTS		ADULTS	
		PRE	POST	PRE	POST
Pill	25	21.4	74.7	42.9	62.9
IUD	71	0.8	1.8	3.7	6.7
Diaphragm	172	0.3	1.1	0.6	1.9
Foams, creams, jellies	184	1.9	0.8	2.3	2.4
Rhythm	250	0.2	0.0	0.2	0.2
Sterilization	0	0.0	0.1	1.7	6.9
Condom	123	5.9	6.5	4.8	7.9
Other	189	0.8	0.6	1.1	1.2
None	490 to 640	68.7	14.4	42.6	9.9
Total	—	100.0	100.0	100.0	100.0

EXPECTED NUMBER OF ANNUAL PREGNANCIES PER 1,000 PATIENTS	ADOLESCENTS		ADULTS	
	PRE	POST	PRE	POST
Low estimate	357	103	237	90
High estimate	460	124	301	104
Midpoint estimate	408.5	113.5	269.0	97.0
Pregnancies averted	295		172	

Source: Forrest, Hermalin, and Henshaw (1981) for expected number of annual pregnancies per 1,000 women.

Note: Based upon surveys of contraceptive failures among married women using the methods listed. The estimates of pregnancy rates among users of no method are based upon surveys of unmarried, sexually active adolescents.

method was coded. In addition, the table gives the expected number of pregnancies expected in 12 months among sexually active women using the various methods.

For both adolescents and adults, the table shows a dramatic drop in the percentages of women reported to be using no method. For example, when entering the program over two-thirds of the adolescents did not use any contraceptive method, but when leaving only 14 percent were still not using any method. The method most often used when leaving the program was the pill for both age groups. These percentages were roughly comparable to the findings of other surveys of contraceptive use.

One might consider the women leaving the program not using a contraceptive method to be program failures. Clinic personnel, however, report that some women seek pregnancy tests at the centers and that some others did not receive any method for medical reasons. It is not possible to distinguish these patients from true program failures.

The lower section of Table C4-1 is based on the rates of use data across methods. The numbers of expected pregnancies per 1000 users for each method was projected to be the number of expected pregnancies in 12 months among 1000 patients of the clinics supported by Title XX funds. These expected values are calculated for patients if they had continued with the methods they used when they came to the clinics ("pre" columns) and if they continued with the methods in use when they left the program ("post" column). Since the estimates for "no method" vary widely, both a high and a low number of estimates of pregnancies per 1000 women for a year are given. For purposes of this study, the midpoint between the high and the low estimates was taken. The differences between the number of pregnancies expected for women using the preclinic methods and for women using the postclinic methods are the numbers of pregnancies averted for adolescents and adults, 295 and 172 per 1000 patients per year, respectively. Table C4–2 converts these pregnancy rates into number of pregnancies averted for the entire patient population of Title XX programs.

Births averted. The number of pregnancies averted, however, is not the same as the number of births averted. On the basis of national data for low-income women, the numbers of pregnancies averted were divided into numbers of averted births, abortions, and miscarriages. The assumption had to be made that these national rates are applicable to the women who attended the Title XX clinics. On the basis of these estimates, it was concluded that the clinics were responsible for averting 22,398 births, or 99 per 1000 patients, per year. Or in other words, the program averted almost one birth for every ten patients served.

Estimate of the Benefit of Title XX

Births to Title XX women create costs to TDHR in several ways. Some women qualify for Medicaid payments for some delivery expenses. TDHR will pay AFDC and Med-

TABLE C4–2. Estimated Number of Pregnancies, Births, Abortions, and Miscarriages Averted by the Title XX Family Planning Program

AGE GROUP	NUMBER IN PROGRAM	PREGS. AVERTED	TOTAL BIRTHS, ABORTIONS, AND MISCARRIAGES AVERTED			BIRTHS AVERTED PER 1,000 PATIENTS
			BIRTHS	ABORTS.	MISCAR.	
Adolescents	63,176	18,637	6,784	9,542	2,311	107
Adults	164,077	28,221	15,614	8,592	4,015	95
Total	227,253	46,858	22,398	18,134	6,326	99

U.S. PREGNANCY OUTCOMES	PERCENT DISTRIBUTION OF UNINTENDED PREGNANCIES BY OUTCOME		
AGE GROUP	BIRTHS	ABORTS.	MISCAR.
Adolescents	36.4	51.2	12.4
Adults	55.3	30.4	14.2
Total	47.8	38.7	13.5

Source: Dryfoos (1982) for distribution of unintended pregnancies by outcome.

Note: Pregnancies averted are calculated by multiplying program counts by Title XX rates in Table C4–1.

icaid benefits for each mother and her child for one year. Last, a birth will qualify some women for additional food stamps. Births to women who qualify for AFDC will be called "AFDC births." Women who do not qualify for AFDC will still qualify for increased food stamps. Births to these women will be called "non-AFDC births."

Costs of AFDC Births to TDHR. The average direct cost of births to TDHR in FY 1981 was $1304 for each delivery and $807 for inpatient care for premature babies and treating birth defects. Thus, the average cost associated with each birth was $2111.

An AFDC mother with one child received $86/month, or $1032 for 12 months. In addition, non-birth-related Medicaid benefits were estimated to be $1006 for each AFDC mother and child. Welfare maintenance, thus, totals $2038 for a year.

The maximum food stamp allotment for increasing the family size from one to two members is $50/month. However, only 87 percent of AFDC cases receive food stamps, and the average case receives 91 percent of the maximum allowed. Therefore, the average AFDC birth was estimated to lead to an additional cost of $50/month × 12 months × 0.87 × 0.91, or $475 for the first year.

In total then, the average AFDC birth was expected to lead to an increase of $2111 plus $2038 plus $475, or $4624, during the 12 months after the birth.

The percentage of births to clinic patients who will become AFDC cases. Since not all of Title XX patients would have qualified for AFDC, these costs must be reduced to reflect only the proportion of mothers who would have qualified for AFDC. It was believed that the percentage of Title XX patients who were already mothers and were qualified for AFDC would be the best estimate of the proportion of child-bearing Title XX women who would have entered AFDC if a child had been borne. These percentages are 35.8 percent and 28.3 percent for adolescents and adults, respectively.

Combining the costs of an AFDC birth and the proportion of Title XX patients who probably would have qualified for AFDC yielded the following average expected benefits for each averted Title XX birth: for adolescents, 0.358 × $4624, or $1655; for adults, 0.283 × $4624, or $1309.

Costs of non-AFDC births to TDHR. The maximum food stamp allotment was $600/year. However, only 27.4 percent of Title XX patients qualify for food stamps, and the average non-AFDC case only qualifies for 50 percent of the maximum allotment. Therefore, the average yearly increase in food stamp allotments for each non-AFDC birth will be about $82, i.e., $600 × 0.274 × 0.50.

Percentages of non-AFDC Title XX Patients. Since the percentages of AFDC cases were estimated above, the percentages of non-AFDC Title XX cases will simply be 100 percent minus 35.8 percent, or 64.2 percent for adolescents and 100 percent minus 28.3 percent, or 71.7 percent, for adults. Applying these percentages to the $82 figure yields the second component of the cost of the average Title XX birth for adolescents of $53,[2] and $59 for adults.

As shown in Table C4–3, the total benefit to TDHR for each Title XX birth averted was $1655 plus $53, or $1708, for adolescents and $1406 plus $59, or $1368, for adults.

Cost-Benefit Analysis of Title XX

Since each patient could not be considered to have a birth averted through the services of the Title XX-supported clinics, the benefits need to be scaled down from the benefit of each birth averted to the average for each Title XX patient. Table C4–3 includes the average saving for each adolescent and adult family planning patient.

[2]The published article erroneously gave this figure as $43.

TABLE C4-3. Costs and Estimated Savings Associated with the Title XX Family Program for Adolescents and Adults

	ADOLESCENTS ONLY (19 AND UNDER)	ADULTS ONLY (20 AND OVER)	ALL PATIENTS
Savings			
Total estimated savings per birth averted	$1,708	$1,368	$1,463
Births averted per family planning patient	0.107	0.095	0.099
Savings per family planning patient	$ 183	$ 130	$ 145
Costs			
Average Title XX expenditure per family planning patient (including sterilizations)	$ 75	$ 75	$ 75
COST-BENEFIT RATIO	1:2.44	1:1.73	1:1.93
Total cost and savings in FY81			
Number of patients	63,176	164,077	227,253
Total cost	$ 4,778,000	$12,410,000	$17,188,000
Total estimated savings	$11,658,000	$21,469,000	$33,127,000
Net estimated savings	$ 6,880,000	$ 9,059,000	$15,939,000

The balance of the analysis is easy to complete. In FY 1981 227,253 patients were served at a cost of $17,187,782; an average cost per patient of about $75. The cost-benefit ratios can then be readily calculated by dividing the benefits by costs. For example, $183 divided by $75 yields a cost-benefit ratio of 1 to 2.44. For each dollar spent on Title XX services, TDHR is estimated to have gained a benefit of $2.44 in the 12 months following the provision of services to adolescents. For adults the ratio was 1 to 1.73.

Final Comments on the Method.

Many potential benefits of Title XX family planning services were not included in this analysis. There were benefits from avoiding nearly 22,000 abortions and over 7,000 miscarriages that were not included. Some of the expenses of the averted births that would have been covered by counties and cities (not TDHR) were ignored since the focus was on the benefits of savings to TDHR, not on benefits to cities and counties. Last, when possible, estimates were compared to other studies of family planning clinics. These comparisons [largely omitted from this condensation] generally supported the findings of the study.

REFERENCES

DRYFOOS, J. G. 1982. Contraceptive use, pregnancy intentions and pregnancy outcomes among U.S. women. *Family Planning Perspectives* 14, 81–94.

FORREST, J. D.; HERMALIN, A. I.; AND HENSHAW, S. K. 1981. The impact of family planning clinic programs on adolescent pregnancy. *Family Planning Perspectives* 13, 109–116.

CASE STUDY 5

Many evaluations rightfully focus on the reactions of the program participants as a major aspect of an evaluation. There are times, however, when the views of the participants cannot reflect crucial aspects of the quality of the program. Furthermore, the self-interest of the participants may not coincide with the interests of other important stakeholders. The authors of this case study found that the program participants (medical residents) were quite pleased with their training. The observations of the evaluators, on the other hand, indicated clear discrepancies between the goals of the program and the actual training the residents received. Inadequacies in training could result in less competent performance as the residents completed their programs and began to function as independent physicians. By identifying the residents' future patients as an important stakeholder group, the evaluators concluded that the residency program had many deficiencies that were not recognized by the residents themselves.

Crucial points to note in this case study include: the contrast between the participants' and evaluators' views of the quality of the training, the evaluators' concern to identify the stakeholders more broadly than just those groups immediately involved in the program, and the use of naturalistic research methods as described in Chapter 12.

AN EVALUATION OF A FAMILY PRACTICE RESIDENCY PROGRAM USING A NATURALISTIC INQUIRY PARADIGM[1]

Summary

Naturalistic observations and ratings of quality of education were used to evaluate a residency program for family practice physicians. The curriculum committee of the program requested an evaluation in order to identify curriculum areas in which

[1]Based on Bussigel, and M., Filling, C. 1985. Data discrepancies and their origins: An evaluation of a family practice residency program using a naturalistic inquiry paradigm. *Evaluation & the Health Professions* 8, 177–192. Copyright 1985 Sage Publications, Inc.

improvements could be made and themes that could be used in faculty development. This concern was important since (a) family practice is a new, still developing, specialty, (b) family practice residents serve rotations, gaining hands-on experience and instruction from specialists in internal medicine, pediatrics, and obstetrics/gynecology, and (c) greater emphasis is placed on the development of interpersonal skills in family practice residencies compared to other specialties.

Program expectations were developed with the curriculum committee, the director, two family practice physicians, and the psychologist associated with the residency. The degree to which these expectations were carried out was examined through structured interviews with 11 of the 12 family practice residents and through nine days of observations of the activities of the residents and their supervising physicians and program faculty.

Residents rated their experiences in quite favorable terms. However, the evaluators observed many examples of (a) poor teaching strategies among the faculty from non-family-practice specialties, (b) inadequate feedback from supervising physicians, and (c) low interest on the part of residents in psychosocial issues related to patient care.

Possible reasons for these discrepancies include: different implicit standards for teaching and different implicit views of the primary stakeholder group. Residents seemed to be basing their ratings of the quality of instruction on their experiences with medical education. It seems unlikely that they could recognize the need for a better quality of instruction without appropriate experience with other, more effective instructional methods. Second, residents may have been making the favorable ratings because they were comfortable with the learning climate rather than on the basis of the amount of learning taking place. The evaluators felt that future patients should be viewed as the primary stakeholder in evaluations on the quality of residency programs. This orientation made the evaluators especially sensitive to lost opportunities for training.

Program Descriptions and Evaluation Questions

Residency programs for physicians are hands-on training programs to be completed by graduates of medical school before becoming licensed medical doctors. Hospitals sponsor residency programs in which the residents provide the primary patient care under the direction of attending (i.e., licensed) physicians. [Note: Family practice residencies are for medical school graduates who plan to offer "primary" medical care to children and adults whose problems do not require the attention of specialists. Family practice physicians also treat patients with chronic conditions requiring monitoring and periodic medical assessments.] Residents work under attending family practice practitioners as well as serving rotations (e.g., three months) in such specialties as obstetrics/gynecology and internal medicine. Since family practice is a fairly new form of medical care, many family practice residencies are rather new. This evaluation was part of a larger project aimed at improvement and expansion of a new residency program.

The curriculum committee contacted the evaluators (a) for help in identifying those curriculum areas in which modification was most likely to improve the program and (b) for suggestions of promising themes for faculty development. To carry out this evaluation, explicit statements of program expectations were developed. Since family practice physicians are responsible for initial diagnosis of illnesses, routine medical care for children, and on-going care of chronic illnesses, their interpersonal relations with their patients are more important than for other specialist physicians. Specifically, the evaluation was designed to (a) identify the fit between expectations and program components, (b) identify the major learning experiences of the residents, (c) identify major strengths and weaknesses of the program with a particular focus on areas in which expectations and what actually occurs do not match, and (d) offer preliminary suggestions for improving the residency program.

The Inquiry Procedure

Four data sources were used. One, documents describing the program structure were reviewed. Two, key faculty members (specifically, the curriculum committee, program director, two family practitioners, and one psychologist) were asked to describe the program components and how each one contributed to achieving specific program goals. This group later responded to the initial draft of the findings and their interpretation. Three, one resident from each of the three classes was observed for three full days. The purpose of these observations was to gain insight into the learning experiences of the residents. Observations were conducted in the out-patient clinic as well as in patient hospital rooms. Both family practitioner settings and specialty rotations were observed. Four, all residents (except one who could not be reached) were interviewed. They were asked to evaluate various aspects of the program and to list major strengths and weaknesses.

Evaluation Findings

[Note: Many of the findings of this evaluation have not been included in this condensation, which stresses the way qualitative observational data changed the interpretation of the interviews.]

Areas for program improvement were considered to be most promising when program expectations and the residents' reports were most discrepant with the evaluators' direct observations.

Comprehensive Care and Continuity of Care

A major goal of the family practice residency was to provide training that emphasized care for the whole person and care that followed the patient throughout the treatment. Since major portions of the residency are spent in rotations outside the family practice department, it was necessary to learn whether the goals of family practice were carried out in all rotations included in the residency. When interviewed, residents affirmed that comprehensive care and continuity of care were stressed in all rotations. Residents reported that these goals were most in evidence in family practice settings, but had little criticism for the training in other settings. The observations of the evaluators contrasted with the residents' views about the non-family-practice rotations. Since all agreed on the goals, the disagreement reflected different standards for measuring adequacy. For example, since no attempt was made to be sure that patients would see the same resident at each visit, the evaluators felt that continuity of care, a major family practice goal, was being ignored.

Formal Teaching Sessions

Besides the hands-on training in clinics and patient rooms, two formal teaching seminars focusing on patient-physician relations and psychosocial topics were held weekly. [These training experiences are especially important to this residency since family practice practitioners are physicians who need to distinguish between medical diagnoses and problems of a psychological origin or health problems compounded by psychological issues.] The residents again described the sessions as very valuable. All but one of the 11 residents claimed to usually attend and to seldom have a schedule conflict with the sessions. However, of the three teaching sessions observed, two were attended by only half or fewer of the residents. One resident mentioned that average attendance was up from the former level of two or three residents per session. In addition, the residents described the sessions as very interesting, a marked contrast to the observed low level of engagement in the discussions of the case studies. It appeared that the residents were describing their interest in positive terms compatible with what they thought the ideal family practice resident ought to believe.

Quality of Clinical Teaching and Training

Residents were asked to rate the quality of teaching and opportunities for hands-on inpatient and outpatient contact.

Obstetrics/gynecology rotation. Residents were quite positive about the degree of patient contact and mildly critical to very positive about the quality of the teaching. Overall, residents evaluated the OB/Gyn rotation in favorable terms. In contrast, the evaluators concluded that the residents received virtually no feedback on their work. Although contact between residents and Ob/Gyn attending physicians was mandated by a sign-off procedure, this contact was not used for teaching. Moreover, attending physicians were not found to express much concern about the development of interpersonal skills among the residents.

Internal medicine rotation. A similar contradiction between resident assertions and evaluator observations occurred for the internal medicine rotation. Residents rated teaching in internal medicine as good to excellent. There was some concern about the limited opportunity to do "procedures." This point did match the evaluators' view in that the patient load was light and included contact with only a limited variety of problems. Observations suggested that attending internal medicine physicians were motivated to teach; however, they displayed undeveloped teaching skills. Cases presented for discussion seemed to be chosen on an ad hoc basis, and teaching sessions were poorly structured.

In general, although the residents rated their experiences in favorable terms, the qualitative observations of the evaluators were quite unfavorable.

Interpretations of the Findings

Contrasts between the residents' views and the evaluators' conclusions based on their observations requires interpretation. Two likely reasons were suggested to lie behind the discrepancies.

Variations in Standards

Asking residents about the quality of their educational experiences assumes that the residents know what a good residency would be. This assumption is not valid since residents have been exposed to many nonoptimal educational situations for several years. In fact, their experiences in the residency may be similar to many instructional settings in medical school during past years. Second, there is no reason to believe that residents should be able to intuit a medical educational system better than the systems they have known.

Variations in Definitions of Goals and Clients

The evaluators became aware that they may have held different goals for the residents than the residents held for themselves. Furthermore, the evaluators discovered that they often identified with patients and thus viewed future patients of the residents as the primary stakeholder group of the evaluation. It is likely that residents saw themselves as the primary beneficiaries of the residency program. Thus, residents may have responded to the interview questions in terms of their own level of comfort with the form of instruction they experienced.

Recommendations[2]

In the light of the findings it is recommended that instructional methods be given close attention by the residency curriculum committee. The expectations for the residency seemed well known by all, but attending physicians not in family practice do not seem to be tailoring their teaching to meet family practice expectations. In some cases, teaching itself needs to be instituted since it isn't occurring.

Second, the focus of the family practice curriculum committee on the importance of psychological and sociological issues is not shared by the residents. Psychosocial issues may become more important to the residents if they see such issues being taken seriously by attending physicians in all of the rotations in which family practice residents serve.

[2]Recommendations were not part of the published report. These recommendations were added to make this condensation conform to the style of an evaluation report.

Epilogue

This text has sought to provide the groundwork for the development of the technical skills necessary to conduct program evaluations in human service and business settings. The organization of the book reflects the authors' view of the most useful approaches to conducting such research. A brief reexamination of the flow chart in Part I can give the reader a quick review of the main points of the material covered. The flow chart can also help evaluators explain to staff the services evaluators can provide.

Perhaps equally as important as technical skills are the evaluator's attitudes and orientation toward the role of program evaluator. While these are referred to throughout this book, it may be of help to draw these themes together in this section.

Humility won't hurt. Evaluators work in service settings. These settings are not designed to facilitate the conducting of research. Because this is true, the evaluator can expect to be seen as filling a marginal role in the service delivery setting. Because the evaluator is always working on someone else's turf, arrogance will effectively block the exercise of even superb technical skills.

Impatience may lead to disappointment. Program and facility administrators have many constituencies, all expecting attention. Program evaluation is only one source of information on which decisions and plans are based. Financial concerns, community pressures, political realities, bureaucratic inertia, and so forth are all powerful influences on program planners and administrators. Evaluators who have patience are less likely to feel ignored and un-loved when their recommendations do not receive immediate attention.

Recognize the importance of the evaluator's perspective. Evaluators have some skills that may be lacking in human service settings. Service staffs focus on individuals and often do not understand the overall program. Evaluators have a social orientation that can provide the staff with a new viewpoint. Administrators, on the other hand, do seek an overall perspective. However, administrators have a far better grasp of financial and other tangible matters than of social variables affecting the patient/client/student/trainee population served. Evaluators can provide information to administrators on social variables that are usually unavailable to administrators.

Focus on practical questions. People working in human service organizations are seldom concerned about matters of only theoretical interest. Evaluators can work most effectively when they are oriented toward practical questions about the program being studied. Try not to forget that seeking to initiate and sustain change in people's lives is hard work. Faced with pressing human needs and with criticism from governmental bodies or insurance companies for excessive costs and alleged inefficiencies, agency staff and management desire practical assistance.

Work on feasible issues. If an evaluation is not feasible, do not attempt it. Do not waste your time and that of the staff. However, although it may not be feasible to work on a particular issue, it might be feasible to work on a less ambitious question. For example, if outcomes cannot be handled, it may be possible to develop a procedure to monitor the delivery of service.

Avoid data addiction. It is tempting to seek to gather a great amount of information about the program or about those served by the program. It might be nice to know everything possible about the program, but there are two compelling reasons to limit the amount of data sought to that which is essential. First, asking for too much information will increase the percentage of potential respondents who will refuse to cooperate and consequently will provide no information. Second, evaluators will often find themselves under too much time pressure to analyze all the data gathered. Thus, the effort of the cooperative respondents will be wasted. If the information is not essential to the evaluation, do not try to gather it.

Evaluators are information channels. There are many things that can get in the way when new information is presented to potential users. Social science jargon and esoteric analyses can reduce the flow of information to those not acquainted with the jargon or schooled in statistics. Readers and listeners will be bored with a presentation that seems planned to display the evaluator's knowledge and technical skills. Save that for meetings of professional societies. To be effective, presentations to staff should be relevant to the program, and recommendations should be practicable.

Encourage an evaluation orientation.   Ideally, evaluation encourages honest relations among staff, clients, administrators, and program sponsors. These groups often act as though all failures could have been avoided. Although failures cannot always be avoided, people can always learn from failures. The essence of the concept of the experimenting society is the recognition of the inevitability of failure. Instead of hiding failures or condemning them, help staff and administrators to treat honest attempts as experiments and to learn from failures as well as successes.

Adopt a self-evaluation orientation to your own work.   When evaluation results and recommendations seem to be ignored, evaluators will benefit by asking themselves: Was my presentation clear? Did I address the right questions? Were my answers right? At times the honest answer to these questions will be "No." Evaluators are like service staff people in some ways: neither can always avoid failures, and both can learn from their errors.

References

ABELSON, P. H. 1977. Commission on federal paperwork. *Science* 197: 1237.

ABRAHAM, B. 1980. Intervention analysis and multiple time series. *Biometrika* 67: 73–78.

ABT, C. C. 1977. Applying cost/benefit paradigms to social program evaluations. Paper presented at the meeting of the Evaluation Research Society, October, Washington, D.C.

ADLER, N. E., and STONE, G. C. 1979. Social science perspectives on the health system. In *Health psychology: A handbook*, ed. G. C. Stone, F. Cohen, and N. E. Adler. San Francisco: Jossey-Bass.

ALBRIGHT, J. 1982. Citizen evaluation from the inside. Paper presented at meeting of the Evaluation Research Society, October, Baltimore.

ALEXANDER, H. A. 1986. Cognitive relativism in evaluation. *Evaluation Review* 10: 259–280.

ALLPORT, G. W. 1954. *The nature of prejudice*. Reading, Mass.: Addison-Wesley.

AMERICAN PSYCHOLOGICAL ASSOCIATION. 1982. *Ethical principles in the conduct of research with human participants*. Washington, D.C.: Author.

ANASTASI, A. 1982. *Psychological testing*. 5th ed. New York: Macmillan.

ANDERSON, C. A. 1987. Temperature and aggression: Effects on quarterly, yearly, and city rates of violent and nonviolent crime. *Journal of Personality and Social Psychology* 52: 1161–1173.

ANDERSON, J. F., and BERDIE, D. R. 1975. Effects on response rate of formal and informal questionnaire follow-up techniques. *Journal of Applied Psychology* 60: 225–57.

ARMOR, D. J. 1972. The evidence on busing. *The Public Interest* 28: 90–126.

ATTKISSON, C. C. et al., eds. 1978. *Evaluation of human service programs*. New York: Academic Press.

BALL, R. M. 1978. National health insurance: Comments on selected issues. *Science* 200: 864–73.

BALL, S., and BOGARTZ, G. A. 1970. *The first year of Sesame Street.* Princeton, N.J.: Educational Testing Service.

BANK, A. 1987. A case study: The review of the Los Angeles Bureau of Jewish Education. *Evaluation and Program Planning* 10: 169–178.

BANK, A., and WILLIAMS, R. C., eds. 1987. *Information systems and school improvement: Inventing the future.* New York: Teachers College Press.

BARBOUR, G. P., and WOLFSON, S. M. 1973. Productivity measurement in police crime control. *Public Management* 55: 16, 18, 19.

BARZANSKY, A.; BERNER, E.; and BECKMAN, C. R. R. 1985. Evaluation of a clinical program: Applying the concept of trustworthiness. *Evaluation & the Health Professions* 8: 193–208.

BASS, B. M. 1981. *Stodgill's handbook of leadership.* New York: The Free Press.

BECKER, H. S. 1986. *Writing for social scientists.* Chicago: The University of Chicago Press.

BECKER, H.; HARRELL, W.; and KIRKHART, K. 1982. Evaluators in grey flannel suits: Implications of changes in roles and evaluation priorities for training evaluators. Paper presented at the meeting of the American Psychological Association, August, Washington, D.C.

BERK, R. A. 1977. Discretionary methodology decisions in applied research. *Sociological Methods and Research* 5: 317–34.

BERK, R. A., and ROSSI, P. H. 1976. Doing good or worse: Evaluation research politically re-examined. *Social Problems,* February, pp. 337–49.

BERMAN, J. J. 1978. An experiment in parole supervision. *Evaluation Quarterly* 2: 71–90.

BIGELOW, D. A., and CIARLO, J. A. 1975. The impact of therapeutic effectiveness data on community health center management: The systems evaluation project. *Community Mental Health Journal* 11: 64–73.

BINNER, P. R. 1977. Outcome measures and cost analysis. In *Emerging developments in mental health evaluation,* ed. W. Neigher, R. Hammer, and G. Landsberg. New York: Argold Press.

BLOM, B., and MOORE, M. 1979. Evaluating mental health services through patient care audits. In *Impacts of program evaluation on mental health care,* ed. E. J. Posavac, Boulder, Colo.: Westview Press.

Blue Shield News. 1977. Routine payment to be discontinued for the following procedures. June, p. 3.

BOK, S. 1974. The ethics of giving placebos. *Scientific American,* 231(5), 17–23.

BORUCH, R. F. 1975. On common contentions about randomized field experiments. In *Experimental testing of public policy,* ed. R. F. Boruch and H. W. Riecken. Boulder, Colo.: Westview Press.

BORUCH, R. F., and CORDRAY, D. S. 1982. *An appraisal of educational program evaluations: Federal, state, and local agencies.* New York: Cambridge University Press.

BORUCH, R. F., et al. 1983. Recommendations to Congress and their rationale. *Evaluation Review* 7: 5–35.

BORUCH, R. F., and RINDSKOPF, D. 1977. On randomized experiments, approximations to experiments, and data analysis. In *Evaluation research methods,* ed. L. Rutman. Beverly Hills, Calif.: Sage.

BRAITHWAITE, R. L.; PATTON, J. M.; and FANG, W. L. 1982. Evaluating a human service program: Employing the judicial evaluation model. *Evaluation and Program Planning* 5: 81–89.

BRINKERHOFF, R. O., et al. 1983. *Program evaluation: A practitioner's guide for trainers and educators—a design manual.* Boston: Kluwer-Nijhoff.

BROTMAN, B. 1983. "Workfare": What state terms success others call boondoggle. *Chicago Tribune,* January 2, sec. 3, pp. 1, 4.

BROWN, F. G. 1983. *Principles of educational and psychological testing.* 3rd ed. New York: Holt, Rinehart and Winston.

BRYK, A. S., ed. 1983. *Stakeholderbased evaluation.* San Francisco, Calif.: Jossey-Bass.

BUNDA, M. A. 1983. Alternative ethics reflected in education and evaluation. *Evaluation News* 4 (1): 57–58.

BURNS, M. L. 1977. The effects of feedback and commitment to change on the behavior of elementary school principals. *Journal of Applied Behavioral Science* 13: 159–66.

BURTLE, V., ed. 1979. *Women who drink.* Springfield, Ill.: Charles C. Thomas.

BUSSIGEL, M., and FILLING, C. 1985. Data descrepancies and their origins: An evaluation of a family practice residency program using a naturalistic inquiry paradigm. *Evaluation & The Health Professions* 8: 177–192.

CAGLE, L. T., and BANKS, S. M. 1986. The validity of assessing mental health needs with social indicators. *Evaluation and Program Planning* 9: 127–142.

CAIDIN, M. 1960. *Let's go flying!* New York: Dutton.

CAMPBELL, D. T. 1969. Reforms as experiments. *American Psychologist* 24: 409–29.

CAMPBELL, D. T. 1983. The problem of being scientific in program evaluation. Paper presented at the meeting of the Evaluation Research Society, October, Chicago.

CAMPBELL, D. T. 1986. Relabeling internal and external validity for applied social scientists. In *Advances in quasi-experimental design and analysis,* ed. W. M. K. Trochim. San Francisco: Jossey-Bass.

CAMPBELL, D. T., et al. 1977. Confidentiality-preserving modes of access to files and interfile exchange for useful statistical analysis. *Evaluation Quarterly* 1: 269–300.

CAMPBELL, D. T., and ERLEBACHER, A. 1970. How regression artifacts in quasi-experimental evaluations can mistakenly make compensatory education look harmful. In *Compensatory education: A national debate,* ed. J. Hellmuth, pp. 185–210. Vol. 3 of *Disadvantaged child.* New York: Brunner-Mazel.

CAMPBELL, D. T., and STANLEY, J. C. 1963. *Experimental and quasi-experimental designs for research.* Chicago: Rand-McNally.

CAPORASO, J. A. 1973. Quasi-experimental approaches to social science: Perspectives and problems. In *Quasi-experimental approaches: Testing theory and evaluating policy,* ed. J. A. Caporaso and L. L. Roos. Evanston, Ill.: Northwestern University Press.

CAPPER, J. 1983. Marketing evaluation skills and services. *Evaluation News* 4(2): 57–60.

CAREY, R. G. 1972. *Hospital chaplains: Who needs them?* St. Louis, Mo.: Catholic Hospital Association.

CAREY, R. G. 1974. Emotional adjustment in terminal patients. *Journal of Counseling Psychology* 21: 433–39.

CAREY, R. G. 1976. Presterilization interviewing: An evaluation. *Journal of Counseling Psychology* 23: 492–94.

CAREY, R. G. 1979. Evaluation of a primary nursing unit. *American Journal of Nursing* 79: 1253–55.

CAREY, R. G., and POSVAC, E. J. 1977a. *Cancer care center: An evaluation of support to patients and relatives.* Park Ridge, Ill.: Lutheran General Hospital.

CAREY, R. G., and POSAVAC, E. J. 1977b. *Evaluation of the Medical Ecology Program.* Park Ridge, Ill.: Lutheran General Hospital.

CAREY, R. G., and POSAVAC, E. J. 1978. Program evaluation of a physical medicine and rehabilitation unit: A new approach. *Archives of Physical Medicine and Rehabilitation* 59: 330–37.

CAREY, R. G., and POSAVAC, E. J. 1979. Holistic care in a cancer care center. *Nursing Research,* 28: 213–16.

CARTER, D. E., and NEWMAN, F. L. 1976. *A client-oriented system of mental health delivery and program management.* Rockville, Md.: National Institute of Mental Health.

CENTRA, J. A. 1977.   Plusses and minuses for faculty development. *Change* 9(12):47, 48, 64.

CHAPMAN, C., and RISLEY, T. R. 1974.   Anti- litter procedures in an urban high-density area. *Journal of Applied Behavioral Analysis* 7: 377–83.

CHAPMAN, L. J., and CHAPMAN, J. P. 1967.   Genesis of popular but erroneous psychodiagnostic signs. *Journal of Abnormal Psychology* 72: 193–204.

CHAPMAN, L. J., and CHAPMAN, J. P. 1969.   Illusory correlation as an obstacle to the use of valid psychodiagnostic signs. *Journal of Abnormal Psychology* 74: 271–80.

CHAPMAN, R. L. 1976.   *The design of management information systems for mental health organizations: A primer.* Rockville, Md.: National Institute of Mental Health.

CHELIMSKY, E. 1978.   Differing perspectives of evaluation. In *New Directions for Program Evaluations,* no. 2, ed. C. C. Rentz and B. R. Rentz. San Francisco: Jossey-Bass.

Chicago-Tribune. 1978.   Postal Service may dump billion-dollar parcel plan. June 14, sec. 4, p. 1.

CICARELLI, V. G. 1970.   The relevance of the regression artifact problem to the Westinghouse-Ohio University evaluation of Head Start: A reply to Campbell and Erlebacher. In *Compensatory education: A national debate,* ed. J. Hellmuth, pp. 211–16. Vol. 3 of *Disadvantaged child.* New York: Brunner-Mazel.

CICARELLI, V. G.; COOPER, W. H.; and GRANGER, R. L. 1969.   *The Impact of Head Start: An evaluation of the effects of Head Start on children's cognitive and affective development.* Westinghouse Learning Corporation, OEO Contract No. B89-4536.

COLBURN, D. 1987,   Jan. 20. Who pays? Insurance coverage varies widely. *Washington Post, Health: A weekly journal of medicine, science, and society,* p. 18.

COLEMAN, J. S. 1976.   Recent trends in school integration. In *Evaluation studies research annual,* vol. 1, ed. G. V Glass. Beverly Hills, Calif.: Sage.

COLEMAN, J. S., et al. 1966.   *Equality of educational opportunity.* Washington, D.C.: Government Printing Office.

Community Mental Health Plan. 1977.   Spoon River, Ill.: Spoon River Community Mental Health Center.

CONNER, R. F., et al. 1985.   Measuring need and demand in evaluation research. *Evaluation Review* 9: 717–734.

COOK, T. D., et al. 1975.   *Sesame Street revisited.* New York: Russell Sage.

COOK, T. D., and CAMPBELL, D. T. 1979.   *Quasi-experimentation.* Chicago: Rand-McNally.

COOK, T. D., and GRUDER, C. L. 1978.   Metaevaluation. *Evaluation Quarterly* 2:5–51.

COOK, T. D.; LEVITON, L. C.; and SHADISH, W. R. 1985.   Program evaluation. In *Handbook of Social Psychology,* 3rd ed. ed. G. Lindzey & E. Aronson. New York: Random House.

COOK, T. D., and REICHARDT, C. S., eds. 1979.   *Qualitative and quantitative methods in evaluation research.* Beverly Hills, Calif., Sage.

COOK, T. D., and SHADISH, W. R. 1986.   Program evaluation: The worldly science. *Annual Review of Psychology* 37: 193–232.

CORDRAY, D. S. 1986.   Quasi-experimental analysis: A mixture of methods and judgment. In *Advances in quasi-experimental design and analysis,* ed. W. M. K. Trochim. San Francisco: Jossey-Bass.

CRANO, W. D., and BREWER, M. B. 1986.   *Principles and methods of social research.* Newton, Mass.: Allyn and Bacon.

CRONBACH, L. J. 1975.   Beyond the two disciplines of scientific psychology. *American Psychologist* 30: 116–27.

CRONBACH, L. J. 1977. Remarks to a new society. *Evaluation Research Society Newsletter* 1: 1–3.

CRONBACH, L. J. 1980. *Toward reform of program evaluation: Aims, methods, and institutional arrangements.* San Francisco: Jossey-Bass.

CRONBACH, L. J. 1982. *Designing evaluations of educational and social programs.* San Francisco: Jossey-Bass.

CULLITON, B. J. 1978. Health care economics: The high cost of getting well. *Science* 200: 883–85.

DARLINGTON, R. B., et al. 1980. Preschool programs and later school competence of children from low-income families. *Science* 208: 202–4.

DATTA, L. 1976a. Does it work when it has been tried? And half full or half empty? *Journal of Career Education* 2: 38–55.

DATTA, L. 1976b. The impact of the Westinghouse/Ohio evaluation on the development of project Head Start. In *The evaluation of social programs*, ed. C. C. Abt. Beverly Hills, Calif.: Sage.

DAVID, E. E. 1975. One-armed scientists? *Science* 189: 679.

DAVIS, D. D. 1982. *Primary prevention through organizational change: Improving program evaluation practices.* Paper presented at the meeting of the American Psychological Association, August, Washington, D.C.

DAWES, R. M., and CORRIGAN, B. 1974. Linear models in decision making. *Psychological Bulletin* 81: 95–106.

DAY, C. R., JR. 1981. Solving the mystery of productivity measurement. *Industry Week*, January 26, pp. 61–66.

DEMONE, H. W., JR., and HARSHBARGER, D. 1973. *The planning and administration of human services.* New York: Behavioral Publications.

DENISTON, O. L., and ROSENSTOCK, I. M. 1973. The validity of nonexperimental designs for evaluating health services. *Health Services Reports* 88: 153–64.

DICKEN, A. 1978. Why patients should plan their own recovery. *RN* 41: 52–55.

DIXON, M. G. 1977. Medical records guaranteed to ruin any malpractice defense. *Medical Economics* 54: 79–83.

DIXON, R. H., and LASZLO, J. 1974. Utilization of clinical chemistry services by medical house staff. *Archives of Internal Medicine* 134: 1064–67.

DRUCKER, P. F. 1954. *The practice of management.* New York: Harper.

DRUDE, K. P., and NELSON, R. A. 1982. Quality assurance: A challenge for community mental health centers. *Professional Psychology* 13: 85–90.

DRYFOOS, J. G. 1982. Contraceptive use, pregnancy intentions, and pregnancy outcomes among U.S. women. *Family Planning Perspectives* 14: 81–94.

EDWARDS, W. 1977. Social utilities. *The Engineering Economist* (Summer Symposium Series) 6: 119–29.

EDWARDS, W.; GUTTENTAG, M.; and SNAPPER, K. 1975. A decision-theoretic approach to evaluation research. In *Handbook of evaluation research*, vol. 1, ed. E. L. Struening and M. Guttentag. Beverly Hills, Calif.: Sage.

EGAN, G. 1985. *Change agent skills in helping and human service settings.* Monterey, Calif.: Brooks/Cole.

EGDAHL, R. H. and GERTMAN, P. M. 1976. *Quality assurance in health care.* Germantown, Md.: Aspen Systems.

EGELHOF, J. 1975. Cop layoffs spur slayings. *Chicago Tribune*, July 10, sec. 1, p. 2.

EISENBERG, L. 1977. The social imperatives of medical research. *Science* 198: 1105–10.

ELLSWORTH, R. B. 1975. Consumer feedback in measuring the effectiveness of mental health programs. In *Handbook of evaluation research*, vol. 2, ed. M. Guttentag and E. L. Struening. Beverly Hills, Calif.: Sage.

ELLSWORTH, R. B. 1979. Evaluating treatment outcomes in mental health services. In *Impacts of program evaluation on mental health care*, ed. E. J. Posavac. Boulder, Colo.: Westview Press.

ENDICOTT, J., and SPITZER, R. L. 1975. Designing mental health studies: The case for experimental designs. *Hospital & Community Psychiatry* 26: 737–39.

ERS STANDARDS COMMITTEE. 1982. In Standards for practice, ed. P. H. Rossi, pp. 7–20. No. 15 of *New Directions for Program Evaluation.* San Francisco: Jossey-Bass.

Ethical principles of psychologists. 1981. *American Psychologist* 36: 633–38.

EVANS, J. W., and SCHILLER, J. 1970. How preoccupation with possible regression artifacts can lead to a faulty strategy for the evaluation of social action programs: A reply to Campbell and Erlebacher. In *Compensatory education: A national debate,* ed. J. Hellmuth, pp. 216–20. Vol. 3 of *Disadvantaged child.* New York: Brunner-Mazel.

EVANS, R. G., and ROBINSON, G. C. 1980. Surgical day care: Measurements of economic payoff. *CMA Journal* 123: 873–880.

FAIRWEATHER, G. W., and DAVIDSON, W. S. 1986. *An introduction to community experimentation.* New York: McGraw-Hill.

FITZGERALD, J. M. 1973. *Fundamentals of systems analysis.* New York: Wiley.

FLAY, B. R., and BEST, J. A. 1982. Overcoming design problems in evaluating health behavior programs. *Evaluation & the Health Professions* 5: 43–49.

FLEISS, J. L. 1973. *Statistical methods for rates and proportions.* New York: Wiley.

FORREST, J.; HERMALIN, A. I.; and HENSHAW, S. K. 1981. The impact of family planning clinic programs on adolescent pregnancy. *Family Planning Perspectives* 13: 109–116.

FOXX, R. M., and AZRIN, N. H. 1973. Dry pants: A rapid methods of toilet training children. *Behavior Research and Therapy.* 11: 435–42.

FREEMAN, R., and HOLLOMON, J. H. 1975. The declining value of college going. *Change* 7(7): 24–31, 62.

FRIEDMAN, H. 1982. Simplified determinations of statistical power, magnitude of effect and research sample sizes. *Educational and Psychological Measurement* 42: 521–26.

FREIMAN, J. A., et al. 1978. The importance of Beta, the Type II error and sample size in the design and interpretation of the randomized control trial. *The New England Journal of Medicine* 299: 690–694.

FRY, L. J., and MILLER, J. 1975. Responding to skid row alcoholism: Self-defeating arrangements in an innovative treatment program. *Social Problems* 22: 673–687.

GARWICK, G. 1973. *Commentaries on Goal Attainment Scaling.* Minneapolis: Program Evaluation Resource Center.

GERSTENFELD, A. 1977. MBO revisited: Focus on health systems. *Health Care Management Review* 4: 51–57.

GILBERT, J. P.; LIGHT, R. J.; and MOSTELLER, F. 1975. Assessing social innovations: An empirical base for policy. In *Evaluation and experiment,* ed. A. R. Lumsdaine and C. A. Bennett. New York; Academic Press.

GLASS, G. V 1976. Introduction. In *Evaluation studies research annual,* vol. 1, ed. G. V Glass, Beverly Hills, Calif.: Sage.

GLASS, G. V; McGAW, B.; and SMITH, M. L. 1981. *Meta-analysis in social research.* Beverly Hills, Calif.: Sage.

GOLD, N. 1983. Stakeholders and program evaluation. *New Directions in Program Evaluation,* no. 17, pp. 63–72.

"Good News—crime is up!" 1983. *Chicago Tribune,* May 8, sec. 2, p. 2.

GOSFIELD, A. 1975. *PSRO: The law and the health consumer.* Cambridge, Mass.: Ballinger.

GOTTMAN, J. M., and GLASS, G. V. 1978. Analysis of interrupted time-series experiments. In *Single subject research: Strategies for evaluating change,* ed. T. R. Kratochwill. New York: Academic Press.

GRAY, B. H.; COOKE, R. A.; and TANNENBAUM, A. S. 1978. Research involving human subjects. *Science* 201: 1094–1101.

GREELEY, A. 1972. *American priests: A sociological analysis*. Washington, D.C.: National Conference of Catholic Bishops.

GREENE, J. C. 1987. Stakeholder participation in evaluation: Is it worth the effort? *Evaluation and Program Planning* 10: 379–394.

GUBA, E. G., and LINCOLN, Y. S. 1981. *Effective evaluation*. San Francisco: Jossey-Bass.

GUTTENTAG, M. 1977. Evaluation and society. *Personality and Social Psychology Bulletin* 3: 31–40.

GUTTENTAG, M., and SNAPPER, K. 1974. Plans, evaluations and decisions, *Evaluation* 1(1): 58–64, 73, 74.

HAGEDORN, H. J., et al. 1976. *A working manual of simple evaluation techniques for community mental health centers*. Rockville, Md.: U.S. Department of Health, Education, and Welfare.

HAKEL, M. D., et al. 1980. *Making it happen: Designing research with implementation in mind*. Beverly Hills, Calif.: Sage.

HANKE, S. H., and WALKER, R. A. 1974. Benefit-cost analysis reconsidered: An evaluation of the Mid-State project. *Water Resources Research* 10: 898–908.

HARGREAVES, W. A.; ATTKISSON, C. C.; and SORENSON, J. E., eds. 1977. *Resource materials for community mental health program evaluation*. Rockville, Md.: U.S. Department of Health, Education, and Welfare.

HARRIS, M. B., and BRUNER, C. G. 1971. A comparison of a self-control and a contract procedure for weight control. *Behavior Research and Therapy* 9: 347–54.

HASTORF, A. H., and CANTRIL, H. 1954. They saw a game. *Journal of Abnormal and Social Psychology* 49: 129–34.

HAVEMAN, R. H., and WATTS, H. W. 1976. Social experimentation as policy research: A review of negative income tax experiments. In *Evaluation Studies Research Annual*, vol. 1, ed. G. V. Glass, Beverly Hills, Calif.: Sage.

HAWKINS, J. D.; ROFFMAN, R. A.; and OSBORNE, P. 1978. Decision makers' judgments: The influence of role, evaluation criteria, and information access. *Evaluation Quarterly* 2: 435–54.

HAYS, W. L. 1981. *Statistics*. 3rd ed. New York: Holt, Rinehart and Winston.

HELMICK, E., et al. 1975. A monitoring and evaluation plan for alcoholism programs. *British Journal of Addiction* 70: 369–73.

HORST, P., et al. 1974. Program management and the federal evaluator. *Public Administration Review* 34: 300–308.

HOUSE, E. R. 1976. Justice in evaluation. In *Evaluation Studies Review Annual*, vol. 1, ed. G. V Glass. Beverly Hills, Calif.: Sage.

HOUSE, E. R., et al. 1978. No simple answer: Critique of the follow through evaluation. *Harvard Education Review* 42: 128–60.

ILLICH, I. 1976. *Medical nemesis*. New York: Pantheon Books.

ISAACSON, W. 1983. The winds of reform. *Time*, March 7, pp. 12–16, 23, 26–30.

ISR Newsletter. 1978. Telephone helps solve survey problems. 6: 3.

JACOBS, C. M.; CHRISTOFFEL, T. N.; and DIXON, N. 1976. *Measuring the quality of patient care*. Cambridge, Mass.: Ballinger.

JASON, L. A., and LIOTTA, R. F. 1982. Assessing community responsiveness in a metropolitan area. *Evaluation Review* 6: 703–12.

JOGLEKAR, P. N. 1984. Cost-benefit studies of health care programs: Choosing methods for desired results. *Evaluation & the Health Professions*, 7: 285–303.

JOHNSON, R. A. 1967. *The theory and management of systems*. New York: McGraw-Hill.

JOHNSTON, J. 1983. The status of evaluation as an enterprise. *ERS Newsletter* 7(2): 1, 7.

JOINT COMMITTEE ON STANDARDS FOR EDUCATIONAL EVALUATION. 1981. *Standards for evaluations of educational programs, projects, and materials*. New York: McGraw-Hill.

JUDD, C. M., and KENNY, D. A. 1981. *Estimating the effects of social interventions.* New York: Cambridge University Press.

KAHNEMAN, D., and TVERSKY, A. 1974. Judgment under uncertainty: Heuristics and biases. *Science* 185: 1124–31.

KANE, R. L., and KANE, R. A. 1978. Care of the aged: Old problems in need of new solutions. *Science* 200: 913–19.

KEATING, K. M., and HIRST, E. 1986. Advantages and limits of longitudinal evaluation research in energy conservation. *Evaluation and Program Planning* 9: 113–120.

KELLING, G. L., et al. 1976. The Kansas City preventive patrol experiment: A summary report. In *Evaluative studies review annual,* vol. 1, ed. G. V. Glass. Beverly Hills, Calif.: Sage.

KERSHAW, D. N. 1972. A negative income tax experiment. *Scientific American* 227: 19–25.

KIRESUK, T. J. 1973. Goal attainment scaling at a county mental health service. *Evaluation,* Monograph no. 1, p. 15.

KIRESUK, T. J., and SHERMAN, R. E. 1968. Goal Attainment Scaling: A general method for evaluating comprehensive community mental health programs. *Community Mental Health Journal* 4: 443–53.

KIRK, R. E. 1982. *Experimental design: Procedures for the behavioral sciences.* Rev. ed. Belmont, Calif.: Brooks/Cole.

KIRSCHT, J. P.; HAEFNER, D. P.; and EVELAND, J. D. 1975. Public response to various written appeals to participate in health screening. *Public Health Reports* 90: 539–43.

KIVENS, L., and BOLIN, D. C. 1977. Profile of a change(d) agent. *Evaluation* 4: 115–19.

KNAPP, M. 1977. Applying time-series research strategies to program evaluation problems. Paper presented at a meeting of the Evaluation Research Society, October, Washington, D.C.

KORAN, L. M., et al. 1983. Changing hospital work environments: An example of a burn unit. *General Hospital Psychiatry* 5: 7–13.

KRAUSE, M. S., and JACKSON, J. C. 1983. The validity of some routine evaluative data: A study. *Evaluation Review* 7: 271–76.

KREITNER, R. 1977. People are systems, too: Filling the feedback vacuum. *Business Horizons* 20 (November): 54–58.

KYTLE, J., and MILLMAN, E. J. 1986. Confessions of two applied researchers in search of principles. *Evaluation and Program Planning* 9: 167–177.

LAWLER, E. E. III, and HACKMAN, J. R. 1969. Impact of employee participation in the development of pay incentive plans: A field experiment. *Journal of Applied Psychology* 53: 467–71.

LAZAR, I. 1981. Early intervention is effective. *Educational Leadership,* January, pp. 303–5.

LENIHAN, K. J. 1977. Telephones and raising bail. *Evaluation Quarterly* 1: 569–86.

LEVIN, H. M. 1975. Cost-effectiveness analysis in evaluation research. In *Handbook of evaluation research,* vol. 2, ed. M. Guttentag and E. L. Struening. Beverly Hills, Calif.: Sage.

LEVIN, H. M. 1982. A world without evaluation. Paper given at the meeting of the Evaluation Research Society, October, Baltimore.

LEVIN, H. M. 1983. *Cost-effectiveness: A primer.* Beverly Hills, Calif.: Sage.

LEVINE, M., et al. 1978. Adapting the jury trial for program evaluation: A report of an experience. *Evaluation and Program Planning* 1: 177–86.

LEVITON, L. C., and BORUCH, R. F. 1983. Contributions of evaluation in education programs and policy. *Evaluation Review* 7: 563–598.

LICHT, M. H. 1979. The Staff-Resident Interaction Chronograph: Observational assessment of staff performance. *Journal of Behavioral Assessment* 1: 185–198.

LIGHT, R. J. 1983. Introduction. In *Evaluation studies review annual*, vol. 8, ed. R. J. Light. Beverly Hills, Calif.: Sage.

LIGHT, R. J., and PILLEMER, D. B. 1984. *Summing up: The science of reviewing research*. Cambridge, Mass.: Harvard University Press.

LIGHT, R. J., and SMITH, P. V. 1971. Accumulating evidence: Procedures for resolving contradictions among different research studies. *Harvard Educational Review* 41: 429–71.

LINCOLN, Y. S., and GUBA, E. G. 1985. *Naturalistic inquiry*. Beverly Hills, Calif.: Sage.

LIPSEY, M. W., et al. 1985. Evaluation: The state of the art and the sorry state of the science. In *Utilizing prior research in evaluation planning*, ed. D. S. Cordray. San Francisco: Jossey-Bass.

LOCKE, E. A. 1968. Toward a theory of task motivations and incentives. *Organizational Behavior and Human Performance* 3: 157–89.

LOHR, K. N.; BROOK, R. H.; and KAUFMAN, M. A. 1980. Quality of care in the New Mexico Medicaid program. *Medical Care Supplement* 18: 1–129.

LOVE, A. J. 1986. Using evaluation to identify service gaps in mental health services to youth. Paper presented at the meeting of the American Evaluation Association, October, Kansas City, Mo.

LUCAS, H. C., JR. 1975. *Why information systems fail*. New York: Columbia University Press.

LUFT, L. L. 1979. The effects of peer review in a community mental health center. In *Impacts of program evaluation on mental health care*, ed. E. J. Posavac. Boulder, Colo.: Westview Press.

LUND, S., and KIRESUK, T. J. 1979. Individualized Goal Attainment as a method of program evaluation in mental health. In *Impacts of program evaluation on mental health care*, ed. E. J. Posavac. Boulder, Colo.: Westview Press.

MAGER, R. F. 1972. *Goal analysis*. Belmont, Calif.: Fearon Publishers.

MAJCHRZAK, A. 1986. Keeping the Marines in the field: Results of a field experiment. *Evaluation and Program Planning* 9: 253–265.

MALITZ, D. 1984. The costs and benefits of Title XX and Title XIX family planning services in Texas. *Evaluation Review* 8: 519–536.

MARK, M. M., and COOK, T. D. 1984. Design of randomized experiments and quasi-experiments. In *Evaluation research methods: A basic guide*, ed. L. Rutman. Beverly Hills, Calif.: Sage.

MARK, M. M., and SHOTLAND, L., eds. 1987. *Multiple methods in program evaluation*. San Francisco: Jossey-Bass.

MARKSON, E. W., and ALLEN, D. F. 1976. *Trends in mental health evaluation*. Lexington, Mass.: Lexington Books.

MARSHALL, T. O. 1979. Levels of results. *Journal of Constructive Change* 1 (1): 5.

MAXWELL, G. S. 1985. Problems of being responsive: Reflections on an evaluation of a program for training motorcycle riders. *Evaluation and Program Planning* 8: 339–348.

MAZUR-HART, S. F., and BERMAN, J. J. 1977. Changing from fault to no-fault divorce. *Journal of Applied Social Psychology* 7: 300–12.

MCCALL, R. B. 1986. *Fundamental statistics for the behavioral sciences*. 4th ed. New York: Harcourt Brace Jovanovich.

MCCARTHY, M. 1978. Decreasing the incidence of "high bobbins" in a textile spinning department through a group feedback procedure. *Journal of Organizational Behavioral Management* 1: 150–54.

MCCLEARY, R., and HAY, R. A., JR. 1980. *Applied time series analysis for the social sciences*. Beverly Hills, Calif.: Sage.

MCCLINTOCK, C. C. 1983. Internal evaluation: The new challenge. *Evaluation News* 4 (1): 61–62.

MCCONKEY, D. D. 1983. *How to manage by results*. 4th ed. New York: AMACON.

McGregor, D. 1960. *The human side of enterprise*. New York: McGraw-Hill.

McKay, H., et al. 1978. Improving cognitive ability in chronically deprived children. *Science* 200: 270–78.

McKillip, J. 1987. *Need analysis: Tools for human services and education*. Beverly Hills, Calif.: Sage.

McKillip, J., et al. 1985. Evaluation of a responsible alcohol use media campaign on a college campus. *Journal of Alcohol and Drug Education*. 30: 88–97.

McLaughlin, M. W. 1974. *Evaluation and reform: The Elementary and Secondary Education Act of 1965. Title I*. Santa Monica, Calif.: The Rand Corporation.

Meadows, D. L., and Perelman, L. 1973. Limits to growth. In *The future in the making: Current issues in higher education*, ed. D. W. Vermilye. San Francisco: Jossey-Bass.

Mechanic, D. 1975. Evaluation in alcohol, drug abuse, and mental health programs: Problems and prospects. In *Program evaluation: Alcohol, drug abuse, and mental health services*, ed. J. Zusman and C. Wurster. Lexington, Mass.: Lexington Books.

Medical World News. May 30, 1977. Hypertension compliance. 18: 20–22; 24–25; 28–29.

Miles, M. B., and Huberman, A. M. 1984. *Analyzing qualitative data: A source book for new methods*. Beverly Hills, Calif.: Sage.

Millenson, M. L. 1983. New Medicare rules. *Chicago Tribune*, April 7, sec. 4, p. 16.

Millenson, M. L. 1987, June 15. System puts doctors, cost cutters at odds. *Chicago Tribune*, Section 1, pp. 1, 11.

Miller, S. I., et al. 1975. An evaluation of alcoholism treatment services for Alaskan natives. *Hospital and Community Psychiatry* 23: 829–31.

Mirvis, P. H., and Berg, D. N., eds. 1977. *Failure in organizational development and change: Cases and essays for learning*. New York: Wiley-Interscience.

Mitchell, E. J. Jr., ed. 1985. *The ninth mental measurements yearbook*. Lincoln, Neb.: Buros Institute of Mental Measurements of the University of Nebraska, Lincoln.

Mitlying, J. 1975/76. Managing the use of staff time: A key to cost control. *Alcohol Health and Research World*, Winter, pp. 7–10.

Moeller, A. D. 1982. Quality assurance—A view from the forest. *Forum*, May/June, pp. 43–45.

Moore, P. D., and Staton, T. 1981. Management by objectives in American cities. *Public Personnel Management Journal* 10: 223–32.

Moskop, J. C. 1987, April. The moral limits to federal funding for kidney disease. *Hastings Center Report*, pp. 11–15.

Mosteller, F., and Moynihan, D. P., eds. 1972. *On equality of educational opportunity*. New York: Vintage.

Mueller, D. J. 1986. *Measuring social attitudes: A handbook for researchers and practitioners*. New York: Teachers College Press.

Nagel, S. S. 1983a. Nonmonetary variables in benefit-cost evaluation. *Evaluation Review* 7: 37–64.

Nagel, S. S. 1983b. Factors facilitating the utilization of policy evaluation research. Paper presented at the meeting of the Evaluation Research Society, October, Chicago.

National Institute of Mental Health. 1971. *Planning for creative change in mental health services: A distillation of principles on research utilization*. Washington, D.C.: Department of Health, Education, and Welfare. Publication No. (HSM) 73-9148.

National Standards for Community Mental Health Centers. 1977. Rockville Md.: Department of Health, Education, and Welfare.

The nation's toughest drug law: Evaluating the New York experience. 1978. Washington, D.C.: U.S. Department of Justice, Law Enforcement Assistance Administration.

NEIGHER, W., et al. 1982. Evaluation in the community mental health centers program: A bold new reproach? *Evaluation and Program Planning* 5: 283–311.

NEWMAN, D. E., and LUFT, L. L. 1974. The peer review process: Education versus control. *American Journal of Psychiatry* 131: 1363–66.

Newsweek. May 9, 1977. Health-cost crisis. 89: 84, 89, 90.

NICHOLSON, N. 1977. Absence behavior and attendance motivation: A conceptual systhesis. *The Journal of Management Studies* 14: 231–252.

NIENSTEDT, B. C., and HALEMBA, G. J. 1986. Providing a model for agency program evaluation. *State Evaluation Network* 6(1): 2–4.

NUNNALLY, J. C. 1975. The study of change in evaluation research: Principles concerning measurement, experimental design, and analysis. In *Handbook of Evaluation Research*, vol. 1, ed. E. L. Struening and M. Guttentag. Beverly Hills, Calif.: Sage.

NUNNALLY, J. C., and DURHAM, R. L. 1975. Validity, reliability, and special problems of measurement in evaluation research. In *Handbook of Evaluation Research*, vol. 1, ed. E. L. Struening and M. Guttentag. Beverly Hills, Calif.: Sage.

NUNNALLY, J. C., and WILSON, W. H. 1975. Method and theory for developing measures in evaluation research. In *Handbook of Evaluation Research*, vol. 1, ed. E. L. Struening and M. Guttentag. Beverly Hills, Calif.: Sage.

OKRENT, D. 1980. Comment on societal risk. *Science* 208: 372–75.

PATTON, M. Q. 1980. *Qualitative evaluation methods.* Beverly Hills, Calif.: Sage.

PATTON, M. Q. 1986. *Utilization-focused evaluation* 2nd ed. Beverly Hills, Calif.: Sage.

PAUL, G. L., ed. 1986. *Assessment in residential settings: Principles and methods to support cost-effective quality operations.* Champaign, Ill.: Research Press.

PENDERY, M. L.; MALTZMAN, I. M.; and WEST, L. J. 1982. Controlled drinking by alcoholics? New findings and a reevaluation of a major affirmative study. *Science* 217: 169–75.

PERLOFF, R. 1983. The uses of roles for evaluation research in the private sector. Paper presented at the Eastern Evaluation Research Society Conference, June, New York.

PERLOFF, R., and PERLOFF, E., eds. 1980. *Values, ethics, and standards in evaluation.* San Francisco: Jossey-Bass.

PETERSON, R. D. 1986. The anatomy of cost-effectiveness analysis. *Evaluation Review* 10: 29–44.

PETTIGREW, T. F., et al. 1973. Busing: A review of the evidence. *The Public Interest* 30: 88–118.

PETTIGREW, T. F., and GREEN, R. L. 1977. The white flight debate. In *Evaluation studies review annual*, vol. 2, ed. M. Guttentag, Beverly Hills, Calif.: Sage.

PITZ, G. F., and MCKILLIP, J. 1984. *Decision analysis for program evaluators.* Beverly Hills, Calif.: Sage.

POISTER, T. H. 1982. Performance monitoring in the evaluation process. *Evaluation Review* 6: 601–23.

POPHAM, W. J. 1975. *Educational evaluation.* Englewood, Cliffs, N.J.: Prentice-Hall.

POSAVAC, E. J. 1974. *A study of the coronary classes.* Park Ridge, Ill.: Lutheran General Hospital.

POSAVAC, E. J. 1975. *Survey of past residents in the Clinical Pastoral Education Program.* Park Ridge, Ill.: Lutheran General Hospital.

POSAVAC, E. J., and CAREY, R. G. 1978. Trading evaluative specificity for statistical power. *Evaluation & the Health Professions* 1: 89–95.

POSAVAC, E. J.; CAREY, R. G.; and MARIN, B. V. 1980. Use of resident physicians: An evaluation of the effects of a significant increase. *Evaluation & the Health Professions*, 4: 433–52.

POSAVAC, E. J., and HARTUNG, B. M. 1977. An exploration into the reasons people choose a pastoral counselor instead of another type of psychotherapist. *The Journal of Pastoral Care* 31: 23–31.

POSAVAC, E. J., et al. 1985. Increasing compliance to medical treatment regimens. *Evaluation & the Health Professions* 8: 7–22.

PRUE, D. M., et al. 1980. Managing the treatment activities of state hospital staff. *Journal of Organizational Behavior Management* 2: 165–181.

QUAY, H. C. 1979. The three faces of evaluation: What can be expected to work. *Criminal Justice and Behavior* 4: 341–54.

RAHE, R. H. 1978. Life stress and illness. Presented at the Stress and Behavioral Medicine Symposium, May 20, Chicago, Ill.

RAY, M. 1973. Marketing communication and the hierarchy of effects. In *New models for mass communication research*, ed. by P. Clarke. Beverly Hills, Calif.: Sage.

REZMOVIC, E. L.; COOK, T. J.; and DOBSON, L. D. 1981. Beyond random assignment: Factors affecting evaluation integrity. *Evaluation Review* 5: 51–67.

RHEINSTEIN, M. 1959. Divorce and the law in Germany: A review. *American Journal of Sociology* 65: 489–98.

RICE, S. A. 1929. Contagious bias in the interview. *American Journal of Sociology* 35: 420–23.

RIECKEN, H. W., and BORUCH, R. F., eds. 1974. *Social experimentation: A method for planning and evaluationg social intervention.* New York: Academic Press.

ROBERTSON, L. S., et al. 1974. A controlled study of the effect of television messages on safety belt use. *American Journal of Public Health* 64: 1071–80.

ROSENHAN, D. L. 1973. On being sane in insane places. *Science* 179: 250–258.

ROSENTHAL, R. 1984. *Meta-analytic procedures for social research.* Beverly Hills, Calif.: Sage.

ROSENTHAL, R., and RUBIN, D. B. 1982. A simple, general purpose display of magnitude of experimental effect. *Journal of Experimental Psychology* 74: 166–169.

ROSS, H. L. 1975. The Scandinavian myth: The effectivness of drinking-and-driving legislation in Sweden and Norway. *Journal of Legal Studies* 4: 285–310.

ROSSI, P. H. 1972. Testing for success and failure in social action. In *Evaluating social programs: Theory, practice and politics*, ed. P. H. Rossi and W. Williams, New York: Seminar Press.

ROSSI, P. H., ed. 1982. *Standards for evaluation practice.* San Francisco: Jossey-Bass.

ROSSI, P. H. 1983. Pussycats, weasels or percherons? Current prospects for social science under the Reagan regime. *Evaluation News* 4 (1): 12–27.

ROSSMAN, G. B.; and WILSON, B. L. 1985. Numbers and words: Combining quantiative and qualitative methods in a single large-scale evaluation study. *Evaluation Review* 9: 627–644.

ROTHCHILD, M. L. 1979. Advertising strategies for high and low involvement situations. In *Attitude research plays for high stakes*, ed. by J. Maloney and B. Silverman. New York: American Marketing Association.

SALASIN, S. E., and DAVIS, H. R. 1979. Achieving desired policy or practice changes: Findings alone won't do it. In *Impacts of program evaluation on mental health care*, ed. E. J. Posavac. Boulder, Colo.: Westview Press.

SCHMIDT, R. E.; SCANLON, J. W.; and BELL, J. B. 1979. Evaluability assessment: Making public programs work better. *Human Services Monograph Series*, no. 14, November.

SCHNEIDER, A. L., and DARCY, R. E. 1984. Policy implications of using significance tests in evaluation research. *Evaluation Review* 8: 573–582.

SCHNELLE, J. F., et al. 1977. Patrol evaluation research: A multiple-baseline analysis of saturation police patrolling during day and night. *Journal of Applied Behavior Analysis* 10: 33–40.

SCHNELLE, J. F., et al. 1978. Police evaluation research: An experimental and cost-benefit analysis of a helicopter patrol in a high crime area. *Journal of Applied Behavior Analysis* 11: 11–21.

SCRIVEN, M. 1967. The methodology of evaluation. In *Perspectives of curriculum evaluation*, ed. R. W. Tyler, R. M. Gagne, and M. Scriven. Chicago: Rand-McNally.

SCRIVEN, M. 1980. *The logic of evaluation*. Inverness, Calif.: Edgepress.

SCRIVEN, M. 1981. *Evaluation thesaurus*. 3rd ed. Inverness, Calif.: Edgepress.

SECHREST, L. 1984. Social science and social policy: Will our numbers ever be good enough? In *Social science and social policy*, ed. L. Stotland and M. M. Mark. Beverly Hills, Calif.: Sage.

SECHREST, L. B. 1987. Research on quality assurance. *Professional Psychology: Research and Practice* 18: 113–116.

SECHREST, L., et al. 1979. Introduction. In *Evaluation Studies Review Annual*, vol. 4, ed. L. Sechrest et al. Beverly Hills, Calif.: Sage.

SELIGMAN, C., and DARLEY, J. M. 1977. Feedback as a means of decreasing residential energy consumption. *Journal of Applied Psychology* 62: 363–68.

SELIGMAN, C., and HUTTON, R. B. 1981. Evaluating energy conservation programs. *Journal of Social Issues* 37: 51–72.

SELLS, S. B. 1975. Techniques of outcome evaluation in alcohol, drug abuse, and mental health programs. In *Program evaluation: Alcohol, drug abuse, and mental health services*, ed. J. Zusman and C. R. Wurster, Lexington, Mass.: Lexington Books.

SHADISH, W. R., JR., et al. 1985. The subjective well-being of mental patients in nursing homes. *Evaluation and Program Planning* 8: 239–250.

SHIPLEY, R. H. 1976. Effects of companion program on college student volunteers and mental patients. *Journal of Consulting and Clinical Psychology* 4: 688–89.

SHRAUGER, J. S., and OSBERG, T. M. 1981. The relative accuracy of self-predictions and judgments by others in psychological assessment. *Psychological Bulletin* 90: 322–51.

SIMON, H. A. 1976. *Administrative behavior*. 3rd ed. New York: Macmillan.

SINGH, B.: GREER, P. R.; and HAMMOND, R. 1977. An evaluation of the use of the Law in a Free Society materials on "responsibility." *Evaluation Quarterly* 1: 621–28.

SJOBERG, G. 1975. Politics, ethics, and evaluation research. In *Handbook of evaluation research*, vol. 2, ed. M. Guttentag and E. L. Struening. Beverly Hills, Calif.: Sage.

SLOAN, S., and SCHRIEBER, D. E. 1971. *Hospital management—An evaluation*. Monograph No. 4. Bureau of Business Research and Service, Graduate School of Business. Madison, Wisc.: The University of Wisconsin Press.

SLOANE, R. B., et al. 1975. Short-term analytically oriented psychotherapy versus behavior therapy. *American Journal of Psychiatry* 132: 373–77.

SMITH, M. L., et al. 1976. Evaluation of the effects of Outward Bound. In *Evaluation research studies annual*, vol. 1, ed. G. V. Glass, Beverly Hills, Calif.: Sage.

SMITH, M. L., and GLASS, G. V. 1977. Meta-analysis of psychotherapy outcome studies. *American Psychologist* 32: 752–60.

SMITH, N. L. 1981. The certainty of judgments in health evaluations. *Evaluation and Program Planning* 4: 273–78.

SMITH, N. L., ed. 1982. *Communication strategies in evaluation*. Beverly Hills, Calif.: Sage.

SMITH, W. G. 1975. Evaluation of the clinical services of a regional mental health center. *Community Mental Health Journal* 11: 47–57.

SOBEL, M. B., and SOBEL, L. C. 1978. *Behavioral treatment of alcohol problems*. New York: Plenum.

SOLOMON, A. 1975. Charges of resigned aide on prisons will be probed. *Madison Capitol Times*, September 12.

SPEER, D. C., and TRAPP, J. C. 1976. Evaluation of mental health service effectiveness. *American Journal of Orthopsychiatry* 46: 217–28.

SPIELBERGER, C. D., ed. 1972. *Anxiety: Current trends in theory and research*, vol. 1 New York: Academic Press.

"Spotlight: Program evaluation and accountability in Minnesota." 1982. *State Evaluation Network*, 2(5), 2.

Staff working papers of the Drug Law Evaluation Project. 1978. Washington, D.C.: U.S. Department of Justice, Law Enforcement Assistance Administration.

STANLEY, J. C. 1982. Education in the fast lane: Methodological problems of evaluating its effects. *Evaluation News* 4 (1): 28–46.

STRAW, M. 1978. Informal presentation delivered at Loyola University, May 22, Chicago, Ill.

STRUPP, H. H., and HANDLEY, S. W. 1977. A tripartite model of mental health and therapeutic outcomes: With special reference to negative effects in psychotherapy. *American Psychologist* 32: 187–96.

STUFFLEBEAM, D. 1978. Meta evaluation: An overview. *Evaluation & the Health Professions* 1: 17–43.

STULL, R. J. 1977. Many concepts mold multiinstitutional systems. *Hospitals* 51: 43–45.

SUDMAN, S., and BRADBURN, N. M. 1982. *Asking questions.* San Francisco: Jossey-Bass.

SULLIVAN, J. M., and SNOWDEN, L. R. 1981. Monitoring frequency of client problems. *Evaluation Review* 5: 822–33.

SUSSNA, E., and HEINEMANN, H. N. 1972. The education of health manpower in a two-year college: An evaluation model. *Socio-Economic Planning Science* 6: 21–30.

The Potemkin Factory. 1980. *Time*, February 25, p. 36.

THOMPSON, M. S. 1980. *Benefit-cost analysis for program evaluation.* Beverly Hills, Calif.: Sage.

Time. August 4, 1975. More guinea pigs, experiments with LSD. 108: 66.

Time. July 24, 1978. Psst! Wanna good job? 112: 18, 19.

TOONG, H. D., and GUPTA, A. 1982. Personal computers. *Scientific American* 247 (6): 86–107.

TRIANDIS, H. C. 1978. Basic research in the context of applied research in personality and social psychology. *Personality and Social Psychology Bulletin* 4:383-87.

TROCHIM, W. M. K. 1984. *Research design for program evaluation: The regression-discontinuity approach.* Beverly Hills, Calif.: Sage.

TROCHIM, W. M. K., ed. 1986. *Advances in quasi-experimental design and analysis.* San Francisco: Jossey-Bass.

TUKEY, J. W. 1977. *Exploratory data analysis.* Reading, Mass.: Addison-Wesley.

TURNER, A. J. 1977. Program goal setting in an evaluation system. Paper presented at the Conference on the Impact of Program Evaluation in Mental Health Care, January, Loyola University of Chicago.

TYSON, T. J. 1985. The evaluation and monitoring of a Medicaid second surgical opinion program. *Evaluation and Program Planning* 8: 207–216.

U.S. News & World Report. April 21, 1975. $301 million a day for HEW—and no end in sight. 79: 45–47.

WALDO, G. P., and CHIRICOS, T. G. 1977. Work release and recidivism: An empirical evaluation of a social policy. *Evaluation Quarterly* 1: 87–108.

WALLIS, C. 1983. Death of a gallant pioneer. *Time*, April 4, pp. 62, 63.

WALSH, J. 1983. Congress questions NBS [National Bureau of Standards] budget cuts. *Science* 220: 176, 177.

WASKOW, I. E., and PERLOFF, M. B., eds. 1975. *Psychotherapy change measures.* Rockville, Md.: National Institute of Mental Health.

WEBB, E. J., et al. 1981. *Nonreactive measures in the social sciences.* 2nd ed. Boston: Houghton-Mifflin.

WEISS, C. H. 1975. Evaluation research in a political context. In *Handbook of evaluation research,* vol. 1, ed. E. L. Struening and M. Guttentag. Beverly Hills, Calif.: Sage.

WERTHEIMER, M. 1978. Psychology and the future. *American Psychologist* 33: 631–47.

WHOLEY, J. S. 1979. *Evaluation: Promise and performance.* Washington, D.C.: Urban Institute.

WHOLEY, J. S. 1981. Using evaluation to improve program performance. *Evaluation Studies Review Annual,* vol. 6, ed. H. E. Freeman and M. A. Solomon. Beverly Hills, Calif.: Sage.

WHOLEY, J. S. 1983. *Evaluation and effective public management.* Boston: Little, Brown.

WINCH, R. F., and CAMPBELL, D. T. 1969. Proof? No Evidence? Yes. The significance of tests of significance. *The American Sociologist* 3: 140–53.

WORTMAN, P. M. 1983. Evaluation research: A methodological perspective. *Annual Review of Psychology* 34: 223–60.

YIN, R. K. 1984. *Case study research: Design and methods.* Beverly Hills, Calif.: Sage.

YUKL, G. A., and LATHAM, G. P. 1978. Interrelationships among employee participation, individual differences, goal difficulty, goal acceptance, goal instrumentality, and performance. *Personnel Psychology* 31: 305–23.

ZAMMUTO, R. F. 1982. *Assessing organizational effectiveness.* Albany, N.Y.: SUNY Press.

ZIGLER, E., and TRICKETT, P. K. 1978. IQ, social competence, and evaluation of early childhood intervention programs. *American Psychologist* 33: 789–98.

ZIMRING, F. E. 1975. Firearms and federal law: The Gun Control Act of 1968. *Journal of Legal Studies* 4: 133–98.

ZINOBER, J. W., and DINKEL, N. R., eds. 1981. *A trust of evaluation: A guide for involving citizens in community mental health program evaluation.* Tampa, Fla.: The Florida Consortium for Research and Evaluation.

Name Index

Campbell, D.T., 22, 34, 46, 55, 72, 136, 137, 138, 142, 144, 147, 153–5, 155, 157, 158, 161, 162, 164, 165, 169, 173, 176, 178, 180, 187, 238, 279
Cantril, H., 180
Caporaso, J.A., 158
Capper, J., 23
Carey, R.G., 21, 29, 31, 76, 78, 111, 175, 185, 248, 255, 261, 262, 271, 274
Carter, D.E., 61, 68, 196, 197
Centra, J.A., 144
Chapman, C., 82
Chapman, J.P., 179
Chapman, L.J., 179
Chapman, R.L., 120, 128
Chelimsky, E., 4
Chiricos, T.G., 273
Cicarelli, V.G., 81, 164, 165, 279
Ciralo, J.A., 279
Clarke, P., 299
Colburn, D., 197
Coleman, J.S., 43, 279, 283
Conner, R.F., 90
Cook, T.D., 4, 8, 15, 19, 22, 29, 32, 39, 40, 50, 72, 83, 89, 93, 138, 144, 150, 153, 161, 162, 168, 169, 173, 187, 190, 226, 228, 238, 241, 242, 244, 282, 283
Cooke, R.A., 49
Cordray, D.S., 170, 190
Corrigan, B., 100
Crano, W.D., 164, 184
Cronbach, L.J., 20, 22, 35, 43, 48, 137, 260, 272
Culliton, B.J., 197

D

Darcy, R.E., 81
Darley, J.M., 124
Darlington, R.B., 81
Datta, L., 13, 60, 164, 185, 277
David, E.E., 88
Davidson, W. S., 25
Davis, D.D., 15
Davis, H.R., 182
Dawes, R.M., 100
Day, C.R., Jr., 200
Demone, H.W., Jr., 25, 193
Deniston, O.L., 175
Dicken, A., 211
Dinkel, N.R., 79
Dixon, M.G., 114, 161

Drucker, P.F., 218
Drude, K.P., 221
Dryfoos, J.G., 313, 315
Durham, R.L., 68

E

Eckert, P.S., 294
Edwards, W., 98, 101
Egan, G., 108, 285
Egdahl, R.H., 16
Egelhof, J., 155
Eisenberg, L., 139
Ellsworth, R.B., 49, 61, 151
Endicott, J., 50
Erlebacher, A., 164, 165, 176, 279
Evans, R.G., 165, 204

F

Fairweather, G.W., 25
Filling, C., 315
FitzGerald, J.M., 17
Flay, B.R., 177
Fleiss, J.L., 260
Forrest, J., 312, 315
Foxx, R.M., 210, 212
Freeman, R., 202
Freiman, J.A., 138
Fry, L.J., 243

G

Garwick, G., 215
Gerstenfeld, A., 218
Gertman, P.M., 16
Gilbert, J.P., 179, 180, 181, 182, 190
Glass, G.V., 161, 254, 274, 279, 283
Gold, N., 73
Gosfield, A., 18
Gottman, J.M., 161
Gray, B.H., 49
Greeley, A., 35
Green, R.L., 279
Greene, J.C., 241
Greer, P.R., 138
Gruder, C.L., 282
Guba, E.G., 59, 66, 76, 226, 233, 238, 240, 241, 243, 244
Gupta, A., 128
Guttentag, M., 4, 23, 25, 68, 103, 153

McConkey, D.D., 16, 212, 223
McGregor, D., 218
McKay, H., 185
McKillip, J., 98, 108, 294
McLaughlin, M.W., 18
Meadows, D.L., 14
Mechanic, D., 110
Miles, M.B., 244
Millenson, M.L., 204
Miller, S.I., 219, 243
Millman, E.J., 15, 238
Mirvis, P.H., 269
Mitchell, E.J., Jr., 68
Mitlying J., 196
Moeller, A.D., 211
Moore, P.D., 218
Moos, B., 289
Moos, R.B., 289
Moskop, J.C., 197
Mosteller, F., 179, 190, 283
Moynihan, D.P., 283
Mueller, D.J., 68

N

Nagel, S.S., 203, 277
Neigher, W., 4
Nelson, R.A., 221
Newman, D.E., 61, 68, 196, 197, 221
Nicholson, J.M., 301, 308
Nicholson, N., 308
Nienstadt, B.C., 19
Nunnally, J.C., 68, 140, 153

O

Okrent, D., 207
Osberg, T.M., 47

P

Patton, M.Q., 65, 66, 77, 129, 226, 234,
    238, 239
Paul, G.L., 60
Pendery, M.L., 72, 80
Perelman, L., 15
Perloff, E., 84
Perloff, M.B., 60, 61, 68
Perloff, R., 84
Peterson, R.D., 200
Pettigrew, T.F., 279, 283

Phillips, J., 294
Pillemer, D.B., 242, 284, 285
Pitz, G.F., 98, 108
Poister, T.H., 109, 209
Popham, W.J., 194, 196
Posavac, E.J., 21, 29, 31, 48, 59, 78, 95,
    188, 261, 248, 262, 284
Prue, D.M., 124

Q

Quay, H.C., 93

R

Rahe, R.H., 188
Ray, M., 296, 299
Reichardt, C.S., 162, 242, 244
Rezmovic, E.L., 186, 189
Rheinstein, M., 155
Rice, S.A., 76
Riecken, H.W., 46, 168, 184, 187
Rindskopf, D., 176
Risley, T.R., 82
Robertson, L.S., 60
Robinson, G.C., 204
Roen, S.R., 25
Rosenhan, D.L., 232
Rosenstock, I.M., 175
Rosenthal, R., 254, 283
Ross, H.L., 273
Rossi, P.H., 23, 43, 51, 84, 210
Rossman, G.B., 242
Rothchild, M.L., 296, 299
Rubin, D.B., 254

S

Salasin, S.E., 182
Scanlon, J.W., 31
Schiller, J., 165
Schmidt, R.E., 31
Schneider, A.L., 81
Schnelle, J.F., 160, 197–199
Schrieber, D.E., 218
Schulberg, H.C., 25
Scriven, M., 10, 15, 16, 93, 276
Sechrest, L.B., 51, 93, 223, 255
Seligman, C., 124, 273
Sells, S.B., 110
Shadish, W.R., Jr., 4, 8, 19, 22, 32, 39, 40,
    46, 50, 89, 93, 150

Subject Index